TINA STANBERY

Brief Therapy: Lasting Impressions

Brief Therapy: Lasting Impressions

edited by

Jeffrey K. Zeig

The Milton H. Erickson Foundation Press
Phoenix, Arizona
2002

Library of Congress Cataloging-in-Publication Data

Brief therapy, lasting impressions / edited by Jeffrey K. Zeig.
p. cm.
Includes bibliographical references.
ISBN 0-9716190-4-2 (alk. paper)
1. Brief psychotherapy. I. Zeig, Jeffrey, K., 1947–
RC480.55 .B748 2002
616.89'14--dc21 2002033924

Published by
The Milton H. Erickson Foundation Press
3606 North 24th Street
Phoenix, AZ 85016

Manufactured in the United States of America

10 9 8 7 6 5 4 3 2 1

Table of Contents

Therapeutic Approaches

Contributors

David H. Barlow, Ph.D.: Professor of Psychology, Director of Clinical Training, and Director of the Center for Anxiety and Related Disorders, Boston University.

Laura S. Brown, Ph.D.: Private practice, Seattle, Wash.

Simon H. Budman, Ph.D.: Innovative Training Sytems, Inc., Newton, Mass.

Emil Chiauzzi, Ph.D.: Innovative Training Systems, Inc., Newton, Mass.

Nicholas A. Cummings, Ph.D., Sc.D.: Foundation for Behavioral Health and University of Nevada, Reno.

Steve de Shazer: Senior Research Assistant, BFTC, Milwaukee, Wis.

Barry L. Duncan, Psy.D.: Institute for the Study of Therapeutic Change, Chicago, Ill.

Albert Ellis, Ph.D.: President of the Albert Ellis Institute, New York.

Betty Alice Erickson, M.S., LPC: Private practice, Dallas, Tex.

Stephen Gilligan, Ph.D.: Private practice, Encinitas, Calif.

Mary McClure Goulding, M.S.W.: Social worker and psychotherapist.

Emily Hoffman Stern, Ph.D.: The American Institute for Cognitive Therapy, New York.

Lynn Hoffman: Adjunct Lecturer, Smith School of Social Work, Northampton, Mass., and the Family Therapy Program, St. Joseph's College, West Hartford, Conn.

Michael F. Hoyt, Ph.D.: Kaiser Permanente Medical Center, San Rafael, Calif., and University of California School of Medicine, San Francisco.

Mark A. Hubble: Institute for the Study of Therapeutic Change, Chicago, Ill.

Lynn D. Johnson, Ph.D.: Institute for the Study of Therapeutic Change, Chicago, Ill.

Robert Langs, M.D.: Psychoanalyst.

Stephen Lankton, M.S.W., DAHB: Licensed marriage and family therapist, Phoenix, Ariz.

Jill T. Levitt, Ph.D.: The Institute for Trauma and Stress, New York University Child Study Center.

Joseph LoPiccolo, Ph.D.: Professor of Psychology, University of Missouri, Director of Psychological Services, Sexual Medicine Center, Columbia, Missouri.

Michael J. Mahoney: Department of Psychology, University of North Texas, Denton.

William J. Matthews, Ph.D.: Professor, Department of Psychology, University of Massachusetts, Amherst.

Leigh McCullough, Ph.D.: Associate Clinical Professor, Department of Psychiatry, Harvard Medical School, Boston, Mass.

Monica McGoldrick: Director, Family Institute of New Jersey, Associate Professor of Clinical Psychiatry, Robert Wood Johnson Medical School, Visiting Professor, Fordham University School of Social Work.

Scott D. Miller, Ph.D.: Institute for the Study of Therapeutic Change, Chicago, Ill.

John C. Norcross, Ph.D.: Department of Psychology, University of Scranton, Scranton, Pa.

Maureen O'Hara, Ph.D.: Saybrook Graduate School, San Francisco, Calif.

Peggy Papp, ACSW: Co-Director, Brief Therapy Project, Ackerman Institute for Family Therapy, New York.

James O. Prochaska, Ph.D.: Director of Cancer Prevention Research Consortium, and Professor of Clinical and Health Psychology, University of Rhode Island.

Ernest Lawrence Rossi, Ph.D.: Diplomate of the American Board of Examiners in Clinical Psychology.

Michael D. Yapko, Ph.D.: Private practice, Solana Beach, Calif.

Jeffrey K. Zeig, Ph.D.: Director of the Milton H. Erickson Foundation, Phoenix, Arizona.

Introduction

As Conference organizer and editor of these proceedings, it is my pleasure to introduce this book, *Brief Therapy: Lasting Impressions*, which contains the proceedings of the Fourth Brief Therapy Conference held August 26–30, 1998, in New York City. These proceedings consist of 26 invited addresses from the Conference.

The authors are among the most renowned practitioners of brief therapy in the world and represent a wide variety of brief therapy orientations. Both the advanced practitioner and tyro are sure to benefit from the clinical expertise of the contributors whose wisdom graces these pages.

HISTORY OF THE BRIEF THERAPY CONFERENCES

The Milton H. Erickson Foundation sponsored the first Brief Therapy Conference in San Francisco in 1988. That meeting doubled as the Fourth International Congress on Ericksonian Approaches to Hypnosis and Psychotherapy. Approximately 2200 professionals from United States and 24 countries met at that meeting to learn various aspects of brief therapy. The proceedings of that Conference, edited by Stephen Gilligan, Ph.D. and myself, were published in *Brief Therapy: Myths, Methods, and Metaphors* by Brunner/Mazel in 1990.

The Second Brief Therapy Conference was held in Orlando, Florida, in 1993. It was organized as a brief therapy conference in its own right, separate from an Erickson Congress. The Third Brief Therapy Conference was held in December 1996 in San Francisco. These two Conferences were each attended by approximately 200 professionals.

The Fifth Brief Therapy Conference is scheduled for December 2003 in Orlando and the Sixth is planned for December 2004 in San Francisco.

CONFERENCE FORMAT

The program for the 1998 Fourth Brief Therapy Conference was designed so the attendees could select from a wide variety of training courses. Registrants picked the format that best suited their needs; there were academic and experiential components to the meeting area.

The academic component consisted of keynote addresses and invited addresses. There were three keynote presenters: Helen Fisher, Ph.D.; Arnold Lazarus, Ph.D; and Frank Sulloway, Ph.D. There were 27 invited addresses, which are the chapters that appear in these proceedings.

The experiental component of the Conference consisted of three-hour workshops and one-hour interactive events. Forty-seven workshops and short courses were offered.

A format change of the third day of the Conference gave attendees an opportunity to witness interactive events. One-hour clinical demonstrations, conversation hours, and panel discussions were featured.

Short courses also were presented during the Conference. There were twenty 90-minute mini-workshops covering a wide range of topics on brief therapy.

The entire faculty consisted of more than 59 members, including moderators, co-presenters, and keynote faculty.

ACKNOWLEDGEMENTS

The success of the meeting was due in part to the input of a great many individuals. I would like to take this opportunity to thank those people.

On behalf of the Board of Directors, our heartfelt thanks again go to the distinguished faculty. Their efforts resulted in an excellent and memorable meeting.

The following professionals reviewed proposals of short courses submitted for presentation at the Conference: Jon Carlson, Ed.D.; John Edgette, Psy.D.; William Matthews, Jr., Ph.D.; and Dan Short, Ph.D.

The Erickson Foundation staff worked tirelessly to ensure the success of the Conference. Under the direction of Executive Director Linda Carr McThrall, the following staff deserve special recognition: Sylvia Cowen, Diane Deniger, Jeannine Elder, Karen Haviley, Alice McAvoy, Julia Varley, Susan Velasco, and Lori Weiers.

A number of volunteers worked with the Foundation staff members both prior to and at the Conference. Special thanks go to Ed Hancock who has provided enormous support to the Foundation over the years. Additionally, more than 21 graduate student volunteers served as monitors and staffed the registration and continuing education tables.

The Board of Directors provided great support during the planning phases of the Conference. Many thanks go to Elizabeth M. Erickson, Roxanna Erickson Klein, and J. Charles Theisen.

Jeffrey K. Zeig, Ph.D., Director
The Milton H. Erickson Foundation
3606 North 24th Street
Phoenix, AZ 85016
USA

For more information about the Foundation and its programs, newsletter, other publications, web-based activities, audio- and videotapes, bibliographies, and the location of Erickson Institutes around the world, please visit www.erickson-foundation.org.

PRINCIPLES AND PRACTICE

1

The Recovered Memory Debate: Where Do We Stand Now?

Laura S. Brown

In the late 1970s and early 1980s, a series of books appeared that called attention to the reality of incest and childhood sexual abuse. Each of these small volumes, arising from the women's movement's speakouts on sexual assault, provided first-person accounts of experiences of childhood violation that had long been ignored, silenced, or minimized (Bass & Thornton, 1983; Rush, 1980; Armstrong, 1978; Butler, 1978; Herman, 1981; Brady, 1979; McNaron & Morgan, 1982). The heritage of the adult survivor movement, they furnish the framework for today's debates over trauma and memory.

In these candid books, their authors spoke of memories long lost that had begun to return in adulthood. The cues for memory were many: attaining sobriety, the birth of a child, participating in a women's sexuality retreat, attending a rape speak-out, a smell, a sound. The experiences of remembering, as described by the writers, in the absence of cultural cues, seemed remarkably similar: the intrusion of images, feelings, and unwanted knowledge that a trusted, loved, and sometimes also feared, family member had violated them sexually.

It was out of such books that the incest-survivor movement was born. Nominally feminist, but also encompassing traditions from 12-step recovery programs and from fundamental Christianity, the movement was a springboard for many people, both women and men, either to identify their never-forgotten recollections as memories of abuse, or to find support for the possibility that new and frightening images coming to their minds were true stories of violation. The movement served as a catalyst for research (Briere & Conte, 1993; Briere & Zaidi, 1989; Herman & Schatzow, 1987) as well, and for the development of enhanced clinical awareness of the presence of survivors of incest and child sexual abuse among clinical populations (Briere, 1989, 1996; Courtois, 1988). It also sparked an awareness among survivors that there were legal strategies that they might pursue to obtain financial damages from those who had perpetrated the sexual abuse. By the early 1990s, more than half of the states had changed their laws so that an adult who had only recently realized, or recently remembered, childhood sexual abuse could still sue. Sexual abuse that had been invisible to or ignored by the legal system decades earlier was being brought to the fore. It was inevitable that there would be a backlash against this social movement as it began to exact material prices from abusers.

In the spring of 1992, a small group of people met in Philadelphia. Among them was a man whose adult daughter believed that he had sexually abused her; another in that group was the man's wife. A third was the psychiatrist who had treated both of them over the years. A fourth was a psychologist who frequently testified for the defense in the criminal trials of men accused of sexual abuse of children. Together, they created the term False Memory Syndrome, founded an organization to promote the concept, and catalyzed a social movement that arguably has had more effect on psychotherapists than any other in this century, one that has become a powerful backlash to the incest-survivor movement and a threat to the use of psychotherapy with adult survivors. We have since seen tremendous upheaval in the practices of psychotherapists, particularly those who work in the fields of trauma and dissociation. Therapists who believed that they were simply treating clients and trying to help them heal from profound childhood wounds found themselves besieged by complaints, litigation, and assertions of new standards of practice according to which almost everything known to assist trauma survivors came to be labeled as dangerous malpractice. Laws were proposed to forbid any treatments that evoked delayed recalls of trauma (Hinnefeld & Newman, 1997). Risk-management experts began to advise therapists to avoid treating anyone who presented with a history of sexual abuse. And in just a few years, adult survivors of childhood sexual abuse had moved from being the heroes of their own lives to being suspect and untrustworthy "hysterics" who had been easily convinced by unscrupulous therapists that they had been the victims of terrible crimes.

Before 1992, there was little questioning in the professional world that memory for a traumatic event could be delayed in its return to consciousness. It had long been observed that exposure to trauma frequently led to disturbances in recall, with both hyperamnesia and/or amnesia being manifest. The recall of traumas was accompanied by either psychic numbing or emotional intensity. The process of remembering traumatic events was often different from that of remembering everyday occurrences; memories for trauma were frequently somatosensory in their presentation, rather than cognitively integrated into the individual's autobiographical narrative.

Over time, the memory effects of trauma have been described by such terms as posttraumatic amnesia, dissociative amnesia, and repressed memory, indicating different hypotheses for the mechanisms causing the delay. But there has been little debate among students of trauma over the principle that this particular manifestation of traumatic stress was real and observable across the range of traumatic events. Some trauma survivors had insufficient "forgettery;" others could only remember when the circumstances of their lives shifted in some manner so as to allow the painful materials to come to consciousness.

Since the spring of 1992, however, the question of how trauma affects memory has ceased to be a matter of unremarkable observation and clinical consensus among trauma researchers and therapists. Instead, with the founding of the False Memory Syndrome Foundation (FMSF), there has been a remarkable flurry of highly politicized debates about whether or not all such delayed recall of trauma is merely an iatrogenic phenomenon arising from poorly conducted, suggestive psychotherapy, the position advanced by the FMSF and its various supporters. Most of the debate has centered on whether long-delayed recall of sexual abuse in the childhoods of certain psychotherapy patients is real. Adherents of the false-memory position have asserted that not only are traumas memorable and unlikely to be forgotten (Loftus & Ketcham, 1994), but also that most child sexual abuse is not traumatic for children, and could not possibly be affected by traumagenic memory dynamics (Ceci, Huffman, Smith, & Loftus, 1994). The false-memory position has also been that sexual abuse of children is a negligible factor in the development of later life distress (Pope & Hudson, 1995); that Dissociative Identity Disorder (DID, formerly known as Multiple Personality Disorder) is mostly iatrogenically created (Merskey, 1992), and that any therapy in which a client experiences a recovery of a memory of abuse must be a form of malpractice (McHugh, 1993).

The false-memory position frequently has been asserted to represent the science of psychology (Loftus & Ketcham, 1994), in juxtaposition to the views of clinicians who are supposed to hold erroneous, or even dangerous, beliefs about the nature of memory, and whether or not memories of traumas can be lost to consciousness and later recalled (Poole, Lindsay, Memon & Bull, 1995; Yapko, 1994). But what do scientific findings tell us when a thorough and unbiased review of research is conducted? Is there a False Memory Syndrome? Are thousands of therapists engaging in dangerous techniques? Should therapists fear working with clients who report recovered memories of abuse? What is the current state of our knowledge about memory for trauma, and in what direction is the debate over recovered memory moving today?

WHAT SCIENCE SAYS ABOUT TRAUMA AND MEMORY

Cognitive Science

The level of physiological arousal present at the time of learning mediates storage, recall, and retention. Traumata by their very definition are not ordinary events, but rather ones in which people experience profound distortions in their levels of arousal owing to some combination of pain, fear, dissociation, and/or confusion. While the ordinary rules of memory creation, storage, retention, and retrieval likely also apply to the recollection of trauma, the trauma itself, with its impact on both consciousness and physiology, interacts with those rules to produce outcomes different from those for memories of ordinary experiences. Emerging brain research indicates that brain involvement in the perception, storage, and retrieval of traumatic events differs from that in the perception of ordinary nontraumatic experience.

Not everything that is remembered, or stored, is recalled, no matter what the circumstances of the event. Most of what we remember has become so implicit and automatic that it is not perceived as a memory per se. For instance, our knowledge of how to place a long-distance telephone call is in fact a memory, yet few people would describe it as: "Today I remembered how to place a long-distance call." Memories are often recalled from long-term storage when something in the intra- or interpersonal environment makes them salient and cues them. Thus, memory is state-dependent, with recall for events that are long in the past contingent on the presence of certain internal or external cues associated with the original event or experience.

Because the states of arousal associated with trauma are frequently unique and demarcated from those of ordinary life, they serve an important function in the storage and later retrieval of memory for the traumatic event. A certain level of high arousal, such as is experienced by some persons at the time of the trauma, may be helpful in retaining the event in long-term memory (Christianson, 1992). However, as Marmer and his associates (Marmar, et al., 1994) have noted, many experience a *decrease* in affective arousal at the time of trauma. This numbing peritraumatic dissociation also has an impact on storage into long-term memory. When the traumatic event is accompanied by both hyperarousal and peritraumatic dissociation, the stage is set for distortions, deletions, or gaps in the material that is retained in long-term memory.

Once material is stored, it does not remain static. New personal narratives place a new slant on stored data; as a story is retold, the relative importance and salience of certain events change, as does the content of the stored memory. Working hard to remember one thing can suppress knowledge of other topics (Anderson, 1998); if an abuser is also a caretaker, a child may need to focus on the caretaker aspects of the relationship, thus actively inhibiting access to knowledge of the abuse. Time leads to the decay of memory traces, with recall for some very remote events becoming less clear. The lack of opportunity to remember, and thus rehearse an event yet again, also can weaken a memory trace. Weaker memory traces may require stronger or more specific cues to elicit recall (Dalenberg, Coe, Reto, Aransky, & Duvenage, 1995), even when an event has been retained in long-term memory, thus leaving an individual with the impression that he or she had forgotten, and then remembered, an event that was always technically remembered but was difficult to recall to conscious awareness. Finally, traumatized people often avoid material that will remind them of a trauma, or actively attempt to suppress knowledge of the traumatic event or process. This, too, deprives the trauma survivor of cues to activate the memory to emerge from storage.

Findings from Neuroscience

In the past decade, with the development of sophisticated neuroimaging techniques that allow study of the living brain at work, new evidence has also emerged about the effects of trauma on brain structures implicated in memory storage and retrieval, as well as about the integration of affect and cognition in memory. The limbic system has been identified as the core of human memory. Research indicates that damage to that system, or to its links to the neocortex, both of which are caused by trauma exposure, can offer physiological models for hyperamnesia and posttraumatic amnesia, as well as for the difficulties experienced by trauma survivors in integrating and consolidating new learning.

Research by Van der Kolk (1998), Bremner and his colleagues (Bremner et al., 1995), and others has found that adults with a history of trauma and symptoms of Posttraumatic Stress Disorder (PTSD) have a decreased volume of the hippocampus, a brain structure that serves the function of integrating cognition and sensorimotor information from experience, and that also has connections to the prefrontal cortex of the brain. While it is as yet unclear as to whether or not these reduced volumes represent a preexisting propensity to develop PTSD in response to trauma exposure or atrophy caused by stress, the neuroimaging data argue more strongly for the latter. Whichever might be the case, what is abundantly clear is that damage to this organ leads to fragmentation of memory, or the failure of memories to store in the prefrontal cortex as declarative verbal memories, leaving them instead stored in unintegrated somatosensory forms. Van der Kolk's neuroimaging studies of brain function during the recall of trauma also suggest ways in which memories for traumatic events may be both differentially stored and retrieved. For example, during trauma recall in persons with PTSD, the limbic system and the visual cortex are activated; however, the prefrontal cortex and left-hemisphere speech areas do not function, in sharp contrast to the brains of nontraumatized individuals. These findings suggest that memories for trauma are stored in nonverbal ways, and recalled as affect and sensation, unintegrated into a verbal narrative.

Thus, the basic science of memory demonstrates from both cognitive and neuroscientific data that the emotions and cognitions surrounding a trauma could lead to the development of posttraumatic amnesia and a subsequent return of access to the memory when the survivor of trauma is exposed to certain cues. The specific cognitive mechanisms by which posttraumatic amnesia occurs are still poorly understood. This gap in the knowledge base has become the place on which the false-memory movement has frequently taken its stand. For example, some authors have argued that there is no scientific evidence for the mechanism of repression, and, consequently, that there must not be such a thing as repressed memory (Loftus & Ketcham, 1994; Ofshe & Watters, 1994).

Freyd (1996, 1998) and others (Brown, 1995; Brown, Scheflin, & Hammond, 1997; Pope & Brown, 1996) have argued that to confuse the *mechanism* causing delayed recall with the *phenomenon* of delayed recall misrepresents the state of scientific knowledge. I analogize the current situation to the flight of the bumblebee. A bee's flight cannot be explained by the laws of aerodynamics; in fact, according to those laws, bees cannot fly. However, since well before humans evolved bees have been empirically observed to take flight. The mechanisms by which bees fly were eventually discovered, and, in the interim, no one alleged that bees could not fly. Similarly, there is excellent empirical evidence for the phenomenon of delayed recall across time, situations, and types of trauma (Brown, Scheflin & Hammond, 1997; Elliott & Briere, 1995); the fact that cognitive science and neuroscience have yet to determine the mechanism simply tells us that our understanding of the "whys" of human memory is still in its early stages of development.

A very promising cognitive science model for the delayed recall of memories of childhood abuse has been proposed by Jennifer Freyd (1995, 1996). Her Betrayal Trauma (BT) paradigm for posttraumatic amnesia and the return of memory in the specific case of childhood sexual abuse uses testable basic cognitive science principles to predict accurately which sexually abused persons are likely to develop amnesia for the abuse. Freyd's model attends to the unique situation of the child sexually abused by a trusted caregiver. She argues that because children must maintain their attachments to caregivers, the betrayal of the relationship with regard to sexual abuse cannot be known by the child. The information thus is stored in a manner that is inaccessible to the abuse victim until such time that the dependency relationship is no longer felt to be necessary for survival. Applications of this model to current information about adult survivors predict with a high degree of accuracy those who will experience delayed recall (Freyd, 1996). Additionally, recent empirical research by Freyd and her colleagues (Anderson, 1998; Freyd & DePrince, 1998) indicates that memory and information-processing phenomena that would be predicted by BT theory are consistently found in persons with delayed-recall experiences. While much further research is required on the question of mechanisms for delayed recall, BT theory provides at least one model based solidly on well-accepted concepts of cognitive science.

MEMORY AND SUGGESTIBILITY

One of the assertions made by false memory advocates is that it is relatively simple for therapists, even well-meaning ones, to make suggestions of abuse to clients that are then transformed into false memories. What does cognitive science tell us about human suggestibility, and how might this apply to the practice of psychotherapy?

The fact that memory for events can be affected by intentional, as well as inadvertent, suggestions has long been established. However, what is less well known is that a number of factors can either increase suggestibility, or decrease it. For example, it is more difficult to change a memory via suggestion if the memory is a well-learned one, such as might happen with repeated exposures to an event. In addition, it is very difficult to suggest to people something that is extremely inconsistent with expectations; for example, for many people, the idea of having been sexually abused by a family member is inconsistent with their expectations, and a suggestion of this nature is not likely to be accepted. Suggestions coming from persons of authority are more acceptable, and the characteristics of some individuals, such as being a high scorer on the Dissociative Experiences Scale, appear to make them more open to suggestion. Since a number of the factors influencing suggestibility are potentially present in the psychotherapeutic context, these data can be important for clinicians who work with adults discovering their recollections of abuse.

Most clinicians are now familiar with Loftus' studies, in which adults accepted suggestions from older family members that they had been, while a child, lost in a shopping mall (Loftus & Pickrell, 1995). These findings have been replicated and extended (Hyman, Husband, & Billings, 1995; Pezdek & Roe, 1994), with suggestions of such events as accidentally spilling the contents of a punch bowl on the parents of the bride at a wedding, being taken to the hospital in the middle of the night with an earache, and, in Pezdek and Roe's study, being given a rectal enema. What appear to be consistent in these studies are the following:

- No more than about 25% of those receiving the suggestions accept them, across studies and conditions. Even when the attempt to suggest is made forcefully and repeatedly, most people do not accept these suggestions.
- When suggestions are made that are unfamiliar or seem implausible to the target person, they are not accepted. Suggestions of the rectal enema were completely rejected by the person to whom they were made.
- A suggestion must be made repeatedly, and the target person invited to elaborate on it for the suggestion to take effect; Hyman (1998) found that asking people to visualize the suggested event increased the likelihood that the suggestion would be adopted as a memory.
- Persons who score higher on measures of dissociation are more likely to accept the suggestions than those who do not.

Hyman (1998) reported that while such studies do indicate that it is possible to create an entire false memory of a moderately unpleasant event (although transcripts of some of his research interviews [Hyman, 1998] suggest that some of his subjects enjoyed creating false memories of having knocked over the punch bowl at a wedding), they are not sufficiently analogous to what occurs in therapy to demonstrate that it is, as some have argued (Loftus, 1993; Loftus & Ketcham, 1994), easy for a therapist to implant a false memory of sexual abuse in a client. Few therapists make repeated, direct suggestions; memories of sexual abuse in childhood are worse than unpleasant, they disorganize a person's entire relationship to an apparent abuser, to self, and often to the family of origin, in ways that being lost in malls and knocking over punch bowls cannot. However, some of the factors that increase suggestibility, such as power differentials, suggestions to visualize, and higher scores on measures of dissociation, may be factors in a particular therapy context. This bring us to our next question.

Is There a Recovered Memory Therapy?

The false-memory movement has also asserted that there is a form of therapy called Recovered Memory Therapy (RMT) that is inherently likely to cause false memories of childhood abuse. This assertion is frequently backed up by reference to studies in which therapists report their recollections of what they have done with clients who remembered abuse. Poole,

Lindsay, Memon, & Bull (1995), positing that certain psychotherapeutic techniques were likely to be suggestive of childhood sexual abuse, surveyed U.S. and British therapists and determined that approximately one-quarter were engaging in what these authors considered risky, suggestive practices, such as hypnotherapy, guided imagery, and journaling. Polusny & Follette (1996) have also raised concerns about therapists' practices, although they interpret their data more cautiously with regard to the degree of risk to clients.

This line of research itself has problems. None of the techniques described in the studies have been shown empirically to be capable of creating entire false memories of abuse (Olio, 1996). While hypnosis, one of the allegedly risky techniques, has long been shown to increase suggestibility, and more recent research demonstrates similar effects of asking people to visualize the suggested event (Hyman, 1998), Brown (1995a, 1995b) has noted that a review of the research on this topic shows that acceptance of suggestions is due more to individual differences in client suggestibility than to the use of any specific allegedly risky technique, including hypnosis. None of these studies indicate whether or not the therapists in question were responding to clients' requests for assistance in retrieving a memory that the *clients* believed a priori to be in hiding, in contrast to therapists who thrust onto clients the unasked-for assertions that they must have been abused.

Since the inception of the false-memory movement, more than 200 lawsuits have been filed against therapists, by both the parents of adult clients and by clients themselves, alleging that the therapists implanted harmful false memories of abuse. Examination of the reports in cases where therapists lost the lawsuits, particularly suits brought by the clients themselves, suggests that some of the sued therapists were not simply using an occasional guided visualization with clients, or merely suggesting that a client with no memories of abuse read a self-help book. Rather, there are accounts of the use of bizarre and problematic mind-control techniques, insistence by the therapist that the client must have been abused and was now in denial, the fostering of extreme dependency, and repeated overt suggestions to clients that abuse must have happened. In some of these cases in which I served as an expert witness, sexual abuse of clients by the therapist and other forms of serious boundary crossing also took place. However, as noted by Pezdek (1998), for most reports of memories of abuse to have been the results of suggestion, suggestibility would need to be an extremely robust cognitive phenomenon, which it is not. Cases such as the ones cited by the false-memory movement probably represent extreme outliers, rather than examples of usual practice with adults remembering childhood trauma.

There is no dispute that serious malpractice by a therapist can lead to a variety of types of cognitive confusion and distortions of reality in vulnerable clients. Techniques such as those advanced by some authors (Blume, 1990; Fredrickson, 1992) may place clients at risk by identifying a large range of symptoms as evidence of hidden sexual abuse that must be uncovered using precisely the sorts of strategies that increase the power of suggestion and decrease clients' abilities to know their own realities. But as Olio (1996) noted in her critique of studies by Poole and her colleagues, the assertions made by those authors that approximately one quarter of psychologists are practicing a risky "recovered memory therapy" appear to be without empirical foundation.

However, this does not mean that therapists can ignore issues raised by this debate. Clients who believe themselves to be recovering memories of abuse, like any psychotherapy clients, deserve careful and thorough assessment, and a treatment plan that is focused on containment, self-care, and the improvement of functioning. As noted by Gold & Brown (1997), Harvey (1996), Harvey & Herman (1994), Pope & Brown (1996), and others in the field of sexual abuse recovery, psychotherapy is not archeology, and remembering per se is not what will assist people in recovering from childhood trauma. Therapy with adults who report delayed (or continuous) recall of childhood sexual abuse needs to focus on enhancing the client's capacity to function. This may or may not require extensive processing of the sexual abuse experience, and no therapist can use a one-size-fits-all methodology for his or her work with clients.

However, such treatment will require working with a client to identify and remediate deficits in self-care that might have arisen from exposure to abuse; the identification of survival and coping strategies that have now become self-sabotaging behaviors, such as dissociation, or the use of alcohol, drugs, food, or overwork to numb; and the integration of the experience of abuse into a coherent adult-life narrative. If individuals present to treatment with what appear to be intrusive recalls of long-forgotten abuse experiences, the job of the therapist is to assist them in gaining a sense of safety, and in making their own sense of the meaning, reality, and weight of the materials that have appeared in this intrusive manner. Therapists must resist the urge to become the new arbitrar of clients' realities; if a perpetrator insisted that "nothing happened," it does not empower a client to have a therapist insist that something did happen. Rather, clients require assistance in becoming their own best experts and sources of authority, using the therapist as a source of reality checking (e.g., "Yes, for an adult to have sex with a child is not a loving act") rather than reality construction (e.g., "I know what happened to you, even if you do not").

Therapists working with traumatized populations need to stay current with the research on suggestibility, and acknowledge that because of the power of their role, their words, even spoken lightly, may carry enormous weight. Therapists must resist their own and their clients' desires to put premature closure on this painful experience by allowing a space in which ambiguity and uncertainty are possible, and empower clients to make their own decisions about what degree of corroboration they wish to obtain for what they now believe to be memories of their earlier lives. Therapists also need to keep aware of the current research regarding treatment for the range of posttraumatic conditions. Whereas in the 1980s and early 1990s, there were few, if any, empirically validated treatments for the sequelae of trauma, clinicians can now choose from a range of techniques with strong research support, including exposure therapies (Foa, Rothbaum, Riggs, & Murdock, 1991), EMDR (Shapiro, 1995), and for the longer-term characterological effects of trauma, Dialectical Behavior Therapy (Linehan, 1993a, 1993b). All of these models of treatment can be incorporated into a range of theoretical orientations.

Finally, therapists need to be forensically savvy. Although most clinicians shudder at the possibility that they might have to testify in court, some clients who have recovered memories of abuse will wish to pursue litigation against the alleged perpetrators. Therapists must be able to delineate for themselves and their clients the differences between the roles of treating therapist and forensic expert, and forbear crossing over the line from one into the other (Brown, 1995). Therapists also need to attend to legal standards for informed consent, notetaking, and the inclusion of third parties in therapy sessions (Pope & Brown, 1996), in order to protect their clients, themselves, and the integrity of the therapy, when working with remembering adults.

Is There a False Memory Syndrome?

The answer to this question is a resounding "No." As Pope (1996) noted in his exhaustive review of this literature, all of the alleged cases of this so-called disorder arose from assertions made by third parties about the state of mind, beliefs, and behaviors of the labeled individual. Usually, those third parties were the persons accused of sexually abusing the individuals labeled as having FMS. The FMSF's assertion that it has documented evidence of thousands of cases of FMS, in this author's opinion, appears to be primarily evidence that there are thousands of instances in which accused adults deny the accusation. As Salter (1995) notes, denial by perpetrators of childhood sexual abuse should never be taken as evidence that the abuse did not occur, since such denials can also be issued in instances where there is incontrovertible evidence that such abuse happened. Members of the FMSF include persons who have been found by the courts to have probably committed sexual abuse and to be liable for its damages (Hoult, 1998). It is impossible to know which, if any, of the denials in FMSF's files are accurate, and which are untrue. Andrews (1998) and her colleagues, who carried out a direct review of the files of the British False Memory Society, found that in very few cases could an objective observer conclude that false allegations arising primarily from therapists' suggestions might be considered to be involved (Andrews, 1998).

No memory, whether continuous or delayed, can be assumed a priori to be either accurate or inaccurate. Any person can have memories that are wrong, or beliefs that are based on erroneous assumptions. Therapists confronted with a client's report of delayed recall of childhood or other trauma must respond with an open mind, neither assuming the role of arbiter of reality by declaring the memory true or false, nor requiring a client to make such experience a sole focus of treatment when this is not the client's desire.

Where Do We Stand Now?

While there continue to be highly polarized partisans on each side of the memory debate, the trend toward covergence and multidirectional cooperation between scientists and clinicians is growing stronger. One of the extremely exciting developments to emerge from the memory debate has been the interest by cognitive scientists in studying memory for traumatic experiences, a topic previously of little interest to the field of cognition. The Conference on Trauma and Cognitive Science held in July 1998 at the University of Oregon exemplifies this tendency for cognitive scientists to interact with trauma clinicians, leading to more sophisticated models of the cognitive mechanisms that underlie the delayed recall of trauma. Additionally, as leading clinicians in the field of trauma integrate these scientific findings into practice with trauma survivors, more effective methods of treatment are developed. Although the memory wars have yet to reach a point of truce, they have evolved to a place of detente among enough of the parties that the crisis ultimately will benefit both the science of memory and the practice of therapy with survivors of trauma.

Author's Note

Those interested in learning more about well-corroborated cases of recovered memories of abuse are referred to the Recovered Memory Online Archive maintained by Professor Ross Cheit of Brown University: http://www.brown.edu/Departments/Taubman_Center/Recovmem/Archive.html

References

Anderson, M. (1998, July). *Active forgetting: Evidence for functional inhibition as a source of memory failure.* Presented at the 1998 Conference on Trauma and Cognitive Science, Eugene, OR.

Andrews, B. (1998, July). *The process of memory recovery and characteristics of the memories among adults in therapy.* Presented at the 1998 Conference on Trauma and Cognitive Science, Eugene, OR.

Armstrong, L. (1978). *Kiss daddy goodnight: A speakout on incest.* New York: Pocket Books.

Bass, E., & Thornton, L. (Eds.) (1983). *I never told anyone: Writings by women survivors of child sexual abuse.* New York: Harper Colophon.

Blume, E. S. (1990). *Secret survivors: Uncovering incest and its aftereffects in women.* New York: Wiley.

Brady, K. (1979). *Fathers' days.* New York: Seaview Books.

Bremner, J. D., Randall, P., Scott, T. M., Bronen, R. A., Seibyl, J. P., Southwick, S. M., Delaney, R. C., McCarthy, G., Charney, D. S., & Innis, R. B. (1995). MRI-based measurement of hippocampal volume in patients with combat-related post-traumatic stress disorder. *American Journal of Psychiatry, 152*, 973–981.

Briere, J. N. (1989, 1996). *Therapy for adults molested as children.* New York: Springer.

Briere, J. N., & Conte, J. (1993). Self-reported amnesia for abuse in adults molested as children. *Journal of Traumatic Stress, 6*, 21–31.

Briere, J., & Zaidi, L. Y. (1989). Sexual abuse histories and sequelae in female psychiatric emergency room patients. *American Journal of Psychiatry, 146*, 1602–1606.

Brown, D. (1995a). Pseudomemories: The standard of science and standard of care in trauma treatment. *American Journal of Clinical Hypnosis, 37*, 1–24.

Brown, D. (1995b). Sources of suggestion and their applicability to psychotherapy. In J. L. Alpert (Ed.), *Sexual abuse recalled* (pp. 61–100). Northvale, NJ: Jason Aronson.

Brown, D., Scheflin, A., & Hammond, C. (1997). *Memory, trauma, treatment and the law.* New York: Norton.

Brown, L. S. (1995). The therapy client as plaintiff: Clinical and legal issues for the treating therapist. In J. L. Alpert (Ed.), *Sexual abuse recalled: Treating trauma in the era of the recovered memory debate* (pp. 337–362). Northvale, NJ: Jason Aronson.

Butler, S. (1978). *Conspiracy of silence: The trauma of incest.* San Francisco: New Glide Publications.

Ceci, S. J., Huffman, M. L. C., Smith, E., & Loftus, E. F. (1994). Repeatedly thinking about a non-event; Source misattributions among preschoolers. *Consciousness and Cognition, 3*, 388–407.

Christianson, S-A. (1992). Emotional stress and eyewitness memory. *Psychological Bulletin, 112*, 284–309.

Courtois, C. (1988). *Healing the incest wound: Adults survivors in therapy.* New York: Norton.

Dalenberg, C., Coe, M., Reto, M., Aransky, K., & Duvenage, C., (1995, January). *The prediction of amnesiac barrier strength as an individual difference variable in state-dependent learning paradigms.* Presented at Conference on Responding to Child Maltreatment, San Diego, CA.

Elliott, D. M., & Briere, J. (1995). Posttraumatic stress associated with delayed recall of sexual abuse: A general population study. *Journal of Traumatic Stress, 8*, 629–647.

Foa, E. B., Rothbaum, B. O., Riggs, D., & Murdock, T. (1991). Treatment of posttraumatic stress disorder in rape victims: A comparison between cognitive-behavioral procedures and counseling. *Journal of Consulting and Clinical Psychology, 59*, 715–723.

Fredrickson, R. (1992). *Repressed memories: A journal to recovery from sexual abuse.* New York: Simon and Schuster.

Freyd, J. J. (1995). Betrayal-trauma: Traumatic amnesia as an adaptive response to childhood abuse. *Ethics and Behavior, 4*, 307–329.

Freyd, J. J. (1996). *Betrayal trauma theory: The logic of forgetting abuse.* Cambridge, MA: Harvard University Press.

Freyd, J. J., & DePrince, A. (1998, August). *Dissociative tendencies and attentional context: A crossover interaction for Stroop interference.* Presented at the 1998 Conference on Trauma and Cognitive Science, Eugene, OR.

Gold, S. N., & Brown, L. S. (1997). Therapeutic responses to delayed recall: Beyond recovered memories. *Psychotherapy: Theory, Research, Practice, Training, 34*, 182–191.

Harvey, M. R. (1996).An ecological view of psychological trauma and trauma recovery. *Journal of Traumatic Stress, 9*, 3–24.

Harvey, M. R., & Herman, J. L. (1994). Amnesia, partial amnesia and delayed recall among adult survivors of childhood trauma. *Consciousness and Cognition, 3*, 295–306.

Herman, J. L., & Schatzow, E. (1987). Recovery and verification of memories of childhood sexual trauma. *Psychoanalytic Psychology, 4*, 1–14.

Hoult, J. (1998). Silencing the victim: The politics of discrediting child abuse survivors. *Ethics and Behavior, 8*, 125–140.

Hyman, I. E., Jr. (1998, July). *False memories of childhood experiences.* Presented at the 1998 Conference on Trauma and Cognitive Science, Eugene, OR.

Hyman, I. E., Jr., Husband, T. H., & Billings, F. J. (1995). False memories of childhood experiences. *Applied Cognitive Psychology, 9*, 181–197.

Koss, M. P., Tromp, S., & Tharan, M. (1995). Traumatic memories: Empirical foundations, forensic and clinical implications. *Clinical Psychology: Science and Practice, 2*, 111–132.

Linehan, M. M. (1993a). *Cognitive behavioral treatment of borderline personality disorder.* New York: Guilford.

Linehan, M. M. (1993b). *Skills training manual for treating borderline personality disorder.* New York: Guilford.

Loftus, E. F. (1993). The reality of repressed memories. *American Psychologist, 48*, 518–537.

Loftus, E. F., & Ketcham, K. (1994). *The myth of repressed memory: False memories and allegations of abuse.* New York: St. Martins Press.

Loftus, E. F., & Pickrell, J. E. (1995). The formation of false memories. *Psychiatric Annals, 25*, 720–725.

Marmar, C. R., Weiss, D. S., Schlenger, W. E., et al. (1994). Peritraumatic dissociation and post-traumatic stress in male Vietnam theater veterans. *American Journal of Psychiatry, 151*, 902–907.

McHugh, P. (1993, October 1). To treat. *FMS Foundation Newsletter*, p. 1.

McNaron, T., & Morgan, Y. (Eds.). (1982). *Voices in the night: Women speaking out about incest.* Minneapolis: Cleis Press.

Merskey, H. (1992). The manufacture of personalities: The production of multiple personality disorder. *British Journal of Psychiatry, 160,* 327–340.

Olio, K. (1996). Are 25% of clinicians using potentially risky therapeutic practices?: A review of the logic and methodology of the Poole, Lindsay, et al., study. *Journal of Psychiatry and Law, 24.*

Pezdek, K. (1998, July). *The recovered memory/false memory debate.* Presented at the 1998 Conference on Trauma and Cognitive Science, Eugene, OR.

Pezdek, K., & Roe, C. (1994). Memory for childhood events: How suggestible is it? *Consciousness and Cognition 3*, 374–387.

Polusny, M., & Follette, V. (1996). Remembering childhood sexual abuse: A national survey of psychologists' clinical practices, beliefs, and personal experiences. *Professional Psychology: Research and Practice*, *27*, 41–52.

Poole, D., Lindsay, D., Memon, A., & Bull, R. (1995). Psychotherapy and the recovered memories of childhood abuse. *Journal of Clinical and Consulting Psychology, 63*, 426–438.

Pope, H. G., & Hudson, J. I. (1995). Can individuals "repress" memories of childhood sexual abuse? An examination of the evidence. *Psychiatric Annals*, *25*, 715–719.

Pope, K. S. (1996). Memory, abuse and science: Questioning claims about the false memory syndrome epidemic. *American Psychologist, 54*, 957–974.

Pope, K. S., & Brown, L. S. (1996). *Recovered memories of abuse: Therapy, assessment, forensics.* Washington, DC: American Psychological Association.

Rush, F. (1980). *The best-kept secret: Sexual abuse of children.* New York: McGraw-Hill.

Salter, A. (1995). *Transforming trauma: A guide to understanding and treating adult survivors of child sexual abuse.* Thousand Oaks, CA: Sage.

Scheflin, A., & Brown, D. (1996). Repressed memory or dissociative amnesia: What science says. *Journal of Psychiatry and Law, 24.*

Shapiro, F. (1995). *Eye movement desensitization and reprocessing: Basic principles, protocols and procedures.* New York: Guilford.

Van der Kolk, B. A. (1998, July). *Neurobiological dimensions of traumatic memories.* Presented at the 1998 Conference on Trauma and Cognitive Science, Eugene, OR.

Yapko, M. (1994). *Suggestions of abuse: True and false memories of childhood sexual trauma.* New York: Simon & Schuster.

Yates, J. L., & Nasby, W. (1993). Dissociation, affect and network models of memory: An integrative proposal. *Journal of Traumatic Stress, 6,* 305–326.

2

Freedom of Thought and Joy in Living

Stephen Lankton

This chapter is about how people solve problems and how they experience themselves and the world. I'll begin by explaining "freedom of thought and joy in living" as ways of interrupting an unfortunate social norm that has become a significant way of life for almost all of our clients and, for that matter, most of us. I describe this way of life without freedom of thought and joy, the harm it does, and basic interventions to transcend into joy.

The most basic interventions deal with ways of disrupting negative thought, clearing the mind of "busy" or pointless thought, stopping thought entirely, and inputting preferred thought. In addition, each of us must develop a personal recognition of the need, build the skills to choose freely what we think, and be able to pass it on to our clients in a way that is relevant for them.

Finally, the chapter details the experience of joy in living. Simply put, joy can be both the by-product of chosen thought and one of the most appropriate things to experience instead of common thought. Most of all, as therapists, we ought to address this directly with ourselves and our clients. And if we are to be effective, we must do it in a way that reduces conventional therapy to brief therapy and reduces brief therapy to conversation.

THE PROBLEM STATE

Most clients I see are victims of a crime. They are the perpetuators of that crime, as well. It is the crime of not knowing. The don't know themselves. They don't know how to use their own minds for solving problems of living, and they don't know how to experience joy. I think it is a kind of crime, or perhaps a sin, that they have not been trained in this skill. It is frightening sometimes to realize how far we have *not* come in education, family teaching, and the art of psychotherapy. It is evidenced by the almost total lack of awareness by people who get lost in repetitious thought and mazes of experience while under the impression that they are solving their problems. But there is no dominant socializing institution that teaches otherwise.

Sociologist Lewis Yablonsky (1972) referred to this trend as:

> . . . the growing dehumanization of people to the point where they have become the walking dead. This dehumanized level of existence places people in roles where they are actors mouthing irrelevant platitudes, experiencing programmed emotions with little or no compassion or sympathy for other people. People with this condition suffer from the existential disease of robopathology. (p. 6)

This rather awkward term never caught on. More unfortunate, however, is that the ideas behind the concept were not widely recorded either. For Yablonsky, robopaths differ from psychopaths in two distinct ways. They are highly predictable and they are nondeviant.

People generally don't think about the sort of freedom I am talking about or Yablonsky feared they were losing. They think they have freedom when some extremely mundane criteria are met.

In today's America, it seems that the definition of free thought is the right to have an uncensored opportunity to shout obscenities or to publish a book of nude photos. It seems that the experience of joy has become confused with the experience of thrill. People who have thrilling surges of adrenaline do, most certainly, report that they are happy, joyful, and higher than usual at those moments. This should not be confused with happiness. Happiness is a hard term to define since it is often attached to the consequences of success reached by means of hard work or by acquiring the symbols of that success by any means available. It is very idiosyncratic and elusive. Happiness for some might be spending a day with the family, quietly fishing, and for others, it might be winning a lucrative employment contact.

Joy, however, refers less to the cognitive and social elements than it does to the experiential, and even spiritual, element of private life. Joy is associated with pleasure and an agreeable sensation or emotion — it need not have an antecedent, consequence, or thought. Nevertheless, I am using the term "happiness" to mean the habitual mental state that gives rise to the feeling of joy.

FREEDOM FROM WHICH THOUGHTS?

I've implied that something about conventional thought is undesirable. But I haven't yet been clear about which type of mental activity this involves. Undesirable thoughts are those that come from social programming and replace and limit experience and awareness.

Most individuals have only a few favored states of consciousness. In some of these states, there is conscious awareness of cognitive activity, with combinations of visual and auditory images. These are images of the past, imagined past, and imagined futures.

Whereas the content varies greatly between individuals, the process of experiencing cognition probably varies less. People differ in consciousness for combinations of these images, mixtures of auditory and visual qualities, chunk sizes, and degree of lucidness for each. There will also be a different quality and intensity in bodily components associated with these cognitions. In fact, some people are more conscious of their bodily components than of their associated cognition. Despite individual variations, limitation on thought affects both the *content* of thought and, to a different degree, the *process*.

Before discussing these two logical levels for an opportunity of change (content and process), it is important to make the problem more explicit. The thoughts about which people do not have a choice can be characterized in several distinct layers.

The Most Common Layer: Referents to Reality

The most tenacious limits on thinking are those imposed by the world view we unconsciously absorb. I have discussed, elsewhere, the history of scientific thought and the logical positivism, reductionism, and chauvinism upon which it is formed (S. Lankton, 1998). The by-product of chopping up the world in this way is immensely important for therapists, and even in common household conversation.

In *The Revolution of Hope*, Erich Fromm (1968) writes:

> In the search of scientific truth, man came across knowledge that he could use for the domination of nature. He had tremendous success. But in the one-sided emphasis on technique and material consumption, man lost touch with himself, with life. Having lost religious faith and the human values bound up with it, he concentrated on technical and material values and lost the capacity for deep emotional experiences, for the joy and sadness that accompany them. The machine he built became so powerful that it developed its own program, which now determines man's own thinking. (p. 2)

This pervasive machine that Fromm writes about is a layer of mindless, or even thoughtful conformity to reality defined by our socializing processes. From the continual propaganda of well-meaning education, we learn that the world consists of things and processes. We learn nouns and verbs. A chair, a table, and even a personality, are labeled as nouns and denote things that basically don't change. Processes, labeled by verbs, consist of such actions as sitting, standing, digesting, and so on. Presumably, the nouns are never events.

This rule is satisfying enough for the young and the simple, but the problem is that everything should be a verb. Everything is in the process of change. Nothing is solid. This distinction becomes especially problematic when we try to make sense of physical reality events, like atoms, electrons, photons, stars, and gravity. Thinking, as we do, that photons and electrons are wave particles results in the seeking of answers for questions that don't make sense, such as, "What holds the energy to the electron?" "What makes the wave become a particle?" "How do energy and matter interact?"

But whereas these problems of physical science are interesting, they probably don't affect joy, well-being, or freedom of our thoughts. Right? Wrong. Over the last few centuries, we have come to think about the existence of love, courage, forgiveness, happiness, and the like as nouns. As such, we think that they are caused by other nouns. Our explanations attest to this. Consider these examples: "He has so much anger in him."

"I don't have enough love." "I don't feel as though I have any forgiveness." People don't often think of love as a process (outside of the thought that it is somehow the same as the sexual act). Our culture doesn't provide information about how to facilitate achieving or experiencing love.

At the same time, we are expected to feel love and to tell our partners about it. This results in a bind: how to say we feel love when we were never sure we felt "it" as a thing within ourselves. But the bind is easily escaped: all we need to do is acquiesce and say we feel it. Then we must fool ourselves a bit and believe what we have said.

This scenario does not apply to all of us at all times. Occasionally, a sense of compassion and pride, mixed with excitement and awe, fills our experience, and we know that the label "love" is truly the best word for what we feel. Then we say, "I love you," and we mean it. Indeed, at these times, we feel love as a verb. Memory of these moments may give rise to a comment like, "I have a lot of love for you." Yet we still use "love" as a noun.

But, more typically, the term is used in a thoughtless conformity to what one ought to say or mean. This is well expressed by R. D. Laing (1967) in *The Politics of Experience* when he writes about why this happens:

> We . . . take action on the world through behavior itself. Specifically this devastation is largely the work of *violence* that has been perpetrated on each of us, and by each of us on ourselves. The usual name that much of this violence goes under is *love*. (p. 59)

Laing uses the word *violence* in a manner that is shockingly liberal. He means that mindless conformity to labels that are not based in experience further obfuscates our understanding of our experience and this is a betrayal of (or violence to) the self. As a result of the world view, people live in a fantasy created by the label given to them by others.

Other examples of thinking of our experience as a thing can go something like this: "When my relationship broke up, it broke my heart and gave me depression." "There is no way that I can trust women." "It's just like a man to drop a bomb on you when you tell him you love him." and "I'm never going to show my feelings again." People accept such self-thoughts and communications as accurate. They accept them without question when they hear them spoken by others. These sorts of meanings are not challenged and the validity of the underlying labels are taken to be useful communications.

But the worst aspect of this arrangement is that such thoughts are never questioned by the user. The validly of the underlying "substance" is not questioned, and the thoughts are constructed from a social reality due to the apparent fit of the meaning. Rational thinking about these nouns is limited and solutions to personal or relational problems are inhibited.

But this "fit" is not generated from the person's own introspection and effort — it is not "true" in the person's experience. It is as if the person's own experience is mashed this way and that way in an effort to use conventional language to express it. After all, one might say, "Everyone else is satisfied with conventional language, why shouldn't I be too?" But without the freedom to think and come to know our own experience, how can we expect to benefit by mindlessly manipulating the labels and thoughts given to us by the impersonal other that society represents?

The Second Layer of Thought Control Is More Personal: Families

The family teaches us that much of our experience is not real. It informs us inaccurately that joy, happiness, and satisfaction are just around the corner (or never available to us at all), and that all we need do to reach it is to labor a bit more, study a bit longer, work more efficiently, exercise a new way, and so on. The largest category of thought limitation comes from the accepted values of the socializing forces from the family.

> Our capacity to think, except in the service of what we are dangerously deluded in supposing is our self-interest and in conformity with common sense, is pitifully limited: our capacity even to see, hear, touch, taste, and smell is so shrouded in veils of mystification that an intensive discipline of unlearning is necessary for anyone before one can begin to experience the world afresh, with innocence, truth and love. (Laing, 1967, p. 27)

Here is an example. I recently had a client who brought in his six-year-old daughter. She was in first grade and presumably was having nightmares in which she screamed. The parents had tape-recorded the child's utterances and brought the tape to me. This was not a child screaming in fear. This was a child who was whimpering to attract attention. Her crying would bring her parents to her room. Then they would leave and she would do it again and they would return.

I wasn't at all alarmed when I heard her cries, and I am a parent who can become alarmed when children make sounds that aren't normal. These were manipulative little whines to which the best response would probably be: "Go on to sleep and we will see you in the morning," or "Please close your door while you make that sound so we can talk without hearing you."

Upon discussion, it became clear that concern for the child was actually a displaced bit of fighting with the wife's ex-husband, the child's father. The daughter visited her father from time to time and the mother was fearful of and angry at him. So she hovered around the daughter looking for signs that might indicate the ex-husband's meanness. But there were none here and the mother was fairly easily satisfied about that.

The case would have been closed except that, with the stepfather in the office, I took the opportunity to ask how things were going in this newly constructed family. I inquired about the daughter's school, family members' health, work, and so on. He volunteered that her school grades were terrible and that she had an attention problem. She just couldn't put her mind to anything, and if she thought about something, within a second, she'd be thinking about something else. And in this way, he added, she was just another stupid woman, like her mother. That, he insisted was what was affecting her school work. He added that he'd be happy if I would try to help her.

He said all this in the presence of his daughter and wife. Not only was it untrue, but it was also extremely damaging to self-image, of course. But such beliefs become true and inhibit freedom of thought. It's the hypnosis of the family. It's the way socializing institutions train us to limit our range of thought and problem solving. We are taught labels, concepts, and causal relations between them, and how to behave toward all of them. As Eric Berne (1972) wrote, "The child is, in effect, hypnotized by his parents into carrying out a certain life pattern" (p. 343).

Each person learns with a different degree of emotional tolerance, so that some people can question and some don't even dare to. Thinking back to the family with the schoolgirl, consider the difference it would have made if the father had said, "She has been improving her ability to pay attention, little by little. Sometimes she doesn't even know that she's improving, but we know she is. She'll see." If he had followed that line of thinking, his family hypnosis would have been positive instead of negative — expansive instead of limiting.

The Third Layer of Thought Control

This layer includes therapists, physicians, and other change professionals. The layers of thought control I've suggested are like skin on an onion. You can peel from the most removed outer shell of world view to the deeper shell of the historical family to the individual's most immediate and intimate shell. This layer concerns the personal re-examination that goes on in therapy.

Specialists

Eric Berne used an anecdote about a make-believe client who had a pebble in his shoe to highlight the absurdity of specialists' obfuscating the simple and obvious. The story explained that because of the pebble, the man walked oddly. Because of that, he threw his hip out and that caused stress on his back, which caused tension in his neck and gave him headaches. He went to see a specialist about the headaches, who prescribed medication for the headaches. But Berne's point was that someone should have simply taken the pebble out of the man's shoe.

Simple efficiency is often lost as specialized helping professionals inadvertently overlook solutions that looking at the whole person in context might reveal. The majority of my clients are being medicated by more than one physician, each a different specialist. In every case, the client has been led to believe that the medical doctor can do no more at this time but prescribe medication. The clients continue to visit each physician to complain about the effects or lack of effects of the medication. None of these clients has reported that any of the doctors has taken a holistic or system-wide approach to their problems. Each doctor has labeled a problem, and most problems are to then be "solved" with prescription drugs. The most distressing for me are clients with pain.

The clients may be impressed, in awe, confused, frustrated, or angry with their diagnosis. But, they either resign themselves to living with these diagnosed "diseases" or ask how they can get rid of them. How can I live with my lupus, myalgia, myasthenia, arthritis, degenerative bone disease, cluster headaches, acid reflux, pinched nerve, slow metabolism? The presence of seemingly obvious factors, such as excess weight, smoking, lack of proper diet and exercise, self-criticism, and neglectful or aggressive others in the client's life, may not even be addressed. This is often true even in blatant cases where pain would most certainly be decreased if the client were to lose weight. In other cases, sleep problems related to medication go uncorrected, except for a referral to a sleep clinic! The general well-being of the client, in my view, is not considered and the often unhelpful labels create further mind control. It doesn't matter whether clients accept or challenge the label. In either case, its reality guides their behavior and experience.

Observable Truth

Alan Watts (1972) provided an interesting illustration concerning a cat crossing behind a fence from which a board was missing. An observer first saw a cat's head, then a cat's body, then a cat's tail. The cat turned around and walked back, and again the observer saw the cat's head, cat's body, and cat's tail. Upon subsequent passes that seemed to be exactly the same, the observer concluded that the cat's head caused the cat's tail since this event comes and then that event comes. Never did the cat's tail occur without the cat's head. The cat's head always led to the cat's tail. "Thereupon, he reasons that the event head is the invariable and necessary cause of the event tail, which is the head's effect. This absurd and confusing gobbledygook comes from his failure to see that head and tail go together: they are all one cat" (p. 27).

The illustration is similar to what we do when we look at the world through filters and assume that we see relationships of cause and effect where there are none. We have been under an illusion that events can be broken down into small pieces. We are, in this reductionistic way, led to believe that one piece causes the next piece, and that any piece had some antecedents that caused it to happen and some consequences and conclusions that it will reach.

As caregivers, it is important to be comfortable not knowing any truth. It is easy to say this, but harder to do. Many people have not learned to be comfortable with ambiguity and no truth to hold on to. But remember how misinformed we believed science to be only 100 years ago. If we must insist on a truth, let it be the truth that our clients can change, improve, and enjoy.

More Labels

Reductionist science, with its proclivity toward assuming that it can know a truth about reality, has given rise to reductionistic subcategories.

It is often unnecessarily difficult to see a client who, in previous therapy, had been labeled and accepted that label. For instance, at a therapy workshop, the person in charge of organizing a demonstration for me asked if I were willing to work with a manic depressive woman. I asked on what problem the woman wanted to work. The organizer replied, "She's manic depressive."

The problem with this conversation is that I don't treat labels, I work with people. Even though the organizer was trying to be helpful by sharing this label, the client (and I) was further alienated from direct experience. For every minute of talk time given to considering aspects of that label, the client is missing out on creative problem solving.

Erickson emphasized the importance of treating each person as an individual. That means finding the uniqueness of the person. Diagnostic categories (labels) are all about finding the similarities between people. Sharing these labels in word, or even in deed, are ways to help clients become more conforming, past oriented, self-conscious, and alienated.

Therapists who foster thinking processes that further limit clients constitute a problematic category of their own. Beyond issues of iatrogenic problems and countertransference in therapy, another, broader problem arises when therapists inadvertently limit thinking by labeling and attribution. Introducing a concept to a client focuses awareness on that concept. To continue communicating, a client has no choice but to agree with or dispute the concept. In both cases, the client's thinking is subsequently bound to that concept.

As a result of these three major layers of worldview socialization, family propaganda, and professional jargon, people think about what they have been told to think about. They ruminate on concepts that are not of their own choosing. They attempt to answer questions with cause-and-effect thinking that can never resolve the concerns. They fret, worry, wonder, puzzle, obsess, muse, fume about ideas, concepts, topics, relationships, duties, faults, and plans. They even seek professional help to get answers to questions that should not ever have been asked. For example, the person presents a goal: "I just want you to help me find out whose fault it was." "Can you tell me why my wife left me?" And one of my favorites, "If I could just understand why I do such stupid things, I'd be happy." These kinds of distractions limit mature and appropriate decision making. However, people don't know anything else to think or any other way to think.

PRACTICAL AND PSYCHOTHERAPEUTIC POINTS OF VIEW

From a practical point of view, everyone would agree with the basic idea of gaining control of their own mental activity. Believing it is possible, knowing how, and putting that knowledge into consistent action are often another matter. For example, long ago, before my son grew to be six feet tall, he was bullied by a particular child at school. And he would come home and talk about it for 10 or 20 minutes or more. Later, he would bring it up again. Finally, after this had gone on for almost a month, I said, "You know, there is something that I really dislike about all of this talk. You are really smart and you've got a great brain, but your brain time is limited and you can only entertain a finite number of thoughts and ideas between now and the time you become an old man. And you're using a lot of your brain time on problems that are somebody else's. You shouldn't have to think about what's wrong with Billy, what Billy does, what Billy did, what Billy's going to do, and what Billy said. You shouldn't let Billy use *your* brain and fill it up with what he'd have you think about. You should have a choice about what you let occupy your brain." Although Shawn no doubt recognized the wisdom of that advice, he was not immediately able fully to implement it and apply it to the disruption of those thoughts that were stealing his brain time. But the point was not lost.

From the psychotherapeutic viewpoint, most of our clients don't know how to disengage their attention from those things about which they think redundantly, whether self-image, an alleged inability to concentrate, manic depression, multiple personality, or depression. They don't know how to step behind that thought process and let it go by without them, to be free of those thoughts, and then to think the thoughts they want to think.

We may tell them they should do it, but we rarely show them how, probably because we don't know how ourselves. We don't have role models for it. For example, the role models of communicators we see when we turn on television to watch "Crossfire" don't even demonstrate people who can discuss things and reach a useful conclusion. They just argue. Now and then, you can get a sophisticated argument on "Crossfire," more often you get several experts trying to interrupt someone. But where do we turn for models of people who can use words to solve problems? It's increasingly unlikely that our clients will come to us thinking they can use discussion to solve a problem.

STOPPING THOUGHT

Education

Despite the scarcity of models and well-known guidelines for achieving freedom of thought, we can identify specific steps that facilitate this goal. The first step is education. I find it useful to discuss the goal and the reasons why clients have not thought of it before. Generally, this is a matter of summarizing what has been stated here in more personal terms to reach the goal of being in a state of freedom from thought will require that clients are ready to experience joy. The educational process is especially important to underscore that the way of life the client needs to follow has to be discerned. The education process must include the understanding that obvious models will be scarce. The journey is not lonely, but the traveler will be alone.

Evaluation

Evaluation and awareness are the next step. Clients can inspect their thoughts at some point and recognize those that obviously are limiting. Self-critical thoughts, pessimistic thoughts, thoughts about their pain, worries about their performance, rehashing of the past, all are targets for censorship. And to do that, a client has to notice and evaluate thought. Initially, this may require the aid of relaxation. Sometimes it is helpful for clients to talk to themselves in a fashion similar to the double-chair technique of Gestalt Therapy: The limiting thoughts are easily revealed when a conversation is created between the client who wishes to feel joy and the part of the client that will explain why "it" supposedly can't do so.

Stop Thought

The third step is actually stopping thought. After the initial target thoughts are identified, the more immediately rewarding part of therapy can begin. Introspection reveals that thoughts arise from memories or from sense perception. The sensory-motor mind is very susceptible to changing input. For training purposes, it is best to begin by reducing outside influences, closing the eyes, relaxing the body. Past experience provides a storehouse of experience from which thoughts arise. There are a number of ways to stop thought. We can engage incompatible thoughts, such as reciting mantras or concentrating on objects of meditation. We can slow thought by shifting to the tonal submodality of the thought and syncing it to a slow exhale. For example, one can imagine the voice tone that would accompany the self-talk or "thought." Upon identifying it, let the tone of the self-talk become lower in lock-step with a slowing of breathing. We can dissociate thought by observing it as something that is not a part of the self. I prefer this method as it can be integrated easily with the use of hypnosis and other visual and auditory dissociation practices that I teach.

Choose Thought

Selecting preferred thoughts is the fourth step. There is an old Hindu saying that a nightingale in a golden case is no freer than one in a cage of iron. Some might interpret that to mean that the positive thoughts one creates of self-nurturing and positive affirmation are likely to be as much of a trap as the interrupted negative thoughts. In practice, however, it is sometimes a necessary and valuable intermediary step for clients to achieve this degree of control. Thought structures such as that of our Self-Image Thinking training (Lankton & Lankton, 1983) are an excellent way to facilitate desired experience and create associations for those experiences to be available in future situations. These associations, like most, operate as posthypnotic suggestions and self-programming.

Experience

Initiating, that is, recognizing, experience is the next step. Certainly, one does not lose consciousness when the mind is quiet. More than at any other time, this is the time when one ought to focus awareness on those natural experiences that bring joy and pleasure. These are as simple as inhalation and exhalation experiences, the feeling of the pulse in your limbs, the awareness of your heartbeat, the feeling of warm and relaxed muscles. They quietly convey a powerful foundation for joy. The pleasure and sense of well-being that come from these experiences should not be underrated. In fact, it should be elaborated!

Practice

Practice is the inevitable last step. The mind learns rapidly, but learning to stop thought and replace it with joy once is hardly enough for most people. After all, they have practiced the opposite internal behavior thousands of times a day for decades. Clients need to be encouraged to continue the self-hypnosis and self-control activity until they can achieve the state with a minimal willful effort or until it becomes an expectation and a habit to be happy. There will be no one else to encourage them to practice finding joy, so it is essential that we provide this expectation.

RESISTANCE TO JOY AND FREEDOM OF THOUGHT

Why would anyone resist the practice of routinely knowing joy and freedom of thought? I can best illustrate this by asking you to imagine and compare two scenarios. In the first, imagine two people walking along a beach and see that both heads are filled with images of checkbooks, calendars, childcare chores, past quarrels, anticipated meetings, lost key chains, and so on. Now imagine the people again, but this time have them walk along the beach with only the reflection of the immediate environment in their minds. They would see ever-changing waves, sand, sky. In comparing these scenarios, most would agree that the first scene depicts tension, worry, self-torture, obsession, anxiety. These people would be robbed of their joy. In many ways, it is correct to say that this is crazy. It may be the norm, but it is crazy. It is living outside the moment and feeling inappropriate experiences.

We may think that the scenario of being oriented to the here and now is the path to joy, peace, and sanity, but we often encounter objections to actually taking it. One reason for objecting is that we are not accustomed to proceeding this way, we don't know how to, and we are afraid to because, upon examination, it is scary and leads to insecurity and loss of control.

Loss of Control

"What the Chinese describe as a gentle standing out of the way ... or an emptying of the mind, is probably what the more egocentric personality of Western man sees as the violent death of the ego ..." (Naranjo & Ornstein, 1973, p. 25).

But one need not be fearful. The possibility of experiencing the here and now is known in those brief times when we allow ourselves to be and to feel. But the possibility of maintaining that state of consciousness for extended periods is considered inappropriate for our culture. That argument is based on the belief that we cannot plan for the future if we simply go about living in the present moment without those "out-of- context thoughts." Such arguing is based on a lack of trust in peoples' intelligence. It is based on the failure to notice how much we have learned and stored in our vast set of unconscious patterns of living.

Being Practical

Another possible basis for resistance is simply the idea that experiencing joy and freedom of thought would be impractical. However, there are clients for whom achieving this outcome is highly practical. Here are some examples. One of my clients was vague and confused when he came to therapy. He wanted to find out how victimized he had been and hadn't expected therapy to be more than an opportunity to vent his feelings and publicly clarify why his life was hard. However, he terminated after five sessions, declaring (to my delight and surprise) that coming to see me had been the best thing that had ever happened to him.

Another client was an overweight woman who complained of multiple medical problems. She said she wanted to die because of her inability to overcome her pain and her historical sense of helplessness in the face of a neglectful, and sometimes abusive, environment. "I have no reason to live," she proclaimed almost proudly. Within a few weeks, she had discovered joy and an ability to let go of the thoughts that reinforced her view of herself, her past, and her future. She announced that she had evolved a sense of well-being and that that experience was reason enough to live. As a result, she could control her pain and begin to lose weight. She has now lost over 40 pounds and has reduced her medication by half, with her doctor's approval.

Most clients could achieve similar benefit from such a shift. In fact, this approach to problems is highly applicable to the majority of clients I see. Establishing freedom of thought and a sense of joy does not change the reality of the world. When divorce is necessary, one must divorce. When changing employment, going to college, losing weight, or whatever, is necessary, then those goals must be pursued. But the state of mind that one is in during these times is negotiable. This is exactly where the education and training to have freedom of thought and joy become important.

Ask your clients what they intend to do to become happy and you will find a confusion of unlikely or inappropriate plans. The plans may be interesting, even wise, but they are not needed in order for the person to attain happiness and joy because we all have these available within us. After a person learns to experience joy, his or her other goals can be pursued for their own material payoff or their intrinsic value.

JOY AND HAPPINESS

Isn't it ironic that so many people are less than happy? They do not have much comfort, and even less joy. A simple experiment of asking people if they are happy will yield interesting results. I have done this on numerous occasions and typically get three types of answers: "Yes," and "I would be happy if 'X' were to happen," and "No, I'm never happy."

The individuals who answer "Yes" usually don't actually seem happy. They aren't exhibiting any of the signs we associate with happiness, like smiling, gracefulness, and good health. When the person responds sharply, "Yes, I'm happy," the answer means something other than what we have in mind when we ask if a person feels joy and happiness. It is as if a large number of people have learned that they are expected to say "Yes" to such a question unless they are, at that moment, actively involved in conflict. But happiness does not mean the absence of conflict or the inability to articulate one's inner state.

Those who report they would feel happiness "if" something else were to happen are at least seekers. Unfortunately, the life of continual seeking only ensures that they will be seeking something new in the future when the joy, happiness, and comfort of a recent conquest wear off. Many believe that they will be happy when they earn more money, graduate, get a faster modem, buy that snazzy car, are accepted into this or that group, or just spend a pleasant Sunday with the family. Of course, people do feel better for a short time when a particular goal is reached, and disappointed or depressed when it is not. But they soon find themselves looking for something else. This attitude makes for a lot of difficulty in life and either fully motivates or in large part supports a mass of problems, including jealousy, possessiveness, competition, false pride, deception, intimidation, theft, anxiety, frustration, inadequacy, and hopelessness.

Initially, it seems to many that achieving what one seeks is the true way to confidence, competence, and the accompanying feelings of happiness and joy. So, a bit of clarification is needed about this issue. People do achieve happiness and joy by living through a process or sequence of events that involves the following three steps.

1. Devise a desire, ideal, or goal state that differs from the current state.
2. Identify resources, organize a plan (no matter how casual), and implement the perceptions, behaviors, thoughts, skills, and so on, to reach the goal.

3. Discover that the strategies, skills, planning, ideas, resources, actions, and so on, led to fulfillment of the goal, ideal, or desire state.

However, this sequence, which is the protocol of building a feeling of competence, is mostly useful to help people *discover* the happiness within them and *provide a memory for recovering the experience* at a later time. It is really essential to realize that the feelings of happiness and joy, especially, are available to people independently of these or any other accomplishment. Once these feelings, or any feelings, are learned, they are available through direct recall of the feeling. The extent to which one loses sight of *that* fact is the extent to which one continually seeks to achieve more. And as people seek an awareness of happiness in this manner, through achievement and competency or gain rather than through *retrieving* the learned experience, they will hold on to their successful feelings and their joy for a very short time. The result is the continued need to seek "more."

Webster's Unabridged Dictionary defines happiness as "the enjoyment of pleasure without pain; felicity; blessedness; satisfaction." It is listed as synonymous with felicity, blessedness, bliss, and aptness. No part of the definition suggests that one must work for it by exerting the sort of effort people commonly report.

I am suggesting that it is a state that can be experienced almost continually. What, then, is happiness? Joy and happiness are words that I'm using in a very general way to describe not just some state of bliss, which most people don't attain, but also very low levels of happiness, all the way through extreme happiness, and, for that matter, religious experiences, as well. "If his mind is truly involved in his action, the bliss of the meditation state is a joy beyond pleasure and pain, a sense of attunement with the holy that follows upon surrender of personal preferences" (Naranjo & Ornstein, 1973, p. 26).

For most people, just happiness would be okay. They would never expect a spiritual high and they would not really expect to be even moderately happy all the time. Oddly, not many therapists have ever had clients come to an intake session saying that they wanted to be happy. Most of the time, clients come to us saying that they want to stop fighting with their spouses, stop being depressed, stop overeating, stop being afraid of elevators, snakes, or using public restrooms. Even when we ask them what it is that would make them happy, those few who say they want to be happy generally restate it in terms of removal of something negative. For instance, "I would be happy if my son would stop getting failing grades at school."

But when that negative thing is removed, they aren't actually happy. Many people don't have a sense that their life is meaningful or worthwhile. A few fortunate ones don't even ask that question, but others do, especially depressed people. They ask how one can find anything worth living for. And sometimes therapists take this to be a question of spirituality needing development. I agree that it is. I think that all joy, all psychotherapy, all personal growth, joy included, is part of some developing spirituality.

There are deep cultural and historical influences affecting our perception of and expectation for happiness. Throughout the Judeo-Christian world, we are alerted to the God of Abraham who was an ever-present spirit of love and comfort, the invitation to "good tidings of great joy," and the covenants of grace and peace offered by the blessings of religions. The U.S. Constitution guarantees the right to the "pursuit of happiness." We are told daily, in one way or another, that it is permissible, even preferable, to be happy. And too, the majority of parents would want this not only for themselves, but also for their children. In short, our philosophical, religious, political, and social structures seem to grant us permission to seek joy and freedom.

So why are people not happy? The answer ultimately lies in our lack of training and attention to the feeling, our lack of trust or faith in keeping it when we have it, and the willingness of our environment to rely on misleading myths about happiness. These reasons include the lack of careful examination, ignorance about the alternative, a sometimes outright deception for profit, and, overall, a historical failure to develop language, awareness, and tools for acquiring our own and other's phenomenological experiences.

It seems that the words to a country-western song I recently heard are all too true for most of us. The singer laments: "Everyone knows what to do about my misery, everybody but me!" Isn't it true that if you ask anyone about how to be happy, you end up with some vague generalities that don't really fit your situation? Often, it seems that the person giving the advice really does hope you will be happy (even when the person giving the advice is not). It appears that the reason that most advice is less than successful is that over many centuries we have developed a society based on some myths about happiness.

- That happiness is only in your head

Happiness is a total-body phenomenon. When we are joyful, we know there are changes in several physical, chemical, cognitive, and digestive functions. These include feelings of comfort, well-being, compassion, peace, increased circulation and respiration, a sense of energy, better immune system functioning, pain reduction, increased behavioral congruity, and an intuitive sense of a reason for living.

- That people automatically know how to feel good

Left to their own devices, people certainly learn to avoid pain and to seek pleasure. That is, they maximize their positive experience within learned limits. However, people aren't left to their own devices. They are constrained by the worldview, economics, geography, political oppression, and limitations imposed by social learning, family training, and professional help.

We believe that children are happy or know how to be happy. This seems to be true enough for children who have a sufficiently nurturing atmosphere and are left to their own devices to discover what brings them pleasure. But too soon children compromise their pleasure so they will not be exhibiting joy that is beyond the norm for their families' apparent limit. This sort of compromising leads to defensive adaptations to hide the threatening experiences of joy from the prying eyes of parents and siblings. The entire range of defense mechanisms from ego psychology has to do with hiding experiences that are perceived to be a threat. These include anxiety, fear, anger, and, of course, tenderness and joy, the well-known components of the Oedipal drama. So, it is not wise to assume that unaided children are "out there having fun." Nor is it wise to assume that everyone, by virtue of having once been a child, knows how to attain joy and happiness, blessedness, and felicity.

- That an atmosphere of nurturing support is not required

Has a relative or friend ever reprimanded you: "Why don't you just stop doing that and be happy?" Not only does this suggest that one already knows how to become happy, but it shows a nontolerance of the acquisition of happiness and the supporting atmosphere in which it must be learned.

Once happiness/joy/comfort is learned, it becomes a strong personal resource that can be relied upon to bolster an individual in performing courageous acts and to sustain him or her through times of trouble. Before it is well learned, however, it requires a delicate focus of attention in order to be recognized and an atmosphere of support in order for it to be learned and reused.

Because few people really understand happiness and joy, there are pitifully few times when transactions are designed to focus on it and support it, and few situations that are structured to initiate those types of transactions. When people come to know of it, their sense of compassion helps build that nurturing environment for others.

- That happiness comes from outside oneself

People often fail to realize how they repeatedly construct whatever feelings they have. They may feel frustrated that they do not "achieve" happiness. They may feel depressed that they are never understood, never happy, never successful. They may feel anxious that others will not like their behavior or pretenses. But no matter what the case, this redundant feeling, whether it be frustration, anxiety, depression, jealousy, anger, or helplessness, is being created by their own thinking and acting again and again.

Ironically, the mental machinations used to create these undesirable feelings would also create happiness or joy. The undesirable feelings are often the by-products of so-called problem-solving tactics. For instance, there are people who worry that some calamity will strike their children or families. As a result, they may mentally rehearse the problem and anticipate their possible solutions. They think they are helping to prevent the problem, but the by-products of that attempt are anxiety and worry. The familiar feeling of worry and fear, in this case, will surely reduce their joy, and, ironically, many become depressed and angry and inadequate in attempting to achieve, and helping their children to achieve, joy or happiness! They continue the practice as a never-ending loop because they think it is the most appropriate way to proceed. This self-inflicted unpleasantness is not seen as self-inflicted or as optional. Nevertheless, they realize that happiness and joy are not to be found within them and they go to external sources. In many cases, this accounts for their seeking destructive distractions and people as diversions from their self-inflicted pain.

- That you can have happiness regardless of how you treat others

It is not so much that others are needed for happiness, but that the emotions and tensions that result from anger, bitterness, and hostility will derail the awareness of happiness. Joy and happiness will produce compassion. As such, the way one person treats another can be a type of voltmeter to measure how much happiness, freedom, joy, and peace they are charged with.

- That it's hard to be happy when you have problems

Many postpone their joy until something happens to improve their problems. They consider joy as a dessert. It is something of which you partake after the meal is over or a reward you receive after a job is completed. However, joy is not like a "just reward," but is available at almost all times. In fact, the point of this chapter is that one ought to establish a state of mind of which joy and freedom of thought are constant components.

This is especially true considering the fact that life is, in some manner of observing, a steady stream of problems with which one must deal. This way of observing, by the way, is how life appears when one does not maintain joy and freedom of thought. It is a catch-22 that if one waits for the problems to go away in order to have full-time happiness and joy, one will never achieve them. However, if you do achieve happiness, your problem will be significantly reduced.

- That you don't need to practice to have happiness

So, do people not want to be happy? Why do they do the wrong things if these acts will not lead to happiness? The answer is that people will rely on old learning, habits, and attitudes until they learn alternatives. Once they succeed at feeling happiness and retaining it, they will rely less and less on their previous ways of filling time. Our difficulty in training ourselves for happiness is attributable to several factors. We have no idea how to begin and no personal or lifestyle model is provided, it violates the customary sense of what is normal, there is no social support from the mass of people who feel differently, there is no commercial appeal for joy or freedom, and it is not thrilling or dramatic enough.

Perhaps the most important of these factors is that we have few (or no) models to follow, no support if we succeed. We do have so-called models from the world of entertainment. That is, we are expected to believe what we read in the papers, that some film stars or athletes are happy. At least they are happy for the moment when they are involved in a romance, have conquered an opponent, or shocked us by performing some outrageous deed. We are also expected to believe that we can become happy if we purchase certain products touted in television commercials and magazine advertisements. One wonders at whom these commercials are aimed since we presume that everyone can recognize their idiocy. But perhaps repetition dulls us to the idiocy because the "Madison Avenue" pitch continues. And as it does, it only further obfuscates the path to happiness and joy.

CONCLUSION

Many of the myths about happiness that we have come to embrace are the result of our thoughtlessly accepting the logic, labels, and limits on experience to which we are socialized. Indeed, socialization seems to be the midwife of thought control and experiential slavery. Alternatively, the achievement of joy requires nothing less than a revolution, just as it has for centuries. And, the way to accomplish this revolution is to put back into the hands of therapists those skills and perceptions that have been the province of medicine men, shamans, mystics, and change agents since civilization began.

As therapists, we must teach our clients to seek freedom of thought and the joy of living, and orient them toward these objectives. We can help people to stop limiting their thinking and problem solving. We can help them to stop "external seeking" and to find the simple joys within. We can help people to expect to achieve joy and happiness, to trust the experience when they have it, and to react spontaneously and creatively when they find it. We must help them integrate it into a new lifestyle and generalize it and apply it to heal anxiety, depression, pain, bitterness, mind/ body splits, helplessness, hopelessness, and immorality.

Ironically, the words "mindful" and "mindless" mean almost the opposite of their usual connotations in this new context. A mind full of unconsciously accepted garbage is not the caring and "mindful" person the term suggests. Conversely, a person who has consciously made an effort to avoid mental clutter might be considered mindless in a certain way, but this does not mean that the person is ignorant. In fact, this "mindless" person may be ignoring far less about the self, and the social and physical environments than other, "mindfull" people do. It is the state of mind of great joy, as R. D. Laing (1967) said:

> The experience of being the actual medium for a continual process of creation takes one past all depression or persecution of vain glory, past even chaos or emptiness, into the very mystery of that

continual flip of nonbeing into being, and can be the occasion of that great liberation when one makes the transition from being afraid of nothing to the realization that there is nothing to fear. (p. 42)

References

Berne, E. (1972). *What do you say after you say hello?* New York: Grove.

Fromm, E. (1968). *The revolution of hope.* New York: Harper & Row.

Laing, R. D. (1967). *The politics of experience.* New York: Ballantine.

Lankton, S. (1998). Ericksonian emergent epistemologies: Embracing a new paradigm. In M. Hoyt (Ed.), *Handbook of constructive therapies* (pp. 116–136). San Francisco: Jossey-Bass.

Lankton, S., & Lankton, C. (1983). *The answer within: A clinical framework of Ericksonian hypnotherapy.* New York: Brunner/Mazel.

Naranjo, C., & Ornstein, R. (1973). *On the psychology of meditation.* New York: Viking.

Watts, A. (1972). *The book: On the taboo against knowing who you are.* New York: Vintage.

Yablonsky, L. (1972). *Robopaths.* Baltimore, MD: Penguin Books.

3

Clinical Heuristics

Jeffrey K. Zeig

PROLOGUE

Here's a brainteaser that was published in the "Ask Marilyn" column by Marilyn vos Savant. Place the digits 1 through 8 in the circles shown in the diagram.

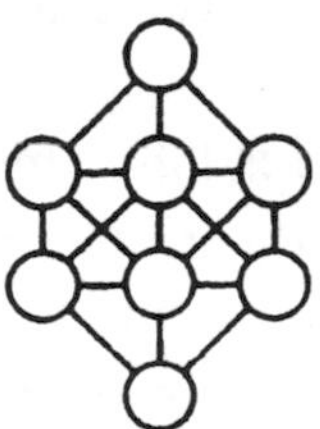

No two digits next to each other in serial order may go into circles that are connected by a direct line. For example, if "3" is placed in the top circle, neither "4" nor "5" may be placed in any of the three circles in the horizontal row beneath it because each of the circles is connected to the top circle by a direct line. There is only one solution.

A computer will take quite some time to solve the problem because there are 40,320 permutations to be analyzed. Most humans can solve it easily, especially with a little hint. (Hint: each digit has two neighbors except for the 1 and the 8.) Why? Two types of "thinking" are involved. The computer process is linear, a tedious step-by-step procedure. The other form of thinking uses a series of "tricks" learned from experience that may foster solutions. Curiously, one may not know consciously the specific details of the tricks one applies to simplify and solve complex problems.

Solving brainteasers requires a different logical process than does solving simple linear problems. Conducting effective psychotherapy is often a "brainteaser." It requires unusual inductive procedures on the part of the therapist.

INTRODUCTION

The practice of psychotherapy can be daunting for the novice and expert alike. Therapy often needs to be inventive, complex, and tailored to the particular patient. Standardizing the task — a preoccupation of psychotherapy in the empirically based, managed care era — misses the point. Consider all the factors involved, including the idiosyncrasies of the personal history and style of both the patient and the clinician; the unique social circumstances of the patient; and variations in biology. Human diversity is so great that it is amazing that one human being can sufficiently understand another to provide adequate counsel.

Even though therapy is often dauntingly complex, clinicians must simplify a lot of data in order to conduct a competent assessment and treatment. How therapists proceed is sometimes based on research, but customarily is based on treasured theories — explicit theories of personality, theories of psychosocial development, and theories of intervention.

Milton H. Erickson diverged from the tradition of basing interventions on research or explicit theories. His modus operandi extolled individual differences. Erickson believed that reliance on theory was slavish, and often led clinicians astray. He believed that interventions should be derived from the unique situations of the individuals seeking help, not from explicit a priori constructs of human behavior. Therapy primarily should be informed by clinical inference rather than empirical reasoning or theoretical constructs.

Erickson's belief in individualizing was tenacious. When I organized the first International Congress on Ericksonian Approaches to Hypnosis and Psychotherapy in 1980, I asked him (personal communication, November 1979) for a quote for the brochure that would summarize his clinical philosophy. He immediately offered, "Each person is a unique individual. Hence, psychotherapy should be formulated to meet the uniqueness of the individual's needs, rather than tailoring the person to fit the Procrustean bed of a hypothetical theory of human behavior." Clinical interventions according to Erickson are profoundly influenced by professional expectations. Therapists often find what they believe they will encounter, and in the process, they may distort or overlook essentials that can facilitate treatment.

Clinical inferences are affected by many factors including overt and implicit theories, prior experiences, mood, and expectations. A study was conducted by Temerlin (1968) in which a videotape was created that portrayed a man who was happy and well-adjusted. Various groups of therapists observed the tape under different conditions: In one instance, a prestigious authority told them that the tape was a "rare case of a mentally healthy individual." In the second, the authority told the observing clinicians that they would see a person who looked neurotic, but actually was quite psychotic. The control group was given no instructions. In the first group, the individual was unanimously deemed healthy. In the second condition, the patient was seen as psychotic or neurotic by 94% of the evaluating clinicians. In the control group, 57% of the clinicians assessed the man healthy, 43% deemed him neurotic.

Expectations are organized into hypotheses that profoundly influence subsequent decision-making, and this process has been tabbed, "behavioral confirmation" (Snyder, 1981). An example of behavioral confirmation is a study in which a person labeled a "job applicant" was seen as significantly less disturbed than the same individual who was labeled a patient (Langer & Abelson, 1974). Reciprocally, client behaviors may conform to the expectations and demand characteristics inherent in the treating clinician's theoretical framework.

Behavioral confirmation can be curtailed by limiting the use of theoretical templates, and relying more on simplifying assumptions that emphasize the uniqueness of patients and their situations.

Of course, conducting therapy without a theoretical template can be disheartening. Erickson succeeded by tailoring therapy to the uniqueness of the individual. In a 75th birthday tribute to Erickson, Margaret Mead (1976) extolled Erickson's style of creating a new therapy for each patient. Tailoring therapy requires creativity and perceptiveness. As previously mentioned, it is also based, in part, on using simplifying assumptions rather than templates.

How can one emulate Erickson's approach? The answer is deceptively simple: Look inside. In fact, therapists may not rely on theory or templates as much as they think. Rather, they are probably already using the simplifying assumptions that guide their practice. But these simplifying assumptions, called "heuristics," can be illuminated and extended in order to strengthen practice. The purpose of this chapter is to help clinicians do just that.

Following is a discussion of some of the heuristics that guide my own assessment and treatment planning, especially those I learned directly from Erickson and from Ericksonian-derived methods. First, let us consider in depth the two kinds of thinking to which I alluded in the brainteasers above.

ALGORITHMS AND HEURISTICS

Human cognitive processes rely on *algorithms* and *heuristics*, uniquely different operations, each suited to address different tasks.

Algorithms

An *algorithm* is a deductive analytical procedure that leads to a concrete solution. A finite number of steps are used to solve a problem. An example of an algorithm is using arithmetic to decide whether or not a specified integer is a prime number.

Algorithms can be used to solve complex problems. For example, one can open a safe by the algorithm of trying all possible combinations. Complexity, however, beckons us to use more inferential tools.

Algorithms can be elegant; they need not be simple. Consider the example of the mathematician, Karl Gauss (reported in Watzlawick, 1997). Even as a grammar school student, he was demonstrating his genius. When the class was given the task of summing the numbers from 1 to 100, Gauss used a masterful algorithm to quickly solve the problem. The rest of the class used the cumbersome algorithm of simple addition. Gauss immediately reported to the teacher's desk with a slip of paper on which was written the correct solution, 5,050. When asked by the teacher how he had derived a solution so quickly, he indicated that 1+100=101; 2+99=101; 3+98=101, etc. Therefore, he derived 50 x 101=5,050. The process he used was an elegant algorithm!

Heuristics

Some problems are so complex that inferential methods are necessary. Such processes are called *heuristics*. Consider chess. The human mind cannot compute all chess possibilities as an algorithm. A series of super computers can compute complex chess permutations and defeat a chess champion. In contradistinction, the human mind uses simplifying assumptions that may or may not lead to a positive outcome. In chess, the aspiring aficionado learns tricks, such as "overprotection of a square leads to an attack," or "control the center squares early in the game," or "don't develop the queen too early." These heuristics are known from experience to more often than not pave the way to positive results. Parenthetically, the last heuristic also is valuable in family therapy.

Heuristics can be processes rather than simple rules. In heuristic processes, a sequence of comparisons may be used, each based on previous experience, and each containing an alternative that is more likely to lead to a solution.

The concept of "heuristics" is not easy to define. To add to that, it shows up in diverse fields with different emphases. The concept is used in computer simulation models where it is applied to artificial intelligence. To create a computer that simulates human reasoning, one must program it to "think" heuristically.

Heuristics are also an area of investigation in social psychology that is used, for example, to understand social inference. Social inference concerns "assessing what information should be gathered to address a given judgement or decision, collecting that information, and combining it in some form" (Fisk & Taylor, 1984, p. 346).

An example of the use of heuristics in social psychology is in the availability heuristic, which addresses biases (Twersky & Kahneman, 1973). Information easy to bring to mind is more "available." If, for example, a person believes that he or she is a failure, that schema is readily available and disconfirming evidence may be ignored with such rationales as, "Well, I did okay, but it was only one time." A clinical example of the availability heuristic might be overestimating the potential of a patient for violence because the therapist recently viewed a newscast about homicide.

The number of literature citations for "heuristics" in computer simulations and social and cognitive psychology is enormous. I entered the term "heuristic" into a computer search engine and found 16,428 entries. A few months later, there were 27,831. A search of Amazon.com uncovered more than 50 books on heuristics. Most of the entries concerned academic psychology and computer models, although some related to mathematics and business. None applied to the practice of psychotherapy.

The only references to heuristics and therapy I could find were based on the work of Clark Moustakas (1990, 1994). He used the concept to refer to "a process of internal search through which one discovers the nature and meaning of experience and develops methods and procedures for further investigation and analysis" (1990, p. 9). To Moustakas, heuristic research is a method of self-discovery within the humanistic tradition, a way of autobiographically investigating human experience.

In general, heuristics are defined as rules or universals. I will use the term *clinical heuristics* to refer to simplifying assumptions for clinical decision-making. Clinical heuristics often are applied without conscious reflection, but they can be used deliberately. Clinical heuristics cannot be easily researched across populations. They are flexible and can be modified for specific situations. They are not universal truths. Which reminds me of a joke ...

The Devil and his compatriot were strolling down the streets of Hell. A poor soul ran in front of them and snatched a piece of The Truth that had been lying there unnoticed. The Devil continued as if nothing had happened. Unable to contain himself, the compatriot asked, "How could you let him get away with The Truth?" The Devil casually replied, "No problem. I will let him keep it a while. He will turn it into a belief."

Having recognized that clinical heuristics guide many of my choices as a therapist, I thought it would be good if I examined these assumptions more thoroughly. I listed, therefore, the ones I use for different phases and operations of therapy, including heuristics specific to hypnosis. I found it an illuminating exercise that helped me evaluate underlying principles so that I could more effectively use them. I thought the list would be instructive for others, but I do not want them to be thought of as rules to be slavishly followed. They are simplifying assumptions that help manage ambiguous complexities and more often than not lead to effective outcomes.

My primary goal in offering this list is to stimulate clinicians to unearth the implicit clinical heuristics that guide their treatment planning. Second, I want to inform therapists about heuristics so that they can apply them clinically.

The heuristics listed below have been gleaned during 30 years of the practice of therapy. Almost all were inspired by Erickson's work. They have been taken from many sources. In the section that follows the list, I provide cases that illustrate heuristically derived treatments.

CLINICAL HEURISTICS WITHIN THE META-MODEL OF THERAPY

The five "choice points" of my meta-model of treatment planning are goal-setting, gift-wrapping, tailoring, processing, and the posture of the therapist. (See Zeig, 1997, for a detailed description of this meta-model of intervention.) Each choice point has a different set of clinical heuristics, although there is overlap because some heuristics pertain to more than one category.

Assessment and Goal-Setting

The purpose of assessment should be treatment planning. A therapy assessment immediately should lead to constructive interventions. Clinical heuristics are based on a social construction of human problems and promote socially based change.

Here is a partial list of Erickson-derived heuristics that primarily concern assessment and goal-setting. Remember that clinical heuristics are not guaranteed to lead to solutions. They are merely known from experience to facilitate assessment (and concomitantly may serve as constructive interventions), and, more often than not, they will prove useful. I encourage the reader to examine and list his/her own assessment heuristics, not merely to rely on mine.

There are two sections of assessment heuristics (presented in no particular order). The first relates to intrapsychic assessment, the second concerns the social/interpersonal aspects of assessment.

Intrapsychic Assessment

1. Structure takes precedence over history. Assess the structure of the patient's complaint rather than its history. Structures in the present can be harnessed to create an effective future.
2. Assessment *is* intervention. Ask assessment questions that are change inducing. Commit the patient to a constructive future: "Picture yourself cured. What specifically does it look like?" Help the patient to access dormant resources: "Respond to this question only in the positive with as many answers as you can provide: How do you *know* you can solve the problem?" Corner the patient to confront unhelpful rationalizations: "Give me five intelligent excuses to continue your habit problem."
3. Intervention *is* assessment. Similar to a Rorschach, patients "pro-

ject" their personalities into their responses to therapeutic assignments, including hypnosis. Assessment is ongoing. It does not stop when treatment begins. Assessment and intervention are two sides of one coin.

4. View the problem as solvable. Presuppose that a solution or adaptive coping mechanism exists. Choose a goal you as a therapist can help the patient achieve.
5. Move in small steps, especially if there is resistance. Divide and conquer. If it is hard work, divide the solution into smaller steps.
6. Minimize formal assessment. Make assessment brief. Get down to work as soon as possible – within the first few minutes of the initial session, if at all feasible. Therapy should emphasize the experience of change at the first possible opportunity.
7. Be recursive, not repetitive. Repeating the same questions in different forms often provides valuable information.
8. Axis. Place the presenting problem on the center of an *XY*-axis. On the *X*-axis to the left extrapolate historical antecedents, and to the right project anticipated evolutions. On the lower part of the *Y*-axis, divide the problem into subparts. On the upper part, ascertain if the problem is just one example of a larger set (e.g., smoking can be an element of the superset of not taking care of one's health).

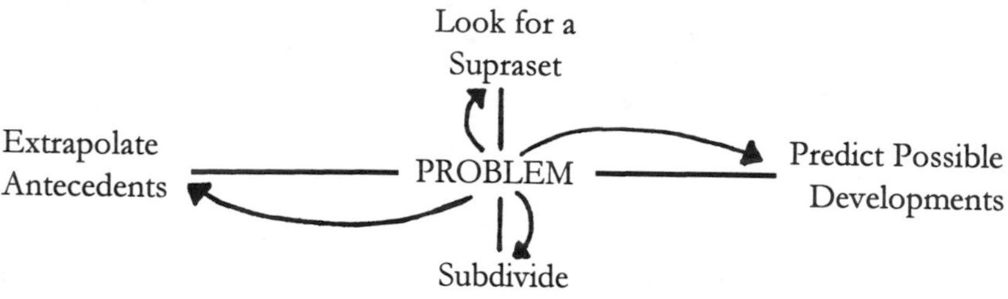

9. Redefine early. Resistance may be tied to the patient's definition of the problem. The patient's depression can be redefined as repressed anger, "bad" thoughts, withdrawal, despair, loneliness, historical familial modeling, a spiritual crisis, etc. It might be easier to change the redefined problem.
10. Notice what is conspicuously absent. There may be a conspicuous absence of aggression, hope, eye contact, gestures, adjectives, self-soothing, etc.

11. A detailed description of the problem generates solutions. It also makes the person overly conscious, which can disrupt the problem. (See Zeig, 1985, for an example of how Erickson used this method to help me stop smoking.)
12. Discern previously attempted solutions. Then you know what not to do in subsequent therapy (Watzlawick, Weakland, & Fisch, 1974).
13. Find examples of exceptions, times when the patient does not do the problem behavior. (See the work of solution-oriented therapists such as de Shazer and his associates.)
14. Goals are co-created by the therapist and the patient. Goals are not definitive "truths."
15. Have multiple descriptions for the problem and solution.
16. Generate analogies for the problem, the solution, the patient's strengths, and the patient's social system. Analogies often generate ideas for interventions.
17. Normalize the problem whenever possible. View problems as blocks in a normal developmental process. Attribute health.
18. Make the symptom/problem into a process. All symptoms are processes, not static things. Processes can be changed more easily than things.
19. Observe, observe, and observe.
20. Ascertain patient strengths. Build on strengths.
21. Ascertain the specific response style of the patient, e.g., to direct suggestions, indirect suggestions, etc.

Social Assessment

1. What is the systemic function of the problem in the family? (For further information, see the work of Haley and Madanes.)
2. What are the patient's relational requirements? What does the patient "pull" from the therapist, e.g., empathy, firmness, concern, humor?
3. Is there anyone in the patient's history who has had similar symptomatic patterns?
4. Note hierarchical conflicts. If a child is in the parent role, it is a hierarchical problem. (Again, see Haley and Madanes for more information.)
5. Solutions are holographic in systems. Treating the couple can change the child; treating the child can change the family. Treating behavior changes cognition, and vice versa.

6. The family is the primary context for change.
7. What is the patient's family structure? Is the patient an only, oldest, middle, or youngest child? How is current behavior consistent with those early patterns?
8. What was the primary trauma in the patient's early life? How is current behavior consistent with the patient's response to early trauma? Look for a repetition compulsion.
9. Foster minimal strategic changes, those that have a snowballing, systemic effect. Such changes can be seeded and even elicited during assessment.

Intervention

1. Make every word and gesture count. Use words and gestures with the same care that a surgeon uses a scalpel.
2. Utilization breeds solutions. Utilize what the patient brings; don't analyze it. (See Zeig, 1992, for more information about utilization, a cornerstone principle of the Ericksonian approach.)
3. Expand choice. Do not limit choice. Rather than telling a patient to limit a habit, indicate, at least initially, how he or she can do it differently. Use modifying rather than proscribing directives.
4. Look for an interactional solution. Involve significant others. For example, a patient giving up smoking can increase the number of compliments to associates by 20 per day.
5. Create experiences; create a safe emergency. Bring the therapy into the present. Patients seek therapy for experiences, not understandings. Make therapy a symbol drama, the imperative of which is, "By living this experience, you will be different."
6. The amount of indirection is proportional to the perceived resistance. The more resistance encountered, the more indirect the therapy should be.
7. Use multilevel communication. Say "X," mean "Y," to get response "Z." A therapist can offer a metaphor about the desired change that indicates how the patient can do something different. Multilevel communication empowers the couched message, and more effectively activates target responses.
8. Intervention can precede assessment. Assessment will be a by-product of intervention.
9. Therapy is messy. Do not sanitize it. Too often therapists try to

make life into a manicured rose garden when it is actually a field of wild flowers.

10. Use a target rifle rather than a shotgun. Be specific.
11. Make the problem worse. If you can make it worse, you can make it better.
12. Change the emotional background. If you cannot change the problem, place it against a different emotional background.
13. Minimize the negative and maximize the positive.
14. Work from the periphery in. For example, in the hypnotherapy of pain, modify peripheral sensations first. There is a military principle that states, "Who controls the rim land, controls the heartland."
15. Work parallel to the problem, e.g., by using metaphors and analogies. Patients activate to personalize the parallel.
16. The severity of the solution should match the severity of the problem. This is especially applicable to the use of ordeals in therapy (Haley, 1984).
17. Play one problem against another. If the patient is both shy and procrastinates, find a way to pit the problems against each other, e.g., "If you procrastinate, you must ask someone on a date."
18. Find reference experiences. Patients commonly report what they cannot do. Help them to access their strengths, which will serve as reference experiences for future adaptation.
19. Access constructive associations. Associations, more than simple thoughts, drive behavior. Build a wealth of constructive associations through indirect techniques, such as anecdotes and metaphors. Once sufficient associations exist, patients may suddenly find themselves behaving more adaptively.
20. Access resources. Therapy is often a matter of identifying and harnessing dormant resources. Patients have within them the elements they need to effect change. All anxious patients have dormant strategies for relaxation.

Hypnosis Heuristics

1. Do the hypnosis first. Erickson admonished students to do the hypnosis in the first part of the session. Discussion of life events can ensue.
2. Induction is a method of therapy, not merely a means. The induction can be a microcosm of the therapy to follow. Intersperse the therapy early in the induction, when defenses may be down.

3. Provide a motivation. Do not merely provide suggestions. Give patients a reason to do things.
4. Smile when you induce trance. Hypnosis need not be grim. It is a pleasure to hypnotize. Erickson even told jokes to patients in trance.
5. Access responsiveness. Especially access responsiveness to innuendo. When the patient responds to minimal cues, it is as if patients accedes to your request to constructively enter their experiential world.
6. Make the trance interactive. Converse with the patient during trance.
7. Whatever the patient does best is a resource for the therapy. Mine for resources. If the pain patient can do age regression best, that patient can regress to a time before the pain.
8. Establish a basis for regression and dissociation in the induction. If therapeutically you will later use the recall of forgotten memories, use an induction that speaks to recollection. If you will use hypnotic phenomena in the therapy, all of which are grounded in dissociation, establish a basis for dissociative experience in the induction.
9. Utilize the patient's words. Therapists can reframe symptom words into both solution words and "hypnosis" words by changing inflections, meanings, and contexts. (See Zeig, 1988.)
10. Hypnotic phenomena can be used symbolically. This was a primary technique that Erickson used in his later years. A simple example: If the patient suffers excess anger and you are doing arm levitation, position the arm to symbolically represent an aspect of anger. Then modify the position of the levitated arm during the therapy. Symbols can serve as a barometer of change.
11. Make things stand out through understatement rather than by overemphasis.
12. Use all output channels of communication. Focus verbal and nonverbal methods in a laser-like fashion.
13. Use gestures while hypnotized patients have their eyes closed. Gestures enhance the message.
14. Hypnosis can be the appetizer, main course, and/or dessert. Hypnosis can be used to set up an intervention, to deliver the intervention, and/or to follow up on a given intervention.
15. Redefine emitted responses as hypnosis. Shape the patient's behavior in the desired direction. Use constructive attributions.

16. Start the induction by increasing tension, then modify the level of tension during the hypnotherapy — for example, by using mild confusion methods. Hypnosis is best effected by modifying the level of tension, not by continually lulling a passive patient.
17. Develop the patient's inherent response to innuendo.

Tailoring

1. Focus the therapy through the patient's lens.
2. Speak the patient's experiential language.
3. Access the flexibility and strengths in the patient's psychosocial system.
4. Hook the therapy to what the patient values. If the patient is logical, explain things in logical terms.
5. Utilize redundant patient patterns. Notice redundancies in language, gesture, style, etc.
6. When motivating, use motivations that are patient-specific. If the patient has to look good, explain that being more empathetic to his or her spouse and children will accomplish that goal.
7. Understanding the symptom phenomenology in specific detail can generate a treatment plan. If the patient is internal, intrapunitive, negative, and speaks a lot about the past, a treatment plan could orient the patient to accessing the opposite characteristics.
8. Almost anything the patient brings in can be constructively utilized, including resistances.
9. Ascertain how the patient "does" the problem, and use that information to establish goals.
10. Ascertain how the patient "does" strengths, and utilize that information.

The Process of Therapy

1. Create a process when offering *every* directive; use the SIFT method: Set up, Intervene, and Follow Through. What you do before and after the intervention determines its effectiveness.
2. Move in progressive steps.
3. Use drama. It makes even simple interventions come alive.
4. Destabilize the habitual set. Enter with mild disruption and exit with concrete wisdom. Change sets quickly, use mild confusion, surprise, etc., to destabilize habitual patterns.

5. Use the patient's process. The process of "doing" the symptom can be used to create an induction (Zeig, 1994).
6. Tie things together. No hanging threads. When you present an idea, follow up on it. Any great novelist/dramatist would.
7. Seed future therapy. Foreshadow, as any great dramatist would.
8. Surgery requires an anesthetic. Enter with contact, caring, and compassion to establish an anesthetic for future "surgery."
9. Build responsiveness early. Get patients to do things.

The Posture of the Clinician

1. Be flexible whenever indicated. Be willing to change your "posture" if you encounter resistance.
2. Respect and voice "baby thoughts." Do not reject or overanalyze your intuitions. Find a way to use them constructively.
3. Observe, observe, and observe. Develop your perceptiveness of details.
4. "Of course you can. . . ." Adopt the attitude that change is inevitable.
5. Have faith in both the therapist and the patient. Presuppose that solutions and mechanisms of constructive adaptation exist.
6. Take charge early. Establish control. Establish structure.
7. Assume the posture of utilization. Utilization is not merely a technique, it is a way of "being" a therapist. (See Zeig, 1997.)
8. Expect generative change. Expect a snowballing effect from a small change in behavior. Expect an interactional effect.
9. The more pathology in the patient, the firmer the therapist's boundaries need to be.
10. Make every word and gesture count. Use words and gestures with the same care that a surgeon uses a scalpel. Develop this skill.
11. Be dramatic. Use gestures to embellish a point. Use your body to communicate. Be dynamic — avoid stiffly sitting in your chair.

CASE EXAMPLES

Two cases illustrate a therapy approach that is informed by heuristics.

Case One: Amazon.com

A patient presented debilitating obsessions with remorse and shame about her failure to speak up for herself at a family gathering. I had her recite the event twice in great detail, the second time in the first person, present tense. I was treating the episode as if it were a dream, and as if we were embarking on dream work. In unresolved dreams, there often are three roles: a persecutor, a victim, and an ineffective rescuer. Therapy sometimes can be accomplished by establishing and strengthening the rescuer.

After the review, I placed a number of objects on her lap. She passively accepted them, and looked at me curiously, waiting for direction. (This technique was brought to my attention by Michael Yapko.) With her lap covered by objects, including my shoe, I hovered over her, and following a method from Erickson, I announced, "If you are walking down the street and someone gives you a gift and you don't want it, do you have to accept it?" She shook her head and I continued, "Then, if you are walking down the street and someone gives you a bag of shit . . ." I let her fill in the blank. She assertively gave me back the objects.

Next, I stood and asked her to sculpt me into the posture of an Amazon Warrior, which she did with a little prompting. Subsequently, I had her close her eyes and symbolically bring that Warrior into her heart. Then she retold the "dream" from the position of the assertive Amazon.

We called the therapy "Amazon.com." Follow-up indicated that one session accomplished her goal.

Comment

A number of clinical heuristics were used to effect this therapy. I assessed what she was missing, namely, assertive behavior. I made the therapy into an experiential symbol-drama of change. I used myself theatrically. I utilized the patient's values. She could especially relate to the image of the Amazon because of the specifics of her background. Also, she worked with computers and liked the idea of calling up "Amazon.com."

Yes, I could have used a behavioral protocol, which could have helped her with her obsessions, but an invented therapy in one session was decidedly effective. Note that the therapy was idiosyncratic in that it could not be generalized. It was patient-specific and situation-specific.

Case Two: Ericksonian Family Therapy with a Problem Child

Harold called me because he was concerned about his ten-year-old son, Bob, who was phobic about gravel roads. Bob's phobia had generalized to the extent that he had become reticent about leaving his home. Harold was the primary caretaker because his blue-collar job allowed him to set his own schedule. The mother, June, was a low-level professional, working full-time.

Baffled by Bob's phobia, Harold and June contacted a psychologist. The psychologist said that he would need four sessions at an exorbitant hourly fee to do an assessment before he could suggest treatment options. Harold and June had limited finances and no insurance. Having heard about hypnosis, Harold called me.

I told Harold that I would be willing to provide a one-hour consultation, if he would bring his wife and his son. I was a bit shocked by my own boldness, but I had faith in Harold's motivation, and my own ability to utilize whatever the family would bring. We confirmed an appointment for two weeks later. I told him that although I used hypnosis, I would not guarantee that it would be needed and that I did not use it in all cases.

The family showed up a week early, justifying my faith in their motivation. Fortunately, my scheduled patient had called to say that she was running late. I explained the situation and she rescheduled.

Bob was the most hyperactive child I have ever seen in my private practice. Based on the phone call, I had no idea that AD/HD was part of the constellation. Bob couldn't stop fidgeting. As he entered my office, he poignantly announced, "I'm the crazy person." My heart went out to him.

I did not want Bob to assume a negative self-definition. I gave him a difficult wooden puzzle consisting of two pieces that fit together to make a pyramid. Bob struggled but could not solve the puzzle. I told him that I could not solve the puzzle either when I first got it. I called the friend who sent it to me and asked, "Where's the third piece?" There was no third piece.

I took Bob out of the office into the waiting room. I showed him how to solve the two-piece pyramid puzzle. I then instructed him to give the puzzle to his mother and father. Smiling, he proudly strolled back into the office. Then Bob and I watched as his mother and father struggled to put the puzzle together. They could not easily do something that he knew how to do. Now Bob was one-up.

Building on the situation, I said to Bob and his parents, "I'm an expert at helping families solve puzzles." I wanted to define the solution as existing within the family.

Harold told me how Bob's problem had begun. The family was driving on a gravel road when a sudden mechanical failure caused the car to spin out of control. An excellent driver, Harold brought the car to a safe stop, but Grandmother, who was in the back seat with Bob, completely panicked, which caused Bob to panic. He subsequently balked when he was asked to get into a car. Eventually, he refused to be in any place where there was a gravel road.

Bob offered that he was afraid of being out of control, leading Harold to a new insight. He had not previously understood that aspect of his son's problem. I asked a few more questions and discovered that Bob was not taking any medication. It was summer, and he was on a medication holiday.

I remembered a clinical heuristic from Gestalt therapy: "If you're in terror, play the terrorizer." If I can get the fearful person to play the part of the internal fear monger, it may breed a solution. Continuing my redefinition of their familial problem, and using the heuristic of externalizing the problem championed by Michael White, I said, "Mr. Fear has attacked this family." Then, bringing the therapy into the immediate situation, I asked Bob to show me Mr. Fear. Bob went to the far corner of the office and became Mr. Fear, attacking his family.

I knew from experience that analogies can generate a solution, so I inquired, "Tell me, what is Mr. Fear like?" Bob asked me if I watched "Power Rangers," which I knew only vaguely. "Mr. Fear is Drilla Monster," he continued. I did not know Drilla Monster, but I proceeded, "Be Drilla Monster and attack your family." So Bob pantomimed being Drilla Monster attacking his family.

Next, I thought about the Ericksonian principle of eliciting resources. I knew that there must be a resource in this family to deal with Bob's fears. Since Bob had offered the metaphor of Power Rangers, I asked him, "What power do you have?" Bob replied, "I know karate." "Show me how you can use karate to fight off Drilla Monster," I said. Bob successfully fought back the imaginary Drilla Monster. Then I asked him, "Please tell me, what power does your mother have?" "My mother has a very powerful scream," Bob replied. Suddenly, a systemic aspect of Bob's situation became clearer. I refrained, however, from interpreting underlying dynamics because I do not believe it to be helpful. I moved on: "Please tell me what power your father has." "Well, my father is a Sumo wrestler," Bob offered. Harold had a wiry build and was of average height and weight, but to this ten-year-old, he looked like a Sumo wrestler.

Next, I explained the therapy. Whenever Mr. Fear, Drilla Monster, attacked the family, they were to stop and convene a meeting of all the Power Rangers who would decide together how to use their powers to defeat Drilla Monster. I then added, "I have two other therapies that I would like you to practice." Because June seemed exhausted and overwhelmed, I directed the tasks to the father and son. Harold seemed to have a lot of energy to devote to Bob. I explained that each morning for a week, Harold and Bob should practice being out of control. Bob would go into the backyard and play act being out of control and Harold would coach him about being better at being out of control. Then Harold would act as if he were out of control, and Bob would coach him on being out-of-control. My covert design was to turn a problem component into a game. They agreed to the therapy.

Then I offered, "I have another therapy for Bob. I want you to write your name in my driveway." I live in Phoenix, Arizona, in the desert. My driveway is made of gravel. I told him that I did not even allow my daughter to write in the gravel, but that I would like him to leave his mark there to show that he had been at my home office. My technique was a symbolic desensitization. Bob would have to slide on my driveway as he shuffled his shoes around to put his name in the gravel. I would have him violate his phobia about gravel. Adequate psychotherapy with a phobia can be achieved when one gets the patient to violate the phobic pattern, even on a symbolic level.

Then I said to the family, "Now that I have given you these assignments, I'm going to give myself an assignment." I said that I was going to Japan two months later, and I would send Bob a postcard of a Sumo wrestler. So I took their address and when I got to Japan, I sent Bob a postcard of a Sumo wrestler.

The entire therapy took 30 minutes. In the remaining time, I asked Bob to play with my daughter, who was a few years his senior. In the meeting with the parents, I empathized with their struggles with a special-needs, highly sensitive child, and we discussed some strategies for providing structure for Bob.

Comment

It would be impossible to recapitulate that highly individualized therapy. I used a series of tricks — clinical heuristics that could generate solutions. I relied on the Ericksonian posture of utilization. I utilized a game in my office. I utilized problem components. I worked through games and symbolic tasks in parallel. I used drama, I harnessed structures in the present, rather than analyzing the past, etc.

A most important heuristic was faith. There were three components to this faith: One, I had faith in my ability to *utilize* whatever they brought me. Most of my professional contributions in print during the past 15 years have been explications of Milton H. Erickson's utilization method. I have made utilization a center point of my therapy. The second aspect of faith also came from what I learned from Erickson. I had faith in the family. I had faith that they had a resource in their system that would be adequate for solving the problem. The job of the psychotherapy would be to help them access that resource experientially. The third part of faith was faith in myself. I knew that I had surmounted difficult problems in my life. I also had used methods to cure myself that were similar to those I prescribed for them. If I could do it, I knew they could, too.

CONCLUSIONS

Contemporary Treatment from the Perspective of Heuristics and Algorithms

Contemporary medical practice is becoming more of an algorithm than a heuristic. If the physician can compile the data correctly, the compilation can be computed and a finite solution can be applied. Medicine is evolving as more of a technical science than as an art.

Contemporary psychotherapy tries to emulate the emerging medical model. Protocols are becoming ubiquitous. Clinicians can now use the DSM and then follow a formulaic procedure such as a protocol-driven therapy for specified diagnostic categories. In short, the zeitgeist practice assumes that therapy is an algorithm. Such an orientation may severely impede socially conceived treatments based on individual differences. Medicalization, moreover, makes clinical entities into diseases; that is, depression is a biochemical brain disorder, rather than a social construction, thereby taking the responsibility for change away from the patient and society.

Viewing therapy as an algorithm is suspect; human behavior is complex, and many lenses, including biochemical and social viewpoints, can be used to understand clinical entities. There is no general agreement among experts about the essential nature of psychological problems and their treatment (Zeig & Munion, 1990). Psychological problems, for example, can be defined in terms of confining behaviors, attitudes, cognitions, images, relationships, developmental problems, spiritual strife, existential dilemmas, affective disturbances, biochemical abnormalities, etc. They can be treated successfully by using methods within any of those domains. For example, one could treat anorexia by family therapy, behavior therapy, cognitive therapy, hypnotherapy, or logotherapy. The availability of such options, however, is not true for medicine. The diagnosis and essential protocol for pneumonia should be relatively similar among patients with the disease, and can be algorithmic.

In therapy, we should rely more heavily on heuristic processes, whereas in medicine, we can use algorithms. The medicalization of psychotherapy unfortunately militates against thinking in terms of heuristics. But for most of life's problems, heuristic processes must be used. Algorithms will not be effective. If algorithms were effective, there would be no need for therapy. One would consult self-help books, which contain algorithms for every known problem, and even for some problems that are constructions of the authors' imagination.

The complexity of human experience is too great to think that algorithms can be the mainstays of psychotherapy. Touting therapy as an algorithm gives patients the mistaken impression that life can be treated similarly.

Heuristics are a necessity for human life. When a large number of processes need to be examined, the search is organized heuristically. Directions most likely to lead to success are explored first. Clinical heuristics are indispensable for therapy.

§

Undertaking therapy informed by heuristics is not an easy task. It requires an experienced clinician with a good sense of self, a therapist who is flexible and creative. All clinicians, however, use heuristics in their practices, some of which are effective and others of which are ineffective habits, and even superstitions. The intent of this chapter was to encourage clinicians to be introspective, to bring to the foreground the heuristics that they use and examine them. Erickson, moreover, can serve as an example of a therapist whose therapy seemed informed by heuristics. By studying his work and their derivations, clinicians may add effective new heuristics to their own practices.

References

Fisk, S. T., & Taylor, S. E. (1984). *Social cognition.* New York: McGraw-Hill.

Haley, J. (1984). *Ordeal therapy: Unusual ways to change behavior.* San Francisco: Jossey-Bass.

Langer, E. J., & Abelson, R. P. (1974). A patient by any other name . . . : Clinical group differences in labeling bias. *Journal of Consulting and Clinical Psychology, 42*, 4–9.

Mead, M. (1977). The originality of Milton Erickson. *American Journal of Clinical Hypnosis, 20*, 4–5.

Moustakas, C. (1990). *Heuristic research: Design, methodology, and applications.* London: Sage.

Moustakas, C. (1994). *Phenomenological research methods.* London: Sage.

Snyder, M. (1981). Seek and you shall find . . . In E. T. Higgins, C. P. Herman, & M. P. Zanna (Eds.). *Social cognition: The Ontario symposium on personality and social psychology* (pp. 277–303). Hillsdale, NJ: Lawrence Erlbaum Associates.

Temerlin, M. K. (1968). Suggestion effects in psychiatric diagnosis. *Journal of Mental and Nervous Disease, 147*, 349–353.

Twersky, A., & Kahneman. (1973). Availability: A heuristic for judging frequency probability. *Cognitive Psychology, 5*, 207–232.

Watzlawick, P. (1997). "Insight" may cause blindness. In J. K. Zeig (Ed.), *The evolution of psychotherapy: The third conference* (pp. 309–321). New York: Brunner/Mazel.

Watzlawick, P., Weakland, J., & Fisch, R. (1974). *Change: Principles of problem formation and problem resolution.* New York: Norton.

Zeig, J. (1985). *Experiencing Erickson: An introduction to the man and his work.* New York: Brunner/Mazel.

Zeig, J. (1988). Phenomenological approach to therapeutic hypnotic induction and symptom utilization. In J. K. Zeig & S. R. Lankton (Eds.), *Developing Ericksonian therapy: State of the art.* New York: Brunner/Mazel.

Zeig, J. (1992). The virtues of our faults: A key concept in Ericksonian therapy. In J. K. Zeig (Ed.), *The evolution of psychotherapy: The second conference.* New York: Brunner/Mazel.

Zeig, J. (1994). Advanced techniques of utilization: An intervention metamodel and the use of sequences, symptom words, and figures of speech. In J. K. Zeig (Ed.), *Ericksonian methods: The essence of the story.* New York: Brunner/Mazel.

Zeig, J. (1997). Experiential approaches to clinical development. In J. K. Zeig (Ed.), *The evolution of psychotherapy: The third conference*. New York: Brunner/Mazel.

Zeig, J., & Munion, S. (1990). *What is psychotherapy?: Contemporary perspectives*. San Francisco: Jossey-Bass.

4

The Power of Vision as an Antidepressant: Rethinking the Focus of Therapy

Michael D. Yapko

The underlying premise of this chapter can be stated explicitly: Our social and technological changes are occurring far more quickly than is our biological evolution, thus affecting our mental health in a variety of specific ways. I believe that one of the primary effects on our mental health is in terms of mood. It does not seem to me to be a coincidence that for several decades reports of depression have been increasing in every age group. It is becoming increasingly apparent that the physical evolution of our brains is too slow to help us deal skillfully with the fast, and often dangerous, world we have created.

What, then, is the solution? I have come to believe that what we must do is change our way of thinking about society, life, the universe, and, more specific to ourselves, people's problems and the focus of psychotherapy. I think we need to enhance our ability to respond to the gradual, longer-term changes taking place in many life arenas that are critical influences on us, and strive to become less reactive to the immediate and dramatic, but less profound, developments. Gradual changes, such as evolving societal values or ecological deterioration, have tremendous potential to affect our lives. But typically such things are quickly dismissed as familiar and not in need of an immediate response, while we pay too much attention to trivial things with a little drama attached to them. There are far more important things taking place in the world that warrant our serious attention, for example, than the private sex lives of government officials or the demise of a popular television program, yet these furnish the fuel for widespread obsession.

What does this say about us, and what, if anything, should mental health professionals do about it?

Here is a joke that captures some of my concerns.

John and Mary are going to go out on their first date. John goes to pick Mary up at her high-rise apartment building, and when he gets to her apartment on the 25th floor, he rings the doorbell. Mary greets John warmly, and shows him around her apartment. She takes him out on the balcony with its lovely view of the city, and introduces him to her dog, Skippy, who can do tricks. Mary tells John that Skippy will roll over, speak, and beg, and that if he forms a hoop with his arms, Skippy will jump through. Mary says, "Isn't Skippy a great dog? He's so much fun!" Then she excuses herself to get ready to leave, and encourages John to enjoy the view and perhaps play with Skippy. As she suggested, John forms a hoop with his arms. Skippy jumps through and right over the edge of the balcony! Just then Mary returns and says, "Isn't Skippy just the happiest dog you've ever met?" Thinking quickly, John answers, "I don't know, he seemed kind of depressed to me!"

In our moments of happy enthusiasm, like Skippy's, we can pitch ourselves over the railing of life. (Falling is a problem, of course, but landing is even worse!) My concerns cover many issues, from social to ecological, but a common denominator of the problems we all face in society, and even in our profession, is a lack of vision, or a meaningful orientation to what is possible — and a common denominator of many of the solutions to these problems is to be more insightfully oriented to the future. We can develop a clearer sense of where the path we're on is leading us while we still have some time to change our direction.

Why have I spent most of my professional life studying, treating, and writing about depression? The answer shouldn't be much of a surprise. Nowhere else is hopelessness more apparent than in the intense suffering of depressives. Nowhere else is the effect on marriages, families, individual physical and mental health, and the ability to contribute to one's community as profound as in the relationship between mood and behavior. Nowhere else can we, as psychotherapists, affect our patients' lives as quickly and dramatically in treatment than when we help to catalyze some vision; vision can be a very powerful antidepressant.

WHY AND WHY NOT?

Robert Kennedy, paraphrasing George Bernard Shaw, once said, "Some people look at the world as it is and ask, 'Why?' Others look at the world in terms of how it *could* be, and ask 'Why not?'" In this chapter, I am essentially wondering whether our profession might be spending too much time on the question of "why," and not enough on "why not," especially with regard to the disorder of depression.

Major depression is the most common mood disorder affecting Americans, and epidemiological research indicates that it is rapidly becoming increasingly prevalent. This is also true in other Western societies. Although the blame is commonly ascribed to some presumed chemical imbalance in the sufferer's brain, I would like to suggest that if you were to take even a cursory tour through the literature on families and depression and on culture and depression, you would find ample evidence that there is considerably more going on than just bad chemistry in people's brains that is responsible for the phenomenon (Yapko, 1999).

In fact, I would suggest that the very culture that can oversimplify a complex phenomenon such as depression, and reduce it to a mere chemical equation while ignoring the greater gender, family, social, and cultural forces known to cause or exacerbate it, is a culture that unwittingly results in higher rates of the disorder. In my opinion, it is a sad thing that people in the mental health profession who should know better help instead to make matters worse by touting the miracles of "better living through chemistry." To reduce a problem as multidimensional as depression to a biochemical anomaly leads people to underestimate it, thereby making it even more difficult to treat. I believe there's a lack of vision evident in such one-dimensional views that no amount of Prozac can resolve. Fortunately, one of the perspectives we as psychotherapists with a brief-therapy affinity tend to share is an orientation toward systemic thinking, to appreciating the multiple interrelated layers of such complex problems.

It makes for more realistic approaches than just medicating everyone with an attitude.

I'd like to raise two key questions for the reader's consideration: First, is it adequate to focus on what I call "mop-up," meaning dealing only with trying to clean up what has already gone wrong in peoples' lives, or should we pay more attention to prevention? Second, should we focus on the smaller picture, treating one individual, family, or couple at a time, or should we focus on the bigger picture, and attempt to influence the larger social and cultural forces that shape peoples' lives?

FUTURE AND POTENTIAL

It is an inescapable truth that "there is no security on earth, there is only opportunity." Opportunity speaks to the future. It addresses possibilities beyond what we currently experience. In the midst of our individual and collective fears and anxieties about what will eventually become of us, we sometimes seem to forget that the future doesn't just happen — it's something we create through the choices we make, or fail to make, today, just as our lives are largely the products of choices we've been making, or neglecting to make, up until now.

Does the future change us, or does it simply gradually reveal us? I believe that it does both; it changes us *and* it reveals us. Most important of all, I think, is that the future provides us with the great challenge to know and value it even more than we do our past. The quality of your vision for the future plays a significant role in the presence or absence of depression in you and your clients, and, therefore, strongly influences, often without your awareness, the choices you make in response to the everyday ambiguities of life.

Psychotherapy provides opportunities for both therapists and their clients. It provides the opportunity to modify the future in positive ways rather than sitting back and believing that you must accept your fate passively. What are the average person's concerns? Pretty much the same as mine and yours: Will I survive and thrive? Will I be able to feed my family? Will I ever achieve a sense of professional and financial security so I can relax a little? Will I be able to have and maintain healthy, supportive relationships? Will I have a high-quality life?

Our clients are worried about their futures. They often become depressed, feeling stuck with the despairing notion that the future holds only the promise that more will go wrong for them. Such hopelessness is a core component of depression, and it's frequently a by-product of having little or no vision about the possibility of deliberately creating a positive future. So, what do we as therapists all too often utilize as our therapeutic interventions? We talk to clients about their pasts! We do genograms and go back multiple generations looking for family legacies to better explain their emotional distress. I think we would do better to apply Robert Kennedy's message; I think we should stop and reconsider whether instead of looking backward and asking "Why?" we should instead be looking forward with our clients and asking, "Why not?"

ARE WE CONGRUENT?

Therapists, it seems to me, have always had a peculiar relationship with the future. One might even say it has been an incongruent relationship. On the one hand, we emphasize the value of therapy as a catalyst for progressive changes, and, on the other, we encourage people to divert their attention from future possibilities by focusing instead on either the burdens of the present or the pains of the unchangeable past. The underlying assumption in doing so has been that understanding the past holds the only key to building a better future. I believe that not only is this assumption no longer useful, but it may even be detrimental to our efforts.

There is an old saying that has become a truism: that is, a statement that seems so obviously true that there is no legitimate basis for either contradicting or rejecting it. If I say, "Where there's a will, there's a way," that is a truism. But uncritically accepted as that statement is, it's *wrong.* Stated more accurately it would be, "Where there's a will, *maybe* there's a way."

The old saying and apparent truism, "Those who do not strive to understand the past are condemned to repeat it," on first consideration may sound like a profound observation. However, I would challenge that apparently true statement that suggests that the past is a reliable predictor of the future as an antiquated viewpoint. It suggests that analyzing past circumstances and using that analysis to extrapolate to present and future conditions will create new choices, but, in my opinion, the ability to extrapolate is not necessarily best developed by looking backward.

Why do I say this? Because our futures no longer are based on what happened yesterday. Subjectively speaking, time is moving faster than it ever has before. I believe that what happens next week will be far more greatly influenced by what happens tomorrow than by what happened even yesterday. And so I state the obvious: tomorrow hasn't happened yet. There's another reason why I say this, too. Therapists have been proceeding on the assumption that treating depression necessitates analyzing the past in order to determine its causes. That is a myth. Whereas there is considerable evidence that, in general, most therapies are roughly equal in effectiveness, the longitudinal treatment data make it overwhelmingly clear that not all therapies specific for depression are equally effective, and the weakest approaches have been shown to be the ones with a past orientation. The strongest approaches for treating depression share the common characteristic of emphasizing a future orientation by focusing more on solutions than on explanations. It is also not especially reasonable in light of current knowledge about depression to spend therapy time sifting the past and doing psychological archeology looking for a single cause. We've come to know that depression has many causes, not just one, and there are also many viable treatments.

I don't believe we can afford to use our positions of considerable influence to give our clients advice that diverts them from paying greater attention to the future. Our profession has the unique capacity to promote change and encourage vision, but instead, therapists are telling their clients the very things that prevent them from developing vision. Too often we tell them, directly or indirectly, that it's all right "just to live life one day at a time." I think it's too easy to ignore detrimental trends, such as the devaluing of families, by reducing them to minor inconveniences with which we merely must cope. That is the very mechanism of denial: reducing something important in scope in order to make it manageable while ignoring the associated critical issues.

Actually, although therapists pushing the "one day at a time" philosophy may be helping people to cope on one level, they unwittingly are contributing to their inability to cope on another. To counter that effect, I believe that we, as therapists, both individually and collectively, must transmit the message to the greater society of which we are a part that it's time we learned to live *beyond* one day at a time, at least in certain critical contexts (bearing in mind that it is not an all-or-none phenomenon of being *all* present or *all* future oriented). I further believe that the artistry of living well involves the ability to move back and forth easily between future goals and the things to do today that can help make the present a steppingstone to a satisfying tomorrow. An important aspect of our job is to help people create the ability to choose the best point on which to focus based on current circumstances and the results they desire. And more often than we might think, we'll find that the best focal point is out there in front of us.

CHANGES, BUT NOT IMPROVEMENTS

The world has changed dramatically over the past several decades, and one of the liabilities associated with those social changes has been the state of America's national mental health. A major research finding of a startling nature, even to the mental health field, which uncovered it, is that the rate of depression in America has increased by a factor of nearly 10 in those born in the years following World War II (the so-called "baby boomers") in comparison with their grandparents. The 1950s and 1960s were times of rapid economic and social developments that forever altered American values and lifestyles — and apparently people's feelings about themselves and their world, as well. The 1970s, 1980s, and 1990s saw life becoming more complicated ever faster, and no doubt the 21st century will continue that momentum. The numbers are similar in other Western cultures. This contradicts yet another myth about depression: realistically, we can't treat depression as if it is only one person's neurochemical problem. It isn't. The social context of depression simply cannot be ignored without further aggravating the issue. The bio-reductionism evident in saying that depression is a disease caused by a biochemical imbalance in the brain is, at best, only partially true. How can we ignore the relevant marriage and family contributions to depression? And how can we get out of the "mop-up" position and act preventively by prescribing drugs, which are, by their very nature, an after-the-fact treatment tool? Despite the advances in developing antidepressant medications, depression's rate keeps rising. Doesn't that reinforce my point about our missing the more salient influences on the disorder?

Life has gradually become more difficult and stressful for most people. Many have suggested to me that every era has its share of challenges and stressors. That's true. But I believe the kinds of things with which people deal now, and the earlier ages at which they face them, are quite different and more complex than ever before. It is no coincidence that, in demographic terms, depression keeps striking younger and younger targets in terms of its average age of onset.

Our society encourages depression, albeit unwittingly. It is striking to note that there are substantial differences in the rates of depression in various cultures around the world. There are even some cultures where depression is a minimal problem, although invariably, these are societies that are primitive by our standards and place great emphasis on a tight social structure, meaning a strong sense of community. "Self" is not emphasized — only what the "self" does for the greater good of the society. In light of the abundant data that exist about its social aspects, depression no longer can be viewed only from an intrapsychic or intrapersonal view. James Hillman and Michael Ventura (1992) address this same point in a different way. They speak candidly to the emphasis on the self in therapy, and the effects of making social relationships less necessary for some, less desirable for others, and less skilled for yet others in our society. More important, I think, is the authors' provocative point that people who are disenchanted with life are in individual therapy either trying to correct their cognitive distortions concerning life or being medicated until they feel more accepting of their disenchantment. Rather than being encouraged to take social action, to fight to be heard and to try to make a difference, they're told they'll feel better if they just wait for their serotonin level to rise. Is this vision? Is a sense of community or social connectedness eventually just going to be about all of us taking our Prozac together?

THE ABSENCE OF VISION

In the same way that a greater focus on self leads to one's becoming less skilled in relating to others, a focus on "now" leads one to be less skilled in relating to the future. Psychotherapy keeps pushing the tired old mantra, "Be fully present in the moment." In doing so, however, it is missing the point that many, no, *most*, things of an enduring value are not present oriented. (Again, I'd like to remind you that it is not an "either/or" phenomenon. The wisdom is to know when to be present and when to be future oriented. But the best problem-solving capability invariably has an orientation to the future at its base.)

The inability fully to perceive that the future hasn't happened yet, coupled with the lack of awareness of the necessity to do something to create meaningful possibilities, is what I would define as an absence of vision. How might our absence of vision influence the work we do? One way is in what seems to me to be obvious incongruities in our field. We profess to be in the business of change, and then we unintentionally teach people to think of themselves in unchangeable terms. For example, consider the term "adult child of an alcoholic," or ACA. Is this a self-defining term that promotes change? No, because it is an unchangeable self-definition. After all, when exactly does someone stop being the adult child of an alcoholic? What about the overuse and often inappropriate use of the term "inner child?" Isn't the inner child an eternal and unchanging metaphor? When exactly does the inner child grow up and leave home? I readily acknowledge that the idea of the so-called inner child has the potential to be useful to people who need to be more self-nurturing. But it can lead others to become more childish! Such metaphors are too easily responded to as facts, and then we have to work even harder to remind people that the inner child doesn't really exist, but is just a metaphor. (Simply put, *if you're not pregnant, you don't have an inner child*!) But understand my point: any idea or metaphor has an equal potential to hurt or help, depending on how and when it is applied and how the client relates to it. There is nothing inherently valuable about the notion of an inner child, or the 12 steps to recovery. There is nothing inherently valuable about cognitive therapy or family therapy, or any therapy, for that matter. They are only valuable concepts or methods when someone uses them well, which obviously not everyone does, since the treatment success rate isn't 100%. Some people even get worse as a result of treatment. I think it lacks vision on our part when we blame people for failing in therapy when we couldn't see the limitations of our own views. I am optimistic that we, as professionals, can examine our beliefs and modify them when they don't serve us or our clients very well. The first step is noticing that that's the case. Never before has it been so urgent a task that we look more closely at ourselves as agents of change on so many levels.

EXPECTANCY

When I speak clinically about the future, I generally prefer to use the term "expectancy." In the treatment of depression, expectancy is a powerful factor that helps determine in the formal therapy context whether or not someone will recover from his or her problems, how long it will take the person to recover, whether or not the person is likely to participate in therapeutic homework assignments, how complete the recovery will be, and whether or not he or she will be more or less likely to relapse.

Let's put the concept of expectancy into "real world" terms. In January 1994, the city of Los Angeles was rocked by a major earthquake. Although I live in San Diego County, about 100 miles south of Los Angeles, the earthquake nearly knocked me out of my bed! It did cause me, I must confess, to be fully present in that moment. At the epicenter in Northridge, the damage caused by the earthquake was extensive. If you had visited Northridge soon after the event, you would have observed that many people were already repairing their homes and putting the broken pieces of their lives back together. Other people were beating a hasty retreat, picking up and moving to other, presumably safer, parts of the country. Some people sat on their front porches, heads in hands, bemoaning their fate, sinking deeper and deeper into despair and even depression.

How would you explain these different responses of bouncing back, leaving town, or giving up? In a word, that explanation would be "expectancy." If you believe that "an earthquake happened, it's over, and now it's time to get on with fixing things up," then you have an expectation that life can, and will, return to normal. This is an optimistic and motivating perspective. It is the response least likely to lead to depression. If, instead, you believe, "Why bother to fix things? It's just going to happen again," then you have the negative expectation that any effort you expend in the direction of bouncing back and moving forward with your life will be wasted, lost to the pessimistic and depressing prediction of further disaster. There is no reason to bother to repair bridges, freeways, buildings, homes, or lives if you believe that "it's just going to happen again." And, of course, no one can realistically assure you that it won't happen again, so you may even feel justified in having negative expectations.

As you can see, while talking about expectancy, I'm also talking about your mood, your level of motivation, your resiliency in bouncing back from hardship, and your willingness to take new risks, especially intelligent, well-calculated risks. To be willing to do something different to improve your life always involves some risk. Expectancy, though, is clearly at the heart of all that may be possible in responding to difficult or painful life circumstances. Part of our job, I think, is to be visionaries for our clients, motivating and inspiring them with the wondrous possibilities life has to offer. Another part of our job, I believe, is to help them transcend the fears or doubts of the moment to reach those possibilities and create new ones.

LIFE IN THE SHORT RUN

In my judgment, one of the most troublesome aspects of humans is our limited ability to anticipate realistically the consequences of our actions. If you consider the state of the world today, turbulent as usual, you can see the evidence of human shortsightedness nearly everywhere. We seem to realize on some level that our planet's natural resources are irreplaceable, and yet we continue to abuse them. For the sake of short-term convenience, and our emphasis on our own immediate personal well-being and profit, we thoughtlessly continue to pollute our waters and air, and to hunt entire species to extinction. We know, for example, that the rain forests provide half of the world's breathable oxygen, but then we cut them down at the rate of more than 50 acres a minute. You don't really have to be much of a visionary to know that deforestation on such a scale is going to be more than a minor inconvenience one day. How can we protect our irreplaceable resources if people only think in terms of short-term profit at the risk of harming this delicate ecosystem? For short-term satisfaction, we risk disease and death by smoking cigarettes, taking drugs, and finding countless other ways to abuse and destroy ourselves. By choosing to live in the moment, or actively encouraging our clients to live in the moment by telling them to do so, or even passively looking the other way when people make serious decisions without regard for the consequences, we avoid dealing with the critical, and even painful, issues with which we'd prefer not to deal, almost assuring their getting worse over time. Long-term negative consequences seem to be so far removed from people's focus on the now as to be invisible, even though they are often quite predictable. Then, when the inevitable happens, it becomes the basis for human anguish. Most of the depressed clients I see had ample time to act preventively, but never noticed the opportunity because it came disguised as inconvenience.

Can we really teach people to think preventively and yet simultaneously routinely encourage them to be "fully present in the moment?" How will people learn to "think ahead" if we don't actively teach them to? The task before us as therapists is to pull ourselves out of the "mop-up" position of dealing almost exclusively with the consequences of the bad things that have already happened in people's lives, trying to help them come to terms with their negative histories. And, while dealing with their pasts, they may continue to make even more bad decisions on the basis of the impulse of the moment, yielding ever more painful experiences to address in treatment.

I am obviously placing a great deal of emphasis on the value of vision in general, and the therapeutic power of a future orientation with depressives in particular. Why are people so shortsighted? Why do we make decisions recklessly in the moment only to suffer terrible consequences later? "It seemed like such a good idea at the time" is one of the things I hear almost daily that is meant to explain obviously destructive relationships, impulsive business decisions, bad financial judgments, and self-destructive and socially irresponsible behaviors.

What happened to foresight? Why don't people know that it's not a good idea to have an affair with the boss's wife? Why don't they act on the insight that getting drunk or stoned isn't going to make their problems go away? Why don't they know that having unprotected sex or taking unknown designer drugs is potentially fatal? So much of human misery could be prevented with some high-quality foresight. We repeatedly tell people to "be fully present in the moment," and then we wonder why they do such foolish, impulsive things.

In *New World, New Mind*, authors Robert Ornstein and Paul Ehrlich (1989) present the notion that the inability to anticipate consequences in a meaningful way is, at least in part, a product of biology, specifically neurology. They observe that the human nervous system is organized to respond best to the novelty and intensity of a stimulus, and that the habituation (or "tuning out" of routine or ongoing stimuli) that occurs in each of our sensory systems also occurs in response to our immediate environment. Thus, some celebrity's latest fiasco can dominate national headlines and television time, while far more profound events have been taking place: more animal and plant species have become extinct, more people have died from starvation and war, and one year alone saw more than 100 million births added to an already terribly overpopulated planet of more than six billion.

I believe that Ornstein and Ehrlich have made an important point in a context seemingly unrelated to therapy that actually has profound implications for the mental health profession. Mental health professionals frequently stress the importance of "getting in touch with your feelings." We encourage people to "get the most out of life today," even if, over the long run, that advice leads to higher divorce rates, the painful breakup of families, the violation of traditional legal and moral standards of behavior, and other examples of courting long-term decline in the interest of achieving short-term gain. It may not cheer us up much, but I believe the mental health profession has unwittingly facilitated the cultural emphasis on immediate gratification at the expense of a longer-term higher-quality life. We place great emphasis on the right to choose, but do not help people to really learn to anticipate the consequences of their choices and, therefore, how to choose responsibly.

WHAT CAN THERAPISTS DO?

Therapists are in a position to put greater emphasis on the future in our interactions with others. We can rethink the arbitrary hierarchy created by the therapy field that puts people's feelings ahead of their goals or responsibilities. I don't think it's a coincidence that the depression rates have been rising in tandem with such a subjective emphasis. We can encourage the ability to choose which part of ourselves to respond to, context by context, based on the vision of the results we want, and not on what is simply most comfortable or familiar emotionally.

I can easily wish for, and envision, a time when we push hard as a unified profession to have schools routinely offer training in how to think critically, how to solve problems, and how to relate empathetically to people from the time we enter elementary school as children. In fact, it's already been done in some places. When children are taught to think critically and to plan ahead and not just to react to the first thought that flies through their brains, they tend to exhibit less depression, substance abuse, teenage pregnancy, and other common acting-out behaviors that end up getting our attention later for "mop-up." (See *The Optimistic Child* by Martin Seligman [1995].)

In daily-life examples, the positive value of focusing on longer-term goals rather than short-term difficulties is evident. How do you get a college education? The eventual value of the degree allows you to endure boring lectures and the stresses of final exams and term papers. How do you raise a child with healthy self-esteem? The goal of eventually having a child with a healthy self-image virtually precludes a willingness to hit the child or call the child names in a flash of anger or to humiliate or ignore the child. How do you motivate an employee? The goal of having the person eventually feel good about himself or herself and the job overrides the willingness to insult the person or question his or her heritage when a mistake is made.

Daniel Goleman's (1995) book on emotional intelligence is an invaluable ally in my quest to help therapists and clients develop vision and think beyond the moment. Goleman describes how people who know how to handle their feelings skillfully can transcend their day-to-day difficulties more readily. Impulse control, the ability to delay gratification, and the capability of realistically anticipating consequences are specific talents that foster what Goleman calls emotional intelligence. They are life skills that have tremendous preventive value, not only in the case of depression, but for other disorders as well. To me, they are the core components of vision.

Part of my orientation to the future, and perhaps yours as well, is to emphasize the role of prevention in treatment. To do that, it seems important frequently to remind people that they are more than their feelings, and to teach them specific future-oriented skills for developing emotional intelligence. No medication can do that, which is why, when antidepressant medications are prescribed as the sole form of intervention, the rate of relapse is nearly 50% higher than when psychotherapy is also utilized. Antidepressant medications unquestionably are valuable tools, but I am not personally aware of a single depression expert who would advocate their use as an exclusive form of treatment. Therapeutic efficacy studies make abundantly clear the value of good therapy in teaching cognitive, behavioral, and interpersonal skills.

There are many risk factors for feeling bad. In the largest sense, life is a risk factor; as long as you are alive, you face countless circumstances that are potentially hurtful. If you are going to have relationships, you run a risk of losing them. If you are going to live in a human body, you will face the prospects of injury, disease, or death. If you are going to have a job, you run a risk of losing political and economic battles, and of being fired or replaced. If you are alive, you face the inevitable difficulties associated with just being alive.

Whereas one therapeutic goal, then, is to establish positive expectations in our clients that their experience can change for the better, another is for them to learn to think in terms of expectations, predictions, probabilities, and possibilities. Only then can one carefully identify where to invest safely emotionally or when a situation is too hazardous and potentially toxic to become invested in it. My basic definition of future orientation emphasizes the ability to be so realistic and detailed about the future that the future seems almost as real and immediate as the present.

Considering the great emphasis I have placed on the value of positive expectancy, it would be easy to assume that I am advocating the positive value of hopefulness in all cases. In fact, hopefulness *is* a valuable ally when unrealistic hopelessness is a dominant theme for your client. However, I am aware of no single pattern that is unilaterally positive or negative everywhere, and hopefulness is no exception. It, too, can be destructively unrealistic, and it is our responsibility to help our clients evaluate the realism of their visions. They must be able to distinguish clearly between inner fantasy and external reality.

CONCLUSION

Neither you nor I can change anyone's past. But tomorrow hasn't happened yet. What would you like to have happen? What about next week, next month, next year, and the years after that?

The things you do today lead to what happens tomorrow, and in all the tomorrows that follow. You can powerfully use the clinical skills you continue to learn to develop a positive and realistic future orientation in yourself as well as in your clients. All the good things in your life will come from doing things both inside yourself and out in the world that will make your life worthwhile in your own eyes. It starts with your vision of what's possible, and continues with each step you take to bring the vision to life.

References

Dubovsky, S. (1997). *Mind-body deceptions: The psychosomatics of everyday life.* New York: Norton.

Goleman, D. (1995). *Emotional intelligence: Why it can matter more than IQ.* New York: Bantam.

Gross, M. (1997). *The end of sanity: Social and cultural madness in America.* New York: Avon.

Hillman, J., & Ventura, M. (1992). *We've had a hundred years of psychotherapy — and the world's getting worse.* San Francisco: Harper Collins.

Klerman, G., & Weissman, M. (1989). Increasing rates of depression. *Journal of the American Medical Association, 261*(15), 2229–2235.

Ornstein, R., & Ehrlich, P. (1989). *New world, new mind.* New York: Touchstone.

Papp, P. (1997). Listening to the system. *Family Therapy Networker, 21*(1), 52–58.

Seligman, M. (1995). *The optimistic child.* Boston: Houghton-Mifflin.

Yapko, M. (1996). Depression: Perspectives and treatments. In *1997 Encyclopedia Britannica Medical and Health Annual* (pp. 287–291). Chicago: Encyclopedia Britannica.

Yapko, M. (1997a). *Breaking the patterns of depression.* New York: Doubleday.

Yapko, M. (1997b). Stronger medicine. *Family Therapy Networker, 21*(1), 42–47.

Yapko, M. (1999). *Hand-me-down blues: How to stop depression from spreading in families.* New York: Golden Books.

Yapko, M. (2001). *Treating depression with hypnosis: Integrating cognitive-behavioral and strategic approaches.* Philadelphia: Brunner/Routledge.

5

Multimedia Computers, Humanistic Intervention, and Screening: The Future is Now

Simon H. Budman & Emil Chiauzzi

Early on the morning of July 17, 2007, Dr. May Smith, cyberpsychologist for Millennium HealthCare went to work. She pulled on her robe, grabbed a cup of coffee, walked up the stairs from the second floor of her house to the third floor, and instructed Roscoe 47, her computer, to "rise and shine." The monitor immediately woke up and a jazzy version of The Star Spangled Banner *began to play. The computer then pleasantly greeted her: "Good morning May. Hope you slept well. Roscoe can't wait to start the day."*

She could see a bunch of blinking 3-D e-mail messages from five health centers in Massachusetts, six in New Jersey, three in Ireland, and six in New Zealand. These were the centers for which she was the virtual on-site consultant. Roscoe told her, in a male voice with a British accent, that she also had 3,567 screening downloads that the computer had sorted, analyzed, and summarized for her. "I have also written a report on my findings from last night's data and compared this with the last 895 nightly reports. If you like, I can also compare the data by gender, continent, or disorder. I hope this meets with your approval." May Smith nodded absentmindedly in the di-

rection of the computer's microcam. "I am glad you approve," continued the voice.

"Roscoe, change voice!" Dr. Smith commanded. She had become very tired of all of this ultraproper behavior on the part of her computer. It was no longer cute or interesting. "Marlon Brando, in 'On the Waterfront'," she continued. "I coulda been a contenduh," replied Roscoe in a voice identical to Brando's. She rolled her eyes. The Computers Do Have a Sense of Humor Department at Microsoft was still in its infancy, she thought. At least with the voice (and cyberpersonality change), she would be rid of all of that stiff, formal stuff that the computer had been getting into lately.

The 3-D e-mails (or just plain d-mails, as they were now called) were from the behavioral techs whom she supervised at the various centers. The techs advised clients on how to apply the different target-centered clinical programs and assisted them as they made use of the numerous key apps (kiosk applications) available. Most clients would periodically see a regular "think shrink" as they worked with a tech. A number of other primary-care patients, who still saw behavioral treatment as stigmatizing, got all of their input from the techs and kiosks. Once Dr. Smith viewed and reacted to the d-mails, she skimmed through the downloads. Every patient who came to a center received a behavioral screening. It was amply clear that many behavioral problems, such as alcoholism, substance abuse, and depression, had major implications for a client's use of other medical services. Routinely, she skimmed the downloads to find the high-risk patients who had been screened and with whom intervention had begun.

Why had it taken so long for such screening to become part of standard medical practice? She could barely remember the time when banks had no ATMs, and if you didn't get money for the weekend by Friday afternoon, you were out of luck. Every bank that she knew of now had advanced to Virtual Tellers (VERTELS). (The ads promised that VERTELS could set you up with a new home mortgage within 59.5 seconds or you would receive the money interest-free for one full year.) Dr. Smith also could not think of a single medical practitioner or health center that didn't have on-site behavioral kiosk screening or didn't ask patients to use their own home PCs and screen themselves at the Millennium web site prior to coming in for a visit.

Is this scenario science fiction? It is inevitable that the future of health care will be tied inextricably to computers and technology. Behavioral health care also will be centrally tied to the computer revolution in ways that are currently unimaginable. There has been an explosion of computer use in the United States and around the world. The speed with which this use has been accepted and continues to accelerate is startling.

- Nearly half of U.S. households (42%) now have computers (*ZD Net PC Magazine Online*, 1997).
- By the year 2002, it is expected that over 60% will have computers (*ZD Net PC Magazine Online*, 1997).
- With the proliferation of computers that cost less than $1,000 (and soon under $400), larger segments of the population will become users.
- Currently, there are 57 million Internet users in the United States (*Open Market Internet News*, 1998).
- In 1997, 10% of automobile shoppers used the Internet to help them make a decision about which model to buy (Krantz, 1998).
- In 1997, there were about 10 million on-line shoppers. (Krantz, 1998).
- By 2002, there will be some 61 million on-line shoppers (Krantz, 1998).

Even today, there are numerous ways in which clinicians are integrating computers into their care of clients.

- E-mailing interventions
- Assessing and planning treatment via computer
- Downloading psychoeducational information for clients
- Suggesting on-line support groups
- Conducting on-line psychotherapy
- Joining mailing lists and news groups to increase their knowledge of a particular diagnostic problem

When, in this chapter, we discuss computers and multimedia technology, we are referring to home PCs, the Internet and the World Wide Web (WWW), computer kiosks with touch-screen monitors used in medical areas or in public places, WebTV, and any other new information-delivery systems that develop in the next 5 to 10 years.

Prior to the use of multimedia, most computers employed rather dull and unengaging text-based interfaces. Typically, one would see little other than words on a screen. Users generally had to be relatively proficient typists and needed to learn a number of obscure commands in order to operate a program. With the widespread adoption of the graphical user interface (GUI), computers became far more intuitive and easier to use. The uncomplicated point-and-click of a mouse has replaced long sets of esoteric commands and keyboard combinations. Further enhancing the user's experience are programs containing full-motion videos and high-quality audio clips. For programs used in public places, or for those individuals with no computer skills at all, the touch-screen monitor can now do all the tasks of a mouse. Finally, the Internet, once the domain of only the most technologically sophisticated, is now gaining tens of thousands of users each day, which is doubling each year! Attractive graphics and a growing number of remarkable multimedia features on the Web mean that the Internet and the Web will be available to anyone with a computer and access to a modem and a telephone line. Computer multimedia technology is rapidly becoming very simple and intuitive.

There is reason to believe that multimedia technology is not simply a new way of delivering old information. Research with children and adolescents, who are most involved with this technology, indicates better comprehension, longer periods of engagement in the educational process, greater achievement, and improved attitudes toward learning (Liu, 1996; Matthew, 1996; Software Publishers Association, 1996). Programs that offer interactive, immediate, and personalized feedback (all characteristics of popular computer games) are effective in capturing the attention of children, teenagers, and adults (Paperny et al., 1990). Compared with questionnaires, computerized primary-care programs for adolescents have been found to increase self-disclosure in such sensitive areas as high-risk sexual behavior, alcohol and/or marijuana use, family problems, and other emotional issues (Krishna et al., 1997; Paperny et al., 1990; Turner et al., 1998). One study found that almost 90% of teenagers preferred computer-screening and advice to written or interview methods (Paperny et al., 1990)! It is clear that multimedia programs, when constructed on sound theoretical principles, can allow the user to control the learning process in a highly productive and open manner. Unlike many psychoeducational efforts (typically pamphlets and videotapes), which utilize a "shotgun" approach to information-giving, multimedia technology allows its tailoring to the user's tastes and needs.

MAJOR USES OF COMPUTERS AND MULTIMEDIA TECHNOLOGY IN BEHAVIORAL HEALTH CARE

There are several major ways in which we believe that computers and multimedia technology will be used in the future: (1) a screening tool in primary-care, behavioral-care, and work settings; (2) as a direct intervention; (3) as a "clinician advisory" tool to help structure clinician interventions; (4) as part of a self-help process making use of Web-based on-line communities and computer learning environments; (5) as a teaching tool for clinicians. A variety of other uses might also evolve, but these appear to me to be the most likely.

Computer Screening for Primary-Care, Behavioral-Care, and Work Setting

Computers, especially multimedia computers, ask questions well. They can ask questions in the same way each time. They can compute scores instantaneously. They can also "skip" particular questions or add relevant questions as needed. Even before there were simple GUI interfaces, text-based computers were used for screening questionnaires. With the advent of touch-screen technology and on-screen video and graphics, interviewees can have the experience of a "virtual" interview. On-screen characters can ask the client questions and lead the interactions. Also, instantaneous scale scoring and the printouts can help determine immediately what is needed by the client. While the client is still in front of the computer, his or her answers can be scored and recommendations made on the basis of the findings.

At Innovative Training Systems (ITS), a health-care multimedia products company in Newton, Mass., we have several outstanding examples of computerized screening programs. One is the multimedia version of the Addiction Severity Index (ASI; McLellan et al., 1985a, 1985b). The ASI is a structured clinical interview used to measure the severity of a range of problem areas that are typically associated with alcohol and drug abuse. Specifically, the interview covers the client's medical status, employment and support status, drug use, alcohol use, legal status, family and social relationships, and psychiatric status. The substance-abuse client is asked a series of questions in each of these areas. The interviewer uses probes and other questions as necessary to clarify answers. The ASI has become a standard assessment tool in clinical trials and other controlled research involving substance abusers. Clinical settings also have adopted the ASI and are using it on a standard basis. Already, the Veterans' Administration recommends use of the ASI in its facilities, and it is employed by many criminal justice agencies. The Joint Commission on the Accreditation of Healthcare Organizations (JCAHO) recognizes the ASI as part of a comprehensive assessment process for developing treatment plans. In addition, a number of states, including Maryland and Pennsylvania, have specifically mandated use of the ASI as the clinical assessment instrument to be utilized in programs they fund.

Although the ASI has much to recommend it, it involves significant problems. For example, in order to use it correctly, interviewers must be thoroughly trained and calibrated. Administering the scale requires a good deal of costly staff time. Further, the ASI Severity Scores, some of the most important, are highly subjective. The interviewer's impressions are weighted heavily, and these can be strongly biased by other factors. For instance, if a client will not be admitted to a treatment facility without a particular level of severity, ASI interviewers from that facility will be hard pressed to be totally objective in their scoring.

The multimedia version of the ASI, developed by ITS with support from the National Institute of Drug Abuse, addresses many of these issues. Its interesting interactive format is characterized by the extensive use of on-screen video interviewers. The treatment facility does not need to impinge on precious staff time to conduct the ASI interview, as it can all be done by the client working on the computer using a simple touch-screen interface. Additionally, a computerized algorithm for the ASI Severity Scores that was developed by ITS works at least as well as an expert ASI interviewer in generating these scores (Butler et al., in press).

Computer-Directed Intervention

Computer programs can be used to actually " intervene" with clients. One of the first examples of such an intervention was Joseph Weizenbaum's program, Eliza, developed in the 1960s while he was at the Massachusetts Institute of Technology (Weizenbaum, 1976). Eliza simulated a Rogerian therapist in being reflective and restating (in text) the client's words. There have since been a variety of examples of computer behavioral intervention, or what has been called computer-assisted therapy. Many of these predate more user-friendly graphical interfaces and are text-based. The best example of a multimedia computer-assisted therapy package was developed by Wright and Wright (1997). It utilizes video examples and tasks for the user and is based on a cognitive behavioral approach. It is interesting to note that Weizenbaum, developer of Eliza, was a linguist who designed the program as a research tool focused on natural language. He believed that computer-assisted therapy was "immoral" and would detract away from the "interpersonal respect, understanding, and love" of traditional treatment (Slack, 1997, p. 83).

Clinician Advisor

It is exceedingly difficult to get clinicians to practice with any degree of homogeneity. Even under circumstances in which there are clear and concrete parameters for intervention (McLellan & Cacciola, personal communication, July 17, 1997), it remains unlikely that clinicians will act in anything like a unitary way. Computers can provide unambiguous guidelines and real-time recommendations to clinicians. With regard to the ASI, it is clear from McLelland's research that when substance-abuse clients receive appropriate treatment services as determined by the scale (e.g., vocational services, family counseling), they show greater improvement and are less likely to drop out of treatment than when this is not the case (McLellan et al., 1994). However, according to McLellan and his colleagues, it is very difficult to get substance-abuse counselors to actually make use of ASI findings. We believe that this is largely because the counselors are uncertain of precisely how to apply this information and believe that they lack the expertise to organize the data into a coherent treatment plan. At ITS, we are planning an "On-line ASI Consultant." This program would take findings from the ITS multimedia ASI and make clear recommendations to the clinician about content areas to pursue with the client. Once the client has provided this information to the clinician and it has been inputted, the computer will generate a clear, operational set of recommendations and guidelines for intervention. The program would also, based on input from experts, generate the answers to any questions or uncertainties the clinician might have about how to proceed.

Building Cybercommunities and Supporting Self-Help Efforts

The Web is becoming a prime location for patient empowerment and self-help. It has been described as "the world's biggest library . . . with all the books on the floor," and it is also the world's biggest self-help meeting. Patients are able to find and research every possible disorder or disease, and then locate or organize an on-line support group, chat session, or news group regarding that topic. There are countless chats, news groups, mail lists and Web sites on any medical topic, common or obscure. Already there are thousands of on-line AA meetings. Such support and information are available around the clock and from any location in the world with a telephone and a computer. In our view, the future holds numerous on-line "cybercommunities" focused on health issues. These communities will allow the participants to share experiences, mentor others, and try new behaviors or approaches. The emerging field of "cyberpsychology" is beginning to evaluate the unique aspects of interaction in cyberspace, such as its effects on time boundaries, identity, and interpersonal status (Suler, 1996).

Unlike the current chat technologies, which are also heavily text-based, new community support environments will be three-dimensional "worlds" in which the user assumes a stable identity and role, and in which he or she has a graphical representative called an "avatar." This avatar will be a figure who will have facial expressions and will "walk" through the virtual environment and interact with other users' avatars. Such graphical worlds would allow people literally to go to an AA meeting on-line and meet face-to-face (or avatar-to-avatar) with others at the meeting. Lest the reader view our description as something from the long-distant future, he or she has only to go to the Web site for Worlds.com (http://www.worlds.com) or the Microsoft corporate Web site (http://www.microsoft.com/ie/chat/?/ie/chat/vchatmain.htm) and find V-chat for examples of such technology in use today.

As a Teaching Tool for Clinicians

Many of the original efforts in the multimedia area focused on the computer as a teaching tool for clinicians. Since multimedia CD-ROM programs provide clinicians the opportunity to try various interventions in a safe, low-risk environment, learning can be flexible and users can test numerous options without the fear of hurting a client. For example, a program focusing on cognitive-behavioral interventions for anxiety might allow the clinician to try various sets of interventions with an on-screen "virtual client" and thereby learn the outcomes of these strategies in a low-risk setting. There might be a computerized "coach" who critiques the intervention approach and "peer stories" from other clinicians who have used this method of intervention describing how it worked for them (Leake, 1996).

AN EXAMPLE: COMPUTER-ASSISTED ALCOHOL SCREENING AND TREATMENT FOR PRIMARY CARE

The best way to clarify the power of computers in behavioral health care is with another direct example. Computer-assisted alcohol screening and treatment for primary care (CAAST) was developed and tested by ITS with support from the National Institute of Alcohol Abuse and Alcoholism. CAAST was developed to deal with several major problems in the area of alcohol screening, recognition, and intervention in primary care.

Annually, nearly $90 billion, or 20% of the nation's health-care costs, are attributable to the effects of alcohol use and abuse. Alcohol is one of the leading causes of preventable illness and early death in this country. About 10% of ambulatory primary-care patients and 25% of general hospital patients meet the criteria for primary alcohol or drug disorders (Brown, 1992). It is also quite clear that a minimal, nonintensive intervention on the part of the primary-care physician (PCP) can have an important impact in reducing problem drinking. In fact, in a large, multinational study by Babor and Grant (1992) it was found that five minutes of advice by the PCP significantly reduced self-reported drinking. Nonetheless, physicians are unlikely to diagnose those with alcohol problems in primary care. One study found that only 45% of alcoholic patients were even asked about their drinking, only 25% were encouraged to reduce their consumption or were told about possible health risks, and only 3% were referred to a treatment program (Kamerow et al., 1986). Further, PCPs fail to recognize alcohol problems in their patients between 33% and 90% of the time. The failure may be due to low confidence, stereotypes about alcoholics, lack of time, or some combination of issues. However, medical physicians seem unlikely to soon engage in higher levels of screening and intervention for alcohol use, despite the fact that such activities would appear to have extremely beneficial cost outcomes for the health-care system and quality-of-life implications for patients.

If the problem entails getting sufficient numbers of primary-care patients screened for drinking problems, why not just use a simple paper-and-pencil measure? Although there are well-validated paper-and-pencil measures of drinking that could be used in primary care, including the MAST (Selzer, 1971), the SMAST (Selzer, Vinokur, & van Rooijen, 1975), and the AUDIT (Saunders et al., 1993), these are less than ideal solutions for a variety of reasons. First, a remarkably large number of people in this country are unable to read or write, or do so poorly. Mrvos, Dean, and Krenzelok (1993) note that over 60 million Americans (fully one-third of the adult population) are estimated to be functionally or marginally illiterate, but rarely identify themselves as illiterate to health-care professionals. Further, even if those with alcohol problems were identified by a questionnaire, it is still unlikely that the PCPs would feel able to intervene comfortably and skillfully.

We developed the CAAST at ITS with the idea that not only could the computer interactively screen patients in primary care for alcohol problems, but it could also provide the patients with motivational feedback about their drinking. Additionally, we learned from focus groups with physicians and nurses that the primary-care team did not wish to "get into arguments" with patients who were not ready to change or interested in changing. Therefore, we decided to give patients the choice of sharing their alcohol screening with their PCPs. If a patient was unwilling, ashamed, or unmotivated to talk with his or her provider, the patient did not need to do so. From the providers' perspectives, they would be dealing with a more motivated population of drinkers who chose to share their findings on the screening instrument.

CAAST is presented to a primary-care patient on a kiosk using a touch-screen monitor. The kiosk has a headset and partitions on each side so that the patient has ample privacy. CAAST presents a series of health-care-related questions as to diet, smoking, and exercise, and then moves on to take the patient through the AUDIT, a 10-item measure of alcohol-use patterns developed for primary care. The AUDIT was developed by the National Institute of Alcohol Abuse and Alcoholism in conjunction with the World Health Organization. Once the AUDIT and other questions are completed, the patient receives very useful motivational feedback about his or her level of alcohol consumption and, if problematic, what can be done about it. Response to CAAST has been extremely positive. It appears that patients enjoy using the computer and that they are more likely to tell the computer about their alcohol use than to report it on a paper-and-pencil test (6% versus 10%). We also find that whereas our computer program identifies 10%, the physicians only identify 0.1% of the patients in their practices as having alcohol problems!

THE ETHICS OF USING COMPUTERS IN HEALTH CARE

What are the ethical issues that arise in using computers for health care and behavioral health? We believe that most of these concerns are related to Weizenbaum's concerns about the loss of "respect, understanding, and love" from the clinical process and their replacement by the "cold mechanics of computers."

It should be noted that Rene Laennec, who developed the stethoscope in 1816, was ridiculed. Physicians felt that using this "modern device" kept them away from their patients because they no longer needed to place their ear against the patient's chest. Is it not conceivable that objections to using computers in health care will appear as naive 25 years from now, or even sooner?

It seems to us that this issue need not be an either/or situation. Computers can humanize treatment in many ways. If the clinician is freed from endless paperwork and has his or her work enhanced by clients using computers for homework tasks, behavioral strategies, support groups, information, and bibliotherapy, everyone benefits. Every technology has its up side and down side; however, to use computers thoughtfully and skillfully, and to consider the computer a treatment enhancer, is beneficial for all of us.

It would appear that ethical questions arise only if the computer is used as a way to prevent patients from receiving services or to keep them from meeting with providers. Although this certainly could be the case, with vigilance, we will expand the parameters of treatment, while enhancing its accessibility and benefits.

References

Babor, T. F., & Grant, M. (1992). *Programme on substance abuse: Project on identification and management of alcohol-related problems. Report on Phase II: Randomized clinical trial of brief interventions in primary healthcare.* Geneva: World Health Organization.

Brown, R. L. (1992). Identification and office management of alcohol and drug disorders. In M. F. Fleming & K. L. Barry (Eds.), *Addictive disorders* (pp. 25–43). St. Louis: Mosby.

Butler, S. F., Newman, F. L., Cacciola, J. S., Frank, A., Budman, S. H., McLellan, A. T., Ford, S., Blaine, J., Gastfriend, D., Moras, K., & Salloum, I. M. (in press).

Predicting ASI interviewer severity ratings for a computer-administered Addiction Severity Index. *Psychological Assessment.*

Kamerow, D. B., et al. (1986). Alcohol abuse, other drug use, and mental disorders in medical practice: Prevalence, costs, recognition, and treatment. *Journal of the American Medical Association, 255*, 2054–2057.

Krantz, M. (1998, July 20). Click till you drop. *Time,* pp. 34–41.

Krishna, S., et al. (1997). Clinical trials of interactive computerized patient education: Implications for family practice. *Journal of Family Practice, 45*, 25–33.

Leake, D. B. (1996). *Case-based reasoning: Experiences, lessons and future directions.* Cambridge, MA: MIT Press.

Liu, M. (1996). An exploratory study of how pre-kindergarten children use the interactive multimedia technology: Implications for multimedia software design. *Journal of Computing in Childhood Education, 7*, 71–92.

Matthew, K. I. (1996). The impact of CD-ROM storybooks on children's reading comprehension and reading attitude. *Journal of Educational Multimedia and Hypermedia, 5,* 56–78.

McLellan, A. T., Alterman, A. I., Metzger, D. S., Grissom, G., Woody, G. E., Luborsky, L., & O'Brien, C. P. (1994). Similarity of outcome predictors across opiate, cocaine, and alcohol treatments: Role of treatment services. *Journal of Consulting and Clinical Psychology, 62*, 1141–1158.

McLellan, A. T., Luborsky, L., Cacciola, J., Griffith, J. E., Evans, F., Barr, H. L., & O'Brien, C. P. (1985a). New data from the Addiction Severity Index: Reliability and validity in three centers. *Journal of Nervous and Mental Disease, 173*, 412–423.

McLellan, A. T., Luborsky, L., Cacciola, J., Griffith, J. E., McGahan, P., & O'Brien, C. P. (1985b). *Guide to the Addiction Severity Index: Background administration and field testing results.* Rockville, MD: U.S. Department of Health and Human Services.

Mrvos, R., Dean, B. S., & Krenzelok, E. P. (1993). Illiteracy: A contributing factor to poisoning. *Veterinary and Human Toxicology, 35*, 466–468.

Open Market Internet News (no. 22, 1998). Retrieved September 6, 1998, from http://www.openmarket.com/intindex/98-05.htm.

Paperny, D. M., et al. (1990). Computer-assisted detection and intervention in adolescent high-risk health behaviors. *Journal of Pediatrics, 116*, 456–462.

Saunders, W. M., & Kershaw, P. W. (1980). Screening tests for alcoholism: Findings from a community study. *British Journal of Addiction, 75*, 37–41.

Selzer, M. L. (1971). The Michigan Alcoholism Screening Test: The quest for a new diagnostic instrument. *American Journal of Psychiatry, 127*, 1653–1658.

Selzer, M. L., Vinokur, A., & van Rooijen, L. A. (1975). A self-administered Short Michigan Alcoholism Screening Test (SMAST). *Journal of Studies on Alcohol*, *36*, 117–126.

Slack, W. V. (1997). *Cybermedicine: How computing empowers doctors and patients for better health care.* San Francisco: Jossey-Bass.

Software Publisher's Association (1996). *Report on the effectiveness of technology in schools.* Washington, DC: SPA.

Suler, J. (1996). *The psychology of cyberspace.* On-line book retrieved July 17, 1998, from http://www1.rider.edu/~suler/psycyber/psycyber.html.

Turner, C. F., et al. (1998). Adolescent sexual behavior, drug use, and violence: Increased reporting with computer survey technology. *Science*, *280*, 867–873.

Weizenbaum, J. (1976). *Computer power and human reason.* New York: Freeman.

Wright, J. H., & Wright, A. S. (1997). Computer-assisted psychotherapy. *Journal of Psychotherapy Practice Res*, *6*, 315–329.

ZD Net PC Magazine Online (December 23, 1997). A PC in every home. Retrieved September 6, 1998, from http://search.zdnet.com/pcmag/news/trends/t971223a.htm.

6

The Cause and Cure of Affect Phobias in Short-Term Dynamic Psychotherapy

Leigh McCullough

PATIENT: "I never have angry feelings. I'm not that kind of person."

PATIENT: "I don't want to start crying — because I'm afraid I'll never stop."

PATIENT: "Tenderness makes me sick to my stomach. I don't even like the word."

Some people have phobias about spiders — or bridges — or heights. But all of us have some degree of phobia about feelings — about the best and deepest within us. Affects can be so frightening. We want to cry sometimes, but feel foolish for doing so, and so we block it or defend against it. We feel angry and want to say so sometimes, but feel guilty, or afraid to make someone mad, so we defend against it and block it while doing something else. We feel tender toward someone, but are afraid of rejection or too embarrassed to speak up and say so. Instead, we become silent. This goes on day after day, and most of us do not realize that these phobias are always in action.

Thus an affect phobia is being afraid of or inhibited about our internal emotional responses, our feelings. At various times, we might be too afraid to speak up, too guilty to get angry, too pained to bear sadness, or too ashamed to show tenderness. When we respond in this way, it can be useful to think of it as an affect phobia because then we can consider using some of the well-tested methods that have been effective in treating phobias.

In short-term dynamic psychodynamic psychotherapy, we think of the person with an affect phobia as acting defensively. For example, a person may be (1) feeling joy, sorrow, anger, excitement (adaptive affects), that are (2) inhibited by anxiety, guilt, shame, or pain, (so they become phobic affects), and (3) this conflict over the feeling results in defensive or avoidant, phobic behavior.

The goal of this treatment is to alter the avoidant defenses enough so that the person not only can express feelings, but also is able fully to feel them, and contain them when necessary. However, this therapy does not encourage mindless catharsis or venting of feelings. It fosters deeply felt experience that is consciously and maturely guided.

Conflicts about affects and behavior (what I am calling "affect phobias") has been visually depicted by David Malan's "two triangles," which represent the "the universal principle of psychodynamic psychotherapy"; that is, defenses and anxieties block the expression of adaptive impulses and feelings (see Figure 1).

The triangle of conflict represents the behavior pattern that results from intrapsychic conflict. In this model, the term "intrapsychic conflict" refers to the tension between emotional activation and emotional inhibition, which results in "phobic" or avoidant defensive behavior. We feel anger (activation), but also feel guilty about feeling angry (inhibition), so we can either phobically avoid the anger and become withdrawn (defensive behavior), or we can learn to guide the angry feelings to a constructive end. This form of therapy is designed to teach the constructive guidance of all feelings.

These defensive patterns of behavior (which we also refer to as intrapsychic conflicts or "affect phobias") are always associated with specific people in the patient's life, as is represented by the triangle of person. The conflict pattern began with early-life caretakers, and is maintained in current relationships. Furthermore, this pattern inevitably will be acted out in the relationship with the therapist, where there will be an opportunity to examine it and change it.

For example, if we learn to inhibit anger in our early life, with "past

Figure 1. David Malan's two triangles: the universal principle of psychodynamic psychotherapy.

Triangle of Conflict

Defense
Maladaptive Behavior
The avoidant response

Anxiety
Conflict/Inhibition
Due to anxiety, guilt, shame, pain

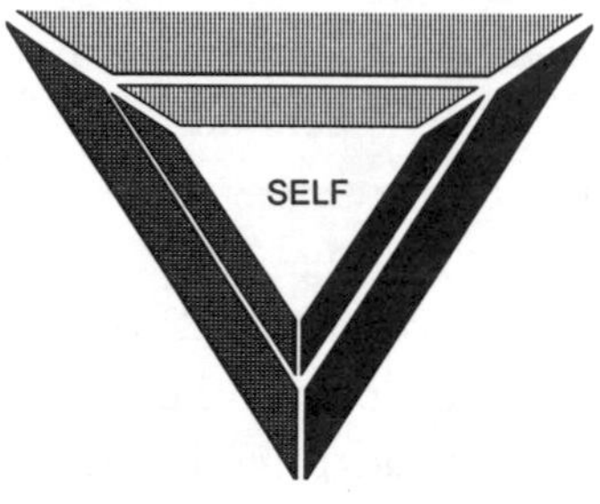

Adaptive Impulse/Feeling
Activation/Excitation
(Anger, sorrow, fear, tenderness, joy, excitement, sexual desire)

Triangle of Person

Therapist
Where patterns can be examined

Current Persons
Current significant others
Where patterns are maintained

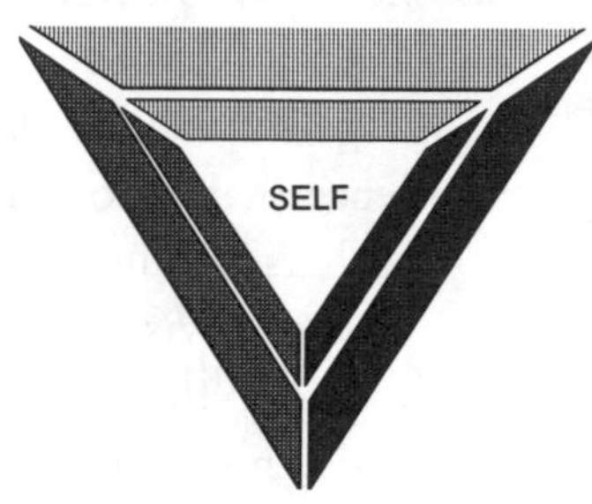

Past Persons
Early-life caretakers where patterns originated

persons," we are probably going to inhibit anger in the same way with "current persons," as well as with the "therapist." So these patterns of 'intrapsychic conflict' that are identified on the triangle of conflict need to be identified as they occur (or have occurred) with the past, current, and therapy relationships. Certain affects (both the inner experience and the outward expression) have become phobically inhibited by anxiety, shame, or pain, and thus — like a phobia — are avoided. We can think of the triangle of conflict as representing an intrapsychic conflict pattern that gives rise to an affect phobia.

TREATMENT MODALITY

This short-term treatment approach is based on the premise that a person's maladaptive behaviors can be understood as attempts to protect the self (*defenses*) by avoiding the experience and/or expression of avoided feelings (*adaptive affects*) that are intolerable because of anxiety or other conflicting feelings that they arouse (e.g., *inhibitory affects*, such as shame, guilt, or fear of rejection). In order to change these maladaptive defensive behavior patterns, the person must recognize them as defensive, feel motivated to modify them, identify the avoided feelings, experience them in the therapy sessions, and learn to express them interpersonally in new and adaptive ways — thus altering the sense of self in relation to others.

If the maladaptive pattern is conceptualized as an affect phobia (i.e., fear of an emotional response because of conflicted feelings associated with it), then we can utilize interventions that abundant research has shown to be useful in curing phobias; namely, systematic desensitization. Although the treatment follows the fundamental structure of psychodynamic psychotherapy (i.e., analysis of defenses blocking conflicted feelings), it employs the technology of behavior change to speed up the therapy process. Interventions involve an exposure (to conflicted feeling) and response prevention (of defensive avoidance) to achieve desensitization of the feared but adaptive affects. The goal of the therapy is a rapid reduction of symptoms, as well as an adaptive change in longstanding character problems.

To achieve these goals, there are three main treatment objectives that have evolved from many years of research and clinical observation. The first is defense restructuring (recognition of and giving up defenses). The second is affect restructuring (the experiencing and appropriate expression of conflicted feeling). The third is self/other restructuring (alteration of the maladaptive inner representations of self and others). These objectives, and the interventions used to achieve them, are not followed in sequential fashion, but are employed as needed by the specific patient.

Defense restructuring can be thought of as a process of response prevention. First, the patient must be made aware of the defensive behaviors that need to be prevented. Patients cannot stop intellectualizing, or smiling to avoid sadness, if they do not know they are doing it. Second, the patient will need to want to give up the defensive response, which is not always the case. So the therapist must help the patient 'uncover' the resistance to giving up the behaviors. For example, I have recommended that the costs and benefits of the defenses be evaluated to see what is holding them in place. In such cases, many patients have discovered that they would rather keep smiles on their faces than feel the depth of pain that they carry. Others prefer to sabotage their job success rather than take on responsibilities that they feel certain will reveal their inadequacies. So the defensive behavior continues until the fear of giving it up is reduced — by regulating the anxieties or inhibitions associated with the adaptive feeling.

Affect restructuring is a process of exposing the patient to the feared inner experience of feeling. The experiencing of affect and the expression of affect are two very different skills, and both need specific exercises to become desensitized. Affect experiencing means the patient links bodily sensations with the correct feeling word. Then the patient must be exposed to the inner felt experience of affect until he or she can tolerate the feeling, without the inhibition of shame, or guilt, or fear. Affect experiencing needs to be done in a step-wise and supportive way, so that the feelings that are uncovered do not become overwhelming or impair the patient's functioning. For example, the therapist must help the patient cry — first a little, and then later, fully sob. The therapist must help the patient get a little irritated, and expand upon it until the patient can feel and control a full burst of anger (because it happens to most of us, and we need to know how to manage it).

The second objective in affect restructuring is affect expression, which exposes patients to the expression of their feelings interpersonally. This is a very different skill from that of experiencing feelings, and requires different mechanisms.

When a patient is too impaired to proceed with either defense or affect work, restructuring the sense of self and of others is often necessary — and may have to be focused on first. One cannot uncover and give up unconscious defenses, if they are shoring up a fragile sense of self: (e.g., "I am not entitled to assert what I want, so I stay silent [defensive behavior] because if I were to ask for my own wants and needs to be met [adaptive affect response], I would be aggressive and hurt others [shame associated with the self]." Such an individual is not going to change defenses if it results in feeling ashamed. First, the sense of self has to be changed by being associated with positive feelings (e.g., feeling entitled to ask for things). The patient's sense of "self" will need to be restructured; that is, desensitized. This means that the self will need to become associated with positive feelings (i.e., healthy pride, self-compassion, self-care) and not with inhibitory feelings (shame, fear, guilt, pain).

Space permits only a brief overview of this treatment model. However, it is described in detail in the psychotherapy manual *Changing Character: Short-Term Anxiety-Regulating Psychotherapy for Restructuring Defenses, Affects, and Attachments* (McCullough Vaillant, 1997). Throughout this manual there are detailed examples of exposure to angry feelings. However, this chapter provides an example of working with a more severely phobic affect than is described there.

The following case example illustrates an extreme affect phobia about anger. This bright, capable young woman is paralyzed by obsessional anxiety. She becomes so flooded with anxiety that she can barely function during the day for weeks at a time. It is crucial that I help her move out of her head and into her feelings that will counter the anxiety, but she is incredibly blocked in doing so. This session is a detailed example of exposing a patient to angry sessions in a very elementary form, just in fantasy. This is almost impossible for her to do — so the exposure is preceded by a lot of teaching and the alleviating of anxiety around the feelings that preceded the anger work. The following is an annotated transcript from this case.

THERAPIST: This is a teaching session about why we get angry and the virtue of having this extreme thought. I've been talking a lot about bringing the feeling up and containing it in fantasy so you have plenty of time to sort it out. Then you can act. The point isn't to go around getting your anger out by screaming, yelling, or being rageful.

PATIENT: I hope you're not training me to be like some "anger soldier."

THERAPIST: Anger soldier? No, not at all!

PATIENT: I didn't think you were, but I just wanted to be clear about what this was going to do in the long run. For me, it is hard not to know where I am going with this and what the point is.

THERAPIST: It's very scary, isn't it?

PATIENT: It scared me a lot because I think, you know, obviously I'm someone who just never could get angry at all. So, to jump in like that really just scared me.

THERAPIST: I try to go painstakingly slow with people who have never been angry. But as soon as possible, I do try to push patients to experience anger fully for several important reasons. First, if you can pull this angry feeling up (or any feeling for that matter) and let it be fully experienced in your body — so you really know exactly what is going on with yourself, — then you don't have to deny the feeling, or minimize how mad you are. If you are comfortable with the inner experience, you can be more comfortable saying, "I am furious!" Then, to kind of explore your body or pay attention: "I'm not a little bit mad, I know what that's like, I'm furious! Or maybe I'm a little bit mad." When the feeling is conscious and contained, you can assess it. You can think about it. "Do I feel like killing her? No. But I do feel like shaking her — or slapping her." Paying attention to these feelings tells you how much the other person is affecting you. So, once you can face these feelings, the issue is what you want to do with them. If you are so mad that you feel like killing this person, that tells you that something has to be done. It might be that you have to sit the person down and say, "We'd better have a talk. Something's gotta change because I'm really upset." That would be the appropriate way. We are never talking about expressing anger in a hostile or violent way.

PATIENT: Right, because that to me feels out of control sometimes, you know?

THERAPIST: What feels out of control?

PATIENT: Well, it could feel out of control to me even when I feel upset. I'm not comfortable with it. It just feels very, you know, upsetting. I think what you're saying is that this helps you become more aware ... instead of being scared or overwhelmed, you feel more in control. Like saying to yourself, "Okay, I've just been violated and I can figure out how I'm going to handle it." Instead of feeling like, "Oh, I deserved that comment and I'm in turmoil because of it." You know?

THERAPIST: Right. Isn't it typical for us to have some type of assault happen and then (rather than standing up and protecting oneselves) we tend to get confused and flustered and not know how to react — or we blame ourselves.

PATIENT: I think the key thing with me that really ruined my ability to handle anger was these girls who were so mean to me in school when I was 12. I *should* have gotten mad at them and said, you know, "What the hell are you saying? Why are you laughing at how I walk up to get my soda?" And I think what you're saying is that like you can learn to access that feeling. But I could not do that back then.

THERAPIST: Those natural protective feelings had already been buried.

PATIENT: Yeah.

THERAPIST: Even the awareness of the feeling.

PATIENT: It was so much, it was so constant that it was this constant feeling like ... confused. ... And I started ... feeling like I deserved being bullied. So it's so hard for me to ... get out of that.

THERAPIST: The natural, healthy anger that would have protected you was so buried that you just got assaulted. Then you felt anxious and ashamed and put yourself down.

PATIENT: So you're saying that this kind of "anger exercise" that you want me to do will teach me how to protect myself?

THERAPIST: Yes, absolutely. And this exercise accesses the feelings that help you protect yourself.

PATIENT: Which keeps you connected with people.

THERAPIST: Yes, it does. You are right. But it is curious that you make that connection.

Most patients — and therapists too — fear that the angry images will hurt relationships. In fact, we repeatedly see that relationships improve when anger is conscious and can be maturely handled. But you are very insightful in realizing that anger helps you stay connected to others.

PATIENT: I guess it means — it's not like you're getting mad at people all the time. It's just teaching you a healthier way of coping with things.

THERAPIST: Again, absolutely. My experience is, after I take people through this "affect exercise," that their relationships get better, not worse, because they're not having to run away and hide. They're not in turmoil. When people speak up about troublesome issues and get them off their chests in a reasonable way they don't end up hating the persons at whom they were mad. And more often than not, these relationships improve.

PATIENT: See, I think the feelings that are really underneath are what get buried. And what you're saying is that, like you said, doing this — [*pulling up the feelings*] helps you to sort out your feelings. I think that's where I'm at a loss. I think that's why it would keep you more connected with people. Because you're really talking about feelings, like, "You hurt my feelings," or "You just did something you shouldn't do, and ... it made me feel bad." Or [there could be] other feelings [that people have trouble expressing] like love, you know?

THERAPIST: [Yes, the same principles apply whether the feelings are positive or negative.] When the feeling being experienced is positive, you can say, "You mean so much to me," or, "You've touched my heart more than anyone." These basic principles are the same with all feelings. It is tremendously helpful to know on a visceral level when your heart feels touched — or when your heart is racing with anger — or when it is beating fast with excitement — or when your heart is broken and you want to cry. If you can make these distinctions in your feeling life, and have the discipline to reflect upon them, then you have the ability to decide how you want to act.

PATIENT: Well, right now, feelings only throw me into turmoil. I guess I could learn to sort them out more and, you know ... cause now, the first thing that comes to my mind is turmoil when I feel anything.

[*As a child, she had to keep such rigid control over herself to manage her chaotic environment that she is terrified of loosening up.*]

THERAPIST: When you have feeling building up inside of you, you tend to say, "No, no, no!"

PATIENT: Because I think all the feelings and everything are connected to, you know, creativity and spontaneity and stuff. I never let myself be spontaneous, so I just have kept to that rigid line. I think anger falls in there, too. To me, anger feels like a creative thing.

THERAPIST: That's a very interesting way of looking at it. I think you're right. Because when feelings come up, they move toward some form of action. That's what creativity is, isn't it? It's freedom to let your feelings drive you or push — or affect you in some way.

[*Of course, the impact we are teaching is mature and adaptive — not regressive and destructive.*]

PATIENT: I think so. I picture that as like a big ball of joy and anger. ... All those emotions, to me, are all connected. And to me, I've covered that ball [*she laughs*] with something and it's like this tantalizing thing for me. Like I know it's there and I know ... I feel, I really feel that there's something that if ... if I can get the needle in there, it's just gonna like open up. To me, I don't know, the talk about anger to me relates to other things, like creativity and spontaneity.

THERAPIST: It sounds like this crystal ball, this special part ... it's the most precious part of you. It's the pulse of life. It's your life spirit.

PATIENT: Right, I think it is. And it's ... and I'm just killing it and crushing it or piling onto it whatever was piled onto it.

THERAPIST: Yeah, you've been piling on, but you didn't start the piling on. It was not your fault. As your mother said, you used to be this outgoing kid. Isn't that tragic to think how at one time in your life you were full of joy and full of tears — and full of anger?

PATIENT: It's tragic that I still feel like I'm that person and I'm trapped. That's even worse to think. I feel like I can just see this little magical thing and I can't get to it. And that's what, that's what is disturbing to me. And I am very inhibited and part of me has been saying I just need to like sit down and write and do things. And I run away from that. It makes me run, you know. Like I wanted all week to just sit and write down before today. The best I could to do was to start jotting things in the car. Because I knew I didn't really have to access it, you know, I could just like spew things off.

THERAPIST: You know this is a part, one of the most magical and precious parts of you that's been pushed away, way under, and you miss it. You know, you're scared to access it ...

PATIENT: And I feel like time is going by.

THERAPIST: Yeah, your life is going by. This is that void you felt ... It's not a void, but it's empty, it's deadened, I'd say. That lifeless place that you want the life to flow back into.

PATIENT: Right. And, I don't know, I was thinking like, what exercises can I do? But that's ... you have one that you ...

THERAPIST: Yeah. That or writing.

PATIENT: It still scares me but ...

[*Now the teaching ends and the therapeutic interventions begin. This first one is called anxiety regulation. She is telling me that she is afraid of angry feelings, so I need to explore those fears in more detail with her until they are "regulated" and she is able to bear the angry feelings, and guide them appropriately. Indeed, all the teaching thus far has been in service of calming her anxiety about exposure to feeling — but in a more indirect and intellectual manner. I was trying to get her "on my side" by teaching her the value of feeling, and how we will go about it. Now I will focus more specifically on the anxieties that arise when anger is felt.*]

THERAPIST: Well, let's go into the fear of it. Like what's ... what's really so bad about feeling anger?

PATIENT: Just — you know, it's just ... I'm still scared to try to fantasize about it, I guess. I don't know.

THERAPIST: Hmm ... Okay, let's look at why. If you fantasized about, what's her name? Is it ...

PATIENT: Julie?

THERAPIST: Julie.

PATIENT: Uh-huh.

[*When trying to access feeling, it is essential to go to a specific example of something that happened with an actual person. Feeling is not as intense when general themes are discussed.*]

THERAPIST: She's ... she's someone you're close to. If you really looked her in the face and felt what you wanted to do to her because she's been so mean to you, what's so scary about that? Because it's just in fantasy. It's safe.

[*This is an attempt at exposure at a very low level. I do not expect her to be able to go very far with it, but I want to see what fears come up.*]

PATIENT: Well, I don't know if it's because I'm really cut off ... Cause like when you ... the key word that you say is, what do you want to do to her? So if you say, what could you do to her? That's where I can't ... I still feel ...

[*She immediately pulls back — saying she can't imagine "doing" something. Because she is pulling back so much, I go on to exploring the fears around the feelings.*]

THERAPIST: What does it mean, if you wanted to hurt her, what does that mean about you?

PATIENT: Um ... what does that mean about me? Hmm ... It wouldn't be me to hit somebody. I'm not that kind of person.

[*This is a very common reaction. People have often been taught since childhood that to be good persons, they cannot act angry or have angry feelings.*]

THERAPIST: But [what about feeling] like hitting them, but *not* hitting them?

PATIENT: Right.

[*I am trying to reduce her anxiety by emphasizing the distinction that feelings are not actions. They are safe if contained in fantasy. Usually, I stay on this focus for a few sentences, but for some reason, I moved on too quickly to her image of herself.*]

THERAPIST: Hmm. And what if it were you? What if you let yourself have these feelings. What would that mean about you [that you could have such feelings]?

PATIENT: If I *really* became that way — or if I only had the feelings in fantasy?

THERAPIST: We're only talking about fantasy here. Letting yourself have these feelings, but *not* acting on them.

PATIENT: I guess I just feel like ... I ... I feel like maybe, I just, I'd be faking it or something to say, well, I want to hit her, I want to do this, I want to shake her.

THERAPIST: Well, that wouldn't be legitimate ...

[*I didn't go into detail here ... but I often say how important it is not to fake anything in therapy. If the patient cannot feel what I am encouraging him or her to feel, that is where we start — at the blocked position, and we look at the inhibition, until the feeling is freed up. However, in this case, I move right to the feeling — because she had said she was angry at a particular friend. (It is difficult to always do what is optimal in the fast pace of the therapy session. That is why watching ourselves on videotape is so valuable a teaching tool.)*]

THERAPIST: But, I mean, you've told me you've been angry.

PATIENT: I can honestly say with Julie in this particular case, I could want to shake her and say, "Why did you ... why did you let this friendship go?" [laughing] I can, in a comical way, imagine myself punching her ...

[*At this point she just pushes past the fears of thinking about this anger — and goes to an imaginal scene of it. This suggests she has become somewhat less afraid.*]

THERAPIST: Um-hm. Interesting that an image of a punch comes up so quickly here.

PATIENT: Yeah.

THERAPIST: But let's go back to the fears. What does it mean about you that you let yourself have these fantasies?

[*I know this patient is very uncomfortable with these feelings, so I am going to persist with "anxiety regulation" to desensitize her a bit more before continuing the exposure to the anger. Also, she has said she doesn't want to "fake it" — so I don't want to push her farther than she can genuinely go.*]

PATIENT: I don't know, it doesn't ... it doesn't like bother me so much. The thing that bothers me about it is just that it feels, it just feels fraudulent to me. Because I don't really want to *do* it, — so I can't say "want" to do it. That's what I mean when I can't say ...

THERAPIST: Well, let's think about that. [There's some confusion between wish and action here.] A person can really feel a feeling and have it be really true. But it can also be really true that the person doesn't want to act it out. [Can you understand that?]

PATIENT: Well, I feel like I could say it as a mantra and pretend to feel that. ... And if I kept doing it, maybe I'd feel it ... really feel that way eventually, like, that could be one way.

THERAPIST: That could be one way of doing it, yes.

PATIENT: Because I could say right now. ... I could say [those things you are encouraging me to say], but ... I just have to say — I wouldn't really be feeling it. I feel like I have to say to you that [the feeling is] not really true.

[*Many patients say this to me, and it is crucial not to push them into faking some feeling.*]

THERAPIST: It's so important [that you keep telling me as long as you are not feeling authentic about the feelings], because ... we don't want you to create a false self [to please me].

PATIENT: Right.

THERAPIST: Nor for you to be just a compliant person — going along with me. [But it sounds like what you are saying now is more like,] "Well, as a creative exploration, I'll play with these ideas and see if my feelings get in line with them."

PATIENT: Right, I mean, cause ... like ... I feel like I can feel more ... I can feel angry about it, but when it comes to like fantasizing about physically doing something, I could do that if it were like, "What could you do to her," but when you put in the word "What do you *want* to do to her?" That changes everything in my mind.

[*The following is a cognitive therapy technique — cognitive restructuring. I am reframing a dysfunctional belief that thoughts are synonymous with action.*]

THERAPIST: Well, let's go to sexual feelings. Have you ever desired a man, but didn't act on it? Have you ever thought someone was very attractive, and you might like to get your hands on him?

PATIENT: Yeah, sure! [*Laughs*]

THERAPIST: But you didn't act on it.

PATIENT: Right.

THERAPIST: Right. So, does that mean you don't have the "want" to act on it? I would ask you the same question that I asked about anger. I'd say, "What would you *want* to do?" or, "What would you *feel* like doing?"

PATIENT: Yeah, you could act that out [in your imagination]. So ... so [with those feelings], I definitely could get into that more [in fantasy] [*laughs*]. But, uh. ...

THERAPIST: But you choose not to act on those feelings.

PATIENT: That, I can totally understand that.

THERAPIST: Well, let me offer you this suggestion. You, in fact, could shake and hit your friend and eventually kill your friend. Humans evolved this way, you know, with the capacity to kill. And it is physically possible.

PATIENT: Right. It is possible.

THERAPIST: Certainly there's a bigger taboo against doing such violent things — even more so than the sexual stuff, but it is physically possible to do it. Each human being has the capacity to be violent. Because you've got anger in you and you've got the capacity to lash out. I'm trying to walk you through this, step by step.

PATIENT: I'm really boiling this down to little details.

THERAPIST: Yeah, but it's really crucial because these feelings are terrifying in our culture. And when I talk like this [focusing on angry imagery], it scares the audience and it scares therapists. What you're making me realize is that you have to ... To do this type of work in therapy, you have to accept that you could be a murderer — or you could be an adulterer. You may choose *not* to be these things — but it has to be acknowledged that we all have that capacity to do both of these things.

PATIENT: Yeah, I wouldn't say ... I'm a pacifist — but [thinking about it] I guess I am. But, you know, like I could say, "I'm not an adulterer," but I can certainly imagine having sex with somebody else — and I have imagined it. So, it's like there is ... there must be something really taboo to me about harming somebody physically. Um ...

THERAPIST: Of course.

PATIENT: So I can't ...

THERAPIST: But to be a pacifist — that has to do with behavior.

PATIENT: Right, I know ... and I know you're not asking me to do anything wrong.

THERAPIST: No, of course not.

PATIENT: And you're not suggesting that I do that.

THERAPIST: Certainly not. — I'm only asking you to make peace with the feelings that are within you.

[*This is the point of this chapter, and the ultimate goal of this therapy model; to make peace with all that is within us.*]

But here's another piece of it. People think that if you're a pacifist or if you're moral, you know, if you're not a murderer, not only do you not do the *behaviors*, but you don't even have the *feelings*. You don't even allow yourself to *feel* it. So they turn off the spigot [on the internal world] way, way down low rather than just [on behaviors as expressed] you know, in the external world.

[*Note how much repetition that I am using here. This deeply held fear of thoughts being unavoidably linked to action will not shift easily. But she is working it through.*]

PATIENT: Well, . . . if somebody came into my house and was trying to kill me, I would have no problems about killing the person.

THERAPIST: Yes. Or if you had a child and they were trying to kill the child?

PATIENT: Yeah, or my dogs. [*Laughs*]

THERAPIST: Or your dogs.

PATIENT: If somebody tried to mess with them . . .

THERAPIST: That's right. Wouldn't you go after them?

PATIENT: Yeah.

THERAPIST: And wouldn't you want that anger free so you could have the power and the energy to fight for those you love?

PATIENT: Yeah.

THERAPIST: Of course, we don't need to have that intensity, except on very rare occasions, if ever. And maybe we wouldn't kill them, but maybe we would get so murderously mad that we'd blast them out or push away or scream or do something effective in an active way.

PATIENT: Right, so I wouldn't be like a pacifist in that situation, for sure.

THERAPIST: So that there are times when these murderous feelingss can be helpful, even when you never intend to murder, but — if you just use the level of the rage to protect yourself.

[*Now she has a memory about such feelings when she was a child. Although this is very slow work — often I would be actively and passionately in the middle of an anger scene by now — she is shifting her perspective on her sense of self, that it is acceptable and human to have such feelings.*]

PATIENT: And I did have fantasies, when I was 12, about killing that girl, Kathy Raynor. I had like . . . like a regular fantasy about chopping her up into little pieces. I really did.

THERAPIST: That must have soothed you at a bad time. Just to have a vent — in fantasy — for all the frustration she was causing you.

[*I accept and validate the feelings.*]

PATIENT: Yeah, I mean, I knew I wasn't going to do it, of course. But I did wish she were dead, I think. So . . .

THERAPIST: So — you were directing the feelings of anger toward her, at least in part — and not taking them out on you.

[*Now I am teaching the positive consequences of allowing these feelings; that is, that no one is hurt — and, in fact, she is helped, because the fantasy brings relief and helps her sort out what she might want to do.*]

PATIENT: Um-hm. Right.

THERAPIST: And you didn't have help from someone to say, "Well, now, let's help you express it to her in some appropriate way. Come on, you can stand up, where's your fight?" You know, a lot of parents do. . . .

PATIENT: No, my father told me never to even say a bad word about anyone. . . . He's stoic. He's a Yankee, you know. But, um, it could have scared me, having those violent fantasies about my friend. Because I have that little obsessive tendency, there have been a few times in my life where I thought I was going to hurt somebody and it scared the hell out of me. I mean, I can't say right now that I'm fearing that, but maybe, somehow in me, it's just . . . I can't . . . I don't want to fantasize about hurting people because I'm afraid I'll do it . . .

[*She has had the lifelong problem of having a negative thought come into her mind and then not being able to stop it. So before we can bring these feelings up strongly, we have to make sure that she has enough control of herself so as not to torture herself with the fear that she might act on them.*]

THERAPIST: That happens a lot to people when they have had "almost" hit someone. Or sometimes one sibling will be beating the other sibling and kind of be aware that they're beating too hard.

PATIENT: Yeah, and it scares them.

THERAPIST: And it scares them and they cut off all their initiative after that.

PATIENT: Well, you know, I think I really did torture my sister psychologically, I don't think I ever beat her up or anything. Maybe I did though? I don't know.

THERAPIST: Maybe you wanted to have someone to torture like they were torturing you. You know, it might have made sense. Where else is it going to go if you can't fight back? What would you do to her?

[*First, I give validating responses to reduce the shame about the feelings, and then I move directly to what the feelings would make her want to do.*]

PATIENT: If I could just do anything. [*Laughs*] I have this picture of her ... of ... I don't know if it's real or if I just ... if it's like a composite of what happened over the years. Of my dad going in to get her up in the morning and ... because ... she couldn't get up on her own. You had to go in and get her up. And, like a little fight would start. She'd say, "I'm not getting up, I'm not going to school today." "Yes you are." And him like coming out with her like trying to grab, like trying to drive her out of the room and like her limbs flailing and it really does make me mad that she's like hurting my father. I guess that made me mad. And it made me feel pain like to be there and to feel like because I'm home, I'm causing this.

THERAPIST: And so what's the feeling toward Marcy? What do you feel like doing? Stay with your body first. Is there any ... is your heart pumping? Is there any energy there?

PATIENT: A little bit. But I'm just like, I feel like I'm observing her instead of like ...

THERAPIST: Well, you are observing her.

PATIENT: She's a very threatening person. She really is, you know like ...

THERAPIST: She might kick you.

PATIENT: She was bigger than me even at that age. She was already taller than me.

THERAPIST: And she was kicking and wild and crazy. So you'd have to be ...

PATIENT: She was hurting my dad.

THERAPIST: You'd have to be *really* angry to stop her.

PATIENT: Yeah. Oh God.

THERAPIST: So let's see, if you went in there with rage. How does your body feel when you think about that?

PATIENT: If you think about it, she's probably oppressed my anger because she really was always such a ball of fury that I could never ...

THERAPIST: Right. You could never feel like you could match it or beat it down.

PATIENT: Yeah. That was her way. My way was words.

THERAPIST: The feelings were so scary. If she can beat up your father ...

PATIENT: Oh yeah. I mean, she ... she was, I mean, she made up for ... she had more physical violence in her than anyone I've ever known.

THERAPIST: So how are you going to outdo Marcy?

PATIENT: Well, I always did with words. And that would frustrate her, so

I guess her physical anger frustrated me.

THERAPIST: So let's see if you can ... you won on the word level. Let's see if we can match her on the physical level. [*Patient laughs*] Because that's been very ...

PATIENT: I keep trying to get back there too, don't I?

THERAPIST: Right.

PATIENT: So what could I do to her?

THERAPIST: What does your body feel like? Just from the neck down. When you think of how mad you were, how does your body feel?

PATIENT: You know, it's ... it's like hard, maybe, because I'm so conditioned not to be physical against her especially.

[*Her defenses immediately come up when I return to try an exposure to feeling.*]

THERAPIST: That's okay. We're digging out from under this pile of defense, so ... Is there anything there at all?

PATIENT: Right now I don't feel like anything physical. Even though I'm picturing probably one of the most disturbing things I could picture.

[*She is revealing that just the image is anxiety provoking to her — even without any visceral feeling attached.*

THERAPIST: There's no anger?

PATIENT: Not that I can really physically access.

THERAPIST: Uh-huh. I've got angry feeling coming up in me just hearing the story. *(I've done this so many times, that I get a very strong feeling response to images of any feelings.)* Why don't we just walk through it intellectually. [Patient: Uh-huh.] You know, so this is one of the practice ones for you to do until the feeling slowly builds and builds and builds. What ... what would you like to do if you were as enraged as you could be, what would you want to do to stop that immediately? You hated to see her kicking and screaming and hitting your father. How would you stop it? How mad would you have to be? And let's let you have at least a visual image.

PATIENT: How mad would I have to be? [Therapist: Uh-huh.] It would ... it would ... you'd have to ... I mean, really because she's taller and she's, you know she's big — bigger than me — and like you'd have to have something in your hand like a baseball bat or something. [*laughs*]

[*I take this image and present it back to her.*]

THERAPIST: O.K. You'd pick up a baseball bat ...

PATIENT: It would be impossible to take her on myself. I'll put it that way.

THERAPIST: Yeah, she sounded too wild for that.

PATIENT: She's wild. She was always like out of control.

THERAPIST: So how would you go over there and what would you start doing with the baseball bat?

PATIENT: Um . . . well, I picture my dad like trying to drag her arms or something. So, just make . . . first, I would try to get her off him [*Laughs*] like bat down her arms and then, um. . . . hm. . . . It's funny, because probably the person I'm really mad at is her, it still hurts for me to imagine hurting her physically.

THERAPIST: What stops you?

PATIENT: I bet she could come right in here and have a total fantasy about beating me up. [*Laughs*]

THERAPIST: Yeah, maybe too easily.

[*If her sister, Marcy, were the patient, I would not have her imagine the angry images at this point, because she has poor impulse control. She would be in too much danger of acting out the feelings. Instead, we would cognitively explore how to control her impulses — and we would never go to the angry images until she had developed sufficient discipline to control the feelings. However, even people with poor impulse control eventually need to learn to have angry images. But such individuals need to learn to direct those impulses into fantasy where they can be safely reviewed and then appropriately guided.*]

PATIENT: Well, we're opposites, see. . . . We just have completely opposite coping strategies, you know. And so . . . and it's so ingrained in both of us. It's so, so entrenched. So it's so hard for me to access . . . it's like the access is just not there. [*Laughs*]

Continued Exposure

THERAPIST: Well, let's just walk through it again. And this is what I do, I just bring someone back and say, well, you're standing there, you want to go over with the baseball bat. Now, swing your arms and imagine some energy in your arms as you're swinging really hard. You're going to go one blow and get those arms, you know, off your father's hands. And now, I mean, she's hurting. Right, she's not kicking much anymore?

PATIENT: Right.

THERAPIST: And what do you want to do to make sure she doesn't kick anymore?

PATIENT: Um . . .

THERAPIST: And let's think, you're standing above her and you're rippling with rage. You're shaking with it. What do you want to say to her at that moment? Not a lot of words, but just what's the first thing that comes to your mind?

PATIENT: Um, . . . um. . . . "Get off Dad!"

THERAPIST: O.K., "Get off Dad." And then what do you want to do?

PATIENT: Um . . . I can hit her in the head with the bat. I can't "want" to do it but I could [*Laughs*] I still can't.

THERAPIST: You're flinching. It seems really hard for you to even imagine.

[*Many patients are able to feel some activation at this point; their hearts racing, their legs and arms energized, and so forth. She is having difficulty accessing physical feelings.*]

PATIENT: It really is. I just . . . can't feel. . . . [*Looking very distressed*]

[*It is remarkable how difficult it is for many people to bear the slightest impact of their angry feelings. Her identity is based on her being 'good' and without negative feelings — so restructuring this feeling will restructure her basic sense of self. When this is the case, the feeling work must proceed more slowly than with people who are less concerned about being a "bad person."*]

THERAPIST: Hm . . . Does it make you feel teary?

PATIENT: It makes me feel that void again, you know, like just . . . like . . . [no feeling].

THERAPIST: That's all right. We're just going to explore it.

PATIENT: Because I'm trying really hard to be as honest as possible. Like I said, I really, like I could totally sit here and tell you a story and I'm just not doing that because . . . you know . . .

THERAPIST: I think that's good that you're being honest and telling me what is really going on with you.

PATIENT: Maybe, you know, maybe I can just keep working on it at home.

[*Because she voiced some desire to keep working on it, I try to go back to the fantasy again.*]

THERAPIST: But if you'd hit her in the head, there's some part of you that would get some release. Think of your sister making so much trouble, and your walking over and hitting her on the head, and thinking whew, well, thank goodness.

[*This time, I just modeled the imagery for her by offering a scene — in a blander way — just so she could continuing facing it and get more comfortable with the fantasy.*]

PATIENT: Well, let's put it this way, if ... if, let's say she kept fighting, okay. Then, I could say, yeah, I'd want to keep hitting her. If she stopped ... I guess the hard part I have is to picture a helpless victim. I picture ... for like some reason I ... when you say that, like go over there. I assume immediately, this person's going to become helpless and I'm just going to be like tramping on them. So if they're still fighting ...

[*Now she discovers one of the reasons it's so hard for her to tolerate these images, much less the feelings. She identifies too much with the victim. So she works to keep the image of the fight continuing.*]

PATIENT: Right, so if she's still kicking, I can say, yeah, I'd want to like keep pounding on her while she's ... until her legs stop. And then if she starts biting, I can, you know, smack her in the head with it.

THERAPIST: And then she'd be in really bad shape. Because you're saying you would smack her in the head — and [remember] you had a baseball bat in your hands. You know, are you really swinging?

PATIENT: Yeah, yeah.

THERAPIST: So you're breaking her bones?

PATIENT: Okay.

THERAPIST: Aren't you? I mean that's the truth of it.

PATIENT: I guess that would happen if you hit someone with a baseball bat.

[*Her "I guess" reveals how hard it is for her to accept the emotional truth of these images — that she could feel like doing damage to someone.*]

THERAPIST: Yeah, imagine swinging. Is there any arousal in your body at all as you imagine swinging hard?

[*I present the image again to see if she can elicit the underlying feeling.*]

PATIENT: Hm ... it doesn't ... it doesn't ... come.

THERAPIST: Sometimes when people have this void feeling, you can go home and wring a washcloth until you get the feeling of "I'm wringing her neck" or swing something and try to get the feeling to start bubbling up in your arms and chest.

[*This is both teaching her a more external way to get to feeling and reassuring her that it is O.K. for now not to be feeling. With repetition, the feeling will come.*]

PATIENT: So maybe just practice physical things.

THERAPIST: Once you are able to have strong feeling along with the fantasy, I don't advise you to use external ways to activate feeling. Then the action will actually reduce the inner experience of the feeling. When a feeling is contained within and the fantasy is allowed to flow, it can get really intense. [Patient: I see.] It decreases the intensity of the fantasy to act it out. But, if you don't have any feeling in fantasy, you need to do some actions sometimes to build it up. [Patient: Uh-huh.] Sometimes you need to get physical first. You know, you need to go jogging and pound the pavement like you're stomping on her skull. You know, let that feeling go through you.

PATIENT: Well, I could, maybe when I'm at the gym try to visualize things, because I do ...

THERAPIST: That's a good thing, then there's a physical release. You're pushing ...

PATIENT: Yeah, because like if I'm on ... there's machines I could be on where I could be trying to fantasize doing things there. That would maybe help.

THERAPIST: You could see. Different things work for different people. But the point is to reaccess that magical part of you that's alive and passionate and intense.

PATIENT: See, I know, like it's hard for me to really feel anything. My feelings are very dead. But I know they are there and I have ... I do experience them from time to time, you know. But I think I need to get easier access to them is what you're saying.

THERAPIST: Well, right, you were so mad at your boss that you didn't have your feelings, they had you. They came up so strong and took it over. Now, you didn't hit him, but, you know, you hit him with your words. So, you see you were even in control there, in that intense situation. But what's my point? The point is for you to have the feelings, not to let the feelings have you. You know, for you to control your feelings, not to have your feelings control you.

PATIENT: Okay.

[*I am referring to an earlier situation when she strongly stood up to her abusive boss after a session where she looked at angry feelings toward him. However, her inner experience was involuntary and scared her so that she shut down again quickly*.]

THERAPIST: So that's why fantasy, that's why pulling the ... having the bodily feeling and having the fantasy route to go is the way you maneuver and guide things.

PATIENT: But I think like the coping that I have always used is to keep things in my head and to try to keep it all under control that way.

THERAPIST: Yeah. It's a good way to keep control, but you pay a huge price for it, in terms of living, in terms of aliveness.

[*I first validate the defense as useful for keeping control, but then point out the costs of the defense – what she loses by maintaining it. This is an example of "defense restructuring."*]

PATIENT: Well it's like, to me, when I ... I feel like everything's all trapped and ugly and like a weed garden in my body because I keep it all in. So, if I can picture the fantasy thing like coming out of me, but it's kind of out of me in a free sense, you know what I mean? Like when you say pushed in and layered down, that's to me like all in, in here.

THERAPIST: Tightened and more compressed. That's interesting. It's like it flows. Because activating energy is a flowing of energy, even if it's joy. Joy is flowing energy. Letting your muscles relax, feeling good, or excitement is like this.

PATIENT: So it's kind of like coming out ...

THERAPIST: Yeah. And the fantasy gives it a place to go that's harmless. [Patient: Right.] It also lets you think about it over and over so you can decide how to act. It also lets you have a feeling of relief.

PATIENT: For me it is a relief. ... But I'm just in jail 90% of the time and I don't want to be there, you know.

I think, you know the factors in my life just came together in such a way that ... I have a spirit inside of me and I've always known that. And I'm just like off-track all the time with dealing with things. ... And to me it is a tragedy.

[*Now she is pointing out the costs of the defenses – which means her inability to feel is becoming increasingly ego-dystonic.*]

THERAPIST: Yeah, it really is.

PATIENT: And that's why I would say I'm in therapy, to desperately, you know, get back here, because I'd rather be dead than living this way. I can't, I cannot go through my life like this ...

THERAPIST: Oh, it sounds horrible.

CONCLUSION

This session achieved an important first step toward the resolution of her phobia about angry feelings. In the beginning of the session, she was very much against having angry feelings. By the close of the session, we see more motivation in her statements that she can't live this way, and that her inability to feel is a tragedy.

In fact, it's been a year since this session took place and she since has had 20 more sessions. She became incrementally more comfortable with her angry feelings. She never was able to handle a series of intensely angry sessions, but she did work with angry feelings in successively stronger doses intermingled with sessions on improving her view of herself, and on anxiety regulation around anger. At one point, I pushed her to face angry feelings too much and she flooded with anxiety during the following week. We then shifted the focus away from the anger onto more supportive interventions until her anxiety subsided. Nevertheless, following this period, she confronted her very difficult father over a major family conflict, and handled it masterfully.

She is now anticipating another 20 sessions over the coming year. (She does not come every week — but every two to three weeks because she travels a long distance.) Her crippling anxiety has been reduced substantially, and more important, her motivation to take risks in her life, loosen up, and become open to new experiences is growing.

Because of her obsessional tendencies and her fears of loss of control, the step-wise procedure of small increments of anger and assertion done in the session, and then acted upon in well-guided ways in her life, were effective in reducing her obsessional defenses and her perfectionism. Because so many patients are frightened of angry feelings, this very careful, incremental approach can offer a useful pathway to resolve affect conflicts.

Reference

McCullough Vaillant, L. (1997). *Changing character: Short-term anxiety-regulating psychotherapy for restructuring defenses, affects, and attachments*. New York: Basic Books.

CONTEMPORARY PERSPECTIVES

7

Expanding Your Psychotherapy Practice Through Medicare

Nicholas A. Cummings

In the current managed-care environment where practice seems to be constricting, Medicare is fertile field for psychotherapists. Most managed-care networks are closed to new applicants, and the fees for those psychotherapists already on the various networks are being ratcheted down annually. Fees in some areas are forcing psychotherapists to work at, or below, cost, while surveillance of practice, intrusion into the therapeutic alliance, and paperwork are on the increase. All of these further constrict practice. On the other hand, the Medicare networks are open to all who are qualified and there are indications that this will remain so for the near future. Surveillance has been modest, although it is expected to increase. Why have therapists not expanded their practices into this rewarding fee-for-service area? Before addressing that question, it would be useful to note some of the important characteristics of Medicare and how therapists need to tailor their practices to be effective with older adults.

GETTING ON A MEDICARE NETWORK

In most areas, Medicare fees have gone up over the last several years (Hartman-Stein, 1998b) in direct contrast to what is happening in managed care. In addition, most of Medicare psychotherapy is under traditional fee-for-service delivery, and will remain so. In 1990, only 3% of the recipients of Medicare were under managed care, and by 1998, this figure had increased to only 16%. It is expected to increase to 25% by the year 2002, but this will leave 75% receiving care through traditional fee-for-service delivery. Not only is this plan remarkable in an era when all other sectors are being devoured by managed care, but there are indications that that 25% may not be attained by the 2002 goal.

Medicare networks are open in almost all areas of the nation. However, once you apply, you must expect several months of red tape before you are accepted. The wait is worthwhile, for if you possess the prescribed qualifications, it is highly unlikely you will be rejected. And once you are in the network, you are essentially secure, unless you commit fraud or behave unethically.

Is there much fraud in Medicare? Hartman-Stein (1998a) meticulously examined that question and found that not only is fraud rampant, but an embarrassing number of psychotherapists have been taking advantage of Medicare's benevolence toward the elderly, and its low surveillance of practitioners. Columbia/HCA, the largest hospital chain in America, is under federal court indictment for highly questionable practices, including double billing. To counter the growing trend toward fraud in Medicare, in 1993, the federal government instituted Operation Restore Trust. By 1997, Medicare had established the first of a number of initiatives designed to increase surveillance: by that time, it was ascertained that over 30% of psychotherapy within Medicare violated the agency's standards for what constitutes medical necessity. Sadly, we as a profession that has complained so bitterly about managed care's intrusion into psychotherapy were, nonetheless, quick to ignore the rules when no one was looking over our shoulders.

MANAGED CARE'S MEDICARE WOES AND THE PRACTITIONER ADVANTAGE

Medicare has been determined to squeeze the capitation rate in its programs as the federal government and the insurers have done in the general health arena. This process has been progressing steadily, discouraging many managed-care companies from bidding on Medicare contracts. It ignores the inescapable fact that the medical bills of older Americans are going to exceed those of a younger, healthier population. Furthermore, the federal government has been laboring under the mistaken belief that Medicare recipients, being from a generation that does not readily seek psychotherapy, do not avail themselves of behavioral health care services. But as we shall soon see, older Americans acutally seek behavioral care at an even higher rate because they are more at risk than their younger counterparts. However, the services must be relevant to the needs of older adults, and not the usual offerings preferred by most independently practicing psychotherapists.

Several years of Medicare miscalculations resulted in the announcement by 90 health maintenance organizations (HMOs), including such giants as Aetna, Humana, and Oxford, that after December 31, 1998, they would stop serving over 400,000 currently eligible enrollees (Gorman, 1998b). With less than a 60-day notice, the government had little alternative but to afford these almost half a million older persons the option of returning to traditional health-care delivery (Gupta, 2001).

In fairness to the government, there is more than just its failure to foresee the negative consequences of its cost-dominated policy. The Medicare HMOs have attempted to administer their services to older adults on a commercial-health-plan model, which has proved to be a financial disaster. Those few plans that changed their delivery models to meet the demands of a Medicare population realistically are thriving, according to the consulting firm of Arthur Andersen (Peck, 1998), which lists 10 steps to Medicare viability. These steps are accessible and doable for the relatively small regional integrated delivery systems that practitioners are forming, whereas for a large, unwieldy and change-resistant HMO, they are improbable, or even impossible.

The crisis in Medicare delivery presents challenges and opportunities to the psychotherapist: (1) Medicare will remain essentially a traditional delivery system in which psychotherapists can have a firm place in the networks. In view of managed-care company defections, it is unlikely that Medicare will achieve its goal of even 25% managed-care penetration by the year 2002. (2) Those psychotherapists who have learned to predict and control their costs, and who can tailor behavioral-care delivery systems to older adults, will have an unprecedented opportunity to become exclusive regional providers for Medicare (Cummings, Pallak, & Cummings, 1996).

COMMON THERAPIST MISCONCEPTIONS REGARDING OLDER AMERICANS

During the years that psychotherapy practices were flourishing, practitioners neglected older adults, favoring the so-called YAVEH patient (younger, attractive, verbal, educated, higher income). Now that practices are shrinking, psychotherapists remain somewhat reluctant to treat Medicare populations because of several myths that prevail.

Myth 1: Older patients have no confidence in younger practitioners. Quite the contrary, older Americans worry that they will not be accepted or valued by the younger therapist. One of the most common complaints of the elderly is: "In public, younger people just seem to look right through me and not even see me." A psychotherapist who accords the older patient the same acceptance, respect, and optimism he or she gives to younger patients will be rewarded by a hard-working, devoted, and sincere treatment recipient. Such a therapist will be surprised by a number of factors. These patients belong to the generation that still respects the doctor, always keeps appointments, is meticulous about following the doctor's advice and regimen, and pays bills on time. The vanishing saying, "The doctor knows best," is very much alive with older Americans. As has been said frequently, this is a remarkable generation of survivors that emerged from the greatest economic depression in history to be flung into the world's most devastating war. The sociopaths among them have long ago done themselves in, so you will never have to see them. They are truly delightful patients.

Myth 2: Not much can be done for the problems of old age. Research demonstrates that a small investment of psychotherapeutic time, properly focused on the needs of the older adult, gives remarkable results (Hartman-Stein, 1997). The greatest psychological needs of the older adult are essentially just two: (1) loneliness, and (2) feeling irrelevant and unneeded. The family is not as cohesive as it was a generation ago, and older adults are more often remanded to a nursing home than cared for at home. On the other hand, their marriages have lasted for a long time, and widowhood usually comes after as long as 40 to 60 years. As one 88-year-old recent widower put it, "I lost my spouse, my lover, and my best friend all at once after 63 wonderful years." Understanding, kindness, and taking the older person seriously, as well as bereavement counseling when appropriate, go a long way for these individuals. Try to bear in mind that someone who has lived depression-free for 60 or 70 years has a lot of resourcefulness that can be activated by surprisingly little psychological attention.

Myth 3: The elderly are not psychologically minded. Such a misconception usually translates into the fact that the therapist is too bound up in a psychotherapeutic straitjacket to do the human thing. When I was in my early 30s, a 73-year-old widow was referred to me by her physician son, who complained that his mother was driving him crazy with her demands. During the first two sessions, the woman berated me with anger she had displaced from her uncaring, too-busy-to-see-his-mother son. At the third session, when she said I looked tired, I confessed that the day had been so busy that I had not had time for breakfast or lunch, even though it was now 3 o'clock in the afternoon. The next day at noon, she was outside my office door with a sandwich and a thermos of soup. She scolded and admonished: "You must eat before you see your next patient." I ate while she sat and made certain I did. When I finished, I hugged her as only an appreciative, repentant son would do. She bonded instantly. Over the next six years before she died, she made certain that all of her needy friends had professional consultations with me, but as she accompanied them, she always asked if I were eating regularly. Her son thanked me because his mother no longer was driving him crazy. She was the center of her circle of older friends; once again, she felt needed and appreciated. This is just one example of the flexibility and sensitivity that are useful in treating older adults. Social workers, trained in casework, are more adept in this regard than are psychologists.

Myth 4: A psychotherapist cannot help the confusion of old age. This is far from the truth. Most confusion seen in the older adult is a befuddlement resulting from too many antagonistic medications having been prescribed. As previously stated, these patients dutifully follow the physician's advice and add a new prescription from a new physician without questioning the continuance of all previous medications. When a family brings in a grandmother or grandfather with a complaint of confusion, do not ask the older person what she or he is taking, as she or he will not remember it all. Rather, have the person bring in the medications. Be prepared to see a full sack, inventory the contents precisely, consult with a medical colleague who specializes in treating older Americans, and arrange for that physician to see your patient. When most of the medications are eliminated, you will often see the confusion clear up in two or three weeks. More often than not, it was not dementia, but iatrogenically induced confusion. The National Institute on Aging (NIA) has a readily available pamphlet listing 78 medications that either should not be prescribed for the elderly, or should be prescribed with a great deal of caution. Most physicians have never seen it. In the absence of anyone taking the responsibility, the psychotherapist can be a psychological primary-care physician, coordinating even this aspect of an older adult's treatment (Gupta, 2001).

Myth 5: Psychotherapy cannot help in the elderly person's preoccupation with death. It is not a generally known fact that older adults are not preoccupied with their own deaths. The older American has seemingly made his or her peace with the inevitable, and the preoccupation with death is more characteristic of the middle and involutional years (45 to 55 years of age) when one worries that there is no longer sufficient time to accomplish things that need to be done. The older adult has become more reflective, recalling life events, and worrying that he or she is no longer wanted or useful. It is usually the countertransference of the therapist, who may be grappling with his or her own fear of death, that leads to the expectation that this is the patient's problem.

PLANNING YOUR PROGRAM

For decades, the conventional wisdom in health care held that older adults did not, and would not, avail themselves of mental health services. This seemed to be supported by the facts: In health plans where psychotherapy was a covered benefit, seldom did the use of the benefit by those over the age of 65 even approach .05%, whereas it would be several times that in the younger population. Furthermore, if an older adult were to see a psychotherapist, he or she was unlikely to return after one or two visits. Now, mental health treatment is one of the fastest growing services in Medicare. What changed?

Meeting the Needs of Older Adults

In times past, psychotherapists did what they liked to do best: long-term therapy. But for the older American who has little time left, long-term treatment might well exceed the remaining life span. Furthermore, the issues that bring most patients to psychotherapy (e.g., courtship, marriage, divorce, parenting, career, job loss, relationships) are not the usual issues that plague one in later life (e.g., loneliness, retirement, widowhood, bereavement, alienation, chronic illness, disability of a spouse or oneself, terminal illness).

When the issues of concern to the elderly are reflected in the behavioral programs made available to them, that population's use exceeds even that of younger patients. The erroneous belief that the elderly do not avail themselves of psychotherapy is forever dispelled in favor of the following truism: the elderly do not avail themselves of *traditional* (irrelevant) psychotherapeutic services. Two successful programs will be presented as examples, but before doing so, it is important to look at the entire question of psychological interventions reducing medical and surgical costs.

The Medical Cost Offset Effect

It has been said that the most compelling reason for the inclusion of psychological services in health care is that they save medical and surgical costs (Dr. Patrick DeLeon, executive assistant to U.S. Senator Daniel K. Inouye, personal communication, September 1992). Since the seminal research demonstrating what has been called the medical cost offset effect (Follette & Cummings, 1967), 91 studies were subjected to meta-analytic review (Chiles, Lambert, & Hatch, in press). There was strong evidence that psychological interventions reduce medical and surgical costs, even after subtracting the cost of the psychological services. Why then does the burden of proof still remain with each individual program?

The answer is simple: Research demonstrates a wide variability in the amount of savings. Furthermore, the Fort Bragg Study (Bickman, 1996) reveals that more is not better, and inappropriate long-term therapy can increase costs. Finally, the Hawaii Medicaid Project (Pallak, Cummings, Dorken, & Henke, 1994), conducted over seven years with 36,000 Medicaid recipients and 90,000 federal employees, demonstrates that while focused, targeted therapy can result in impressive cost savings, traditional or nonfocused psychotherapy can increase costs significantly. The savings were the most impressive among six groups of chronic diseases, all of which are common to older Americans. In other words, appropriate psychological treatment can be effective in chronic, and even terminal, physical illnesses.

It is up to each program to demonstrate that it reduces rather than increases costs. A spokesperson for the American Medical Association stated it succinctly, "In God we trust. All others must have data" (Gorman, 1998a, p. 69). Fortunately for the psychotherapist planning a program, there are guides for building into such a program both a medical cost offset study and a demonstration project (Cummings, 1994, 1997b).

The Florida Bereavement Program: A Model for Success

In 1988, the Humana Health Plan, having been awarded one of the earliest Medicare HMO arrangements, became responsible for 140,000 Medicare recipients on the west coast of Florida. Humana then entered into a subcontract with American Biodyne (now part of Merit/Magellan Health Care Systems) to provide the mental health/chemical-dependency portion of the health care. This subcontract predicated its capitation on an aggressively increased annual penetration level, through outreach and provision of relevant services, to at least 5% or 6% of the total population. Surprisingly, the outreach and offered services were so successful that the penetration exceeded 10%. Initially, this placed a severe financial strain on American Biodyne, but eventually the services proved remarkably cost-effective. The early financial crisis was an incentive to tailor and streamline services to older adults, and the result has been a model of success to be emulated (Cummings, 1997a).

The Prevalence of Bereavement

Grief following widowhood is a major issue in later life. With a mortality rate of 5%, these 140,000 older adults yielded nearly 20 widows or widowers every day. The centers in which this study was conducted had to contend with an average of three per day, or more than 20 per week. Of the patients of all ages, from childhood to older adults, 8% of the total were recently widowed. The average length of marriage of those widowed in this population was 46 years, indicating the seriousness of the grieving process. Such a heavy caseload clearly called for immediate and aggressive outreach, assuring there would be early intervention.

The Design of the Experiment

Two Biodyne centers, with populations bearing the same demographics of older adults, were selected. In one center with 22,000 enrollees, an especially tailored group bereavement program was created, which included an aggressive outreach program that enabled the center to contact enrollees within two to three weeks of widowhood. The nearby center with a similar number of enrollees continued to see widowed patients on a traditional individual psychotherapy model, with the usual referral systems in place. Because it lacked the outreach, a smaller number of patients were in the contrasting group.

Once the center received notification of widowhood, the surviving spouse was routinely assigned to one of the psychotherapists (an M.S.W. or a Ph.D. psychologist) for telephone outreach. The call followed a well-tested protocol and was sensitively conducted, ending with an offer to the patient to come to the center for help with his or her mourning. About 7% of those contacted were not available because they had returned, or were about to return, to their states of origin to be with families. Another 16% consistently expressed either reluctance or the inability to come to the center, and a house call was offered. After the house call was made, the procedure yielded about half of those who had expressed initial reluctance. Throughout the study, the outreach was successful in bringing into the Bereavement Program about 85% of the surviving spouses.

Screening for Depression

Unlike mourning, which is nature's healing process, designed to enable a survivor to go on with life, depression can produce lasting, detrimental pain. In depression, there are unresolved psychological issues in the relationship with the deceased, which lead to introjected rage. The repressed anger hides the true object of the unresolved hostility (the deceased spouse), and only a feeling of one's own worthlessness is expressed. Reactive depression prevents, or drastically interferes with, the work of mourning and results in protracted sadness, sometimes for many years after the death.

About one in five widowed patients predominately demonstrated depression rather than mourning, and was seen individually for the treatment of reactive depression. The four out of five who clearly showed mourning were seen in the Bereavement Program. This screening typically involves one individual session, or two in very difficult cases. It is also used to prepare those who will become part of the group Bereavement Program.

The Program

There were five to eight mourners in each group, depending on the patient traffic. Each session was two hours long, with a total of 14 sessions spaced as follows: four semiweekly sessions followed by six weekly sessions, and then by four concluding sessions held monthly. Accordingly, the program lasted six-and-a-half months. About 15% of the patients who completed the program expressed an interest in repeating it, and were allowed to do so. When a group member has already gone through the program, his or her participation enhances the experience for the other patients because the repeater assumes the role of a quasi-cotherapist, often pointing out, "I felt like you do when I first began therapy," and concluding with successful steps taken toward healing. Since women tend to outlive men, the groups were composed of 75% women. This did not seem to deter the men from participating, as men seem to have an even greater difficulty in coping with widowhood than women do.

The program was psychoeducational in nature, imparting information about the process of mourning, encouraging patients to experience it (e.g., crying profusely, giving oneself permission to be alone, reflecting and recalling the good times with the deceased, reliving important dates with the deceased as each date occurs in the present). Relaxation and guided imagery techniques were provided, and a "buddy system" was established. The patients were paired off for mutual support and encouraged to call, and even meet with, each other as needed. Typically, well-meaning physicians had prescribed antidepressants or sleeping pills, both of which can delay the work of mourning. The patients were encouraged to discontinue these, or at least to use them sparingly. They characteristically complied, reflecting the respect this generation has for a doctor's advice.

The patients were encouraged to read from a carefully selected group of titles, and when they showed interest in doing so, this was taken as a definite sign of progress in treatment. The overall objectives of the program were three: (1) *self-efficacy* (Bandura, 1977), which is a process of restoring self-confidence by the performance of discontinued tasks that were once part of daily life; (2) defeating *learned helplessness* (Seligman, 1975), which is the sense of being crippled by overwhelming feelings that dictate, "I no longer can do this"; (3) restoring a *sense of coherence* (Antonovsky, 1987) that there is still meaning to life, but in a different way than before.

Bereavement and the Medical Cost Offset Effect

It has long been observed that widowed persons manifest a sharp increase in physical symptoms, which necessitates frequent visits to a physician. This lasts for one or two years following the death of a spouse, but sometimes persists far beyond that time. It is not unusual for the surviving spouse to experience symptoms resembling the condition from which the deceased suffered, such as cancer, emphysema, or heart disease. These symptoms are persistent and so resemble the actual disease that the physician is compelled to initiate and continue costly diagnostic/medical procedures, with an enormous increase in unnecessary costs.

Results of the Bereavement Project

The medical-care utilization of 323 patients who participated in the Bereavement Program was contrasted with that of a group of 287 widowed patients in an adjacent center who received traditional individual psychotherapy. The medical care of each of the two groups was determined through a straightforward tabulation of all visits to physicians and emergency rooms; all outpatient procedures; use of all laboratory tests, X-rays, and other imaging devices; and all prescriptions issued. For all patients, there was a calculation for the 365 days immediately preceding the death of the spouse, for the first 365 days immediately following the death, and for the 365 days constituting the second year after the death.

Both the Bereavement Program group and the contrast group reveal a somewhat low rate of medical care utilization for this age group in the year preceding the death of the spouse. This reflects the surviving spouse's preoccupation with the medical needs of the dying spouse, to the neglect of his or her own needs. After the death of the spouse, for those in the Bereavement Program, the survivor's medical utilization increases somewhat, again reflecting some "catching up" on the survivor's own postponed medical needs. For those in the contrast group, however, medical utilization rises sharply after the spouse's death to over twice that seen in the Bereavement Program group for the same period. Although it subsides during the second year after the death of the spouse, it remains 40% higher than that of the patients in the Bereavement Program for that same year. Therefore, the Bereavement Program is dramatically effective in preventing a surge in medical-care utilization for an older adult population during the two years after the death of a spouse.

What does this mean in medical cost savings? The investment in behavioral care, focused on the needs of mourners and targeted to that population, is minuscule by comparison with the impressive savings in medical costs. The 14 sessions, doubled to account for their two-hour duration, and then divided by six (the average number of participants), yield the equivalent in cost of 4.3 individual psychotherapy sessions per patient. After subtracting these behavioral care costs, there is a saving in medical care of $1,400 per patient for the two-year period. This amount, extrapolated to the general elderly population covered by this one health plan, translates into a potential saving of several million dollars. Even more important, however, this program can spare widowed older adults two years of avoidable suffering from physical symptoms and ill health.

Another Example of Program Implementation: Early Alzheimer's Counseling

During this same period, one program focused on the caretakers of patients with early Alzheimer's dementia and on the patients themselves (Cummings, 1997a). It has been noted for some time that the hardship imposed on the caretakers of Alzheimer's patients results in an increased rate of illness among the spouses or adult children caring for a person with this dementia. The stress increases with both the length of the caretaking and the severity of the dementia, which is progressive and unpredictable. Some medical authorities suspect that the immune system of the caretaker is compromised by the constant, and often mounting, stress, and this is reflected in a steady increase in the caretaker's use of medical services. The feature of the dementia that leaves the patient incapable of displaying the slightest bit of gratitude or affection places almost unbearable stress on the caretaker. Although the usual period from diagnosis to death is 10 years, some Alzheimer's patients, thanks to excellent physical care, live in such a state for as long as 20 years.

The early Alzheimer's patient also experiences stress. Frequently disoriented when away from home, he or she soon manifests a characteristic "catastrophic emotional response" upon becoming disoriented in familiar surroundings. As this response is evidenced before the dementia has damaged ego functioning, the patient is devastated by the experience, fears its recurrence, and is reluctant to leave home. There is a corresponding narrowing of life space for both the patient and the nonafflicted spouse.

Early Alzheimer's Counseling and the Medical Cost Offset Effect

The typical reaction of both relatives and patients to the unpredictable, often baffling, but always frightening, early symptoms of this dementia is to seek immediate medical help. A counseling program, by imparting information that anticipates the sporadic intrusion of brief episodes of disorientation into an otherwise normal life, and by teaching ways to handle such episodes, brought about a dramatic reduction in the reliance on emergency services. Early Alzheimer's patients who accepted counseling, and who carried two or three telephone numbers of loved ones whom they were to call if they found themselves "lost," did not need to be rushed to the emergency room when these frightening lapses occurred.

The ongoing counseling of caretakers on an as-needed basis, which included initial training in relaxation, guided imagery, and meditation, proved highly successful in reducing the caretaker's incidence of illness and concomitant higher use of medical services. In addition, a hotline was provided so that caretakers could seek immediate advice in the face of the patients' more unpredictable symptoms. It was also noted that the hotline served as an emotional safety valve whenever stress became unbearable. Although the costs of this behavioral care were ongoing over several years rather than the relatively brief six-and-a-half months of the Bereavement Project, so were the consistently significant medical savings, which far more than offset these costs.

SUMMARY AND CONCLUSIONS

Participation in Medicare is an expanding area of opportunity for psychotherapists that not only can be of importance to the well-being of older adults, but also can be highly rewarding and satisfying for the practitioner. While the fee-for-service practice is contracting, that of Medicare is increasing, particularly because managed-care companies have not been able to rise to the requirement of specific programs that are focused on the needs of older adults and are targeted to that population. In abandoning this sector, managed-care companies are creating an unprecedented opportunity for the psychotherapist who has learned to control and predict costs and to design and implement effective interventions and programs and demonstrate their efficiency.

References

Antonovsky, A. (1987). *Unraveling the mystery of health: How people manage stress and stay well.* San Francisco: Jossey-Bass.

Bandura, A. (1977). Self-efficacy: Toward a unifying theory of behavioral change. *Psychological Review, 84,* 191–215.

Bickman, L. (1996). A continuum of care: More is not always better. *American Psychologist, 51,* 689–701.

Chiles, J. A., Lambert, J. A., & Hatch, A. L. (1999). The impact of psychological interventions on medical cost offset: A meta-analytic review. *Clinical Psychology: Science and Practice,* in press.

Cummings, N. A. (1994). The successful application of medical offset in program planning and in clinical delivery. *Managed Care Quarterly, 2,* 1–6.

Cummings, N. A. (1997a). Approaches in prevention in the behavioral health of older adults. In P. Hartman-Stein (Ed.), *Innovative behavioral healthcare for older adults: A guide-book for changing times* (pp. 1–23). San Francisco: Jossey-Bass.

Cummings, N. A. (1997b). Behavioral health in primary care: Dollars and sense. In N. A. Cummings, J. L. Cummings, & J. N. Johnson (Eds.), *Behavioral health in primary care: A guide for clinical integration* (pp. 3–21). Madison, CT: Psychosocial Press.

Cummings, N. A., Pallak, M. S., & Cummings, J. L. (Eds.). (1996). *Surviving the demise of solo practice: Mental health practitioners prospering in the era of managed care.* Madison, CT: Psychosocial Press.

Follette, W. T., & Cummings, N. A. (1967). Psychiatric services and medical utilization in a prepaid health plan setting. *Medical Care, 5,* 25–35.

Gorman, C. (1998a). Is it good medicine? *Time,* November 23, 68–69.

Gorman, C. (1998b). Medicare woes. *Time,* December 7, 238–239.

Gupta, S. (2001). Not for the elderly. *Time,* December 24, 78–79.

Hartman-Stein, P. (Ed.). (1997). *Innovative behavioral healthcare for older adults: A guide-book for changing times.* San Francisco: Jossey-Bass.

Hartman-Stein, P. (1998a). HCFA crackdown on fraud, abuse, suspect billing procedures heats up. *National Psychologist,* November/December, 16–17.

Hartman-Stein, P. (1998b). New Medicare rules disallow "extenders." *National Psychologist,* September/October, 14–15.

Pallak, M. S., Cummings, N. A., Dorken, H., & Henke, C. J. (1994). Medical costs, Medicaid, and managed mental health treatment: The Hawaii study. *Managed Care Quarterly, 2,* 64–70.

Peck, C. (1998). Medicare profitability demands effective investments, relations. *Healthcare Management, 1*(9), 1–5.

Seligman, M. E. P. (1975). *Helplessness: On depression, development, and death.* San Francisco: Freeman.

8

Brief Therapy in Light of the Evolution of the Mind

Robert Langs

Although we seldom think about it, the human mind, like the physical systems of the body, is a product of evolution (Slavin & Kriegman, 1992; Langs, 1996). Even so, we are unaccustomed to tracing the mind's evolutionary history and even less inclined to wonder what this scenario can tell us about the present design of the emotion-related mind and about psychotherapy — and for us, brief psychotherapy in particular.

My discussion in this chapter focuses on a particular module of the mind that I call the "emotion-processing mind." The human mind is composed of specialist modules that are organized around particular adaptive tasks — seeing, hearing, using language, understanding and negotiating one's physical surroundings, understanding what's going on in another person's mind. The emotion-processing mind is a mental module that has evolved to adapt to emotionally charged impingements — gratifying and traumatic events and their implications and meanings. The evolutionary history of this module actually clarifies its present design and operations, which was unexpected, and provides us with new and surprising insights into short-term therapy.

THE THEORY OF EVOLUTION

In brief, Darwin's theory of evolution states that the descent of a species depends on a process called natural selection, in which a larger number of variants compete for resources, survival, and reproductive success under particular environmental conditions. The passive process of natural selection "chooses" for favored reproduction the variant that is most robust under these conditions. Once this is accomplished, new variants appear and a new round of competition and selection takes place in a fresh environment, and so on, ad infinitum.

These are many details of, and debates about, the present-day, revised or neo-Darwinian theory of evolution that need not concern us here (Dawkins, 1976; Dennett, 1995). The essential principles of evolution remain intact, and they have been buttressed by the discovery of the biochemistry of evolution — chromosomes, genes, DNA, RNA. Even the most argued issue of whether evolutionary processes are concentrated on individuals, species, or genes can be set aside for the moment. The point is that organisms and their adaptive systems have heritages. They have evolved and changed, and they have done so along lines "chosen" in response to selection pressures: environmental conditions and other issues that challenge an organism's adaptive resources and account for who and what gets selected and why. In developing an evolutionary scenario for the emotion-processing mind, it is essential to have a clear picture of these selection pressures, which have proved to be the causative factors that shaped the design of that most important mental module.

SELECTION PRESSURE AND ADAPTIVE CHALLENGES

The questions I want to ask are these: When did the emotion-processing mind appear on the evolutionary scene? What were the selection pressures to which it was responding? How have these pressures changed over the time spans of thousands or millions of years? How does defining an evolutionary scenario for this module help us to understand the present state of human emotional adaptations? And finally, what has all of this to do with short-term or brief psychotherapy?

Apes, our closest ancestors, have minds that operate on the basis of a mixture of powerful inherited, fixed, instinctual tendencies and a limited capacity for learning. The earliest hominids, as we are called, had minds not unlike those of these predecessors. Most important, their cognitive capabilities were, and are, confined to what is called event perception: the ability to adapt and use memory when embedded in a situation, but unable to represent that situation in the mind so as to work it over outside of the setting in which it occurred (Donald, 1991). This, in essence, is a relatively simple conscious-system mind.

The history of the various hominid species that culminated in ourselves, *homo sapiens sapiens*, is one of very slow genetic change coupled with very rapid, and of late incredibly fast, intensifications of adaptive demands and traumatic selection pressures. Thus, hominid environments (a term I use to refer to both living and nonliving entities, including settings, happenings, and interactions with others) have become increasingly complex to the point where, probably some 200,000 years ago with the advent of language, the human mind was so seriously threatened with overload that extinction of the species became a possibility.

Among the many new adaptive pressures experienced exclusively by the evolving hominid line were complex social mores and rules, peer pressures, intricate bonding issues with mates and child-rearing demands, the development of weaponry so sophisticated that today we could easily destroy our entire species in one massive attack, as well as increasing demands for resources, food, shelter, and companionship, and much more.

It was, however, the acquisition of language that made these demands so compelling and dangerous. The use of language accounts for almost all of the most critical changes in the hominid environment since that fateful moment. Yet, not only did language bring with it remarkable advances in adaptive resources, but it also is responsible for many of the inordinate dangers faced by humans. Paradoxes like this are quite common in both evolution and emotional life.

The advent of language was accompanied by remarkable cognitive advances, especially the capacity to represent and work over reality and its adaptive challenges in our minds. This capability, and that of language-based reflective awareness, led to many new forms of memory: the ability to anticipate and plan for the future, a definitive sense of self and identity as distinct from others, and such forms of intelligence as symbolic thinking, abstracting, engaging in science — and again, much more.

Most fateful for emotional life and the design of the emotion-processing mind was language's gifts of a well-defined personal identity and the ability to anticipate the future. And along with these developments came the conscious realization of personal mortality and an existential death anxiety that are uniquely human. The adaptive tasks associated with death have wreaked havoc with *homo sapiens sapiens* and their emotional lives, and has been a most compelling selection pressure for the emotion-processing mind with which we adapt to emotionally charged impingements.

There are three forms of death anxiety: *predatory*, which is a response to threats and dangers to one's integrity and survival arising from physical events, as well as from humans and other living beings; *existential*, which is a response to the conscious realization of the inevitability of death for all humans and almost all of the other living species; and *predator*, which is a response to having caused harm to others.

ADAPTIVE RESOURCES

I have briefly outlined some of the main adaptive challenges and selection pressures that were part of the emotional environments to which hominid emotion-processing minds had to adapt. How did these pressures affect and help to shape the design of this mental module and what were the results?

The evolution of the emotion-processing *mind* was, of course, dependent on the evolution of the hominid *brain*, which grew increasingly larger and more complex over millions of years. In evolutionary terms, the mind is the bodily entity or phenotype that negotiates the environment on behalf of the genes (the genotype) that configure both the brain and the mind. As time passed, the emotion-processing mind, which evolved to adapt to emotionally charged triggering events, emerged and gradually changed its design and operations.

Many of these changes took millions of years to effect. They involved the emotion-processing mind and other cognitive capacities that, at first, were isolated from each other and did not share knowledge, but (with certain exceptions pertaining to the deep unconscious system of the emotion-processing mind) they eventually became integrated and increasingly effective.

In the emotional realm, two basic systems evolved for coping with emotionally charged environmental impingements or triggers. The first is called the emotional mind or module because it is the module that responds to triggers with the affects and bodily changes we call emotions.

The most important of these states is responses to danger situations or traumas, which serve to mobilize mental and physical adaptive resources. They are based on immediate instinctive, as well as learned, and automatic, as well as reasoned, adaptive reactions to threat.

The second system is the emotion-processing mind. Its primary adaptive task is to process over extended periods traumatic triggering events that disturb our equilibria and adaptive functioning, to respond to their meanings and create adaptive strategies in thought and behavior so as to resolve the anxieties and other disturbances that they cause. These effects need to be processed in both the short and long term, and they often linger for years or a lifetime.

The emotion-processing mind seems to have emerged first as a single-system conscious module that was confined, as are the minds of apes, to event perceptions. Little by little, a more complex memory system and internal representations were devolved, first crudely expressed through gestures and mime, but then, with language, through words that were used concretely, and eventually symbolically as well. These capabilities are part of the remarkable language-based package of resources that hominids acquired.

Over hundreds of thousands of years, the emotion-processing mind changed from being a general, instinctive processor with minimal learning capabilities to a language-based processor capable of discriminating and detecting definitive events and their particular meanings. Here, it should be made clear that the meanings of human emotion-related experiences are defined both by the nature of the reality impingement and by the inner state of the recipient of a given event. Reality is not simply constructed from within. These constructions are guided and constrained by the nature of the triggering event; the selection of relevant meaning is a better concept than one created solely from within.

Thus, the emotion-processing mind initially was designed as a single-system module — the conscious system — and operated in this way for thousands of years. At some juncture, probably late in its development, its memory capabilities expanded into a memory subsystem capable of internal representations (crude at first, but eventually language-based) and the processing of meaning. This system is called the superficial unconscious subsystem of the conscious system, which, in simple language, means that the conscious mind has its own unconscious storage and processing subsystem from which we retrieve memories that are recalled directly and without disguise or encoding. This is our familiar form of memory, and it entails simply recalling an event as such. It operates with a conscious-system repressive barrier or defensive gradient, in that conscious memory is safeguarded against the direct recall of events or meanings that would evoke excessive anxieties and lead to adaptive dysfunction. But, as we shall see, it is not the only form of memory and recall upon which humans now draw.

Although adaptive demands and selection pressures continued to intensify for the hominid line, they did so very slowly until language came on the scene, after which these burdens expanded at an incredibly rapid pace. The existing protective shield — conscious-system repression — proved to be unequal to the task of maintaining, without undue disruption, the conscious system's main adaptive responsibility, namely, to ensure effective short- and long-term survival. Something more was urgently needed to accomplish this and there was little time for natural selection to make its choices; it had to go with the available variants.

The result was the passive "selection" for favored descent of minds that had two systems for processing the emotionally charged information and meaning contained in traumatic triggering events. One system was linked to awareness, but the other system was not. By bypassing awareness, this second system could relieve the conscious mind of many potentially disruptive impingements and their meanings. It was mainly for this reason that the present two-system emotion-processing mind evolved as a mental module with a conscious system and a second system called the deep unconscious system.

THE TWO-SYSTEM EMOTION-PROCESSING MIND

The evolved design of the emotion-processing mind is both surprising and intriguing. With the conscious-system mind plagued by an overload of triggers and their disturbing meanings, there was a selection for the capability for unconscious or subliminal perception, the receipt of stimuli and their meanings without awareness. In fact, it seems clear that all incoming stimuli and experiences are received subliminally, and that the so-called default position of the system is to allow those experiences and meanings that are tolerable to the individual, or that call for urgent response, to be passed on immediately to awareness, where they obtain in an instant a second moment of registration (unconscious registration being the first).

Those experiences and meanings that are anxiety provoking and potentially disruptive, whether an entire event or some of its meanings, are barred from awareness and receive only an instantaneous moment of unconscious registration. These impingements are relegated to unconscious processing. In this way, the emotion-processing mind and the mind in general are spared and protected from emotional overloads that would render them dysfunctional.

Given that this design protects the conscious mind from disturbing realizations, the present architecture of the emotion-processing mind should be understood fundamentally to use the inbuilt defense of denial in its daily operations. Adaptation is the prime task for all humans and denial is their prime defense. This denial, directed at environmental triggers and their upsetting meanings, is so effective that we do not, and cannot, know that we are using it. In psychotherapy, for example, only a therapist who knows the trigger to which a patient is responding, and who does not deny its existence as well, can recognize and, if necessary, interpret the use of this mechanism.

But there's more. When we deny access to awareness to a meaning of a trigger and send it on for deep unconscious processing, we will never be able to experience that meaning directly in awareness. This is a distinctive feature of deep unconscious repression and it is sustained indefinitely. The only means that the deep unconscious system has of getting its perceptions and adaptive processing activities into awareness is through encoded narratives.

There are, then, two forms of mental repression: one connected with the conscious system, which allows direct recall of events and their meanings, and one connected with the deep unconscious system, which allows only encoded or disguised recall via narrative communications. Thus, when perceptual denial and deep unconscious repression prevail, there can be no direct, conscious recall of an impingement. The only means by which such events and meaning can enter awareness is through disguised or encoded narratives that carry them into consciousness. This means that the stories that patients tell in the course of a psychotherapy session are two-tiered messages, with both a consciously intended meaning and an unconsciously intended one. Each message is different because the triggers are different; patients respond to one set of stimuli consciously and to quite another, more threatening, set unconsciously.

TRIGGER DECODING

This understanding of the nature of unconscious experience, processing, and communication leads to the realization that the only way that therapists can access the deep unconscious meanings of patients' material is by decoding their narratives themes in light of their evocative triggers — a process called trigger decoding. And given the inordinate power of deep unconscious experience, trigger decoding is an invaluable means whereby therapists can help patients to achieve deeply insightful inner change and symptom relief.

As for how to use this process, there's good news and bad news — and some feel that the good news is bad news, too. As it turns out (and this has been confirmed repeatedly), for patients in psychotherapy, whether long or short term, the critical triggers for their deep unconscious experience are always constituted as the interventions of their therapists. We, as therapists, evoke our patients' encoded reactions — and, on occasion, their conscious reactions, as well. And these deep unconscious perceptions and reactions are encoded in the stories patients tell in sessions.

Why do patients encode their stoires? They do so to spare both themselves and us excessive anxiety and emotional pain. This is the case for two reasons. First, we are trained as therapists to do conscious-system psychotherapy and, therefore, offer many interventions that are perceived unconsciously as erroneous and harmful to our patients; and second, every intervention by a therapist, unconsciously validated or invalidated, evokes a measure of anxiety. This is explained in the following, but for now, it should be stressed that there are strong motives on both sides of the therapy dyad to avoid trigger decoding and an understanding of patients' deep unconscious perceptions of the ways in which their therapists behave with and speak to them.

THE IDEAL GROUND RULES

Once you begin to use trigger decoding, a world of discovery is at your beck and call. The deep unconscious system is highly sensitive to the ground rules, settings, and boundaries of the therapy situation and how the therapist manages this important aspect of treatment. Support for this position comes from patients' responses to therapists' ground-rule-related interventions. Holding the frame secured evokes encoded stories of helpful and wise individuals, while modifying the ideal frame consistently evokes images of individuals who are harmful, seductive, and insensitive.

On this basis (and the deep unconscious system is quite consistent in this area), it has been found that there is a universal, evolved, deep unconscious need in humans for secured frames, which means that there is an ideal set of conditions and ground rules for optimal healing in psychotherapy. This does not, however, preclude departures from this ideal — and brief therapy is one of them because the ideal frame calls for treatment to last until the patient has resolved his or her emotional problems and is ready to stop. But it does mean that in the deep unconscious mind, and in reality, as revealed in encoded narratives, patients experience predation, harm, and the like under these frame-modified conditions. At the very least, then, these deep unconscious experiences — and they are valid and not distorted — need to be interpreted to patients and rectified, if possible, in order to resolve the anxieties, conflicts, symptoms, and displaced acting out that they cause.

The other ideal ground rules include a single fee and setting; a set locale for, and the length and frequency of, sessions; the use of free association; total privacy and confidentiality; the neutrality and relative anonymity of the therapist, with no directives, advice, personal opinions, or self-revelations; and the absence of physical contact. As you can see, the deep unconscious system is quite demanding and definitive as to the conditions under which healing best occurs, and secured frames, as they are called, are quite healing in themselves. But you also no doubt realize that few therapists adhere to these unconsciously sought and validated conditions for therapy. This fact reflects the general use of conscious system forms of psychotherapy in which trigger decoding is seldom or never used. But it also is testimony to the unmastered death anxieties that exist in both patients and ourselves, their therapists.

Modified frames, as indicated, create predatory death anxieties in patients. But they also offer patients defenses, however costly, against existential death anxieties, because every frame break implies the ability and privilege of being able to violate ground rules — and the fundamental ground rule of life is that it ends in death. Thus, denial-based defenses flourish in modified frames, which is the main psychological reason that they are so favored by the conscious-system mind, which either ignores or downplays the importance of secured frames and generally tolerates or prefers those that are modified.

Secured frames are healing and optimal for therapeutic work, and they are always validated by the deep unconscious system, as seen in the positively toned encoded stories patients tell after a therapist intervenes to maintain an ideal ground rule or secure a ground rule that is deviant. But secured frames are constricting and entrapping, and they create claustrum-like effects that are similar to life itself; we are all born into a closed space from which, ultimately, death is the sole exit. Thus, secured frames evoke existential death anxieties, and given that we can never fully master these anxieties (we can make peace with them, but we can't defeat death in the long run), they are the most morbid of human experiences.

Patients (and therapists) who have experienced intensely emotional death-related traumas – to others and through their own actions – are especially terrified of secured frames because unconsciously they expect a repetition of the death-related trauma, or retaliation for the harm that they have caused others. Because situations of this kind are so common in today's world, deep-unconscious secured-frame anxieties are extremely common in those involved in a psychotherapy experience. This is a major cause of frame modifications, much to the detriment of all concerned.

Existential death anxiety has been especially fateful for the evolution of the emotion-processing mind and its present design, and for the nature of emotional disorders; it is a root cause of all emotional maladaptations. Unconsciously, it also has had an enormous, although unrecognized, influence on the forms taken by the practices of psychotherapy. Denial of these anxieties in thought and in such actions as frame violations proves to be extremely costly emotionally. People are hurt badly by these actions, but the conscious mind generally is willing to pay almost any price for the momentary relief so gained, and the cost in pain almost always is denied or goes unrecognized as such.

ANOTHER FATEFUL FEATURE

One last evolved feature of the emotion-processing mind is of importance to the new perspectives offered here with respect to brief psychotherapy, many of which may be evident from what has already been described. The deep unconscious wisdom subsystem, which processes the unconsciously perceived inputs of events and meanings with great adaptive wisdom, has no mental tracts that go directly to awareness; all of its outputs to awareness must be encoded. In addition, and this is unexpected, the wise adaptive choices of the deep unconscious wisdom subsystem do *not* unconsciously affect conscious thinking, choices, and adaptations; there are no intuitive or other subtle effects. This unfortunate situation is further aggravated because the unconsciously perceived meanings of traumatic events do have such influence. Unconsciously, they motivate or contribute to many symptomatic maladaptations in patients — and their therapists.

The loss of adaptive resourcefulness can be rectified solely through the aforementioned process of trigger decoding. But to carry out this effort, one must go against the natural, evolved defensive alignment of the emotion-processing mind, and defending against traumatic inputs is its basic mode of operation. The emotion-processing mind is designed for denial and knowledge reduction, rather than for insight, because its main responsibility is to adapt to unbearable inputs by keeping them outside of awareness. In a few words, our emotion-related minds are committed to defense in lieu of understanding. This, too, has greatly influenced the ways in which psychotherapy is practiced.

Some of the detrimental effects of traumas are mediated through a subsystem of the deep unconscious system that does unconsciously affect behavior and conscious coping strategies. This component is called the *fear-guilt subsystem*, and it embodies the human fear of death and the experience of guilt for harm caused to others and oneself. The unconscious fear of death prompts a wide range of denial-serving thoughts and behaviors, of which frame modifications are but one; religions, belief in an afterlife and immortality, and sexual acting out are others. These denial-based mechanisms are the main means that humans have found to deal with human mortality.

As for deep unconscious guilt, it is a dynamic that evokes self-punishing behaviors as the price for hurting others. This vengeful imperative means that the conscious mind is under continual pressure to find and rationalize ways of causing harm and pain to oneself. The selection pressures behind this unusual feature of the emotion-processing mind appears to be the strong inclination of humans to attack and harm others who attack and cause harm to themselves. Conspecific (same-species) violence, both physical and psychological, is the major danger confronting us today. And the impulse to take vengeance and the tendency to harm others in order to survive oneself, whether the issue is one of food or of territory or mate, are so powerful that conscious forms of guilt have had little restraining power. Unconscious guilt appears to have evolved to reduce such tendencies further, although it too has fallen short of achieving this vital goal.

Translated into practical consequences for psychotherapy, patients seek therapies that will, unwittingly and at great cost to themselves, protect them, through denial-based mechanisms, like departures from the ideal frame, against their existential death anxieties. And at the same time, they also seek therapies that unconsciously will damage and cause them suffering in an unrecognized effort to assuage their deep unconscious sense of guilt. Creating and doing sound forms of psychotherapy are, in this light, enormously difficult undertakings that are easily set awry.

IMPLICATIONS FOR BRIEF PSYCHOTHERAPY

Brief psychotherapy is a viable and necessary form of treatment. That said, as therapists, we should deeply understand its nature and structure, and especially its unconscious effects on both our patients and ourselves. Once you begin to engage in trigger decoding your patients' narrative material, you will discover for yourself that brief psychotherapy is, indeed, a departure from the ideal framework of psychotherapy, with many unconsciously mediated, critical consequences. And the effects of these departures from the ideal secured frame often are compounded by other frame modifications. There may be ancillary personnel who are contaminating third parties to the therapy, and/or forms to fill out and information that is released in violation of the necessary total privacy and confidentiality of the therapy. The fee may be low and/or the therapist may engage in self-revelations because he or she consciously believes them to be harmless, or even helpful, although unconsciously they cause harm and often serve the therapist's need for active forms of denial against his or her own existential death anxieties.

Practically speaking, brief therapy should be as secured with regard to frames as possible and unnecessary frame modifications should be eliminated or rectified; the patient's encoded themes will direct the therapist to do so. The frame modifications that are inescapable, when activated, should be used as triggers for the decoding of patients' material and suitably interpreted (and rectified, if possible). This transforms a deviant, short-term therapy without insight into a deviant therapy with deep understanding, and the latter is by far the better way to do deviant-frame therapy.

Patients deeply appreciate these interpretations and they will validate them through their encoded narratives and symptomatic improvement.

The prearranged termination of brief therapy is an ever-present deviant trigger to which patients will continuously adapt, in part through repetitive encoded images and themes embodied in the stories that they tell. Trigger decoding needs to be judiciously applied each time the issue comes up as a trigger. Much of the healing in this therapy modality will come from the interpretation of patients' unconscious perceptions of this aspect of the therapy — and its connection to past traumas, which will emerge in patients' material as these meanings are processed and understood. In essence, then, brief therapy will be most effective when the therapist includes the interpretation of the meanings for patients of the trigger that calls for the time limit to the work.

Therapists should be wary of the direct comments and evaluations of patients in brief therapy. The perspectives of the conscious mind are under the unconscious influence of needs to deny death and receive punishment. With motives like these driving the comments, it is unwise to accept them at face value. On the other hand, patients' stories will continue to encode perceptions and appraisals of their therapists' efforts, and make recommendations for frame rectification and reinterpretation where needed. Properly trigger decoded, these advisories are sound and well worth heeding and carrying out to the greatest extent feasible.

You can see, too, that a brief therapy need not be a manifest-content, conscious-system therapy. Not only is it possible to interpret deep unconscious meaning in this form of therapy, but it is imperative to do so. The world of deep unconscious experience has a far more powerful effect on emotional symptoms, and emotional life in general, than does conscious experience. It follows then that understanding and interpreting the deep unconscious messages from patients are by far the most efficacious way to proceed.

CONCLUSION

The constraints of space have made it necessary only to skim the surface of many complex ideas and issues. My main hope is that I have provided a sense of the complexities of the human mind and its emotion-processing module and have helped the reader to understand their peculiar and rather self-defeating, modern features. The shortness of the time that natural selection has had in which to select language-based emotion-processing minds that are able to ensure the survival of us as individuals, and our species and genes, helps to explain the pervasively defensive and costly design of this mental module. We must rely on our gene-based, yet autonomous, individual and collective intelligences to enhance this vital, but compromised, instrument of adaptation.

References

Dawkins, R. (1976). *The selfish gene*. Oxford: Oxford University Press.

Dennett, D. (1995). *Darwin's dangerous idea*. New York: Simon & Schuster.

Donald, M. (1991). *Origins of the modern mind*. Cambridge, MA: Harvard University Press.

Langs, R. (1996). *The evolution of the emotion processing mind, with an introduction to mental Darwinism*. London: Karnac Books.

Slavin, M., & Kriegman, D. (1992). *The adaptive design of the human psyche*. New York: Guilford.

9

Reality Exists: A Critique of Antirealism in Brief Therapy

William J. Matthews

As I have stated elsewhere (Matthews, 1998), radical social constructivism and its equivalencies of cultural constructivism, deconstructivism, feminist discourse, poststructuralism, postmodernism, and the like have become, in my opinion, a serious blight on the American intellectual landscape. The focus of this chapter will be on (1) outlining the presence of antirealist thought in brief psychotherapy, and then (2) arguing that it is contradictory and irrelevant to the process of psychotherapy.

The argument, which I refer to in general terms as postmodernism, is fallacious logically, and on reasonably close inspection falls under its own nihilistic weight. In essence, the postmodernist position is that truth is only relative and has no general application, given that said truth is a mere construction created by a given social context. As Fox (1996) points out, such a statement, even under the most cursory inspection, is seen to be paradoxical and to fall prey to the same problem as that of our ancient Cretan friend (who told us that all Cretans are liars). Since truth is only relative and subject to various prejudices, the statement that all truths are relative and have no generalizability is itself simultaneously relative and absolute, and as such offers us no reason to accept it.[1] Relativism makes no distinction (because for such folks there is none) between objective (i.e., verifiable) knowledge and superstition (astrology, creationism, and flat-earthers, among others) and is deeply flawed as an epistemology. It is, by definition, a direct attack on science, scientific method, and critical rationality. This view would offer us no way to distinguish between superstition and verifiable knowledge and as such is both nonsensical and intellectually dangerous (c.f., Matthews, 1998).

Postmodern thought has continued to gain prominence and increasing influence within some subsets of the psychological community. For example, with reference to the latter, Prilleltensky (1997), in his discussion of the assumptions of various models of therapy, appeared to feel forced to elevate postmodernism to the status of a model of therapy in the absence of any empirically based evidence to support it. This philosophical view provides the underpinning of the growth of the brief-strategic-therapy movement into its current forms of solution-focused and narrative therapy (Held, 1999).

POSTMODERNISM DEFINED

As Phillips (1995), in his review of the wide range of constructivist thought, reminded us, few believe that we come into the world with our "cognitive data banks fully packed with empirical knowledge, or with pre-embedded epistemological criteria or methodological rules" (p. 5). Conversely, few believe in Locke's *tabula rasa* notion — that knowledge is existent, already formed, and written upon us as passive recipients. Most would agree with the evolutionary notion that humans are born with some inherited cognitive (e.g., language ability) and epistemological capacities (Phillips, 1995). As such, one can safely say that "knowledge" and its criteria, methods of inquiry, and so on, are by definition "constructed." This observation is trivially true and few, if any, scientists

---

[1] This is also exactly the problem of Hegel's dialectic, a belief in which is an underpinning of much of postmodernist writing. There is a logical contradiction in the notion of the dialectic. For Hegel, truth was both relative and absolute. He contended that truth was relative to each historical and cultural framework and that each is incommensurable with the other. However, as Popper (1994) observed, Hegel liked to have things both ways and believed this relative view of truth to be *absolutely* true.

would disagree. It is at this point, however, that the divergence between postmodernists and science begins. Kvale (1992) states that postmo dernism attempts "diverse diagnoses and interpretations of the current culture, a depiction of a multitude of interrelated phenomena" (p. 32). Perhaps, but the question then becomes: By what method and criteria is such interpretation judged?

In its essence, postmodernism and its related concepts of constructivism (radical and social), poststructuralism, and deconstructivism can be characterized by a nonbelief in (1) the objective world and (2) meta-narrative explanations (e.g., the universal theories/explanations generated by science). Kvale (1992) states that in postmodern thought there is no foundation for a universal and objective *reality*. For the postmodernist, there is no pure, uninterpreted datum; all facts embody theory. Thus, in the absence of objectivity, reality is purely a function of social and, by definition, linguistic construction (Anderson & Goolishian, 1988; Kvale, 1992). Kvale (1992) further states that "there exists no standard method for measuring and comparing knowledge within different language games and paradigms; they are incommensurable" (p. 35). He further states that "a postmodern world is characterized by a continual change of perspectives, with no underlying common frame of reference, but rather a manifold of changing horizons. *Language does not copy reality*. Rather language constitutes reality, each language constructing specific aspects of reality in its own way. The focus is on the linguistic and social construction of reality, on interpretation and negotiation of the meaning of the lived world" (p. 35, italics added).

Gergen (1985, 1991; Gergen & Kaye, 1992) has been particularly vocal both in his critique of rational-empirical thought and as a proponent of the so-called postmodern paradigm shift. Gergen and Kaye (1992) conclude, in reference to a noncorrespondence between language and the "real world" (authors' quotes), that "in the case of writing, each style or genre of literature operates according to local rules or conventions, and these conventions will largely determine the way we understand the putative objects of representation. Scientific writing, then, furnishes [a] no more *accurate* [original italics] picture of reality than fiction" (p. 173). These authors conclude that both fiction and science are simply guided by cultural conventions, and as such determine the character of the reality each view (i.e., science and fiction) seeks to depict. Thus, one could legitimately conclude that the narrative of intelligently designed canals on

Mars, for example, is no less true than astronomy's geologically based explanation. According to Gergen and Kaye (1992), since knowledge is socially constructed, the data-based empirical observations of astronomy are simply a "local truth" and, therefore, carry authority only within the scientific community.

Gergen (1985) states: "Constructionism asks one to suspend belief that commonly accepted categories of understandings receive their warrant through observation. Thus it invites one to challenge the objective basis of conventional knowledge" (p. 267). Interestingly, he further states that "accounts of social construction cannot themselves be warranted empirically. . . . the success of such accounts depends primarily on the analyst's capacity to invite, compel, stimulate, or delight the audience, and not criteria of veracity" (p. 272). Gergen's statement is a clarion call to pre-Enlightenment thought. The Popperian canon of refutability upon which science and rational-empirical thought are built is cast aside in favor of that which is "compelling, stimulating, and/or delightful." Such criteria are exactly those used by the jury in the Salem witch trials, for example, (with "delightful" being an exception, at least for the defendants) for which the jury later apologized (Crews, 1997). For Gergen and postmodernists, empirical data and the conclusions thus derived must be subject to "the pragmatic implications of such conclusions within society more generally" (Gergen, 1985, p. 273). One might suggest that it was these "pragmatic implications within society" that created significant difficulty for Galileo — a pragmatic point not lost upon René Descartes who sought in vain to appease the Catholic Church (he repudiated Galileo), but whose writings were banned anyway.

As Held (1995, 1996, 1999) notes in her critique of postmodernism in psychotherapy, postmodernist thought is antirealist at its core, which is to say that reality is either (1) only that which is socially constructed by the observer or (2) may exist, but cannot be known. Since there can be no hierarchy of knowledge and there are only local truths, postmodernists contend that reality should be constructed along certain pragmatic lines (i.e., ethical/egalitarian notions). From this perspective, science, the scientific method, and critical rationality hold no special authority or privilege. This perspective has permeated much of the brief therapy movement and is, at its heart, antithetical to its stated purpose, the individuation of practice (Held, 1995, 1999). In the remaining discussion, the essence of postmodernism, and related concepts, is collapsed into its core epistemological perspective, which is antirealism.

THE EVOLUTION OF BRIEF THERAPY: FROM PRAGMATISM TO ANTIREALISM

In The Beginning

Brief strategic therapy owes much of its development to the work of Milton Erickson (Haley, 1963, 1973; Weakland, Fisch, Watzlawick, & Bodin, 1974). Erickson did not operate from a formal theory of personality, as did, say, Freud, and was much more interested in the uniqueness of the individual and the pragmatics of achieving a positive therapeutic outcome (Lankton & Lankton, 1983; Matthews, 1985; Rossi, 1980). Citing Erickson's unpublished manuscripts from the 1950s and 1960s, Rossi (1980) observed that Erickson rejected the limitations of most schools of psychotherapy in favor of the importance of current realities of the client's life in the process of psychotherapy. With regard to the limitations of most schools of psychotherapy, Erickson rejected the notion held by psychodynamically oriented therapies that "psychotherapy based upon observable behavior and related primarily to the demands of the immediate and future life situations of the patient must necessarily be inadequate, superficial, and lacking in validity — as compared with therapy that restructures the patient's understanding of the remote past" (Rossi, 1980, p. xv).

Erickson was primarily interested in the importance of everyday life (i.e., reality) and its influence on the individual. Rossi, in paraphrasing Erickson, states, "Preoccupation with the past and disregard of the needs, opportunities, and capabilities of the current situation may easily, and often does, prolong psychotherapy" (p. xvii). While these early writings by Erickson suggest a rejection of the importance of past experiences as a necessary or sufficient condition for therapeutic change, there is nothing that suggests that reality is purely a social construction and that antirealism is a requisite principle of brief strategic therapy. Quite the contrary, implicit in this view is that Erickson believed that the current reality of the client was in fact real and frequently had a significant effect (i.e., causality) on the behavior for which the client sought change.

Erickson's most famous student, Jay Haley (1973), defines strategic therapy as that in which "the clinician initiates what happens during therapy and designs a particular approach for each problem. He must identify solvable problems, set goals, design interventions to achieve those goals, examine the responses he receives to correct his approach, and ultimately examine the outcome of his therapy to see if it has been effective" (p. 17). This definition of brief strategic therapy would seem to suggest an observable pragmatic reality-based approach to change.

In their seminal article on brief strategic therapy, Weakland, Fisch, Watzlawick, and Bodin (1974) define their work as based on "two ideas central to family therapy: (a) focusing on observable behavioral interaction in the present and (b) deliberate intervention to alter the going system" (p. 142). Implicit in this definition, as in that of Haley, is that reality exists, is observable, and is subject to causal influences.

Held (1995, 1999), in her critique of antirealism in brief therapy, summarizes four objectives of the brief strategic approach:

1. Brief therapists see and treat each and every case as unique or particular.
2. Brief therapists are careful observers who listen to, are curious about, and are acutely sensitive to their clients.
3. Brief therapists omit general, predetermined theoretical constructs (i.e., those determined prior to any particular therapy case — hence the term "predetermined") that other therapists rely on to guide their interventions; for instance, irrational thoughts in cognitive therapy, cross-generational coalitions in structural family therapy, weak defenses in psychoanalysis, poor self concept in humanistic therapy. Brief therapists avoid such predetermined theory, which allows them to simplify therapy.
4. Brief therapists are active; they directly influence the client (pp. 2–3).

The Point of Departure

I wholeheartedly agree with Held (1999) when she notes, "Objective 4 eventually split the brief therapy movement over the question of whether brief therapists should take a relational/collaborative nonimpositional stance instead of the hierarchical/interventionist/directive and manipulative/strategic stance they started out with."

Nowhere in their article in *Family Process* (Weakland, Fisch, Watzlawick, & Bodin, 1974) do these authors discuss the antirealist notion of radical constructivism or suggest such a notion as a requisite foundational principle. However, in their book *Change*, Watzlawick, Weakland, and Fisch (1974) do make the link between the key therapeutic technique of reframing and antirealism (cf. Held, 1999).

> To reframe, then, means to change the conceptual and/or emotional setting or viewpoint in relation to which a situation is experi-

> enced to place it in another frame which fits the "facts" of the same concrete situation equally well or better, and thereby changes its entire meaning. (p. 95)

As Held (1999) wryly notes, the use of quotes on the word "facts" should alert the reader to the fact that the notion of facts as connected to an existent reality is in doubt. However, their endorsement of antirealism is unmistakable in their later quote:

> On reflection it becomes obvious that anything is real only to the extent that it conforms to a *definition* of reality — and those definitions are legion. To employ a useful oversimplification: real is what a sufficiently large number of people have agreed to *call* real — except that this fact is usually forgotten; the agreed-upon definition is reified (that is, made into a "thing" in its own right) and is eventually experienced as that objective reality "out there." (p. 96) [italics and quotes are original]

> Truth, as Saint-Exupéry remarked, is not what we discover, but what we create. (p. 97)

By 1984, Watzlawick had published three books (Watzlawick, 1976, 1978, 1984) in which reality was under severe criticism. For example, Watzlawick (1978) stated: "Language does not so much *reflect* reality as *create* it" (p. 16). The surrealistic rabbit hole of antirealism is opened and entered.

While their antirealist writings began to emerge during this time, the active interventionist stance presented in objective 4 (Held, 1999) remained quite central to their description of brief strategic therapy. So when did this creeping antirealism challenge the interventionist stance of Erickson, Haley, and the Mental Research Institute (MRI)? I would suggest that the shift began in earnest in 1982 in *Family Process.* In the first article of this issue, Keeney and Sprenkle (1982) offer a very clear critique and rejection of the pragmatic approach to brief therapy as presented by Erickson, Haley, and the MRI group. In a call for more art, more theory, less technique, and conscious manipulation/intention on the part of the therapist, they state: "A brief perusal of the field indicates that numerous schools of therapy are based on attempts to reduce therapeutic artistry to packageable techniques that can be explicitly taught (and evaluated)" (p. 11).

These authors take particular issue with the notion of therapist manipulation (objective 4). They state, "One outcome of pragmatically inspired schools of therapy is that they typically present solutions and cures in left-brain, discursive (digital) terms. That form of presentation assumes that problems and solutions can be known and approached through conscious, purposive thinking. As Bateson (1980) has pointed out, however, the solution, cure, or answer is always partly unknowable. Any attempt to 'know' the answer involves translating it into the left-brain, manipulative side" (p. 15).

The reality of straightforward behavioral change as proposed by the strategic approach is called into question. The notion here is that conscious direct action by the therapist is a violation of the esthetics of the therapy process, and even if successful in bringing about behavioral change is likely to be acting in "ignorance of the larger ecology" (p. 15).

Dell (1982) continues this theme in his rejection of the notion of causation when he boldly states, "[T]he concept of causation is an epistemological error. All causal accounts of phenomena are fundamentally flawed and erroneous" (p. 21).

In lieu of causation, Dell suggest the notion of *fit* that does not reference etiology or causation. He states, "Fit simply posits that the behaviors occurring in the family system have a general complementarity; they fit together" (p. 21).

The underlying antirealist notions of Dell's position becomes more apparent when he later says: "In other words, one cannot say what the system 'is,' One can only choose a particular punctuation and take what consequences come with it" (p. 26).

He rejects the notion of causality and reality when he later states: "Again, however, one must remember that if punctuating the system one way 'works' (i.e., facilitates successful intervention), all we can say is that it works, this it was useful. *The fact that it works does not mean that it is accurate or truthful* [italics added]; it only means that it works" (p. 26).

Dell is quite clear in his rejection of causality and purpose. He is equally clear in his implicit suggestion that reality, if it exists, cannot be known, but is simply a function of the punctuation of the observer. There can be no question as to the implicit antirealism of his view.

By the time we come to the third article in this issue, Allman (1982) is directly challenging the lack of aesthetic preference of the MRI. In referencing Gregory Bateson, he states the problem of being a pragmatic therapist (i.e., interested in defining a problem, and seeking an achievable, observable outcomes). He maintains:

> When we view therapy as if it were only a pragmatic modality rather than as a part of an aesthetic process, we overlook the evolutionary idea implicit in Bateson's open systems epistemology: ... to study in order to do something is irrelevant. The moment you put purpose into what you're studying, you project onto it a pragmatism that leads to a dormative principle by placing your eye on the goal, not the life force." (p. 44)

Allman goes on to criticize the MRI group for engaging in the error of pragmatic reductionism. He further states:

> Family therapy is in danger of losing what is meaningful and artistic in its contribution to clinical understanding as it becomes coopted by the dominant mechanistic epistemology, with its inherent emphasis on pragmatism at the expense of aestheticism. (p. 45)

Allman rejects the reality-based approach of the strategic therapists:

> Effective family therapy is art, in that it serves to find the organic connections that help place self as part of a unified, patterned integrity of nature as revealed in family mental life. ... Finding the particular meanings within a family's contextual arrangements and helping the system stay in touch with the *life-producing forces* [original italics] uniting them is the artistry of family therapy. (p. 46)

To further underscore his point, Allman presents a clear rejection of the realism of science in his quotation of Polyani that is strikingly reminiscent of the 19th-century Romantic rejection of science:

> A quantum-mechanical theory of the universe is just as empty of meaning as a Laplacean mechanical theory. It is simply this sort of mechanical reductionism that is the heart of the matter. It is this that is the origin of the whole system's scientific obscurantisms under which we are suffering today. This is the cause of our cor-

> ruption of the conception of man, reducing him either to an insentient automaton or to a bundle of appetites. This why science can be invoked so easily in support of totalitarian violence, why science has become the greatest source of dangerous fallacies today. (p. 52)

Allman, emboldened by his quote from Polyani, continues:

> Family therapists who seek only to find a scientific base for their assumptions often remove the creative spontaneity of poetic meanings from life. This form of systemic reductionism endangers the creative "twinkle" necessary for an openness to life. (pp. 52–53)

What is interesting in this piece by Allman is that he, via Polyani, invokes scientific reductionism as a cause for the corruption of man, but offers no systematic empirically based evidence to support his hypothesis. One might suggest that he uses (quite badly) the very process (scientific method, at least logically based causality) he condemns. Since Allman, Dell, Keeney, and Sprenkle reject the notion of causality, and therefore, I assume, the empirical evidence by which such a claim could be tested, they can claim the fallacy of pragmatic reductionism with impunity.

In a fourth article in that issue of *Family Process*, Steve de Shazer (1982), a founder of the solution-focused therapy model, criticizes what he calls the "contest model of therapy." He specifically discusses the approach of Erickson, Haley, and the MRI as that which is based on the old "power epistemology," which, we are to understand from the earlier articles, is an epistemological error. De Shazer argues that since these therapists viewed the client's presentation as an attempt at a manipulation of power (i.e., the power of the pathogenic double bind), "The therapist was seen as needing counterpower and thus the problem of who was going to control what is central to the conflict model of therapy" (p. 78).

Objective 4 (the therapist's taking direct action) is abjectly rejected. In the place of the contest/power model of therapy, de Shazer suggests the notion of cooperation. He reframes what was perceived as client resistance as: "Each family, individual, or couple shows a unique way of attempting to cooperate, and the therapist's job becomes first to describe to himself that particular manner that the family shows, and then to cooperate with the family's way, and thus to promote change" (p. 78).

De Shazer then suggests that the concept of cooperation negates cause-

and-effect linearity and the notion that the therapist can, or should, be directive.

By 1986, Lynn Hoffman continued to challenge the brief therapy principle of objective 4. In her article "Beyond Power and Control: Toward a 'Second Order' Family Systems Therapy," Hoffman (1986) criticized the MRI group and Haley for using the vocabulary of war and adversarial games (i.e., power-tactics, strategy, being one up or one down). She makes a rather interesting and provocative observation: "I am often struck by the resemblance between accounts of therapeutic prowess described within this framework (i.e., Erickson, Haley, MRI) to the sexual performance known as 'scoring'" (p. xx).[2]

Clearly, in her view, such an orientation leaves much to be desired. In this article, Hoffman, citing the writings of Gregory Bateson, who rejected the instrumentality of Erickson, Haley, and the MRI, strongly objects to the notion of therapist control (being directive) as being power oriented, linear, and purposive in favor of that which is nonhierarchical, egalitarian, nonjudgmental, and noninstrumental (i.e., that which is not directive). She also suggests a constructivist approach to reality, which is to say, "It is not so important that our constructs match with items in the environment as that they fit sufficiently to ensure survival" (p. xx).

The Full-Blown Antirealism of Solution-Focused and Narrative Therapies

The techniques of reframing and positive connotation (Selvini-Palazzoli, Cecchin, Prata, & Bosclo, 1978) are the smoking-gun connections to the postmodernist antirealism of the solution-focused and narrative therapies of the 1990s (Held, 1995, 1999). While I would not disagree with the importance of these techniques and their bridge to antirealism, I am of the general opinion that this period, beginning with the *Family Process* articles of 1982 and continuing to the present, coincides with the larger intellectual shift in some areas of academia (i.e., literary criticism, some feminist discourse, the deconstructivism of Derrida and Foucault, some aspects of multiculturalism) that rejected out of hand the authority of science and

[2] On a personal note, Hoffman (1986) alluded to the fact that she worked for a number of years with an Ericksonian therapist. I was that therapist. In our many discussions about instrumentality and therapist intentionality, she frequently stated her discomfort with what she experienced as the "alpha male"-oriented instrumental approach of strategic therapy. She never felt completely comfortable with this approach to change and was pleased with the emergence of a more collaborative approach, to which she made significant contributions.

the scientific method as singularly Eurocentric, nonegalitarian, hierarchical, and white-male dominated (for an in-depth discussion, see Gross & Levitt, 1994). It was in this larger context that this epistemological shift in therapy took place. Whatever the pathways of influence, there is no doubt that antirealist notions alluded to in the mid- and late 1980s became the central precepts in the postmodern/constructivist/antirealist approaches of solution-focused and narrative therapies (Held, 1999).

Steve de Shazer certainly can be given credit for creating brief solution-focused therapy (de Shazer, 1985). His commitment to antirealism as an intellectual foundation is clear. "Post-structuralists (i.e., postmodernists) in fact question the opposition of the subject and object upon which the possibility of objectivity depends" (de Shazer, 1991, p. 50). And: "There are no wet beds, no voices without people, no depressions. There is only *talk* about wet bed, *talk* about depression" [italics original] (de Shazer, 1993, p. 89).

In contemporary poststructuralist thought, our world — our social interactional context — is seen as created by language, by words: "Language constitutes 'the human world and the human world constitutes the whole world' " (de Shazer & Berg, 1992, p. 73).

This notion of a reality that is purely constructed by the language of the observer is a key antirealist theme (Anderson & Goolishian, 1988; Efran, Lukens, & Lukens, 1990; Hoffman, 1986). De Shazer would seem to represent the radical constructivist view that there is *no* reality, only that created by the language of the observer.

O'Hanlon and Weiner-Davis (1989) further develop the solution-focused therapy of de Shazer and with it, its antirealism stance. These authors state as part of their assumptions: "There is no way to ascertain which view is most 'correct'; rather , it is evident that each view is merely a small portion of the total picture and is colored by each person's biases and assumptions" (p. 46).

Perhaps it is a less radical view than that of de Shazer, but it is antirealist nonetheless. To underscore their antirealist position, O'Hanlon and Weiner-Davis (1989) use scare quotes (Held, 1999) on such words as "right," "wrong," and "facts." As Held notes in so doing, one can use the words without adopting (or being contaminated by) the realist epistemology that such words imply.

Selekman (1993), in discussing his approach to solution-focused therapy with adolescents, says:

> Assumption 9: Reality is observer-defined and the therapist participates in co-creating the therapy system's reality. (p. 42)
> Assumption 10: There are many ways to look at a situation, none are more correct than others. (p. 43)
> There is no such thing as a "God's eye" view: we can never find an objective outside place from which to look at our clients. (p. 43)

In stating the assumptions underlying his solution-focused approach, Selekman references the authors cited earlier (i.e., Anderson & Goolishian, 1988; Bateson, 1980; de Shazer, 1991; Efran & Lukens, 1985; Hoffman, 1986).

Following on the heals of the antirealism of solution-focused therapies came what O'Hanlon (1994) termed the third wave (psychodynamic and strategic therapies being waves one and two, respectively) — the narrative therapy created by Michael White and David Epston (White & Epston, 1990). Their support for antirealism would seem even more pronounced than that of the second wave. "Since we cannot know objective reality, all knowing requires an act of interpretation" (p. 2).

And White (1993) adds:

> The constitutionalist perspective that I am arguing for refutes foundationalists' assumptions of objectivity, essentialism, and representationalism. It proposes that an objective knowledge of the world is not possible, that knowledges are actually generated in particular discursive fields. . . . And the constitutionalists' perspective proposes that descriptions that we have of life are not representations or reflections of life as lived, but are directly constitutive of life; that these descriptions do not correspond with the world (i.e., they give us no objective truth), but have real effects in the shaping of life.

To sum up all the antirealist notions of all previous authors regarding the antirealism embedded in solution-focused and narrative therapies, Freedman and Coombs (1996, p. 22) present their position regarding truth and reality in unmistakable terms:

1. Realities are socially constructed.
2. Realities are constituted through language.
3. Realities are organized and maintained through narrative.

4. There are no essential truths.

One can at least appreciate the clarity and directness of Freedman and Coombs' position.

INCOHERENCE, RESPONSIBILITY, OSCILLATION

The Incoherence Of Antirealism

In the previous sections, I traced that intellectual development of antirealism from its incipient beginnings in brief strategic therapy to its full-blown and unabashed embodiment of the belief that there are no essential truths in narrative therapies. At this point, one might reasonably ask, to what end? What is the value of antirealism for a psychotherapist?

Joseph Carroll's (1996) book *Evolution and Literary Theory* provides an elegant and straightforward discussion of the incoherence of the antirealism of postmodernism that is quite applicable to our urguments here. Carroll observes that the two fundamental doctrines of antirealist thought — *textuality* (language does not represent experience, but constructs it according to its own internal principles); and *indeterminacy* (language is fraught with gaps that render all text void of specific contingent and/or causal meaning) — are logically incoherent. The chief problem with these principles is, in fact, their shortsighted antirealism.

As stated by Carroll, "Textuality and indeterminacy eliminate the two criteria of truth: the correspondence of propositions to their objects and the internal coherence of propositions" (p. 4). Carroll observes that if there is no correspondence between literature and one's experience of the world then there is no value to, or need of, literature or literary scholarship. Such texts would be completely unstable and, therefore, without meaning. The same argument would apply to psychotherapy, if there are no wet beds or depression, but only talk of wet beds and depression (de Shazer, 1993), then there is no objective reality (only that which is socially constructed in language), no need to consider formal causality (because no such thing exists), and no empirically based practice (which is a mere linguistic construction). Following this line of reasoning, there would be no need for a system of therapy, narrative or otherwise, as the client's narrative is not connected to any real experience and the story itself has no stability and is likely to change in the absence of therapy.

However, more to the point is the lack of internal logic of antirealist thought, which renders its own principles incapable of validation, *conve-*

niently relieving its practitioners of all intellectual responsibility for their pronouncements. A therapy based on antirealism negates not only its own effort at legitimization, but also that of being proved wrong, and herein is the heart of the issue that I will discuss.

If there were no truth, either as stated by the client or by the therapist, then the new story, narrative, or reframing could be anything without fear of being found wrong, or perhaps more important for these therapists, for being manipulative. If causality and objectivity exist, then a given reframing by the therapist would be, by definition, manipulative and intentional, purposely seeking to cause a client's behavior to change in a particular direction. As Held (1999) notes, if there is a knowable reality, then the therapist's reframe should not violate it. However, in the absence of reality, we are without constraints, as there is no objective reality to violate. The ethical implications of such a position are severe.

Antirealism and Responsibility

A second, more insidious problem with antirealist therapy relates to an accumulated body of empirically based knowledge of psychology in general, and of psychotherapy in particular. From the antirealist/postmodernist perspective, there is no objective truth, but only local truths. The accumulated empirically based knowledge of psychology and psychotherapy are in that category, are particular to that community (i.e., scientists), and, as stated by Gergen and Kaye (1992), carry no special authority or privilege. One local truth is as good as another. Thus, the research on psychopathology, its etiology, and its treatment has no special authority. For example, the American Psychological Association Task Force on Psychological Intervention Guidelines (1994) indicated that cognitive-behavioral therapy is a very effective therapy for a range of presenting problems (e.g., anxiety, depression, phobias, obesity). Said report, however, is only a local truth that need have no meaning for the antirealist therapist, who is free to construct any meaning or any narrative in whatever manner he or she chooses. There is only the uniqueness of the client and his or her story with which the therapist has to deal. Could one imagine consulting a medical doctor who dismisses the science-based practice of cancer treatment in favor his or her own local truths?

Epistemological Oscillation

Philosopher John Searle (Levitt, 1997) points out that the antirealist confuses the epistemological with the ontological. Ontological realism is a position that virtually everyone assumes automatically, whereas antirealism is incoherent since it offers no manner of validation and is internally contradictory. Levitt (1997) points out that "realism is not so much a formal doctrine as it is the unspoken ground of all discourse, all attempts at communication" (p. 81). Any sincere declarative utterance is an attempt to give a true account of something presumed to be real. When I state that I drove my car to the store, I am not driving or visiting a symbolic representation or manifestation of "car" or "store." I am driving an actual 3,000-pound vehicle through time and space to a place. Thus, when the antirealist says that science, or the client's given story of personal inadequacy, is just one of many narratives, that antirealist is absolutely conceding that science, scientists, narratives, logical positivism, data, and cars and stores *exist* (i.e., are real). This is what Held (1995) calls "epistemological oscillation" when she says: "Within the postmodern narrative therapy movement, we therefore find a general causal claim: narrative/discourse *itself* — that is, whether or not any particular manifestation of it is extralinguistically true — affects extralinguistic behavior or events" (p. 138).

Consider the simple example of the client's belief/story/theory that her husband yells at her because he feels inadequate in some aspect of his life, which could lead to a different client response than that elicited by a belief/story/theory that he yells at her because he feels she deserves that sort of treatment. The story/belief/theory of the client affects her behavior. Held (1995) notes:

> This claim about the effects of narrative/discourse on extralinguistic behavior is perfectly general precisely because it transcends the unique, particular content of any individual client's narrative; indeed, it is the adoption of this sort of general, predetermined claim that entitles narrative therapy to call itself a *system* of therapy. Thus the fact that the problem and solution narratives — whatever their particular content — may not, according to the postmodern narrative system of therapy, accurately reflect any independent, extralinguistic reality does not diminish the realism behind its claim that narrative/discourse *itself* affects behavior that is external to — independent of — the language/narrative in use. (p. 139)

She drives this point home when she states:

> The narrative metatheory of problem resolution (i.e., that the co-creation of new narratives is the way to solve "problems") retains an underlying realism that is denied but that nonetheless permeates the very tissue of its argument. (p. 139)
>
> They express that extreme explicitly when they speak of epistemology (and not of therapy), and then withdraw that extreme when they speak of their theory and practice of therapy (not epistemology). Evidently, they are caught between a realization that there are many things in life, especially life in therapy, that we cannot know directly or cannot know at all — not even indirectly — and the wish to insist that nevertheless there is some knowledge of reality about the workings of therapy. (p. 161)

She later avers with regard to postmodern narrative therapists:

> They have failed to notice that once formed by rationality's formative function, those stories have a real, independent (of any particular knower), consistent existence *as* stories, or linguistic entities. That is, stories themselves become part of knowable reality, and a direct knowable reality at that. Indeed, dominant discourses would not oppress and so would not be the object of so much postmodern concern if they did not persist — both in their composite parts and in their meanings — over persons, place, and time. They also could not be the object of systematic postmodern study if they themselves — realist or antirealist — were not directly knowable as discourses. (p. 187)

In essence, the client's narrative has *stability over time* (if not, then one would not need therapy to change it), and as such has real ontological status that becomes available to direct rational awareness (Held, 1995). As such, it is inescapable to conclude that the antirealist is, *malgre lui*, as much an ontological realist as any logical positivist, albeit a confused one.

BACK TO THE REALITY WE NEVER LEFT

As discussed earlier, one of Milton Erickson's criticisms of most schools of therapy was their rigidity in theory and in practice, particularly psychodynamically oriented approaches (Rossi, 1980). Within the psychodynamic orientation, the client was made to fit the theory and intervention — a "one size fits all" approach. If the client chafed at such an orientation, he or she was judged to be resistant, which served to provide further proof of the correctness of the theory. Although I agree with Erickson's rejection of theory rigidity in favor of considering the uniqueness of the individual, this does not require a rejection of preexisting knowledge and acceptance of antirealism. Let us briefly consider a general description of a system of therapy.

A complete therapy system has three component parts (Held, 1999):

1. One or more descriptions of what constitutes the problem or pathology.
2. One or more theories about what causes the problem or pathology (from the biological to the psychological). Within this frame, the cause, in order for change to occur, must be at least considered and discussed.
3. One or more methods of intervention to alleviate the problem under discussion.

Thus, in their attempt to individualize practice, the solution-focused/narrative therapies resort to antirealism by claiming that all knowledge is biased and an intersubjective local truth (Held, 1995, 1999). What they really have done is simply to eliminate points 1 and 2 and create an *incomplete* system of therapy. Their practice then, guided by their incomplete system, is, by definition, less systematic, less rule governed, and not replicable (i.e., antisystematic) (Held, 1995, 1999). This is the price to be paid for an exclusionary emphasis on individualized practice. However, the reality of logical incoherence raises its ugly head at this point in the discussion. Are we to believe that the narrative therapist thinks this approach has no effect on the client's life, linguistically or otherwise (i.e., how he or she functions as a result of psychotherapy)? Are we to believe that since all truths are local and there is no external objective truth, the narrative therapist considers this approach to therapy no better or no worse than the most reality based of all therapies — behavior modification? I think one can safely answer "No" to these questions.

As pointed out in footnote 1, Hegel believed his relativistic notion of truth to be absolutely true. And so it is with the antirealist narrative therapist, who, in stating that there is no predetermined external reality, and so therapies taking such a position are in epistemological error, clearly implies this approach to be superior to other therapies (i.e., it really helps clients to live better in the real world). In order for such a claim to be true, it must submit to some systematic form of evaluation (i.e., the scientific method). To make such claims in the absence of empirical evidence (i.e., to dismiss the validity of the scientific method) is simply to make the argument on the basis of special pleading: this is so because it should be so. Although this argument is less than compelling logically, it clearly implies some degree of realism.

If Held (1999) is correct that the purpose of antirealism is to enhance the individualization of practice (i.e., to recognize the uniqueness of the individual), then it is in fact an impediment to this goal. We have learned from Erickson first, followed by Haley, Watzlawick, de Shazer, and colleagues, that careful observation of the individual is central to recognizing the uniqueness of that individual. If there is no external truth, then observation, careful or not, is a contradictory waste of time. This is the problem with antirealism: one cannot apply it in dabs, as one would use a spot remover, but once called upon, it negates all observable and verifiable aspects of existence, including the unique lives of clients. Everything becomes a story that has no more privilege or authority than any other story.

Thus, the development of an individualized approach to the practice of psychotherapy requires a realist epistemology based on two important premises (Held, 1999):

1. There is no basis for thinking that clients have no objective, rational awareness of at least some aspects of their lives. The client's unique view of his or her experience in the world does not necessitate antirealism. As such, the brief therapist should not confuse the issue of individualization in therapy with being antirealist or antisystematic.
2. We have to know what clients really think about their lives. Whether they are correct or incorrect in their understanding of their life experience, we as therapists really have to know how correct or incorrect they are so that reframing/restorying can take place. In order to do this, clear, consistent observation is required so that we can attend to what is truly unique about a given client (Held, 1999).

Solution-focused and/or narrative therapy, in its commitment to an individualized approach, requires both keen observation and an antisystematic belief that dismisses all prior predetermined knowledge. That keen observation is a requirement of all therapists in any system of therapy seems reasonable. However, that an antisystematic approach produces an effective system (i.e., identifiable/measurable therapeutic change takes place) is an empirical question that is realistic in epistemology and needs to be answered by keen (i.e., the scientific method) observation (Held, 1999).

Ultimately, the question regarding solution-focused/narrative therapies is simple, yet very important: "Do clients improve (change their behavior, beliefs, attitudes) as a function of solution-focused/narrative therapies when compared with some other form of therapy and no treatment?" Psychoanalysis, as created by Sigmund Freud, was never interested in such a question, and became merely a form of literary criticism in which its practitioners engaged. If solution-focused and narrative approaches have something to offer as systems of therapy (which I believe they do), then these therapies must be evaluated systematically and compared with other approaches. Antirealist epistemology serves only to detract from a systematic understanding of these methods of therapy, is inherently contradictory, and can be abandoned without detriment to the commitment to individualized practice.

References

Allman, L. R. (1982). The aesthetic preference: Overcoming the pragmatic error. *Family Process*, *21*(1), 43–56.

American Psychological Association Task Force on Psychological Intervention Guidelines. (1994). Washington, DC: Author.

Anderson, H., & Goolishian, H. (1988). Human systems as linguistic systems. *Family Process*, *27*, 271–393.

Bateson, G. (1980). *Mind and nature: A necessary unity*. New York: Ballantine.

Carroll, J. (1996). *Evolution and literary theory*. Columbia: University of Missouri Press.

Crews, F. (1997). The legacy of Salem: Demonology for an age of science. *Skeptic Magazine*, *5*(1), 36–44.

Dell, P. F. (1982). Beyond homeostasis: Toward a concept of coherence. *Family Process*, *21*(1), 21–42.

de Shazer, S. (1982). Some conceptual distinctions are more useful than others. *Family Process*, *21*(1), 71–84.

de Shazer, S. (1985). *Keys to solution in brief therapy*. New York: Guilford.

de Shazer, S. (1991). *Putting difference to work*. New York: Norton.

de Shazer, S. (1993). Creative misunderstandings: There is no escape from language. In S. Gilligan & R. Price (Eds.), *Therapeutic conversations* (pp. 81–90). New York: Norton.

de Shazer, S. & Berg, I. K. (1992). Doing therapy: A post-structural re-vision. *Journal of Marital and Family Therapy*, *18*, 71–81.

Efran, J. S., & Lukens, M. (1985). The world according to Humberto Maturana. *Family Therapy Networker*, May–June, *23–28*, 72–75.

Efran, J. S., Lukens, M. D., & Lukens, R. J. (1990). *Language, structure, and change: Framework of meaning in psychotherapy*. New York: Norton.

Fox, R. (1996). State of the art/science in anthropology. In P. Gross, N. Levitt, & M. Lewis (Eds.), *The flight from science and reason, Vol. 775*. New York: New York Academy of Science.

Freedman, J., & Coombs, G. (1996). *Narrative therapy: The social construction of preferred realities*. New York: Norton.

Gergen, K. (1985). The social constructionist movement in modern psychology. *American Psychologist*, *40*, 266–275.

Gergen, K. (1991). *The saturated self*. New York: Basic Books.

Gergen, K., & Kaye, J. (1992). Beyond narrative in the negotiation of therapeutic meaning. In S. Kvale (Ed.), *Psychology and postmodernism*. Newbury Park, CA: Sage.

Gross, P. R., & Levitt, N. (1994). *Higher superstition: The academic left and its quarrels with science*. Baltimore: Johns Hopkins University Press.

Haley, J. (1963). *Strategies of psychotherapy*. New York: Grune & Stratton.

Haley, J. (1973). *Uncommon therapy: The psychiatric techniques of Milton H. Erickson, M.D.* New York: Norton.

Held, B. S. (1995). *Back to reality*. New York: Norton.

Held, B. S. (1996). Constructivism in psychology: Truth and consequences. The flight from science and reason. *Annals of the New York Academy of Sciences*, *775*, 198–206.

Held, B. S. (1999). How brief therapy got postmodern, or, where's the brief? In W. Matthews, & J. Edgette (Eds.), *Current thinking and research in brief therapy: Solutions, strategies, narratives*. Philadelphia: Taylor & Francis.

Hoffman, L. (1986). Beyond power and control: Toward a "second order" family systems therapy. *Family Systems Medicine*, *3*, 381–396.

Keeney, B., & Sprenkle, D. (1982). Ecosystemic epistemology: Critical implications for the aesthetics and pragmatics of family therapy. *Family Process*, *21*(1), 1–20.

Kvale, S. (1992). Postmodern psychology: A contradiction in terms? In S. Kvale (Ed.), *Psychology and postmodernism*. Newbury Park, CA: Sage.

Lankton, S., & Lankton, C. (1983). *The answer within: A clinical framework of Ericksonian hypnotherapy.* New York: Brunner/Mazel.

Levitt, N. (1997). More higher superstitions: Knowledge, knowingness, and reality. *Skeptic Magazine, 4*(4).

Matthews, W. (1985). A cybernetic model of Ericksonian hypnotherapy: One hand draws the other. In S. Lankton (Ed.), *The Ericksonian monographs. No. 1* (pp. 42–60). New York: Brunner/Mazel.

Matthews, W. J. (1998). Let's get real: The fallacy of postmodernism. *Journal of Theoretical and Philosophical Psychology. 18,* 16–33.

O'Hanlon, W. (1994). The third wave. *Family Therapy Networker,* Nov./Dec., 19–29.

O'Hanlon, W., & Weiner-Davis, M. (1989). *In search of solutions: A new direction in psychotherapy.* New York: Norton.

Phillips, D. C. (1995). The good, the bad, the ugly: The many faces of constructivism. *Educational Researcher, 24*(7), 5–12.

Popper, K. (1994). *The myth of the framework: In defence of science and rationality.* M. A. Notturno (Ed.). London: Routledge.

Prilleltensky, I. (1997). Values, assumptions, and practices: Assessing the moral implications of psychological discourse and action. *American Psychologist, 52,* 517–535.

Rossi, E. (Ed.). (1980). *The collected papers of Milton H. Erickson, M.D.* New York: Irvington.

Selekman, M. (1993). *Pathways to change: Brief therapy solutions with difficult adolescents.* New York: Guilford.

Selvini-Palazolli, M., Cecchin, G., Prata, J., & Bosclo, L. (1978). *Paradox and counterparadox.* New York: Jason Aronson.

Watzlawick, P. (1976). *How real is real?* New York: Random House.

Watzlawick, P. (1978). *The language of change: Elements of therapeutic change.* New York: Basic Books.

Watzlawick, P. (Ed.). (1984). *The invented reality.* New York: Norton.

Watzlawick, P., Weakland, J., & Fisch, R. (1974). *Change: Principles of problem formation and problem resolution.* New York: Norton.

Weakland, J., Fisch, R., Watzlawick, P., & Bodin, A. (1974). Brief therapy: Focused problem resolution. *Family Process, 13*(2), 141–168.

White, M. (1993). Deconstruction and therapy. In S. Gilligan & R. Price (Eds.), *Therapeutic conversations* (pp. 22–61). New York: Norton.

White, M., & Epston, D. (1990). *Narrative means to therapeutic ends.* New York: Norton.

10

Brief Therapy as a Growth Industry

James O. Prochaska

Whether brief therapy survives in its current form or as a growth industry depends, in part, on our readiness to transform ourselves and our field. Business as can only bode ill for the future. Si Budman, a leader in time-effective therapy, was formerly the director of mental health research at the HMO that has been cited as the best in the nation. That HMO has one of the most liberal ratios of subscribers to therapists, about 3,000 to 1. Kaiser-Permanente, which is also considered liberal, has about 5,000 to 1. Budman says that once all mental health is monitored as closely as it is at Kaiser and at his former HMO, there will be twice to three times as many mental health specialists available as health-care systems currently need.[1]

The signs of decline are obvious. In Rhode Island, for example, the largest insurer, Blue Cross, has notified all mental health specialists that their reimbursement rates for psychotherapy will be reduced by at least 15%. Even more unsettling was the announcement that approximately 50% of mental health providers no longer would be covered. In Califor-

[1] The research cited here was supported by National Cancer Institute Grants CA 27821, CA 50087, and CA 63745.

nia, reports are that mental health specialists have been downsized by about 40% in terms of incomes and opportunities.

What is particularly depressing is that such declines are occurring at a time when it is becoming apparent how important brief psychotherapy could be to the health of individuals and their families, communities, companies, and health-care systems. The top 10 killers of our time are all behaviors: smoking, alcohol and drug abuse, obesity, lack of exercise, unhealthy diet, accidents caused by risk taking, stress, chronic hostility, and depression.

The cost of health care in the United States exceeds $1 trillion and is increasing, in part because managed care has invested almost everything in cutting costs and almost nothing in preventing them. Of the total amount, 7–8% is spent on pharmaceuticals, one of the most profitable areas of our economy, but behavior problems account for 50–60% of total health-care costs.

Because behavioral health services reach so few people, however, less than 5% of the total behavior costs are treated effectively. Our first major transformation must be to redefine our field from mental health to all of health. Brief therapy is first and foremost about changing behavior. The more deadly, damaging, or costly the behavior, the higher the priority it must be given by the science and profession of behavioral change.

Fewer than 25% of people with DSM-IV-R diagnoses ever see a professional mental health provider (Veroff, Douvan, & Kulka, 1981a, 1981b), and fewer than 10% of those with high-risk health behavior problems, such smoking or obesity, ever see a behavior health specialist (USDHHS, 1990).

Such statistics could depress us — or they could energize us. Executives of one of the world's largest and most diversified health-care-products companies looked at the figures and envisioned the following future. In 10 to 15 years, the company will be the world's leading health-behavior company, with psychology rather than biology its major innovator. This is a corporation whose research budget is bigger than that of any National Institutes of Health, with the exception of the National Cancer Institute. Until recently, none of its budget for research and development was allotted to behavior. What these business visionaries do not realize is that neither behavior change scientists nor practitioners are prepared for such a transformation.

Managers of the National Health Service in Great Britain looked at similar statistics for that country, and concluded that what is currently in place is a National Illness Service that must be transformed into a Health Promotion Service, with behavioral change its primary business.

If behavior accounts for 50–60% of the costs in health-care systems, imagine what percentage it represents in legal and educational systems. Every major corporation in the world is undergoing at least one significant transformation, such as merging and reengineering, including implementing integrative technologies. Organization-change gurus estimate that about 75% of such transitions will fail — about the same failure rate that our best behavior-change programs report with such major killers as smoking, alcohol abuse, and obesity. A study of 400 corporations found that the prime reason for the failure of organizational-change initiatives is the employees' resistance to changing their behavior. As a result, many organizations turn to downsizing so that they don't have to deal with behavior change.

Behavior change is destined to become a multitrillion-dollar business. But will brief therapists lead in implementing the trend or resist it? Are we so busy trying to hold on to what we have that we cannot see what we could have?

A century ago, those who built horse whips and buggies could not imagine that their age-old business someday would be replaced by the manufacture of automobiles. I am afraid that psychotherapists who are trying to hold on to their age-old ways of practicing will soon be in need of a whipping boy. Managed-care administrators are the first candidates to come to mind.

I am convinced that psychotherapy as a science, and as a practice, must reinvent itself, if it is to be a leader in behavior health and behavior change. Just because we are experts does not make us leaders. Leaders are those who create the future, whereas experts all too often are those who would perpetuate the past.

One of the first things the British did to prepare for behavior change as the number one concern of Great Britain's National Health Service was to turn to the research literature to identify evidence-based practices that could treat high-cost behaviors on a population basis and not just on the basis of individual patients. If such conditions as the addictions and depression are so costly to clients, communities, and health-care systems, then we must be prepared to treat as many of these problems as possible, and not just the small percentage of patients who historically have found their way to psychotherapy.

Depression, for example, has been cited as second only to cardiovascular disease as the most costly complaint in the United States. But most depression goes undiagnosed or is misdiagnosed, remains untreated or is mistreated. Less than 20% of those with major depression ever see a mental health specialist (Veroff, Douvan, & Kulka, 1981a, 1981b). Almost all psychotherapists can manage depression on an individual-case basis, but few are prepared to manage it on a population basis. Thus, the second major transformation we must make is to shift our responsibility from individual patients with problems to entire populations with those problems.

What does the research literature teach us about how to treat problem behaviors from a population perspective? Most of the largest and best clinical trials ever carried out with entire communities, workforces, or at schools have been reporting their results over the past several years. What they can teach us is what not to do, since their outcomes have been almost uniformly disappointing.

Consider the Minnesota Heart Health Program, for example. It had five years and $40 million to intervene in such behaviors as smoking, obesity, and sedentary lifestyles in four communities. After five years of treatment and three years of follow-up, it showed no significant differences in the treated population of smokers as compared with the controls (Luepker et al., 1994). The same pattern was true of almost all of the targeted behavioral risk factors for cardiovascular disease.

"What went wrong?" the organizers of the project wanted to know. Maybe they should have treated only one behavior, such as smoking, rather than spread their resources across multiple behaviors. But aren't people with multiple behavior problems the ones who are at greatest risk, are most costly, and are most in need of help? Furthermore, a report on the COMMIT trial (COMMIT Research Group, 1995), the largest community trial ever completed and which focused on smoking, revealed that there were no significant differences between the treated populations and the controls.

A closer examination of the Minnesota project can provide some clues as to what went wrong (Lando et al., 1995). When asked if they had seen any stories about smoking in newspapers or on television or heard them on the radio, nearly 90% of both the treated and untreated populations reported that they had. So the media are doing a good job of reaching populations with information about behavior health. But when queried as to whether a physician had asked about their smoking in the past year, only about 12% of each population said "Yes." And what about the most powerful approaches to behavior change? What about brief-therapy programs, such as counseling and group clinics, that can provide individualized and interactive help to participants? Only 4% of the treated communities and 3% of the controls had participated in such programs.

When managed-care organizations across the country offer free action-oriented smoking-cessation counseling in clinics, only about 1% of eligible subscribers participate. We simply cannot have an impact on the health of Americans and the high costs of health care if with our best brief therapies we only reach 1–4% of the populations exhibiting the most damaging behaviors.

FROM AN ACTION TO A STAGE PARADIGM

The third transformation we must make, then, is from an action paradigm to a stage paradigm for behavior change. If our profession continues to offer action-oriented therapies to populations that are not prepared to take action, what will result are low participation rates and low impacts for our profession. Table 1 presents the stage distributions of three different populations of smokers (Velicer et al., 1995). Although smoking has been the nation's leading public-health problem for the last 35 years, only some 20% of current smokers are prepared to take action to stop their smoking. About 40% of smokers are in the precontemplation stage and are not intending to take action within the next six months. Approximately 40% are in the contemplation stage and do not intend to take action within the next month.

If we are to help more people, and if we are to help ourselves by identifying more professional opportunities, then we will need to offer services for the 80% who are not ready to take action, and not just the 20% who are.

There are six stages of change in the stage paradigm: (1) precontemplation (not intending to take action); (2) contemplation (intending but not ready); (3) preparation (ready to take action now); (4) action (reached the criterion for recovery in the past six months); (5) maintenance (sustained recovery for more than six months); (6) termination (recovered for more

Table 1. Distribution of Smokers Across Four Different Samples

		Stage		
Sample	*n*	Precontemplation	Contemplation	Preparation
Random digit dial	4,144	42.1%	40.3%	17.6%
Four U.S. work sites	4,785	41.1%	38.7%	20.1%
California	9,534	37.3%	46.7%	16.0%
Rhode Island high schools	208	43.8%	38.0%	18.3%

than six months and zero risk of relapse). Note that the action stage is integrated as one of the six stages. All that we have learned about effective action can be included in this paradigm and can be complemented by the changes that precede and follow the action stage.

In the stage paradigm, behavior change is no longer understood as an event whereby someone dramatically changes by quitting smoking or drinking or by suddenly exercising or losing weight. Behavior change is a process that unfolds over time and involves progress through a series of steps.

Elsewhere we have described in detail each of the stages of change and the 14 principles and processes of change that are most useful in helping people progress from one stage to the next (Prochaska, Norcross, & DiClemente, 1994). Here we shall focus on how a stage approach to brief therapy can help meet five of the most important challenges for behavior health treatment programs: (1) recruitment; (2) retention; (3) progress; (4) process; and (5) outcomes.

Managed care has become increasingly preoccupied with outcomes. But outcomes are a function of inputs. How important are outcomes if the input into programs is only 1–4% of the people with the most costly of conditions?

THE CHALLENGES

Recruitment

We have already seen how action-oriented programs can fail from the start by recruiting or reaching such small percentages of unhealthy populations. This challenge of reaching or recruiting entire populations with high-cost conditions can be met through a fourth transformation. We must shift from a passive-reactive approach to the practice of brief therapy to a proactive approach, where we reach out to people with chronic behavior problems, rather than wait for them to reach us. As has already been shown, practicing passive-reactive therapy results in too few people with behavior health problems ever participating in professional programs.

Here is what the Cancer Prevention Research Center has demonstrated in a series of large-scale clinical trials. With a representative population of about 5,000 smokers, we were able to recruit 82.3% to undergo stage-matched brief interventions. With a population of about 4,500 smokers from an HMO, we were able to reach and recruit 85%. With regard to teenage smokers, the Surgeon General's Report of 1994 concluded that cessation therapies were not a meaningful alternative because so few adolescent smokers would participate. With a population of 6,000 ninth graders in 23 schools in Rhode Island, we were able to recruit over 90% of the teenagers into multiple behavior-change programs that included smoking cessation.

To produce high participation rates involves two of the major transformations: stage-matched programs provided via proactive outreach. What happens if only proactive recruitment is utilized? Kaiser tried this approach with entire populations of smokers (Lichtenstein & Hollis, 1992). Only 1% had been participating in Kaiser's action-oriented cessation clinics.

So every physician was asked to take time with each smoker to get him or her to sign up for a cessation clinic. If that didn't work, nurses would take up to 10 minutes to get smokers to sign up. If that didn't work, health educators with videos would take up to 15 minutes to teach smokers about the benefits of the clinics. And if that didn't work, telephone counselors would call the smokers to persuade them to sign up.

This most intensive proactive recruitment protocol in the research literature resulted in 35% of the smokers in the precontemplation stage signing up. But only 3% attended, of whom 2% finished the protocol and 0% ended up better off. Of smokers in a combined contemplation and preparation group, 65% signed up, 15% showed up, 11% finished up, and a small percentage ended up quitting (Lichtenstein & Hollis, 1992).

Historically, what was the modal number of sessions patients spent in therapy before brief therapy was the prescribed approach? Most therapists guess "one" which is correct, except that the sign is wrong: -1 means call and no show.

In the future, brief therapists may not be responsible for most of the proactive recruitment. But they need to be responsible for matching the therapeutic needs of the vast majority of populations who are identified and referred for therapy and who are in the precontemplation or contemplation stages of change.

One way that brief therapists can participate in proactive recruitment for high cost conditions is with the children of patients with particular problems. If an adult patient with a history of major depression or addiction has a child, that child is at risk of acquiring depression or addiction. If children have two parents with such problems, then their risk factors are over 70%. Proactively reaching out to children of such patients or to adolescents and screening them yearly can be a brief and low-cost approach to prevention or early intervention. Women with just one first-degree relative with breast cancer must be seen yearly for primary or secondary prevention, if health-care systems are to meet the standards for quality health care and avoid potential malpractice charges. The same will be true in the future for children who are known to be at elevated risk for major behavior health problems. In my practice, most parents have welcomed, and been relieved by, my proactively reaching out to their children to develop a brief (single-session) therapeutic relationship. Such parents do not want their problems to be passed on to the next generation, if they can prevent it.

Retention

Once we reach many more therapy participants than ever before, will we be able to retain them until therapy has been completed? Not if we continue with past practices. One of the skeletons in the closet of psychotherapy is that about 50% of clients drop out of therapy (Wierzbicki & Pekarik, 1993). The median number of sessions has been three, meaning that only about 50% of patients complete more than three therapy sessions. Across 125 studies, there was little ability to predict who would drop out, except that minorities, people with less education, and those with addiction problems are more likely to do so, but these groups didn't account for many of our drop outs. One series of studies on alcohol abuse, obesity, heroin abuse, smoking, and general psychotherapy indicated that the best predictor of dropping out is the stage the clients are in. In a study on general psychotherapy, we were able to predict 93% of the patients who would terminate prematurely as judged by their therapists (Brogan, Prochaska, & Prochaska, 1999). The 40% who were premature terminators had a group profile of patients in precontemplation. The 10% who terminated quickly but appropriately had a profile of people in the action stage. Those who continued therapy longer had a mixed profile, with most in the contemplation stage.

We cannot treat people in the precontemplation stage as if they are prepared to take action and expect them to stay with us. We drive them away, and then we blame them as noncompliant, resistant, unmotivated, or not ready for therapy. We now know that it was us who were not ready for them.

With a patient entering therapy already in the action stage for a problem such as addiction, what would be an appropriate therapeutic strategy? Relapse prevention à la Allan Marlott would be recommended. But would relapse prevention make any sense for someone in precontemplation. What clinical strategies would we recommend? Dropout prevention would be appropriate. There are now four clinical trials that show that if we match our therapy to the client's stage of change, then those in precontemplation at the start will complete our brief interventions at the same high rates as those in the preparation stage. Thus, the fifth transformation we will need to make is to match our therapies to the client's stage of change, rather than to expect participants to match our therapies.

Progress

How can we help people progress who have been stuck in the precontemplation or contemplation stage for long periods of time? The same way we would with any effective brief therapy: by setting realistic goals for them and for ourselves. What is realistic is to help people progress through one stage in one brief encounter. If we help them to accomplish that, then we double the chances that they will take effective action within the next six months. If we help them to progress through two stages, we can quadruple the chances that they will take such action. We will see how such progress can produce major impacts on a population basis.

As more and more therapists shift to brief therapy, there is the serious risk that they will feel pressured to define it as action-oriented therapy. We have already seen that if all we offer is brief action-oriented therapies, then the consequences are predictable: most people won't sign up, show up, finish up, or end up better off.

The stage paradigm has been taught to over 6,000 health professionals in Great Britain; that is, to reach out proactively to all patients with problems related to alcohol and substance abuse, smoking, and obesity. These professionals have been taught to set realistic goals of helping each patient progress through one stage in one brief interaction.

The first results have been a dramatic increase in the morale of health professionals because they can see progress with the vast majority of their populations, whereas they saw failure when immediate action was the only goal. The sixth transformation is what I teach my students: We should adopt therapy models that are good for our mental health as well as for our clients' mental health, because clients are in therapy for a brief time, but we are in therapy for a lifetime.

Process

The process of producing progress from one stage to the next goes beyond the scope of this chapter. As indicated earlier, there are 14 principles and processes that need to be applied systematically at each stage of change (Prochaska, Norcross, & DiClemente, 1994). Different principles and processes are emphasized at different stages of change. Learning how to match particular processes of change is the seventh transformation needed to practice population-based behavior health.

Outcomes and Impacts

What happens when we combine all of these principles and processes of change to help patients and entire populations to progress toward action? What are the outcomes that can be produced with groups of patients and the impacts on entire populations when stage-matched interventions are proactively delivered to those populations? We will examine a series of clinical trials applying stage-matched interventions to see what lessons we might learn about the future of behavior health and mental health care.

In our first large-scale clinical trial we compared four treatments: (1) one of the best home-based action-oriented cessation programs (standardized); (2) stage-matched manuals (individualized); (3) expert system computer reports plus manuals (interactive); and (4) counselors plus computers and manuals (personalized). We randomly assigned 739 smokers by stage to one of the four treatments (Prochaska, DiClemente, Velicer, & Rossi, 1993).

In the computer condition, using mail or the telephone, participants answered 40 questions and these answers were entered into our central computers and generated feedback reports. These reports informed participants about their stage of change, the pros and cons of their changing, and their use of change processes appropriate to their stages. At baseline, participants were given positive feedback on what they were doing correctly and guidance as to which principles and processes they needed to apply more in order to progress. In two progress reports delivered over the next six months, participants also received positive feedback concerning any improvement they had made on any of the variables relevant to progressing. So, demoralized and defensive smokers could begin progressing without having to quit and without having to work too hard. Smokers in the contemplation stage could begin taking small steps, such as delaying their first cigarette in the morning for an extra 30 minutes. They could choose small steps that would increase their self-efficacy and help them to become better prepared for quitting.

In the personalized condition, smokers received four proactive counselor calls over the six-month intervention period. Three of the calls were based on the computer reports. Counselors reported much more difficulty in interacting with participants without any progress data. Without scientific assessments, it was much harder for both the clients and the counselors to tell whether any significant progress had been made since their last interaction.

Figure 1 presents point-prevalence abstinence rates for each of the four treatment groups over 18 months, with treatment ending at six months. The two self-help-manual conditions paralleled each other for 12 months. At 18 months, the stage-matched manuals moved ahead. This is an example of a *delayed action effect*, which we often observe with stage-matched programs specifically, and others have observed with self-help programs in general. It takes time for participants in early stages to progress all the way to action. Therefore, some treatment effects as measured by action will be observed only after considerable delay. But it is encouraging to find treatments producing therapeutic effects months, and even years, after treatment has ended.

The computer alone and computer plus counselor conditions paralleled

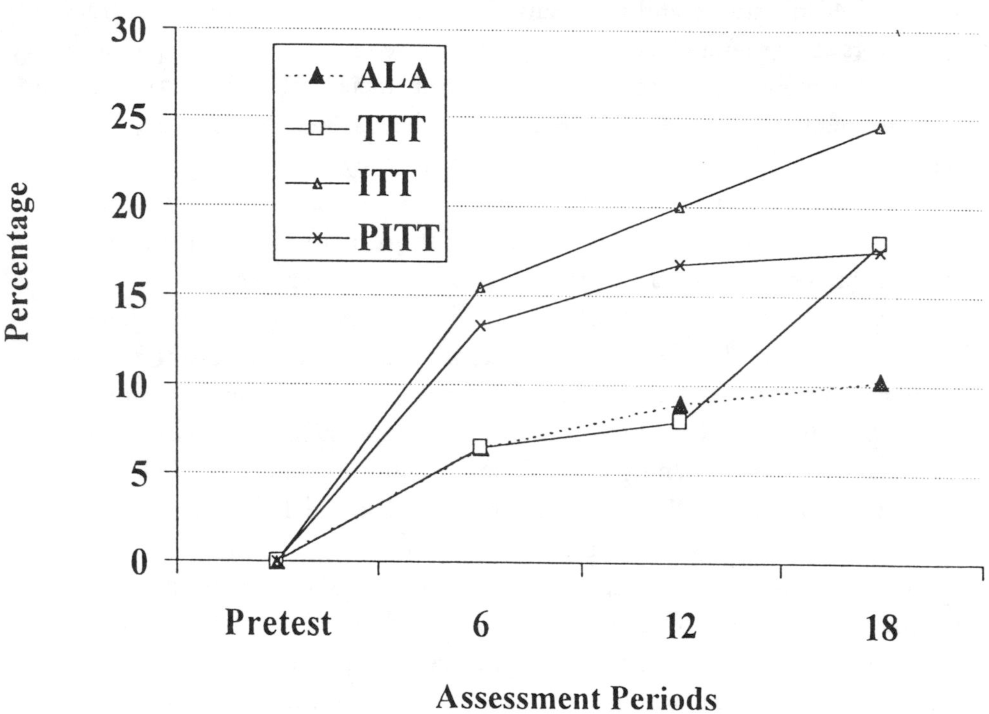

Figure 1. Point-prevalence abstinence (%) for four treatment groups at pretest and at 6, 12, and 18 months. ALA (American Lung Association) + standardized manuals; TTT = individualized stage-matched manuals; ITT = interactive computer reports; PITT = personalized counselor calls.

each other for 12 months. Then the effects of the counselor condition reached a plateau whereas the computer condition effects continued to increase. We can only speculate as to the delayed differences between these two conditions. Participants in the personalized condition may have become somewhat dependent on the social support and control of the counselors' calls. The last call was after the six months of assessment and benefits would be observed at 12 months. Termination of the counselors could result in no further progress because of the loss of the social interaction. The classic pattern in smoking-cessation clinics is that of a rapid relapse beginning as soon as the treatment is terminated. Some of this relapse could well be attributable to the sudden loss of the support or control provided by the counselors and other participants in the clinic.

The next test was to demonstrate the efficacy of the expert system when applied to an entire population that was recruited proactively. With over 80% of 5,170 smokers participating and fewer that 20% in the preparation stage, we demonstrated significant benefits of the expert system at each six-month follow-up (Prochaska, Velicer, Fava, Rossi, & Tsoh, 2000). Furthermore, the advantages over proactive assessment alone were found to be increased at each follow-up over the full two years assessed. The implications here are that expert system interventions may continue to demonstrate benefits long after the interventions have ended.

We then showed remarkable replication of the expert system's efficacy in an HMO population of 4,000 smokers with 85% participation (Prochaska et al., 2000). In the first population-based study, the expert system was 34% more effective than assessment alone; in the second, it was 31% more effective. These replicated differences were clinically significant, as well. While working on a population basis, we were able to produce the level of success normally found only in intense clinic-based programs with low participation rates of more selective samples of smokers (about 25% abstinent). The implication is that once expert systems are developed and show effectiveness with one population, they can be transferred at a much lower cost and produce replicable changes in new populations.

Enhancing Interactive Interventions

In recent research, we have been trying to create enhancements to our expert system to produce even better outcomes. In the first enhancement in our HMO population, we added a personal hand-held computer designed to bring the behavior under stimulus control (Prochaska et al., 2000). This commercially successful innovation was an action-oriented intervention that did not enhance our expert system program on a population basis. In fact, our expert system alone was twice as effective as the system with the enhancement. There are two major implications here: (1) more is not necessarily better, and (2) providing interventions that are mismatched to stage can result in outcomes that are markedly worse.

Counselor Enhancements

In our HMO population, counselors plus expert system computers were outperforming expert systems alone at 12 months. But at 18 months, the effect of the counselor enhancement had declined whereas that of the computers alone had increased. Both interventions were producing identical outcomes of 23.2% abstinence, which are excellent for an entire population. Why did the effect of the counselor condition lessen after the intervention? Our leading hypothesis is that people can become dependent on counselors for the support and monitoring that they provide. Once these social influences are withdrawn, people may do worse. The expert system computers, on the other hand, may maximize self-reliance. In a current clinical trial, we are fading out the use of counselors over time as a way to deal with the dependency on the counselors. If fading is effective, it will have implications for how counseling should be terminated: gradually over time.

We believe that the most powerful change programs will combine the personalized benefits of counselors and consultants with the individualized, interactive, and data-based benefits of expert system computers. But we have not yet been able to demonstrate that the more costly counselors, who had been our most powerful change agents, are actually more efficacious than computers alone. These findings have clear implications as to the cost effectiveness of expert systems for entire populations who need behavior health programs.

Interactive Versus Noninteractive Interventions

Another important aim of the HMO project was to assess whether interactive interventions (computer-generated expert systems) are more effective than noninteractive communications (self-help manuals) when controlling for number of intervention contacts (Velicer, Prochaska, Fava, Laforge, & Rossi, 1999). At 6, 12, and 18 months for groups of smokers receiving a series of one, two, three, or six interactive versus noninteractive contacts, the interactive interventions (expert system) outperformed the noninteractive manuals in all four comparisons. In three of the comparisons (one, two, and three), the differences at 18 months were at least five percentage points, a difference between treatment conditions assumed to be clinically significant. These results clearly support the hypothesis that interactive interventions will outperform the same number of noninteractive interventions.

Thus, these results also support our assumption that the most powerful behavior health programs for entire populations will be interactive. In the reactive clinical literature, it is clear that interactive interventions such as behavioral counseling produce greater long-term abstinence rates (20–30%) than do noninteractive interventions, such as self-help manuals (10–20%). It should be kept in mind that these traditional action-oriented programs were implicitly or explicitly recruiting populations in the preparation stage. Our results indicate that even with proactively recruited smokers, with less than 20% in the preparation stage, the long-term abstinence rates are in the 20–30% range for the interactive interventions and in the 10–20% range for the noninteractive interventions. The implications are clear. Providing interactive interventions via computers is likely to produce a better outcome than is relying on noninteractive communications, such as newsletters, the media, or self-help manuals.

Proactive Versus Reactive Results

We believe that the future of behavior health programs lies with stage-matched, proactive and interactive interventions. Much greater impacts can be generated by proactive programs because of their higher participation rates, even if the efficacy rates are lower. But we also believe that proactive programs can produce outcomes comparable to those of traditional reactive programs. It is counterintuitive to believe that comparable outcomes can be produced with people to whom we reach out to help and with those who call us. But that is what informal comparisons strongly suggest. In comparing 18-month follow-ups for all subjects who received our three expert system reports in our previous reactive study and in our current proactive study, we see that the abstinence curves are remarkably similar (Prochaska, DiClemente, Velicer, & Rossi, 1993; Prochaska et al., 2000).

The results attained with our counseling plus computer conditions were even more impressive. Proactively recruited smokers working with counselors and computers had higher abstinence rates at each follow-up than did the smokers who had called for help. One of the differences is that our proactive counseling protocol had been revised, and we hope, improved, on the basis of previous data and experience. But the point is that, if we reach out and offer people improved behavior change programs that are appropriate for their stage, we probably can produce efficacy or abstinence rates at least equal to those we realize with people who reach out to us for help. Unfortunately, there is no experimental design that could permit us randomly to assign people to proactive versus reactive recruitment programs. We are left with informal, but provocative, comparisons.

If these results continue to be replicated, therapeutic programs will be able to produce unprecedented impacts on entire populations. We believe that such impacts require scientific and professional shifts:

1. from an action paradigm to a stage paradigm;
2. from reactive to proactive recruitment;
3. from expecting participants to match the needs of our programs to having our programs match their needs;
4. from clinic-based to population-based programs that still apply the field's most powerful individualized and interactive intervention strategies.

BUILDING A BEHAVIOR HEALTH CARE DELIVERY SYSTEM

I believe that individualized and interactive technologies will be to behavior health care what medications have been to biological medicine: the most cost-effective approach to bringing optimal science to bear on major health problems in entire populations in a relatively user-friendly manner. Unfortunately, there are therapists who will feel threatened by computers being an integral part of the clinical enterprise. They need to ask themselves: Did the status of physicians decline with the development of such scientific assessment instruments as blood pressure and blood tests or MRIs and CAT scans? Did the salaries of physicians decrease with the widespread use of intervention technologies, such as medication or laser surgery?

On what techniques do psychotherapists rely? They rely on speech and reading matter, such as bibliotherapy. How long have these technologies existed? What advances in medicine would have been made if all physicians could do would be to talk to their patients and give them printed material? Would we go to physicians who had no advanced assessment methods, no medications, and no other technologies for treating us?

Would we continue with clinicians who could only speak to us or provide us with pamphlets to read? The next transformation we have to make is to become the leaders in developing and applying advanced interactive and individualized computer-based technologies that can complement and enhance our work as clinicians.

The final transformation for now will be to build a behavior health care delivery system. Many therapists are angry at managed-care administrators and blame them for the deterioration of behavior health care. However, the fundamental problem is not with the managers, but with the health-care delivery systems they are attempting to manage. What were hospitals designed to deliver? Births, deaths, and surgery. What were outpatient practices designed to deliver? Diagnoses and drugs.

Essentially, then, both of these systems were designed to deliver acute care for acute conditions, such as infectious diseases. The problem is that by the 20th century, these acute conditions no longer were the prime contributors to the death rate, and the acute-care delivery systems upon which we still rely were not designed to treat the behaviors that are the major causes of chronic illness and premature death today.

As history has taught us, out of a need comes a solution, and, thereby, progress. For example, when goods needed to be delivered across the sea, shipping was developed as a major transportation system. When the goods reached land, a new delivery system had to be developed, such as the railroads. When the goods reached the end of the line, another delivery system was needed, namely, highways on which cars and trucks could travel to deliver the goods to the customer.

In behavior health care, we are faced with the equivalent of trying to drive a car down railroad tracks. No wonder it is such a bumpy ride. No wonder we worry about whether or not our vehicle will survive.

Where will be the primary site for behavior health care delivery? Clearly, it won't be hospitals or outpatient clinics. Those are fine for acute care, but they don't reach the many people with the chronic behavioral conditions that can kill them, and that drive the costs of health care up. It is the home that will be the primary site for behavior health care, with telecommunications the primary delivery system.

Who will pay for building this system? Who paid for the new highways? The government paid, through taxes on gasoline. Here is one vision of how the new behavior health care system could be built. Utilizing proactive telephone and mail recruitment, interactive computers, and 40,000 stage-matched counselors paid $60,000 per year, we could reach out to 80% of the smokers in the United States and reduce smoking by 20–25% in 18 to 24 months. This would result in huge public health benefits and savings on health care. The system would also be in place to treat other major behavior health problems, such as depression and addictions, on a population basis. And all of this could be accomplished for less than 10% of the recent settlement of litigation with the tobacco industry.

The 20 transformations outlined in this chapter are all doable right now. The theory is available, the science is available, the technology is available, the professional personnel are available, and the resources to build the system are available. What is needed are therapists and allied health professionals, scientists, and administrators who share a common vision and a common mission to help make these transformations happen.

References

Brogan, M. E., Prochaska, J. O., & Prochaska, J. M. (1999). Predicting termination and continuation status in psychotherapy using the transtheoretical model. *Psychotherapy.*

COMMIT Research Group. (1995). Community Intervention Trial for Smoking Cessation (COMMIT): I. Cohort results from a four-year community intervention. *American Journal of Public Health*, *85*, 183–192.

Lando, H. A., Pechacek, T. E., Pirie, P. L., Murray, D. M., Mittelmark, M. B., Lichtenstein, E., Nothwhyr, F., & Gray, C. (1995). Changes in adult cigarette smoking in the Minnesota Heart Health Program. *American Journal of Public Health*, *75*, 201–208.

Lichtenstein, E., & Hollis, J. (1992). Patient referral to smoking cessation programs: Who follows through? *The Journal of Family Practice*, *34*, 739–744.

Luepker, R. V., Murray, D. M., Jacobs, D. R., et al. (1994). Community education for cardiovascular disease prevention: Risk factor changes in the Minnesota Heart Health Program. *American Journal of Public Health*, *84*, 1383–1393.

Peto, R., & Lopes, A. (1990). World-wide mortality from current smoking patterns. In B. Durstone & K. Jamrogik (Eds.), *The global war: Proceedings of the Seventh World Conference on Tobacco and Health* (pp. 62–68). East Perth, Australia: Organizing Committee of Seventh World Conference on Tobacco and Health.

Prochaska, J. O., DiClemente, C. C., Velicer, W. F., & Rossi, J. S. (1993). Standardized, individualized, interactive and personalized self-help programs for smoking cessation. *Health Psychology*, *12*, 399–405.

Prochaska, J. O., Norcross, J. C., & DiClemente, C. C. (1994). *Changing for good.* New York: Morrow.

Prochaska, J. O., Velicer, W. F., Fava, J., Rossi, J., & Tsoh. (2000). *A stage matched expert system intervention with a total population of smokers.* Manuscript under review.

Prochaska, J. O., Velicer, W. F., Fava, J., Ruggiero, L., Laforge, R., & Rossi, J. (2000). Counselor and stimulus control enhancements of a stage matched expert system for smokers in a managed care setting. Manuscript under review.

U.S. Department of Health and Human Services. (1990). *The health benefits of smoking cessation: A report of the Surgeon General* (DHHS Publication no. CDC 90–8416). Washington, DC: U.S. Government Printing Office.

Velicer, W. F., Fava, J. L., Prochaska, J. O., Abrams, D. B., Emmons, K. M., & Pierce, J. (1995). Distribution of smokers by stage in three representative samples. *Preventive Medicine, 24,* 401–411.

Velicer, W. F., Prochaska, J. O., Fava, J., Laforge, R., & Rossi, J. (1999). Interactive versus non-interactive and dose response relationships for stage matched smoking cessation programs in a managed care setting. *Health Psychology, 18,* 1–8.

Veroff, J., Douvan, E., & Kulka, R. A. (1981a). *The inner America.* New York: Basic Books.

Veroff, J., Douvan, E., & Kulka, R. A. (1981b). *Mental health in America.* New York: Basic Books.

Wierzbicki, M., & Pekarik, G. (1993). A meta-analysis of psychotherapy dropouts. *Professional Psychology: Research and Practice, 29,* 190–195.

11

Revisioning Family Therapy: Culture, Class, Race, and Gender as Hidden Dimensions of Clinical Practice

Monica McGoldrick

I am beginning to realize, slowly and painfully, what Peggy McIntosh (1998) means when she says that we who are white carry around a kind of invisible knapsack of privilege — one that contains special provisions, maps, passports and visas, blank checks and emergency gear. We cannot see it, but those who don't have one can.

So I have been trying to think differently about these issues. To listen, to attempt to learn about my ignorance, so that gradually I can overcome it. I am starting to notice racism in a lot of my work. It may have been unconscious, but I was being racist when I spoke about couples or families and didn't really mean black couples or families, or when I spoke about women and didn't really include black women. In fact, in the mid-1980s, I co-organized conferences for women family therapists, and although we invited women of color, almost none of them came. I kept trying to figure out how to include them — how to get them to recognize the importance of the issues. One who did attend questioned the lack of reference to minority issues. I remember feeling irritated, because I thought how different it was to think about gender inequality, and that if we added race, we'd never get it straight. Now I realize I had it wrong. The truth is, we'll never get it straight if we don't include race in the discussion of gender. Women of color have been saying and showing clearly for a long time that they prioritize gender differently. They have been saying, and showing by their absence and silence, that the field of family therapy hasn't related very much to them. And we have thought it was *their* problem. We thought we could go on with family therapy as usual, even though it was really white family therapy.

I also realize that telling only the stories of the positive values and actions of my family or my culture keeps me part of the problem. Our family trees might include Nazis, as well as victims of the Holocaust; members of the Ku Klux Klan and slave owners, as well as those who suffered racial oppression. Any time I try to distinguish my family or my ancestors from the oppressors, I may be standing next to a person whose ancestors owned slaves, making the acknowledgment of that legacy more difficult. What we need to do is create a crucible that can contain the histories of all of us, noticing our interconnections and helping each other to acknowledge our pasts so that together we can work to change our futures.

But these changes also require that those of us with privilege give up some of our privilege in the interest of social justice. Individually, we will feel less safe or secure, but we will be empowered as a group by our awareness that we are in it together. We will need to realize that we all need to feel secure for any of us to have true security. Our freedom and safety cannot be built on the backs of others. In the words of the Talmud, "It is not our job to finish the work, but we are not free to walk away from it."

REVISIONING THE FAMILY

It takes more than two parents to raise a child. There are 55,000 children in foster care in New York City alone, and they cost the city $300 million a year. If a problem arises, children are removed to a "place of safety." When that happens, the mother has to go into therapy to learn to cope with the removal of her child. Parents need parenting skills groups, groups without children. Mothers can usually visit their children for two hours a week, and it takes an average of 18 months to get the children back. The children then incur the additional scars of losing their mothers, in addition to not having their child-care needs met. We pay our

Some Typical Patterns Whites Use to Avoid Acknowledging Racism:

1. We distinguish ourselves from those with power and privilege by emphasizing ways in which we have personally come from oppressed groups — referring to a great-grandfather who was Cherokee, or to centuries of oppression as Irish or Jewish, or to being gay in a straight world, or to having a mentally ill or abusive parent.
2. We take the moral high ground, saying we do not think of others in terms of their color, culture, or economic class, but as human beings. This makes it impossible to discuss social processes, such as oppression or prejudice, that occur at a group level.
3. We accept criticism and experience deep shame associated with it, but become paralyzed, and then paralyzing to those who raise the issues (Tamasese & Waldegrave, 1993), covertly requesting that they listen to or take care of our pain about our racist behavior.
4. We assume a talking rather than a listening stance in relation to people of color, when the only reasonable position to take is to "listen and believe" (Akamatsu, 1998).
5. We individualize criticisms of oppression, claiming that we can only be responsible for our personal behavior, and then attempt to be individual paragons of cultural or gender equality (Tamasese & Waldegrave, 1993).
6. We say that we feel "unsafe" in an atmosphere of "political correctness," that it makes us feel as though we are walking on eggs, which focuses discussion on our discomfort, implicitly blaming those who are attempting to discuss their oppression for making us uncomfortable, and thus making it impossible to have a discussion about our privileges.

---

zookeepers and janitors more than we pay our child-care workers. Divorced fathers spend more on their car payments than they do on child-care payments.

BELONGING, SACREDNESS, AND LIBERATION: FINDING A PLACE CALLED "HOME"

There were many things about my privilege and about my oppression that I grew up not knowing, or not knowing that I knew, many issues that were obscured or kept out-of-sight by my community and my training. Society's implied structuring of gender, class, culture, race, and sexual orientation limited the relationships in my family, my schooling, and the communities in which I lived. None of these issues was ever mentioned in my childhood, in my adolescence, in my college or graduate experience, or in my study of family therapy. I think "passing" is what everyone in this country has been pressed to do — to accommodate, to fit images, to keep invisible the parts of themselves that do not conform to the dominant culture's values. Historically, some of us have found our safety at the expense of others, mostly without knowing it. We must not seek safety at the risk of jeopardizing others or denying them their own sense of belonging and spiritual connection. I have been wondering what will help us realize, as Susan Griffin (1992) points out, that "our personal stories and the history of the world are all one story" (p. 8). How can we realize that somewhere within ourselves we know the secrets we keep from ourselves and from each other? I have come to realize that "home" is much more than where we live physically. It is not just where we sleep, and it it not just the nostalgic home of our childhood or our wished-for childhood. It is a spiritual and psychological place of liberation. Home is a space where we can all belong — with each other — strengthened by what we take from those who have come before us, creating a safe haven for those who are with us in our time, and ensuring that we leave a safe space for all those who will come after us. I am coming to realize that I must work to create a safe place not just for my own child, but for the children of all of us, who are, as Jorge Luis Borges has put it, "our immortality on earth."

MARGARET BUSH

My primary caretaker, Margaret Bush was another invisible hero of my life. Descended from slaves in, I believe, Asheville, North Carolina, she was the person I was closest to emotionally and physically from the time of my birth until her death the year after I left for college. It was to her I confided my problems — with boyfriends, with teachers, and with my mother. She was always there for me. She loved me unconditionally. She had lost her twin sons and her first husband, and then had to be away from her home with her second husband much of the time in order to live with us. But this was not only Margaret's story. It was a common situation among African Americans who were forced to sacrifice the needs of their own families to those of the white families they served. I miss her every day and she, too, lives in my soul and helped to make me who I am. When I speak, you hear her voice, her struggles, her silences, as they have filtered down to me, as you hear the others who loved and cared for me. And I know I have an ongoing responsibility to her to seek the right relationships among things — and people.

But how do I deal with the shadow side of my relationship with Margaret, who gave to my family the love and care that should have gone to her own. This is the story of racism. What I received was what my African American friends whose mothers or fathers had to serve white families were denied at their own expense. And it is painful to realize that the love and care I received were at the cost of someone else's loss, and that the two — my benefit and the other's deprivation — are intertwined.

I grew up thinking I was innocent, that I had nothing to do with racism, and certainly not with slavery. I did not recognize Margaret's white uniform as a symbol of her status in our family. Nor did I question the fact that she did not learn how to read until after I did, when she was 50 years old. This, too, was a heritage of slavery; slaves could be killed for learning to read, as could anyone who taught them. How ignorant I was not to sense her dilemma. Her invisible life made mine visible. I realize that I am a part of all that came before, that I have benefited from racism, and continue to do so in the unearned privileges I receive merely by being white. These include the fact that most books are written for white readers, so even when Margaret did learn to read, she was forced to begin by reading about Dick and Jane and their white middle-class families, leaving invisible, yet again, her history and the courageous efforts of her ancestors to survive, which would have been an even greater inspiration in her desire to become literate.

We need to learn how to listen to the everyday experiences of people of color and think about the inherent privilege of being white in our society, rather than focusing on how we ourselves are exceptions and are not as privileged as others might think.

I remember when women first spoke out about sexism and men responded by telling us that we were overgeneralizing because they, for example, loved their mothers, were never abusive to women, and did many chores around the house. We used to want to say to them: "Just sit down and give a listen. Rather than focusing on the exceptions, try to take in the pain of what we are saying in terms of the overall situation. When we speak of men's violence, for example, give some acknowledgment, rather than getting irate because we have not mentioned women's violence."

The same admonition applies to those accorded unearned privileges based on their skin color. Of course, accusations of racism are painful for those of us used to feeling like the "good guys." Most white people's image of racism is lynching or the Klu Klux Klan, whereas when people of color use the term, they are often referring to such things as being treated as invisible, being ignored in a store, or being the targets of careless insults that may slip out unconsciously owing to our ignorance of their history or experience. In fact, until recently, whenever I discussed culture, I would preface my comments by confessing my fear that others would hear them as prejudiced or racist, and would appeal to them not to think in those terms. That was when I still thought I wasn't a racist.

And it put the burden on others to make me feel okay. If the subject of racism did come up, I wanted the other person somehow to make peace with the issue by the end of the discussion, just as in our discussions about gender, men assumed that their comments would somehow resolve the issue, so that women no longer would be upset, which assumes that the issues are small, rather than pervasive, and can be resolved by talk, rather than by transforming our social arrangements. More recently I have noticed that if an African American complains of frustration, anger, or pain to a white person, the latter will respond by trying to get him or her feeling "okay" within the course of the conversation. Although I have done this myself, now I realize that I was being arrogant. The problems that are being described can't be taken care of in the space of one conversation. How can we demand that the pain or anger cease, if the issues remain? I realized that my invisible knapsack of privilege must disappear before the conversation can be over. To men who insisted that they were not sexist, I used to say: "Until you are actively working against gender inequality, you are part of the problem." I realize now that unless my own life is about overcoming racism, I am also part of the problem. My privilege will not disappear of its own accord. I must work to ensure that everyone is entitled to the same privileges. Then we all will have a home.

Many white people say that if they allow themselves to become conscious of their unrecognized racism, they will suffer overwhelming guilt and shame. They feel that they would have to give up everything they've acquired to become congruent with the notion of "liberty and justice for all." And so denial becomes an easier approach. They move away from the issues, which is very easy for whites, because our society is so segregated that we can generally live our lives quite oblivious to our connectedness to people of color. We can walk away and pretend that these issues do not relate to us. We can do this as long as we do not think about who cares for us when we are ill, helpless, or old; who sees to our comfort when we are staying in hotels or are on vacation; who makes our shoes and clothing and the home products that keep us comfortable. But our denial will surely hurt us in the long run. So we need to do what we can to stay conscious of the situation, and for that we need each other. Alone, we will get picked off. We will be mystified, silenced, invalidated. We will burn out in the struggle. Together, there is nothing we cannot do. So we must overcome our denial. Thus, I have been trying to think differently about these issues: to listen, to attempt to learn about my ignorance, so that gradually I can overcome it.

ECONOMIC CLASS

We must transform our thinking to become aware of our multiple cultural selves and how we can move marginalized cultural experiences and ideas to the center of our awareness. The dimension of economic class is one of the essential and, until now, most invisible elements of revisioning family therapy from a cultural perspective. It goes unacknowledged that many societal groups are not represented in our political institutions and do not have the same entitlements to participate even in the world of family therapy. It goes unsaid that where you come from does matter, that you cannot shed your past, become whatever you want, or move up just through hard work and desire.

Without my knowing it, my entire life has been organized by class hierarchies. The clothes I wear are a class statement, just like the car I drive or would feel comfortable driving, my house, my furniture, the pictures on my walls. The music I listen to is a class statement: If I say I like opera, it is a class statement. If I say I like country-and-western music, it is a class statement. The same is true of sports — bowling says one thing, tennis or golf another. Where we feel comfortable eating or spending our vacations is all about class (and race and gender, of course). Yet I never acknowledged it nor was it ever mentioned in my training. Everyone knows the class code for all the degrees in our field, yet we don't talk about it: M.D., Ph.D., Ed.D., D.S.W., M.S.W., M.A. We also know the complex code for rating colleges and universities. We all learn the hierarchy: the Ivy League, the Seven Sisters colleges, Harvard, Duke, Berkeley, Georgetown, Notre Dame, Howard, Morehouse, Spellman, Trenton State. Class hierarchies are exquisitely comprehensive. They govern all our social interactions. How we celebrate life-cycle rituals, such as death or marriage, is a matter of class (as well as of gender, race, culture, and sexual orientation). In my family, since the early 1960s, it would be "declassé" to have a fancy wedding, with prescribed outfits, food, drink, and music. But for other classes, these are a necessity.

I realized how pervasively and how insidiously the rules of class influence our feeling of "otherness," of not being "okay," in one situation or another, and how much we feel the need to hide who we are – whether to hide Anglo roots or money that would distance us socially in the mental health field, or to hide our poverty or working-class origins. In addition to the invisibility of class as an issue, there is the fact that most of us have changed class. We cannot change our race, our gender, our culture, or our sexual orientation. We can lie about them, but we cannot change them. However, we can, and most Americans do, change class frequently. My parents rose two classes from their parents, who rose one class from *their* parents. My generation moved down half a class, having less social status than my parents had, because of my father's political and academic status. Like most families, mine included members who were in different classes, and the social distance this created was almost never dealt with directly.

Whatever we cannot acknowledge — the secrets we feel we must keep about class, about how much or how little money we have, about class contempt and class elitism, about the pain of unacknowledged class distance from other family members — keeps us from being free. I believe that we should dare to put our prejudices on the table, to examine them, to see their price. I believe we must change our training radically to help trainees muster the courage to discuss these issues. A first step is to acknowledge our prejudices and to know that we will make mistakes — we will blurt out racist comments, sexist comments, and unconscious insults. If we are lucky, someone will draw this to our attention, and we will move along in overcoming our prejudice.

Our entire society, our entire business world, and our entire educational system are organized to accommodate a type of family structure that represents only 3% of U.S. households — nuclear family units with employed fathers and homemaker mothers who devote themselves to the care of their husbands and children. Most family therapy, like our dominant social ideology in general, has tended to be oriented toward this view of families as self-sufficient, usually nuclear, units. However, our definition that two parents are critical for child development has always been a euphemism for a mother who is perpetually on call for everyone, emotionally and physically, and a distant money-providing father. Families with such a structure cannot help being problematic. Poor families are seen as deficient, because they are obviously and critically dependent on systems beyond themselves for their survival. The reality is that more American children die from causes directly related to poverty than American soldiers died during the Vietnam war.

Actually, all families depend for their survival on systems beyond themselves, but those of us who are of the dominant groups fail to realize this, because of the ways in which the government and others support us. Our needs are met, taken for granted, and the mechanisms rendered invisible to us (Coontz, 1992). Schools, courts, the police, and all the other institutions of society basically operate for the protection and benefit of the dominant groups. Thus, those of us who make the rules and create the definitions remain unaware or our privileges (see McIntosh, 1998, Chap. X) and of our dependence on others to take care of us. So the real problem is not the dependence of certain people on the society, but the delusion of autonomy. The dominant groups are depleting the world's resources with no awareness or feeling of accountability (Ehrlich & Ehrlich, 1991; Ehrenreich, 1989). The economic system, the prison system, the drug rehabilitation industry, the gun industry, the legal structure, and the government make money for the dominant groups in society at the expense of the poor and the disenfranchised, who serve us in our homes, hotels, hospitals, and factories, while we remain blind to our connection to them, and to our exploitation and the racism implied by our behavior.

Paradoxically, the ideals stated in the U.S. Constitution could be the foundation of a truly egalitarian society, perhaps the first in human history, but only if we acknowledge and deal with the pernicious, unspoken exclusions. To do this, however, we must acknowledge the issues. Our history books brag about the founding of our nation, while minimizing the slaughter, slavery, and forced invisibility of more than half of the population. This is hard to see, because what we espouse overtly obscures the underlying facts of exclusion. Everything we profess falls at the intersection between the spoken and the unspoken. But our society makes it very difficult to notice the unspoken words or to hear the silent voices.

Along with all other institutions, we in family therapy need to revise our books to make room for the underside of what has been spoken — the unspoken secrets that have structured the cultural-, racial-, class-, and gender-biased hierarchies that are the underpinnings of society. It goes unacknowledged that African Americans are not represented in our formal institutions and do not have the same entitlements to participate, even in the world of family therapy.

REVISIONING FAMILY THERAPY

The failure of society to tolerate diversity is the greatest single threat to the survival of civilization. We have been feeling an increasing need to break out of the constraints of our traditional monocular vision of families as white, heterosexual, and middle class, and to redefine the boundaries of our field, taking into account that diversity and the way that societal oppression has silenced the voices and constrained the lives of family members, whole families, and entire communities.

The larger forces of racial, sexist, cultural, classist, and heterosexist power hierarchies define the boundaries of our clients' lives and determine what are to be considered problems and what services will be established to respond to the problems. We need to enlarge the focus of our work to go beyond the interior of the family so that we can begin to see how our clients' lives are constrained by these larger societal structures and develop new ways of working based on a revised understanding of our society, ourselves, our history, and our clients' lives.

Over the past few years, we have been struggling to envision a theory and practice that would be a part of transforming our field so that we might see ourselves and our clients more clearly and so provide services that would be more healing, offering a sense of hope and belonging for all who seek our help. In this chapter, I can only allude to the complexity of these ideas, which are laid out more fully in *Ethnicity and Family Therapy* (McGoldrick, Giordano, & Pearce, 1996), *The Expanded Family Life Cycle* (Carter & McGoldrick, 1998), and *Revisioning Family Therapy* (McGoldrick, 1998). These books provide much more detail about our expanding view of families and of family therapy from more inclusive cultural perspectives, helping us pay attention to those who have been hidden from history.

Family therapy, which, like every institution, set of ideas, and practice of society, is always evolving, originally developed primarily in reaction to Freudian psychology, which had concentrated primarily on intrapsychic processes. It offered a kind of corrective perspective, focusing attention on interpersonal processes between family members as central to understanding psychological functioning. Whereas some family therapists eschewed any level of analysis other than the interpersonal/family level, most came to think in terms of multiple systemic levels, from the biological to the familial to the cultural. However, it has been very difficult to shift our thinking about therapy beyond the family to consider the therapeutic implications of the context in which families are embedded.

BEYOND POLARIZATION: BLACK/WHITE, MALE/FEMALE, GAY/STRAIGHT

We have attempted in our work to address not only our cultural diversity, but also the diverse ways in which we practice as family therapists. I have, however, been troubled by two common pitfalls encountered in discussions of diversity. The first is to be so inclusive that it trivializes racism or leads to its being ignored owing to the multiplicity of "isms." This often happens in discussions of cultural diversity, where proposals for inclusiveness are so extensive that the institutionalized racism that is destroying our society is ignored in the presence of other inequalities.

The second pitfall is for the discussion to become polarized. As Beverly Tatum (1997) has noted in another context, those who have focused on the development of racial identity have done little to address gender, and feminist theorists have often done little to address race. I have noticed that in discussions of diversity the "black/white" issues can predominate, leaving others feeling that their issues are considered less important. Sexism, anti-semitism, and homophobia are pushed into the background as people argue over which oppression is the worst or most important.

We still find it difficult to raise some issues in cases that involve yet other issues. The question of how one can discuss sexism with a couple whose partners have been targets of racism is a hot topic. And the question of how to address the negative attitude toward homosexuality in the

African American community is equally challenging. Finally, Hall and Greene (1994), writing from a feminist family therapy perspective, consider the ethical imperative for attending to the complexities around issues of feminism, racism, and homophobia in relation to African American families:

> The African American woman may perceive that feminists and the feminist movement underestimate the integral role of cultural traditions and racism in her life. In a parallel experience, many African American males equate feminism with lesbianism, anti-male and white perspectives. It is imperative that feminist family therapists examine how much of the negative perception of therapy and feminist family therapy within the African American community is based on realistic experiences as opposed to sexist attitudes and misconceptions. . . . The ethical inclusion of cultural pluralism, a cultural context for therapy, as well as the examination of the influence of white privilege in feminist family therapy is essential in the provision of appropriate and meaningful treatment. (pp. 6–7)

I believe we need to maintain a multidimensional perspective, which can highlight the horror of institutionalized racism, while not, at the same time, minimizing the impact of other forms of oppression. We have to hold African American men accountable to women, and yet understand the particular oppression to which they have been subjected for generations. While moving against sexism, we have to hold white feminist family therapists accountable for the ways in which their privileged position and their unintentional racism perpetuate the very oppression of which they should be well aware. We must also not humiliate or dehumanize white men, even as we respectfully hold them accountable for their entitlement and lack of awareness of their role in perpetuating the current system. Their lack of consciousness is part of the structure of our society, which functions in such a way that the oppressed always know much more about the dominant groups than the dominant groups know about them, for the very reason that their survival depends on this understanding. This means that just as we must ask white men to take responsibility for learning to be uncomfortable with organizational structures that are dominated by white men, white women, as well, must learn to become uncomfortable in segregated situations, such as when reading books, including books about feminism or homosexuality, that pertain only to white people. We must become so uncomfortable that we are moved to do something about it.

I am hoping that we will keep working toward finding ways to contain opposites, contradictions, and ambiguities — not oversimplifying the issues and, at the same time, not obfuscating the prejudices and oppression that are defining and destroying us.

REVISIONING FAMILY THERAPY

Issues of transcendence, spirituality, hope, and resilience have also long been eschewed in our theory and practice. For thousands of years, such ideas have been the primary resources for people in emotional distress. It is high time we reintegrated them into our conceptual formulations. The belief in something beyond our individuality and our personal self-interest is our only hope for a future. We trust that within the next few years, this area will begin to receive the attention it deserves, as more and more therapy incorporates transcendant ideas in the clinical assessment of families under stress and in approaches to healing.

CHALLENGING RACISM IN TRAINING

Racism is perhaps the most pernicious element of our culture, and the hardest to deal with in our segregated society. The forces for racial segregation are so powerful that, unless we make strong and deliberate efforts to nurture diversity, they will prevail. Whites have tended to keep themselves unaware of racism. It is not a category in our diagnostic manuals and has been invisible in our developmental theories and in our psychotherapy. We cannot assume that racism will disappear just by our being "good people," or by leaving it to be dealt with by its victims, people of color. It is time for us to come to grips with our role in perpetuating the problems of racism by refusing to let ourselves see them.

Unwittingly, our training programs have been part of the problem, reproducing the racist, sexist, and heterosexist structures of the larger society. Clearly, we cannot make revisions just by modifying our reading lists. We must change our programs radically so that our trainees can break through the dominant culture's blinders. We must transform our training to remove these blinders and, in turn, to transform our theory and practice.

WHAT IT MEANS TO BE WHITE

Typically, discussions of culture and racism focus on the marginalized group as the "other." Revisioning our field will require that we explore instead those who see themselves as the norm or who have established the norms. That we must turn the tables on the dominant versions of our stories seems particularly appropriate for the new vision we require. We often need to stand on our heads, flipping things upside down, in order to notice the most obvious facts. We must consider what must change so that white men can be collaborative partners with everyone else in families and communities in the 21st century.

"Whiteness" is a political descriptor of those who have enjoyed unearned privileges in relation to others. It is a characterization that exists because racism exists. Unfortunately, whiteness is also something that defines and characterizes the practice of our profession. We cannot continue to train white therapists to work primarily with white families. Most family therapy training gives minimal lipservice to cultural issues. Probably not even 5% of the faculty of most family therapy training programs and courses, and less than 10% of family therapists and psychologists, are people of color. Yet 25% of the U.S. population, and a much higher percentage of the families in need of psychological help, are ethnic minorities. As Hall and Greene (1994) pointed out in their call for training in cultural competence as an ethical mandate of our times:

> The mental health professions [are] representative of the cultural norms and values of the dominant culture. Both African American and white therapists have been trained in institutions representative of the dominant culture's values, which for the most part embrace and support rather than explore or challenge the status quo. (pp. 24–25)

THE PROBLEMS OF NAMING

We in family therapy get paid by the names we give to the problems our clients present to us. This naming is a powerful issue. An early-19th-century physician in the United States, Samuel Cartwright, described two mental disorders prevalent among slaves (Tavris, 1992; Thomas & Sillen, 1974):

1. *Drapetomania* — characterized by a single symptom, the uncontrollable urge to escape slavery. This was literally a "flight-from-home mania."
2. *Dysathesia aethiopia* — for which many symptoms were described, including destroying property on the plantation, being disobedient, talking back, fighting with their masters, and refusing to work.

These diagnoses turned the desire for liberty into a sickness that afflicted the slaves, not the slave owners. The slave owners — the oppressors — become completely invisible in this nomenclature. But using labels to control others still continues, even in family therapy. We are much readier to diagnose the victims of abuse than the abusers. We have our favorite acronyms — MPD (multiple personality disorder), PTSD (posttraumatic stress disorder), SCS (survivors of child sexual abuse) — to define the life course of those who have experienced trauma, but leave out of our descriptions those who traumatize others, just as we did with slavery. Not only is racism not a diagnosis, it is not even listed in the index to the 800-page fourth edition of the *Diagnostic and Statistical Manual of Mental Disorders* (DSM-IV). We also obscure who does what to whom in our nomenclature by our naming: "alcoholic family," "violent family," "schizophrenic family" — terms I myself have used for years.

The DSM-IV claims that its naming is based on "scientific evidence," although a significant part of this research was funded by drug companies (Kupers, 1995)! This diagnostic manual includes diagnosis number 301.6: Dependent Personality Disorder for the person who "has difficulty expressing disagreement with others because of fear of loss of support or approval." The description adds a note that this does not include "realistic fears of retribution," but gives no guidelines as to how one would assess whether or not a person's fears are realistic, perhaps because of race or gender. The DSM-IV has no comparable diagnosis for those who are pathologically fearful of intimacy or dependence, those who are unable to develop friendships, or those who need to make sexual conquests or who react to their fear of aging by leaving their mate and establishing a relationship with a person the age of their children (Kupers, 1995). The manual also has failed to come up with a diagnosis not only for those who are racist, but also for those who are misogynists or homophobic.

Indeed, it is not sufficient, according to the DSM-IV, to have been physically or sexually violent to receive the diagnosis of "Conduct Disorder" or "Antisocial Personality." The most one can give is a V-code, number 61, which mentions without description or explanation "sexual or physical abuse of child or adult." And this is the case in spite of the fact that, on the average, every 18 seconds, somewhere in the country, a woman is beaten, and physical abuse is the most common cause of disability among women, surpassing breast cancer and automobile accidents.

At the same time, families of color, families of the poor, and immigrant families, whose norms and values are different from ours, remain peripheralized, invalidated, and pathologized as deficient or dysfunctional, or, worse yet, invisible. Many family therapists are still trained without reference to the insidious role that hierarchies related to culture, class, race, and gender play in the United States. We are taught concepts of human development, psychopathology, and family functioning in the totally skewed patriarchal, classist framework of the dominant white groups in our society. We are taught that you can learn about "men's issues," but that does not include issues of African American men, because their experiences are never mentioned. In general, when we have talked about "couples therapy," "child sexual abuse," "the family life cycle," "dual-career families," or "genograms," we have meant only white families.

CULTURAL LEGACIES

Our attempt to revision families and family therapy has led us to seek new ways to discuss our work. Personal narratives are a major part of this attempt to shift our paradigm. From Murray Bowen's first account of his own family at a 1967 research meeting, which stunned the field by breaking the rules of academic and professional discourse, we have gradually been stretching and transforming the boundaries of our dialogues to create more inclusive ways of thinking. Clearly, the individualistic models of "scientific" discourse about therapy have proved inadequate to the realm of healing. These models are of limited relevance in a world where our lives are so profoundly interconnected. It is often through personal narratives that we learn most about those aspects of our experience that do not fit our theoretical and clinical models. These stories may be the key to liberating us from the past to move toward new visions of our efforts.

MIGRATION

Immigrants, more than anyone else, experience our society from a multicultural perspective. Their bicultural lens could be a model for the cultural flexibility we require as family therapists in the most culturally diverse nation that has ever existed.

Coming to terms with our diversity as a nation transforms our awareness of what it means to be quintessentially American. As Sanford Ungar (1997) writes of becoming conscious of the meaning of his family's migration for him, a third-generation grandchild of Eastern European Jewish immigrants: "I was no less American than ever before, of course, but now, in middle age, I had discovered my own immigrant consciousness. Indeed, in that sense, I could now feel more authentically American" (p. 18).

Only by attending to the multiplicitous voices that have until now been silenced in the story of who we are as a nation can we become "more authentically American." While African Americans, Hmong refugees, and recent immigrants from Sri Lanka have their own cultures and particular experiences of migration and/or dislocation, they need equally to feel themselves included in the definition of "American."

The recent dramatic increase in immigration to the United States is forcing us to come to terms with our multiculturality. At no time in U.S. history have we had so many residents who were born outside the country (Roberts, 1994). And never before, despite previous waves of immigration, has our nation been so diverse. This is forcing us to challenge our assumptions about who we are and what our values should be. The cultural richness and complexity of the immigrant generation, especially those whose cultures are different from the dominant European-American values of our society, offer us the greatest possibilities for revisioning who we are and who we can be. Our diversity can become our greatest strength. But when we fear our diversity, our prejudices and rigidities as a nation are highlighted. Our fears bring out our ability to exclude others and to dehumanize those whom we feel do not belong.

Family therapy has ignored this multicultural dimension, and has proceeded to develop models without accounting for their cultural limitations. We have failed to notice that families from many cultural groups never come to therapy or find our techniques helpful. It is we who must change — to include them.

The disruptions of migration and the complexities of being bicultural are profound. When families belong to more than one culture, as most families in the United States do, we must consider their cultural differences, and acculturation. If we read them carefully, they can help us rethink the nature of our identity (Tataki, 1994). Instead of dismissing immigrants as "others," we will use their experiences to revision our notions of assessment and intervention.

NEW APPROACHES TO THERAPY PRACTICE

The good news is that a number of therapists have begun to propose intervention models based on a revisioning of families from a contextual viewpoint. Building their work around an acceptance of the need for social accountability, they attempt to integrate into it the multiplicity of considerations presented in this chapter, while avoiding the polarizing pitfalls. Nollaig Byrne and Imelda McCarthy (1998) have been developing their fifth-province model for some years and collaborating with others in the community to expand their perspectives. They have worked especially with an innovative Catholic nun who defies traditional boundaries in her community work. Charles Waldegrave (1998) and his colleagues in New Zealand (Tamasese & Waldegrave, 1993) have for some time been on the cutting edge of a revisioning of our field in their "Just Therapy" model, an approach that includes social justice in their thinking and practice and provides a profound challenge to traditional family therapy approaches by factoring in the impact of oppression on women, on cultural groups, and on poor families, and intentionally countering these oppressions in their ways of working.

Rhea Almeida, Robert Font, Theresa Messineo, and Rosemary Woods (1998) have developed an extraordinarily creative approach to family problems, including domestic violence. Their Cultural Context Model places clients in a cultural context, through a socioeducational training program, before they even describe their problems. Problems are thus contextualized from the first moment of assessment. The program creates a new healing community to counter the dominant culture's oppressive messages, and challenges the rules of privacy of traditional therapies, validated by professional associations, that so often maintain the status quo of oppressive relationships within families and in relation to the larger social context. In Hartford, Connecticut, Ramon Rojano has also expanded the boundaries of traditional family therapy, developing collaborations between businesses, informal community organizations and health-care systems to heal families in a community context (Markowitz, 1997).

References

Akamatsu, N. (1998). The talking oppression blues: Including the experience of power/powerlessness in the teaching of cultural sensitivity. In M. McGoldrick (Ed.), *Revisioning family therapy: Race, culture and gender in clinical practice*. New York: Guilford.

Almeida, R., Font, R., Messineo, T., & Woods, R. (1998). The cultural context model. In M. McGoldrick (Ed.), *Revisioning family therapy: Race, culture and gender in clinical practice*. New York: Guilford.

Byrne, N. O., & McCarthy, I. C. (1998). Marginal illuminations: A fifth province approach to intracultural issues in an Irish context. In M. McGoldrick (Ed.), *Revisioning family therapy: Race, culture and gender in clinical practice*. New York: Guilford.

Carter, B., & McGoldrick, M. (Eds.). (1998). *The expanded family life cycle: Individual, family and social perspectives*. Boston: Allyn & Bacon.

Coontz, S. (1992). *The way we never were: American families and the nostalgia trap*. New York: Basic Books.

Ehrenreich, B. (1989). *Fear of falling: The inner life of the middle class*. New York: Harper.

Ehrlich, P., & Ehrlich, A. (1991). *Healing the planet*. New York: Addison-Wesley.

Griffin, S. (1992). *A chorus of stones: The private life of war*. New York: Doubleday.

Hall, R. L., & Greene, B. (1994). Cultural competence in feminist family therapy: An ethical mandate. *Journal of Feminist Family Therapy, 6*(3), pp. 5–28.

Kupers, T. A. (1995). The politics of psychiatry: Gender and sexual preference in DSM-IV. *Masculinities, 3*(2), 67–78.

Markowitz, L. (1997). Ramon Rojano won't take no for an answer. *The Family Therapy Networker*, Nov.–Dec.

McGoldrick, M. (1995). *You can go home again*. New York: Norton.

McGoldrick, M. (Ed.). (1998). *Revisioning family therapy: Race, culture and gender in clinical practice*. New York: Guilford.

McGoldrick, M., Giordano, J., & Pearce, J. K. (1996). *Ethnicity and family therapy* (2nd ed.). New York: Guilford.

McIntosh, P. (1998). White privilege: Unpacking the invisible knapsack. In M. McGoldrick (Ed.), *Revisioning family therapy: Race, culture and gender in clinical practice*. New York: Guilford.

Tamasese, K., & Waldegrave, C. (1993). Culture and gender accountability in the "just therapy" approach. *Journal of Feminist Family Therapy, 5*(2), pp. 29–45.

Tataki, R. (Ed.). (1994). *From different shores: Perspectives on race and ethnicity in America* (2nd ed.). New York: Oxford University Press.

Tatum, B. D. (1997). Racial identity development and relational theory: The case of black women in white communities. In J. V. Jordan (Ed.), *Women's growth in diversity*. New York: Guilford.

Tavris, C. (1992). *The mismeasure of women*. New York: Simon & Schuster.

Thomas, A., & Sillen, S. (1974). *Racism and psychiatry*. Secaucus, NJ: Citadel.

Ungar, S. (1997). *Fresh blood: The new American immigrants*. New York: Simon & Schuster.

Waldegrave, C. (1998). The challenges of culture to psychology and postmodern thinking. In M. McGoldrick (Ed.), *Revisioning family therapy: Race, culture and gender in clinical practice*. New York: Guilford.

12

Why the Field of Therapy Is On the Verge of Extinction and What We Can Do to Save It

Scott D. Miller, Barry L. Duncan, Lynn D. Johnson, & Mark A. Hubble

"Dinosaurs ... were less malleable. They had changed before, in previous ecological crises, but this time the stresses were overwhelming."

— John Noble Wilford (1986), *The Riddle of the Dinosaur*

On a cold, wintery December day in 1799, the 67-year-old former president of the United States, George Washington, returned to his mansion from his usual morning ride on the grounds of the Mount Vernon estate. Everything seemed normal as he and the other members of his household went about their daily routine. As the day wore on, however, a minor sore throat the president had been experiencing since his morning ride worsened. By early the next morning, his condition was so grave that a doctor was summoned.

The doctor — together with two other physicians who eventually made it through the snowy weather to Mount Vernon — administered the accepted therapy of the day. When no results were observed, the three agreed that more of the same treatment was indicated. Several hours and two treatments later, the president was dead. The cause of death? Historians agree that George Washington did not die of some strange or exotic disease. Instead, he died of the competently and skillfully delivered treatment he received while in an already weakened state. This intervention, of course, was the accepted "standard of care" for late 18th-century medicine — blood letting (Flexner, 1974).

It is tempting to believe that the modern healing arts have evolved beyond such primitive and misguided practices. However, strong evidence exists that the very same forces that led Washington's physicians to administer (and then readminister) an ineffective (and ultimately lethal) treatment not only continue to operate, but now also threaten the very survival of the mental health professions. These forces, in particular, have led the field to focus primarily on the *competence* of service delivery rather than on the effectiveness of the services delivered.

The bias favoring the process of treatment over outcome can clearly be seen in the ethical codes of the three largest mental health provider organizations (the National Association of Social Workers, the American Psychological Association, and the American Association of Marriage and Family Therapy). At no place in these codes are social workers, psychologists, or marriage and family therapists explicitly required to practice *effective* treatment. Indeed, as Dawes (1994) points out in his critical analysis of the field, existing ethical codes neither mandate the use of effective therapeutic approaches nor require therapists to subject their practices to any systematic assessment of outcome. Curiously, the codes require only that therapists practice "within the boundaries of their competence and experience" (p. 1600, APA, 1997 [Principle A], emphasis added; NASW, 1996 [Principle 1.04]; AAMFT, 1991a [Principle 3.4]).

Conventional wisdom suggests that competence engenders, if not equals, effectiveness. Notwithstanding, this conflation of competence with effectiveness has occurred so often in professional discourse and training that the difference between the two has become blurred. In this regard, consider the continuing education workshops that clinicians must attend to maintain their professional licenses. In theory, the continuing education requirement is designed to ensure that clinicians stay abreast of developments that enhance treatment outcome. Even so, in practice, the vast majority of approaches taught at these workshops have themselves only rarely, if ever, been tested scientifically and determined to be effective.

A recent issue of *The Family Therapy Networker*, for example, contains ads for continuing education training in nearly 30 different therapeutic modalities, including EMDR, Thought Field Therapy™, Divorce Mediation, Biofeedback, Solution-Focused Therapy, Advanced Energy Therapy, Light Therapy, Systematic Applied Kinesiology, and NLP. Few of these have been rigorously evaluated and shown to be effective. And rarely do these workshops teach therapists a practical, systematic method for either evaluating the effectiveness of or making informed modifications in the approach they are learning. Sole emphasis is placed on the attendees' becoming proficient at using the skills or techniques of a particular brand or style of treatment. In the world of continuing education, competency is king.

As the story of the death of George Washington illustrates, however, competence is no guarantee of effectiveness, as even ineffective or dangerous treatments can be used competently. More important perhaps, the story shows that having no systematic method in place for evaluating the outcome of a treatment approach (either overall or as applied to a specific case) may create an illusion of success that blinds practitioners to corrective feedback. During Washington's day, there was no accepted method for evaluating the overall effectiveness of a given treatment, much less for determining the efficacy of that treatment when applied to a particular case. As a result, Washington's physicians relied on their training and clinical judgment first to choose and then to continue with what was, at best, an inert treatment.

As surprising as it may be, until the middle of the 20th century, there was little interest in the empirical study of psychotherapy outcome. The utility of a given method was taken for granted, if the practitioner administered the treatment correctly. Training and supervision were considered the keys to success and the experience of the teacher the "gold standard" by which the quality of the practitioner could be measured. All this changed dramatically, however, when, in 1952, English psychologist Hans Eysenck published a study that purportedly showed that competently administered psychotherapy was no more effective than no treatment at all. Although later found to contain methodological flaws that called his conclusions into question, Eysenck's research did serve as a catalyst for increased interest in the study of psychotherapy outcome.

Now, almost 50 years and thousands of studies later, the overall effectiveness of psychotherapy has been well established. Indeed, in most quantitative studies, the average treated person has been found to be better off than 80% of those who do not have the benefit of psychotherapy (Asay & Lambert, 1999; Lambert & Bergin, 1994). Unfortunately, the mountain of evidence that researchers have amassed in support of psychotherapy has had very little impact on direct service delivery (Barlow, 1996; Ogles & Lunnen, 1996). In fact, in the practice of psychotherapy, outcome information is seldom formally assessed or utilized. A variety of reasons can be found for the current state of affairs; chief among them is that standard research methods are time consuming, costly, impractical, and often irrelevant to clinical work. Yet whatever the reasons, the unfortunate result is that individual therapists have been rendered incapable of demonstrating convincingly that their services are effective and efficient.

Even worse, available evidence suggests that the failure to employ outcome information may (1) decrease effectiveness and efficiency, and (2) limit the growth of individual therapists. Most therapists, for example, would say that their own clinical ability has improved with time and experience. In reality, however, a sizable body of research finds little or no relationship between the experience level and the effectiveness of therapists (Berman & Norman, 1985; Clement, 1994; Garb, 1989; Hattie, Sharpley, & Roberts, 1984; Stein & Lambert, 1984). If anything, the data indicate that increasing the amount and type of training and experience that most therapists undergo may *lessen* therapeutic effectiveness (Christensen & Jacobsen, 1994).

Consider a 1995 study conducted at a large health maintenance organization (HMO) to examine the qualities of effective therapists (Brown, Dreis, & Nace, 1999). Using clients' self-reports and peer ratings, researchers Hiatt and Hargrave successfully distinguished between the therapists who were most and least effective (as determined by clinical outcome). The results of their study were both surprising and distressing. In brief, therapists in the *low*-effectiveness group tended to have been in practice for *more* years than those in the high-effectiveness group (18.2 versus 12.9 years respectively). Most distressing, however, was the finding that the clinical outcomes of the most and least effective therapists were identical when the providers' own ratings were used as the basis for comparison. This means that the ineffective therapists were unaware that they were ineffective!

Although discouraging, awareness of these and similar findings affords front-line practitioners a critical "window of opportunity." Therapists have the chance to improve the quality of direct clinical care while simultaneously ensuring the survival and viability of the profession in the next millennium. As is news to no one, mental health service delivery has been undergoing dramatic change over the last 10 years (Berkman, Bassos, & Post, 1988; Cummings, 1986; Zimet, 1989). Third-party payers have become increasingly cost-conscious and now stridently insist that, if they are to be paid, therapists must substantiate the effectiveness of their services. In the battle with the cost-cutters and corporate nay-sayers, the routine, systematic assessment and utilization of outcome information are shaping up as the single best weapon that average practitioners have both for ensuring the continuation of quality services and for proving the value of their individual work. To do otherwise not only risks exclusion, but also ultimately may hasten the transfer of control over clinical decision making from mental health professionals to accountants and actuaries.

TOWARD AN OUTCOME-INFORMED THERAPEUTIC PRACTICE

"Data talks and bullshit walks."
— *Geraldo Rivera*

During the 1950s and 60s, a series of intriguing experiments were conducted on the nature and effect of feedback on human activity. In one representative study, Professor Alex Bavelas simultaneously exposed two participants to a series of pictures of either healthy or sick cells (Watzlawick, 1976). Neither person in the study could observe the other while the experiment was under way, and each was given the assignment to learn to distinguish between the two types of cells through trial and error. Small lights marked "right" and "wrong" provided feedback to the participants about their respective choices.

There was just one "wrinkle" in the experiment, of which both participants were unaware. Only one of them received accurate feedback about the guesses. When the light in this person's cubicle indicated that the "right" choice had been made, the person had indeed guessed correctly. On the other hand, feedback for the second participant was based not on that participant's own guesses, but on those of the first participant! No matter the person's choices, this person was told the choices were "right" if the other person had guessed correctly and "wrong" if the other had been incorrect. Data collected without the knowledge showed, at the conclusion of the experiment, that the first participant had learned to distinguish healthy from sick cells with an 80% rate of accuracy. The second continued to guess at no better than a chance rate.

These were not the only results. The two types of feedback also had a distinct and interesting impact on the theories that each participant developed during the study for differentiating between " healthy" and "sick" cells. The participant who received accurate, reliable feedback ended the experiment with a very simple, concrete, and parsimonious explanation. In contrast, the second participant developed a complicated, subtle, and elaborate theory. This person, it is recalled, had no way of knowing that the feedback received was not contingent on the participant's own responses. Sometimes, as luck would have it, the responses happened to coincide with the correct answer. However, given the inconsistent and unreliable feedback, this participant was prevented from learning anything about the person's own actions and choices.

Even these results are not all that surprising. Something more troubling occurred when the two participants shared their respective theories with each other. Contrary to what one might hope and expect, the first participant was impressed with the complicated, mysterious, and unreliable theoretical formulations of the co-participant. The second, on the other hand, dismissed the statistically accurate theory of the first as "naive and simplistic." In later retests during which both participants received accurate feedback about their own guesses, the second continued to guess at little better than a chance rate. The performance of the first, however, who was now attempting to put some of the "brilliant" insights of the co-participant into practice, significantly worsened.

The parallels between the results of this study and the field of psychotherapy are striking. Divorced from systematic, reliable, and valid feedback about the outcome of most standard therapeutic practices, the field has become a jumble of competing, complicated, and often contradictory theories of treatment. Since the 1960s, for example, the number of available treatment approaches has increased a whopping 400%, with no end in sight. Depending on the way models are counted, some estimates are actually much higher (Garfield, 1982; Kazdin, 1986). For all this phenomenal growth, the actual overall effectiveness of psychological intervention has not improved in the least.

Reliable and valid means do exist for evaluating progress and overall effectiveness in treatment (cf., Brown, Dreis, & Nace, 1999; Howard, Moras, Brill, Martinovich, & Lueger, 1996; Johnson & Shaha, 1996). Rather than repeating the failures of the past and attempting to determine a priori "what approach works for which problem," these methods typically focus on how well a given treatment is working for an individual client at a specific point in time. While each of the various approaches for tracking outcome is different, all take advantage of the fact that despite the treatment approach or theoretical orientation, the general trajectory of change in successful treatment is consistent and highly predictable.

Studies that have tracked its occurrence have consistently found that most change takes place earlier in the treatment process rather than later. Nearly all large-scale meta-analytic studies, for example, have found that 60–65% of clients experience significant symptomatic relief within one to seven visits — figures that increase to 70–75% after six months and 85% at one year (Howard, Kopte, Krause, & Orlinsky, 1986; Howard, Moras, Brill, Martinovich, & Lueger, 1996; Smith, Glass, & Miller, 1980; Steenbarger, 1992, 1994; Talmon, Hoyt, & Rosenbaum, 1990). These same data (Howard, Kopte, Krause, & Orlinsky, 1986) also show "a course of diminishing returns with more and more effort required to achieve just noticeable differences in patient [sic] improvement" as time in treatment lengthens (p. 361).

Such results should not be construed as an indictment of all therapies that extend beyond a handful of sessions. On the contrary, they indicate that, in cases where progress is being made, more treatment is better than less. At the same time, the data strongly suggest that therapies in which little or no change (or even a worsening of symptoms) occurs *early* in the treatment process are at significant risk for a null, or even negative, outcome (Lebow, 1997). Indeed, early improvement — specifically, the client's experience of meaningful change in the first few visits — is emerging as one of the best predictors of treatment outcome (Garfield, 1994). In one study of more than 2,000 therapists and thousands of clients, researchers found that clients reporting no improvement by the third visit on average showed no improvement over the entire course of treatment (Brown, Dreis, & Nace, 1999)! In addition, clients who worsened by the third visit were twice as likely to drop out of treatment than those experiencing improvement.

Developing an outcome-informed therapeutic practice need not be complicated, time consuming, or expensive. Neither is a background in statistics nor sophisticated research methodology required. Therapists can simply choose from among the many paper-and-pencil rating scales already available. Most of these instruments are in the public domain or can be had for a small fee. More important, however, such measures have the advantage of being standardized, psychometrically sound, and accompanied by an abundance of normative data that can be used for comparative purposes. Several good sources exist that front-line practitioners can consult for information about existing instruments (c.f., Fischer & Corcoran, 1994a, 1994b; Froyd, Lambert, & Froyd, 1996; Ogles, Lambert, & Masters, 1996).

The choice of instruments depends on several important factors. The first is the type of outcome one wants to measure. In this regard, there are two basic types of outcome: (1) clinical and (2) client satisfaction. Clinical outcome measures, as the name implies, assess the impact or result of the service a therapist offers a client. Customer-satisfaction measures assess the client's personal experience of how well he or she was served, including such factors as courtesy, timeliness, accessibility, professionalism, the strength of the therapeutic relationship, and qualities of the treatment facility (Hill, 1989; Lebow, 1982; Pasco, 1984). In short, measures of clinical outcome tell the therapist how he or she is doing, whereas customer-satisfaction scales provide feedback about what a therapist actually did to obtain a particular result.

A second factor to consider when choosing outcome measures is the nature of the service being assessed. In an article in the *Family Therapy Networker*, Mary Sykes Wylie (1997) worried that the marketplace atmosphere currently surrounding mental health care was gradually redefining a good therapist as "the one with the most magazines and videos in the waiting room" (p. 41). As far as outcome and client satisfaction are concerned, Wylie's observations are only likely to be true if reading material and popular videos happen to correspond with the expectations and goals of the people being served in a particular practice. Therapists may need to survey their clients before choosing measures.

The best measure of client satisfaction ultimately will be one that is sensitive to how well the unique aspects of the therapy match the clients' expectations for care. Research shows, for example, that the quality of the therapeutic relationship accounts for as much as 30% of treatment outcome (Lambert, 1992; Miller, Duncan, & Hubble, 1997; Duncan, Hubble,

& Miller, 1997). In particular, clients give the highest ratings to therapeutic relationships they experience as caring, affirming, flexible, accommodating, and collaborative. Obviously, an instrument that measures these aspects of the therapeutic relationship will provide helpful feedback about client satisfaction.

The Session Rating Scale (SRS) (Johnson, 1994)[1] is just one example of a customer-satisfaction survey specifically designed to be sensitive to clients' perceptions of the therapeutic relationship. Briefly, the 10-item instrument assesses client perceptions regarding the overall flow and helpfulness of the visit (e.g., session depth, smoothness). It also taps how well the therapist succeeded in establishing a therapeutic atmosphere (e.g., warmth, acceptance, positive regard) and in working on issues that the client wanted to address.

With regard to clinical outcome, therapists can choose from among a host of well-established and inexpensive instruments. Here again, they are best served when they select measures that fit the nature of their clinical practice. For example, the Beck Depression Inventory (BDI) is a short and reliable instrument that might be administered at some point during each session for clients whose presenting complaint is depression (Johnson & Shaha, 1997). Declining scores over time could be considered proof of the efficacy of the type of treatment being given. A lack of change or an increase over time would indicate that the course of treatment needs to be evaluated and altered in some way. Finally, and perhaps most important, as long as a particular client is making progress, but has not yet reached a score indicative of recovery (a raw score of 10 or less), the instrument would make a strong case for continuing treatment.

Consider the case of Linda, a woman in her 40s, an executive and the mother of two, who presented for treatment with complaints of depression. In the first interview, she explained how her current symptoms resulted from serious problems at work. She related how once friendly coworkers had turned against her, accusing her of having sex with a senior executive to gain a promotion. Her score on the BDI at the beginning of the visit was 37 — indicative of a serious level of depressive symptoms.

Linda also completed the SRS, but at the end of the first session. The instrument was not scored promptly because both the therapist working with Linda and another observing from behind a one-way mirror thought

---

[1] The SRS can be obtained without charge at www.talkingcure.com.

the session went quite well. After completing the measure, Linda simply was asked to return the following week for a second appointment.

Later that day, the therapist did score the SRS and learned that Linda was quite *dis*satisfied with the session (see Figure 1). Specifically, her answers indicated that she had expected the therapist to give her some advice and suggestions for dealing with the situation – something that had not taken place.

The therapist phoned Linda and offered to meet the following day during lunch hour. She agreed, showing up on time for the scheduled appointment. Together, they worked on specific strategies for addressing the problems at work. However, Linda's scores on the BDI already were on the decline. Results of the SRS taken at the conclusion of this session indicated that she was satisfied with the visit. As Figure 1 illustrates graphically, Linda's scores on the BDI continued to decline over the next four visits, finally reaching the recovery level (10) by the eighth. At the same time, after the first visit, Linda's scores on the SRS improved, remaining high throughout the treatment process.

One final factor to consider when choosing an instrument is how long the measure will take to administer, score, and interpret. No clinician has the time, for example, to use a clinical-outcome measure such as the Hamilton Depression Rating Inventory, which must be administered through a structured interview. Neither is there any advantage to be gained from using such lengthy measures as the Millon Clinical Multiaxial Inventory, the Minnesota Multiphasic Personality Inventory, or the Rorschach. In the real world of clinical practice, the best instrument is one that can be administered and scored in a few minutes (Brown, Dreis, & Nace, 1999).

One measure that shows particular promise in this regard is the Outcome Questionnaire 45 (OQ-45.2; Lambert & Burlingame, 1995).[2] The *OQ-45* is reliable, well-validated, and inexpensive measure that costs less than three cents per administration. The 45-item checklist takes clients about three to four minutes to complete and can be scored by hand in less than two minutes. Unlike problem-specific measures such as the BDI, the OQ-45 has the advantage of being applicable to a broad range of clients

[2] The OQ-45 can be obtained from American Professional Credentialling Services, P.O. Box 346, Stevenson, MD 21153-0346. Other outcome scales are available without charge at www.talkingcure.com.

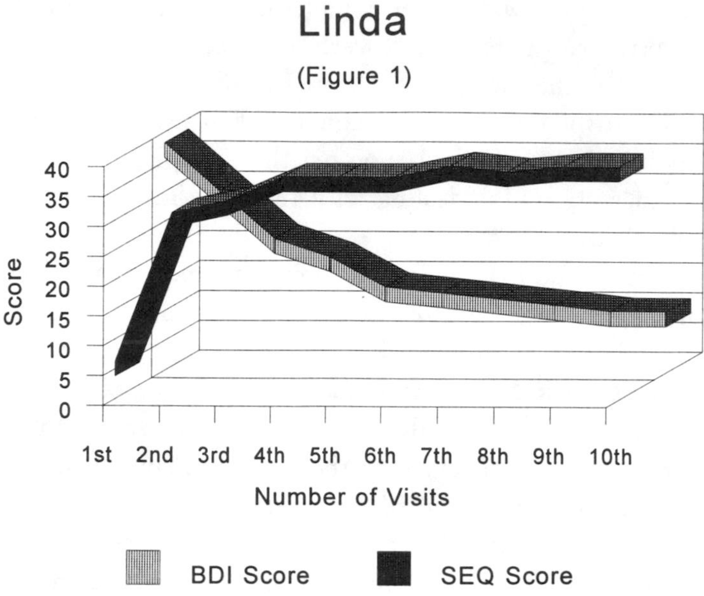

and presenting complaints. This means that clinicians do not have to master a long list of instruments. More important, research has established that whereas the OQ-45 is stable in nontreated individuals, it is sensitive to change in those undergoing successful treatment.

Three different dimensions of client functioning are assessed by the OQ-45: (1) symptoms (measuring depression, anxiety, alcohol and drug use, and other symptoms); (2) interpersonal relationship (measuring how well the client thinks he or she gets along with the important person[s] in his or her life); and (3) social role (how well the client rates his or her functioning at work or school). As such, the measure taps into the three variables that researchers and practicing therapists consider relevant and strong predictors of client progress (Orlinsky, Grawe, & Parks, 1994).

Clients are typically given the measure before the beginning of each session. Scores on each dimension of the OQ-45 are then plotted on a graph and compared with the scores of people who are not distressed. As with the BDI, declining scores over time show successful treatment. No change or increasing scores are a sign that treatment is off course.

An example of using the OQ-45 to inform treatment is that of Barbara, a 36-year-old woman who presented for therapy with complaints of depression, lapses in memory, difficulty with concentration, mood swings, and low self-esteem. Her score on the symptom dimension of the OQ-45 was significantly elevated as compared with people not in distress (see Figure 2). In the first interview, she related how a family member had victimized her sexually from the age of 13 to age 16. During the session, she expressed a strong desire to bring her mood swings under control and to learn to cope better with her history of abuse. The therapist used a combination of competency-oriented and cognitive-behavioral treatment methods to highlight times when Barbara had coped unusually well with her memories and symptoms. At the conclusion of the visit, Barbara was asked to "do more of what had worked" for her previously.

The following week, Barbara returned. She looked and sounded better and her score on the OQ-45 confirmed the changes. These positive changes continued through the third visit. Then Barbara said that she wanted to remember more about the abuse she had suffered. Barbara and the therapist considered whether or not exploring the abuse was appropriate at that time in the treatment. Eventually, they decided to try recovering some memories.

As illustrated in Figure 2, Barbara returned for her fourth visit in even greater distress than she had been at her first. Together, Barbara and the therapist spent the session reviewing the scores on the OQ-45 and discussing whether they should continue the recovered-memory work or return to the approach used in the first three sessions. They eventually decided to focus again on what had been working for Barbara. Over the next two visits, her scores on the OQ-45 decreased.

In the sixth session, Barbara once more expressed a desire to recover memories about her abuse. The therapist cooperated with her desires and they explored the memories. When her scores were elevated the following week, however, Barbara and the therapist decided to stop pursuing the memories. Barbara was unusual in that her symptom-distress scores were elevated, but her social-role scores were not. That is, she was the sort of person who shows up for work and does what needs doing whether she feels like it or not. The therapist commented on this quality to Barbara, and together they decided that the best course would be to foster that active coping strategy, rather than explore her past. By the eighth and final visit, her score on the OQ-45 had decreased. A routine telephone contact a year later found her living comfortably without any further complaints.

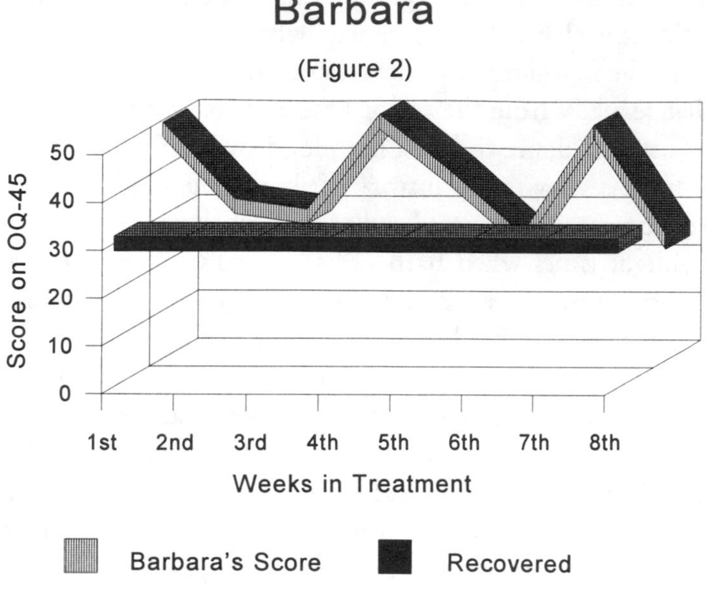

Barbara's case says nothing about the absolute value of competency-oriented, cognitive-behavioral, or recovered-memory treatment approaches. Instead, it merely shows what worked for this client seen at a given point in time by a single therapist using one type of treatment modality versus another. The measures promoted an open discussion with Barbara of the costs and benefits of different methods and allowed her to make an informed choice. The process was simple, it strengthened the therapeutic relationship, and it improved the treatment process.

Practicing therapists can begin monitoring their own practices with similar results. No special training is needed. No significant expense need be incurred. Such monitoring would have several immediate advantages. To begin, the systematic collection and use of outcome information would effectively mute current public and professional debate over the value of therapy (Johnson & Shaha, 1997). Therapists would have actual proof of their effectiveness. Over time, individual practitioners would even be able to document any special abilities for working effectively with certain client populations or types of presenting complaints.

Treatment informed by outcome would also greatly simplify the interaction between mental health professionals and managed-care entities.

For instance, most managed behavioral health care organizations (MBHOs) currently require that clinicians complete lengthy reports and comprehensive treatment plans before authorizing payment for services. Clinicians agree that the process is time-consuming, repetitious, and, frankly, busy work. Only rarely do these reports reflect what is going on in treatment. Even less often do they serve to improve treatment in any way. Indeed, the reports continue to focus on factors that have *no* relationship to outcome (e.g., type of treatment, DSM-IV diagnosis; Miller, Duncan, & Hubble, 1997). The process does not even control the cost of outpatient care. In fact, proof grows that the typical review of outpatient mental health care actually increases costs (Johnson, 1995; Johnson & Shaha, 1997). Each time a care manager contacts a therapist, it costs an MBHO approximately $60 to $70. This money is wasted in a superstitious pursuit of information that is of no value in helping to improve therapy outcome. Worse yet, there is a constant risk of harm to clients attendant to any breaches in confidentiality during the authorization and review process.

Using standardized measures would eliminate the need for therapists to submit detailed reports containing sensitive and potentially damaging personal information. For their part, MBHOs would finally have something other than cost to consider when authorizing treatment; they would have hard data about the effectiveness and efficiency of particular therapists and provider groups.

As an example of the latter, consider what happened at the Brief Therapy Center of Utah (BTCU), a member clinic of the Institute for the Study of Therapeutic Change. Clinicians at the center discovered that they were being excluded from referrals by one of their area's MBHOs because they charged more per session than did a competing specialty group. Fortunately, clinicians at the BTCU had been collecting outcome data for some time. Their results suggested that most of their clients fully recovered within a few visits. Although less expensive, the competing group had no outcome data to speak of other than the average number of visits per client. After meeting with the provider relations representative at the MBHO, the BTCU not only was returned to the provider list, but also was given more referrals than ever before. There can be no doubt: data talks.

Besides improving relationships between therapists and third-party payers, becoming informed about outcome would help the nonmedical helping professions establish an identity separate from the field of medicine. For most of the last 100 years, the field of therapy has been caught in a never-ending game of "catch up" – gaining acceptance by adopting much of the questionable language and practices of American psychiatry. Take, for example, the widespread use and acceptance of medicine's *Diagnostic and Statistical Manual of Mental Disorders* (DSM-IV) (APA, 1994). In spite of its being plagued by poor reliability and unknown validity, and having absolutely no predictive power for treatment outcome (Kirk & Kutchins, 1992; Kutchins & Kirk, 1997), this book, and its accompanying emphasis on pathology, is now a fixed part of most graduate training programs in therapy.

More recently, the American Psychological Association was quick to publish a list of "approved" treatments for specific DSM disorders after the American Psychiatric Association beat it to the punch and published its own list first. The idea of having a specific psychological intervention for the treatment of a given type of problem is one that resonates with the public and government policy makers. The truth is, however, "that forty years of sophisticated outcome research has not found any one theory, model, method, or package of techniques to be reliably better than any other" (Miller, Duncan, & Hubble, 1997, p. 2).

Neither is the APA content with possessing the mere psychological equivalent of a pill for emotional distress. Movers and shakers within the organization are now attempting to wrestle prescription privileges away from the field of medicine (DeLeon & Wiggins, 1996; Klein, 1996; APA, 1992; Lorion, 1996). This latest example of "follow the leader" is particularly baffling because the data so clearly show that being able to prescribe will neither reduce costs nor make psychologists one bit *more* effective or accountable (Greenberg, 1999; Hubble, Duncan, & Miller, 1999)! Only the development of reliable and valid alternatives to the poorly substantiated practices of American psychiatry will enhance effectiveness and ensure accountability, thereby enabling nonmedical professionals to compete effectively in the next millennium. Continuing to envy the field's economically more successful half sibling will simply make permanent the second-class status to which therapists have been relegated since Freud.

The time has come to "Just say no." No, to diagnosis and pathology. No, to empirically validated treatments. And No to medical conceptualizations of therapy. Outcome-informed practice offers a way to legitimize therapy without parroting the medical profession. In the end, the greatest beneficiaries of outcome-informed clinical practice most likely will be the clients. They would clearly benefit from a field that trained and credentialed practitioners based more on the ability to achieve results than one based on the mastery of various theories and techniques. They would also benefit from treatment innovations that, when introduced and used, already had proved to result in better outcomes.

In the past, clients have been the unwitting victims of clinical myths and superstitions — from Freud's mistreatment of Dora to the primal scream, from orgone therapy to "epidemics" of addictions and multiple personalities, and from the treatment of past-life traumas to survivors of highly secretive, but well-organized satanic cults (Carlinsky, 1994; Morrock, 1994; Roper Organization, 1992; Weiss, 1988). As a more practical example, consider the widespread practice of conducting comprehensive intake evaluations before treatment commences. This practice is still called state-of-the-art and necessary, as it is supposed that an extensive history and psychological workup (sometimes as long as two hours of data collection) improve treatment. However, in centers where such a system is in place, the average client usually attends only five to six sessions. In addition, more than a third of the clients leave after the initial screening and evaluation without receiving any treatment at all! Such practices, which cost as much as $500 per client, cause harm by squandering scarce clinical resources.

Being outcome-informed, dependent as such a system would be on clients' experiences and reports, would also invite the users of therapy to become full and equal participants in the treatment process. After all, research suggests that they are the most potent contributors to outcome in treatment — more important than the therapeutic relationship (30%), placebo (15%), or approach (15%). They are the real "heart and soul" of change. Making their voices a routine part of the evaluation of treatment outcome would do a great deal to energize professional discourse and ensure the survival of the field.

References

American Association of Marriage and Family Therapy (1991a). *AAMFT code of ethics*. Washington, DC: AAMFT.

American Association of Marriage and Family Therapy (1991b). *Ethical principles for marriage and family therapists*. Washington, DC: Author.

American Psychiatric Association (1994). *Diagnostic and statistical manual of mental disorders.* Washington, DC: American Psychiatric Association Press.

American Psychological Association (1992). *Report of the ad hoc task force on psychopharmacology.* Washington, DC: APA Press.

American Psychological Association (1997). *Ethical principles for psychologists.* Washington, DC: APA Press.

Asay, T., & Lambert, M. J. (1999). The empirical case for the *common factors in therapy: Quantitative findings.* In M. Hubble, B. Duncan, & S. Miller (Eds), *The heart and soul of change: A handbook of common factors in treatment.* Washington, DC: APA press.

Barlow, D. H., & Wolfe, B. (1981). Behavioral approaches to anxiety disorders. *Journal of Consulting and Clinical Psychology, 49,* 448–454.

Barlow, D. H. (1996). Healthcare policy, psychotherapy research, and the future of psychotherapy. *American Psychologist, 51,* 1050–1058.

Berkman, A. S., Bassos, C. A., & Post, L. (1988). Managed mental health care and independent practice: A challenge to psychology. *Psychotherapy, 25,* 434–440.

Berman, J. S., & Norman, N. C. (1985). Does professional training make a therapist more effective? *Psychological Bulletin, 98,* 401–406.

Beutler, L. E., Crago, M., & Arizmendi, T. G. (1986). Research on therapist variables in psychotherapy. In S. L. Garfield and A. E. Bergin (Eds.), *Handbook of psychotherapy and behavior change (3rd ed.),* (pp. 257–310). New York: Wiley.

Brown, J., Dreis, S., & Nace, D. (1999). What really makes a difference in psychotherapy outcome? Why does managed care want to know? In M. Hubble, B. Duncan, & S. Miller (Eds), *The heart and soul of change: A handbook of common factors in treatment.* Washington, DC: APA Press.

Carlinsky, J. (1994). Epigones of orgonomy. *Skeptic, 2*(3), 90–92.

Christensen, A., & Jacobsen, N. (1994). Who (or what) can do psychotherapy? The status and challenge of nonprofessional therapies. *Psychological Science, 5*(1), 8–14.

Clement, P. W. (1994). Quantitative evaluation of 26 years of private practice. *Professional Psychology: Research and Practice, 25*(2), 173–176.

Cummings, N. A. (1986). The dismantling of our health system: Strategies for the survival of psychological practice. *American Psychologist, 41*(4), 426–431.

Dawes, R. M. (1994). *House of cards: Psychology and psychotherapy built on myth and tradition.* New York: Free Press.

DeLeon, P. H., & Wiggins, J. G. (1996). Prescription privileges for psychologists. *American Psychologist, 51*(3), 225–229.

Duncan, B. L., Hubble, M. A., & Miller, S. D. (1997). *Psychotherapy with impossible cases.* New York: Norton.

Eysenck, H. J. (1952). The effects of psychotherapy. *Journal of Consulting Psychology, 16*, 319–324.

Fischer, J., & Corcoran, K. (1994a). *Measures for clinical practice, Vol. I: Couples, families and children*. New York: Free Press.

Fischer, J., & Corcoran, K. (1994b). *Measures for clinical practice, Vol. II: Adults*. New York: Free Press.

Flexner, J. T. (1974). *Washington: The indispensable man*. New York: Little, Brown.

Froyd, J. E., Lambert, M. J., & Froyd, J. D. (1996). A review of practices of psychotherapy outcome measurement. *Journal of Mental Health, 5*, 11–15.

Garb, H. (1989). Clinical judgement, clinical training, and professional experience. *Psychological Bulletin, 105*, 387–392.

Garfield, S. L. (1982). Eclecticism and integration in psychotherapy. *Behavior Therapy, 13*, 610–623.

Garfield, S. (1994). Research on client variables in psychotherapy. In A. Bergin and S. Garfield (Eds.), *Handbook of psychotherapy and behavior change (4th ed.)*, (pp. 190–228). New York: Wiley.

Greenberg, R. (1999). Common psychosocial factors in drug therapy. In M. Hubble, B. Duncan, & S. Miller (Eds), *The heart and soul of change: A handbook of common factors in treatment*. Washington, DC: APA Press.

Hattie, J. A., Sharpley, C. F., & Rogers, H. F. (1984). Comparative effectiveness of professional and paraprofessional helpers. *Psychological Bulletin, 95*, 534–541.

Hill, C. E. (1989). *Therapist techniques and client outcomes: Eight cases of brief therapy*. New York: Sage.

Howard, K. I., Kopte, S. M., Krause, M. S., & Orlinsky, D. E. (1986). The dose-effect relationship in psychotherapy. *American Psychologist, 41*(2), 159–164.

Howard, K., Moras, K., Brill, P., Martinovich, Z., & Lueger, R. (1996). The evaluation of psychotherapy: Efficacy, effectiveness, patient progress. *American Psychologist, 51*, 1059–1064.

Hubble, M., Duncan, B. L., & Miller, S. D. (1999). Directing attention to what works. In M. Hubble, B. Duncan, & S. Miller (Eds), *The heart and soul of change: A handbook of common factors in treatment*. Washington, DC: APA Press.

Hubble, M., & Miller, S. D. (1995). Science and psychotherapy (letter). *Family Therapy Networker, 19*(1), 8.

Johnson, L. D. (1994). *Session rating scale*. Salt Lake City, UT: Author.

Johnson, L. D. (1995). *Psychotherapy in the age of accountability*. New York: Norton.

Johnson, L. D., & Shaha, S. H. (1996). Continous Quality Improvement in Psychotherapy. *Psychotherapy, 33*, 225–236.

Johnson, L. D., & Shaha, S. H. (1997). Upgrading clinician's reports to MCOs. *Be-*

havioral Health Management (July/August), 42–46.

Kazdin, A. E. (1986). Comparative outcome studies of psychotherapy: Methodological issues and strategies. *Journal of Consulting and Clinical Psychology, 54*, 95–105.

Kirk, S., & Kutchins, H. (1992). *The selling of DSM: The rhetoric of science in psychiatry*. New York: Aldine de Gruyter.

Klein, R. G. (1996). Comments on expanding the clinical role of psychologists. *American Psychologist, 51*(3), 216–218.

Kuhn, T. S. (1970). *The structure of scientific revolutions* (2nd ed.). Chicago: University of Chicago Press.

Kutchins, H., & Kirk, S. (1997). *Making us crazy*. New York: Free Press.

Lambert, M. J. (1992). Implications of outcome research for psychotherapy integration. In J. C. Norcross & M. R. Goldfried (Eds.), *Handbook of psychotherapy integration*. New York: Basic Books.

Lambert, M., & Bergin, A. E. (1994). The effectiveness of psychotherapy. In A. E. Bergin, & S. L. Garfield (Eds.), *Handbook of psychotherapy and behavior change (4th ed.)*, (pp. 143–189). New York: Wiley.

Lambert, M. J., & Burlingame, G. (1995). *The outcome-questionnaire 45*. Stevenson, MD: American Professional Credentialing Services.

Lambert, M. J., Okiishi, J., Finch, A. E., & Johnson, L. D. (1998). Outcome assessment: From conceptualization to implementation. *Professional Psychology, 29*(1), 63–90.

Lebow, J. (1982). Consumer satisfaction with mental health treatment. *Psychological Bulletin, 91*, 244–259.

Lebow, J. (1997). New science for psychotherapy: Can we predict how therapy will progress? *Family Therapy Networker, 21*(2), 85–91.

Lorion, R. P. (1996). Applying our medicine to the psychopharmocology debate. *American Psychologist, 51*(3), 219–224.

Miller, S. D., Duncan, B. L., & Hubble, M. A. (1997). *Escape from Babel: Toward a unifying language for psychotherapy practice*. New York: Norton.

Morrock, R. (1994). Pseudo-psychotherapy: UFO's, cloudbusters, conspiracy, and paranoia in Wilhelm Reich's psychotherapy. *Skeptic, 2*(3), 93–95.

National Association of Social Workers. (1996). *NASW code of ethics*. Washington, DC: NASW.

Ogles, B., Lambert, M. J., & Masters, K. (1996). *Assessing in clinical practice*. New York: Allyn & Bacon.

Ogles, B., & Lunnen, K. M. (1996). Outcome measurement: Research tools for clinical practice. *Newsletter for the Ohio Psychological Association*, 1–3.

Orlinsky, D. W., Grawe, K., & Parks, B. K. (1994). Process and outcome in psychotherapy — noch einmal. In A. E. Bergin and S. Garfield (Eds.), *Handbook of psychotherapy and behavior change (4th ed)*, (pp. 270–376). New York: Wiley.

Pasco, G. C. (1984). Patient satisfaction in primary health care: A literature review and analysis. *Evaluation and Program Planning*, *6*, 185–210.

Roper Organization. (1992). *Unusual personal experiences: An analysis of data from three national surveys*. Las Vegas, NV: Bigelow Holding Co.

Smith, M. L., Glass, G. V., & Miller, T. I. (1980). *The benefits of psychotherapy*. Baltimore: The Johns Hopkins University Press.

Steenbarger, B. N. (1992). Toward science-practice integration in brief counseling and therapy. *The Counseling Psychologist*, *20*, 403–450.

Steenbarger, B. N. (1994). Duration and outcome in psychotherapy: An integrative review. *Professional Psychology*, *25*(2), 111–119.

Stein, D. M., & Lambert, M. J. (1984). On the relationship between therapist experience and psychotherapy outcome. *Clinical Psychology Review*, *4*, 1–16.

Talmon, M., Hoyt, M., & Rosenbaum, R. (1990). Effective single-session therapy: Step-by-step guidelines. In M. Talmon, *Single-session therapy: Maximizing the effect of the first (and often only) therapeutic encounter*. San Francisco: Jossey-Bass.

Watzlawick, P. (1976). *How real is real? Confusion, disinformation, communication*. New York: Vintage.

Weiss, B. L. (1988). *Many lives, many masters*. New York: Fireside.

Wilford, J. N. (1986). *The riddle of the dinosaur*. New York: Knopf.

Wylie, M. S. (1997). Consumer driven therapy. *Family Therapy Networker*, *21*(4), 34–41.

Zimet, C. N. (1989). The mental health care revolution: Can psychology survive? *American Psychologist*, *44(*4), 703–708.

THERAPEUTIC APPROACHES

13

Brief Psychosocial Treatments for Panic Disorder

Emily Hoffman Stern, Jill T. Levitt, & David H. Barlow

Recent health-care policy developments have emphasized the importance of effective short-term therapy. Responding to changes in the emerging health-care system, research initiatives have led to substantial progress in the development of short-term psychosocial treatments. Controlled studies have been conducted providing strong evidence for the efficacy of a variety of brief treatments for different psychiatric disorders. For anxiety disorders, in particular, studies have reported consistently positive results for the efficacy of short-term psychosocial treatments when compared with no treatment, a psychosocial "placebo," or a credible alternative psychotherapeutic intervention (Craske, Brown, & Barlow, 1991; Borkovec & Costello, 1993; Heimberg, Dodge, Hope, Kennedy, Zollo, & Becker, 1990; Foa, Rothbaum, Riggs, & Murdock, 1991). More recently, large-scale studies have evaluated the efficacy of short-term psychosocial treatments in combination with and compared to effective pharmacological treatments (Barlow, Gorman, Shear, & Woods, 1998).

In the area of psychotherapy research, the development of brief therapies for the treatment of panic disorder with and without agoraphobia, in particular, has received substantial interest and attention. Early research on the development of brief effective treatments for panic disorder was conducted by behaviorally oriented investigators who attempted to treat agoraphobic avoidance behavior using in vivo exposure procedures (Agras, Leitenberg, & Barlow, 1968; Marks, 1969). These studies indicated that gradual, systematic exposure to feared situations produced marked clinical improvement in patients with phobic situational avoidance. Compared with no treatment or a placebo, such as attentional control procedures, in vivo (rather than imaginal) exposure-based procedures were consistently effective in reducing agoraphobic avoidance. Treatment gains from exposure therapy were maintained at follow-up points four years and longer after treatment was completed (Barlow, 1988; Jansson & Ost, 1982). Despite the evidence supporting the efficacy of exposure-based treatments, however, as many as 25% to 40% of patients did not show clinical improvement in response to treatment, and few of the patients who responded to treatment were "cured" or symptom-free at the conclusion of exposure therapy. Many patients continued to experience frequent panic attacks and substantial anxiety, suggesting that reducing avoidance behavior was not a sufficient treatment for panic disorder with or without agoraphobia.

During the 1980s, evolving conceptualizations of panic disorder led to the development of brief treatments directed specifically at unexpected panic attacks and the cognitive interpretation of the meaning and consequences of the physical symptoms of panic (Klein, 1967; Barlow, Craske, Cerny, & Klosko, 1989). Cognitive-behavioral treatment (CBT) approaches combine exposure-based procedures with techniques designed to modify cognitive misconceptions of panic and anxiety. Panic Control Therapy (PCT) is a widely disseminated, brief cognitive-behavioral treatment based on a three-component model of panic (Craske, Brown, & Barlow, 1991; Barlow, Craske, Cerny, & Klosko, 1989). According to this model, the three dimensions of anxiety (physical, cognitive, and behavioral) interact in a way that may increase anxiety and perpetuate the experience of panic. The physical component of anxiety consists of somatic sensations, such as shortness of breath and accelerated heart rate, and their underlying hormonal and cardiovascular changes. The cognitive component involves an attentional shift toward possible signs of danger and anxious thoughts about physical or emotional threat. The final component addresses the behaviors motivated by anxiety: specifically, avoidance of anxiety-provoking situations or safety behaviors, such as distraction, designed to reduce or prevent anxiety.

PCT, which typically is conducted over approximately 12 sessions, consists of three primary treatment phases: (1) breathing retraining, (2) cognitive restructuring, and (3) interoceptive or structured exposure to bodily sensations that have become associated with panic attacks. Breathing retraining addresses the physical component of anxiety; cognitive restructuring targets the cognitive shift toward danger and associated misinterpretations; and exposure attempts to reduce avoidance and associated safety behaviors.

Breathing Retraining

Hyperventilation and associated symptoms, such as lightheadedness, are among the most common physical manifestations of panic attacks. Breathing retraining involves a psychoeducational component in which the therapist explains the origins and physiological basis of hyperventilation and demonstrates the effects of hyperventilation during the therapy session. Following this demonstration, patients are taught proper diaphragmatic breathing until they can breathe comfortably at a rate of 8 to 10 breaths per minute. Once patients have mastered the technique of slow diaphragmatic breathing, they can use it regularly in their daily lives and during stressful periods.

Cognitive Restructuring

This component of treatment, adapted from Beck's cognitive therapy for depression, is directed at correcting misinterpretations of bodily sensations as dangerous events that may lead to death or loss of control. Treatment focuses on identifying core, "automatic" cognitions associated with two fundamental cognitive errors: overestimating the probability of dangerous events and "catastrophizing" about the consequences of these events.

Interoceptive Exposure

According to the cognitive-behavioral model of panic from which PCT was developed, physical sensations trigger learned alarms, leading to heightened anxiety. Interoceptive exposure targets the anxiety associated with the experience of somatic sensations. Patients proceed through a standard series of exercises designed to elicit physical sensations similar to those experienced during periods of panic or high anxiety. These exercises include running in place, spinning in a chair, and breathing through a narrow straw. Patients practice these exercises repeatedly in session and at home, and they are encouraged to enter naturalistic situations that may be associated with the experience of anxiety-provoking physical sensations such as watching horror movies or drinking caffeinated beverages.

Situational Exposure

When agoraphobic avoidance accompanies the panic disorder, intensive in vivo exposure is incorporated into treatment until the avoidance is substantially decreased or eliminated. Currently, we are experimenting with condensing this treatment component into a several-day period following the administration of PCT.

CLINICAL TRIAL DATA ON THE EFFICACY OF CBT

Several clinical trials have investigated the efficacy and clinical utility of PCT and other brief cognitive and behavioral treatments of panic disorder. PCT shares similar therapeutic techniques with an independently developed treatment at the University of Oxford (Clark et al., 1994). This approach focuses more exclusively on cognitive restructuring while also addressing physiological and behavioral components. Both PCT and the cognitive therapy developed by Clark and colleagues (1994) seem to be comparably efficacious treatments although the treatments have not been directly compared with one another. Table 1 summarizes data from studies published prior to 1996 that evaluate the variants of cognitive-behavioral therapy for panic disorder utilizing an intent to treat analysis (an earlier version of this table was presented in Barlow & Lehman, 1996). In most studies, CBT resulted in greater treatment gains than did a waitlist condition or a variety of psychotherapeutic placebos, ranging from applied relaxation to drug placebos.

In the first controlled study of PCT (Barlow, Craske, Cerny, & Klosko, 1989), three treatment conditions — PCT alone, progressive muscle relaxation (PMR) alone, and PCT combined with relaxation — were compared to a waitlist control condition. At post-treatment, 36% of the waitlist group, 60% of the PMR group, 85% of the PCT group, and 87% of the combined treatment group were panic-free. The PCT and combined treatment groups differed significantly from the waitlist, while the PMR group did not. At a six-month follow-up assessment, the PCT and combined treatment groups showed maintenance of treatment gains, while the

Table 1. Clinical Trials of Cognitive Behavioral Treatments for Panic Disorder and Intent-to-Treat Analysis*

Source, year	Length of Follow-up, month	Treatment/ No. of Patients/ % Panic Free	Significant Comparison, % Panic Free**: Other Treatments	Significant Comparison, % Panic Free**: Waitlist
Craske et al., 1991***	24	PCT/15/81	Yes: AR=36	...
			Yes: PCT and AR=43	...
Clark et al., 1994	12	CT/17/76	Yes: AR=43§	...
			Yes: IMI=48§	...
Klosko et al., 1990	PT	PCT/15/87	No: AL=50	Yes: 33
			Yes: PL=36	...
Newman et al., 1990	12	CTM/24/87	...	...
		CTNM/19/87	...	...
Cote et al., 1992	12	CBTM/13/92	...	...
		CBTNM/8/100	...	...
Beck et al., 1992	PT	CT/17/94	Yes: ST=25‖	...
Black et al., 1993	PT	CT/25/32	Yes: FL=68	...
			No: PL=20	...
Margraf and Schneider, 1991	4 wk	CT/22/91	...	Yes: 5
Ost et al., 1993	12	CT/19/89	No: AR=74§	...
Telch et al., 1993	PT	PCT/34/85	...	Yes: 30
Craske et al., 1995	PT	CBT/16/53	Yes: NPT=8	...
Shear et al., 1994	6	CBT/23/45	No: NPT=45	...

*AL indicates alprazolam; AR, applied relaxation; CBT, cognitive behavioral therapy; CBTM, cognitive behavioral therapy and medication; CBTNM, cognitive behavioral therapy without medication; CT, cognitive therapy; CTM cognitive therapy and medication; CTNM, cognitive therapy without medication; FL, fluvoxamine maleate; IMI, imipramine hydrochloride; NPT, nonprescription treatment; PL, pill placebo; PCT, panic control treatment (exposure and cognitive restructuring); PT, posttreatment; and ST, standard treatment.

** Yes indicates the comparison was significant; no, comparison not significant; and ellipses, no comparison made.

*** Follow-up study of Barlow et al., 1989

§ Percentage of patients who were panic free at follow-up and who had received no additional treatment during the follow-up period.

‖ At eight weeks, which is the end of supportive therapy. At this time, 71% of patients undergoing CT were panic free.

PMR group evidenced deterioration on measures of clinical severity as well as general and somatic anxiety. At the 24-month follow-up, 81% of patients in the PCT alone group remained panic-free compared to only 43% in the combined group and 36% in the relaxation alone treatment (Craske, Brown, & Barlow, 1991). The authors speculated that patients in the combined treatment did not retain therapeutic gains as well as those who received PCT alone because neither the PCT nor the relaxation therapy was presented as thoroughly in the combined treatment as they were in the two other treatment conditions.

Although this study evaluated the efficacy of PCT conducted in an individual treatment format, other studies have administered PCT in a group context. Comparing the outcome of patients given eight weeks of group PCT to patients in a waitlist control condition, Telch and colleagues (1993) found that 85% of patients in the PCT group and only 30% in the waitlist control condition achieved panic-free status at the conclusion of treatment. These treatment gains were maintained at the six-month follow-up assessment, providing strong support for the efficacy of PCT in a group treatment format.

Other studies have compared the efficacy of PCT or a variant of CBT to pharmacological treatments (Klosko, Barlow, Tassinari, & Cerny, 1990; Clark et al., 1994). These studies report greater efficacy of brief cognitive-behavioral treatment compared to already established pharmacological treatments, such as alprazolam immediately following treatment (Klosko, Barlow, Tassinari, & Cerny, 1990) or imipramine at six months following discontinuation of all treatments (Clark et al., 1994).

Results from a recently completed multicenter clinical trial provide the most definitive data to date on the efficacy of PCT as compared to tricyclic antidepressants and their combination (Barlow, Gorman, Shear, & Woods, 1998). In this randomized, double-blind placebo controlled study that was conducted at four different sites, a total of 302 patients with panic disorder received either imipramine plus medical management (IMI), PCT, a pill placebo (PLA), or a combination of PCT and medication or PCT and placebo (Barlow, Craske, Cerny, & Klosko, 1989). The acute treatment phase comprised 11 sessions conducted within a 12-week period, and a subsequent maintenance phase consisted of six monthly sessions. Following the maintenance phase, all treatment was discontinued, and patients were assessed again six months later.

Results from this study indicated that both treatments (IMI and PCT) were equally effective at the conclusion of the initial three-month period, and both treatments were more effective than the placebo condition after six months of maintenance. At follow-up six months after treatments were discontinued, however, significantly more individuals in the IMI condition deteriorated compared to those who received PCT alone (Shear, 1998). The combined PCT and IMI treatment, as well as the PCT + placebo condition, revealed no clinical advantage over PCT alone. In addition, PCT + IMI also deteriorated significantly at follow-up compared to PCT + placebo or PCT alone. The results suggest that PCT may be the preferred treatment strategy initially due to the non-intrusive nature of psychosocial as compared to psychopharmacological interventions. Pharmacological treatment, then, could be reserved for patients who do not respond optimally to PCT.

A recent review of the literature on combined cognitive-behavioral and benzodiazepine treatments for panic disorder also indicated that there was little evidence to suggest that combination treatment is superior to CBT alone (Spiegel & Bruce, 1997). In fact, some studies recently reviewed reported greater long-term outcomes for CBT alone than for the combination (Otto, Pollack, & Sabatino, 1996), consistent with results from the multicenter collaborative study.

NEW DEVELOPMENTS IN BRIEF TREATMENTS FOR PANIC DISORDER

Recent research in the area of child and adolescent psychopathology has focused on the nature and prevalence of panic disorder in this younger age group. Studies have found that panic disorder occurs prior to adulthood, and that the primary clinical features of panic in youngsters are similar to those seen in an adult population (e.g., high trait anxiety, comorbid depression, and situational avoidance). Patterns of avoidance of everyday situations and the associated psychopathology often present in panic disorder may be particularly detrimental when experienced by adolescents, causing significant interference in daily life and activities essential to normal adolescent development. Building on the promising results of CBT for panic disorder with adults, Ollendick (1995) conducted a controlled multiple-baseline study combining elements of PCT and other cognitive-behavioral treatments to treat four adolescents with panic disorder. Post-treatment assessment indicated a decline in the frequency of panic attacks for all participants and significant reductions in agoraphobic avoidance, anxiety sensitivity, trait anxiety, fear, and depression. Based on consistent reports of the efficacy of PCT with adults and the findings reported by Ollendick (1995), a randomized, controlled study of the treatment of panic in adolescence, using a developmental adaptation of PCT, is underway at the Center for Anxiety and Related Disorders at Boston University. Preliminary data from pilot cases for this study support the efficacy of PCT for an adolescent population (Hoffman & Mattis, 2000).

In addition to the extensive research reviewed above and cited in Table 1, recent developments in panic disorder research have attempted to expand the scope of brief treatments for the disorder. Although many new short-term treatments for panic disorder have been developed from a cognitive-behavioral perspective, some treatments integrate elements from interpersonal and more psychodynamic approaches. Shear and her colleagues have developed an emotion-focused treatment (EFT) that is conducted over the course of 11 sessions followed by six monthly maintenance sessions (Shear, Cloitre, & Heckelman, 1995). EFT addresses emotion regulation, targeting fear and avoidance of negative emotions and triggers of these emotions. Treatment involves a psychoeducational component, which provides information about the nature of panic and panic disorder in a manner similar to PCT, and a component that attempts to identify and clarify emotional reactions in the context of interpersonal relationships and fears of being abandoned, trapped, or of some other negative event. By incorporating techniques addressing interpersonal relationships and emotion regulation, EFT may lead to improvements in the quality of life as well as a reduction of panic attacks and associated anxiety (Shear, 1998). In one study, EFT produced efficacy comparable to an early version of PCT, but drop-out rates were very high in both conditions (Shear, Pilkonis, Cloitre, & Leon, 1994. See Table 1).

THE DISSEMINATION OF EMPIRICALLY SUPPORTED TREATMENTS FOR PANIC DISORDER

Despite empirical support for the efficacy of PCT and other forms of CBT, these treatments are still significantly underutilized in community clinics. Goisman, Warshaw, and Keller (1999) found that while there have been several published reports on empirically supported cognitive-behavioral interventions for anxiety disorders, there have been no significant changes in the delivery of these treatments over the past decade. This conclusion is based on a report from the Harvard/Brown Anxiety Disorders Research Program (HARP) that examined psychosocial treatments delivered to participants in the HARP program in order to determine whether changes in treatments have paralleled changes in treatment recommendations for patients with anxiety disorders (Goisman, Warshaw, & Keller, 1999). Despite increased public and professional awareness of the effectiveness of CBT, the authors found that the utilization of cognitive and behavioral treatments did not increase relative to alternative treatments between 1991 (when the authors conducted a similar study: Goisman, Rogers, Steketee, Warshaw, Cuneo, & Keller, 1993) and 1995–96.

This finding on insufficient dissemination is surprising, considering the mounting evidence that cognitive-behavioral treatments are effective for a variety of anxiety disorders. These findings illustrate the need for a research initiative to study the effectiveness of PCT and other such empirically supported treatments in community settings. Such naturalistic studies can provide evidence of the utility of these treatments for community clinicians. It is important for clinical researchers to demonstrate that empirically supported treatments such as PCT are generalizable to community settings, and are logistically feasible and cost-effective. Evidence supporting the clinical utility of PCT in naturalistic studies should lead to an increase in the dissemination and utilization of PCT in the community.

One method for evaluating the transportability of well-known empirically supported treatments to community mental-health settings is the "benchmarking" research strategy (McFall, 1996). In this approach, treatments of known efficacy are delivered in clinical service settings and comparisons are made between the outcomes obtained in randomized clinical trials versus community settings. Wade, Treat, and Stuart (1998) utilized this strategy by applying PCT to 110 patients at a community clinic. Despite differences between settings, patients, and therapists in the research clinic and community clinic samples, treatment outcomes from the two groups were comparable (Wade, Treat, & Stuart, 1998). This study suggests that PCT can be successfully transported to a community mental-health center and that PCT is a generalizable and feasible treatment that can be utilized successfully in the community.

CONCLUSIONS

A substantial body of clinical research demonstrates the efficacy of brief psychosocial treatments for panic disorder. The majority of this research has focused on cognitive-behavioral therapies, particularly PCT. Current studies are attempting to extend the use of PCT to an adolescent population. In addition, recent research has provided preliminary support for the effectiveness of PCT delivered in a community setting. Finally, the ease of dissemination and cost-effectiveness of PCT and other empirically supported treatments merit future attention from psychotherapy researchers.

References

Agras, W. S., Leitenberg, H., & Barlow, D. H. (1968). Social reinforcement in the modification of agoraphobia. *Archives of General Psychiatry, 19,* 423–427.

Barlow, D. H. (1988). *Anxiety and its disorders: The nature and treatment of anxiety and panic.* New York: Guilford.

Barlow, D. H., Craske, M. G., Cerny, J. A., & Klosko, J. S. (1989). Behavioral treatment of panic disorder. *Behavior Therapy, 20,* 261–282.

Barlow, D. H., & Lehman, C. L. (1996). Advances in the psychosocial treatment of anxiety disorders: Implications for national health care. *Archives of General Psychiatry, 53,* 727–735.

Barlow, D. H., Gorman, J. , Shear, M. K., & Woods, S. (1998, November). Study design and pretreatment attrition. In D. H. Barlow (Chair), *Results from the multi-center clinical trial on the treatment of panic disorder: Cognitive-behavioral treatment versus imipramine versus their combination.* Symposium conducted at the 32nd annual meeting of the Association for the Advancement of Behavior Therapy, Washington, D.C.

Beck, A. T., Sokol, L., Clark, D. A., Berchick, R., & Wright, F. (1992). A cross-over study of focused cognitive therapy for panic disorder. *American Journal of Psychiatry, 149,* 778–783.

Black, D. W., Wesner, R., Bowers, W., & Gabel, J. (1993). A comparison of fluvoxamine, cognitive therapy, and placebo in the treatment of panic disorder. *Archives of General Psychiatry, 50,* 44–50.

Borkovec, T. D., & Costello, E. (1993). Efficacy of applied relaxation and cognitive-behavioral therapy in the treatment of generalized anxiety disorder. *Journal of Consulting and Clinical Psychology, 61*(4), 611–619.

Clark, D. M., Salkovskis, P. M., Hackmann, A., Middleton, H., Anastasiades, P., & Gelder, M. (1994). A comparison of cognitive therapy, applied relaxation, and imipramine in the treatment of panic disorder. *British Journal of Psychiatry, 164,* 759–769.

Cote, G., Gauthier, J., & Laberge, B. (1992, November). *The impact of medication use on the efficacy of cognitive-behavioral therapy for panic disorder.* Presented at the 26th annual meeting of the Association for Advancement of Behavior Therapy, Boston, MA.

Craske, M. G., Brown, T. A., & Barlow, D. H. (1991). Behavioral treatment of panic disorder: A two-year follow-up. *Behavior Therapy, 22,* 289–304.

Craske, M. G., Maidenberg, E., & Bystritsky, A. (1995). Brief cognitive-behavioral versus non-directive therapy for panic disorder. *Journal of Behavior Therapy and Experimental Psychiatry, 26,* 113–120.

Foa, E. B., Rothbaum, E. O., Riggs, D., & Murdock, T. (1991). Treatment of PTSD in rape victims: A comparison between cognitive-behavioral procedures and counseling. *Journal of Consulting and Clinical Psychology, 59,* 715–723.

Goisman, R. M., Rogers, M. P., Steketee, G. S., Warshaw, M. G., Cuneo, P., & Keller, M. B. (1993). Utilization of behavioral methods in a multicenter anxiety disorder study. *Journal of Clinical Psychiatry, 54,* 213–218.

Goisman, R. M., Warshaw, M. G., & Keller, M. B. (1999). Psychosocial treatment prescriptions for generalized anxiety disorder, panic disorder, and social phobia, 1991–1996. *American Journal of Psychiatry, 156*(11), 1819–1821.

Heimberg, R. G., Dodge. C. S., Hope. D. A., Kennedy, C. R., Zollo, L., & Becker, R. E. (1990). Cognitive-behavioral group treatment for social phobia: Comparison to a credible placebo control. *Cognitive Therapy and Research, 14,* 1–23.

Hoffman, E. C., & Mattis, S. G. (2000). Cognitive behavioral treatment for panic disorder in adolescents. *Cognitive and Behavior Practice, 7,* 253–261.

Jansson, L., & Ost, L. G. (1982). Behavioral treatments for agoraphobia: An evaluative review. *Clinical Psychology Review, 2,* 311–336.

Klein, D. F. (1967). Importance of psychiatric diagnosis and prediction of clinical drug effects. *Archives of General Psychiatry, 16,* 118–126.

Klosko, J. S., Barlow, D. H., Tassinari, R., & Cerny, J. A. (1990). A comparison of alprazolam and behavior therapy in treatment of panic disorder. *Journal of Consulting and Clinical Psychology, 58,* 77–84.

Margraf, J., & Schneider, S. (1991, November). *Outcome and active ingredients of cognitive-behavioral treatments for panic disorder.* Presented at the 25th annual meeting of the Association for Advancement of Behavior Therapy, New York.

Marks, I. M. (1969). *Fears and phobias.* London, England: Heineman.

McFall, R. M. (1996, July). *Consumer satisfaction as a way of evaluating psychotherapy: Ecological validity and all that versus the good old randomized trial* (panel discussion). 6th annual convention of the American Association of Applied and Preventative Psychology, San Francisco, CA.

Newman, M. G., Kenardy, J., Herman, S., & Taylor, C. B. (1990, November). *Efficacy of cognitive therapy in reducing panic attacks and medication.* Presented at the 24th annual meeting of the Association for Advancement of Behavior Therapy, San Francisco, CA.

Ollendick, T. H. (1995). Cognitive-behavioral treatment of panic disorder with agoraphobia in adolescents: A multiple baseline design analysis. *Behavior Therapy, 26,* 517–531.

Ost, L. G., Westling, B. E., & Hellstrom, K. (1993). Applied relaxation, exposure in vivo and cognitive methods in the treatment of panic disorder with agoraphobia. *Behaviour Research and Therapy, 31,* 383.

Otto, M. W., Pollack, M. H., & Sabatino, S. A. (1996). *Maintenance of remission following CBT for panic disorder: Possible deleterious effects for concurrent medication treatment.* Presented at the World Congress of Behavioural and Cognitive Therapies, Copenhagen, Denmark.

Shear, M. K. (1998). *Cognitive-behavioral therapy of panic disorder.* Presented at the American Psychiatric Association, Toronto, Canada.

Shear, M. K., Pilkonis, P. A., Cloitre, M., & Leon, A. C. (1994). Cognitive-behavioral treatment of panic disorder. *Archives of General Psychiatry, 51,* 395–401.

Shear, M. K., Cloitre, M., & Heckelman, L. (1995). Emotion-focused treatment for panic disorder: A brief, dynamically informed therapy. In: J. P. Barber, & P. Crits-Christoph (Eds.), *Dynamic therapies for psychiatric disorders (Axis I).* New York: Harper-Collins.

Spiegel, D. A., & Bruce, T. J. (1997). Benzodiazepines and exposure-based cognitive-behavioral therapies for panic disorder: Conclusions from combined treatment trials. *American Journal of Psychiatry, 154,* 773–780.

Telch, M. J., Lucas, J. A., Schmidt, N. B., Hanna, H. H., Jaimez, T. S., & Lucas, R. A. (1993). Group cognitive-behavioral treatment of panic disorder. *Behavior Research and Therapy, 31,* 279–287.

Wade, W. A., Treat, T. A., & Stuart, G. L. (1998). Transporting an empirically supported treatment for panic disorder to a service clinic setting: A benchmarking strategy. *Journal of Consulting and Clinical Psychology, 66,* 231–239.

14

Getting to the Surface of the Problem: The Bricks and Mortar of Our Constructions

Steve de Shazer

Since my job involves doing, teaching, supervising, researching, and writing about Solution-Focused Brief Therapy (SFBT), this is what I know and, therefore, I will focus on the larger world of hypno/family/psychotherapy and on my own particular (and peculiar?), smaller section of that world. (Whether and how this way of thinking might apply in other contexts is beyond the scope of this chapter.)

In this larger hypno/psycho/family-therapy world, there are both constructionists of various types and traditionalists of various types and their interest in the surface of things varies a lot. The traditionalists, the majority of the therapists in the so-called psycho/hypno/family-therapy world (which I will call "therapy" from here on), hold to what is usually called "the medical model," and especially to the accompanying conceptions of "psychopathology"[1] that are still the basis — in fact, the absolute foundation — of most of the psychiatric field, and thus the whole world

[1] Michael White (1993) considers the *invention* of psychopathology as the central and most significant achievement of the whole culture of psycho [family, hypno]-therapy. I couldn't agree more. But, of course, the traditionalists do not see it as an invention.

of therapy (Weakland, 1993, p. 140). The traditionalists have inherited the legacy of Western thought that held that it was important to go deeper and deeper beneath the surface of whatever it was they were trying to explain. This approach is based on their belief that being puzzled by the surface of things means that there is something hidden and, therefore, that there is something very important that cannot be seen.

At least some constructivists agree with Wittgenstein (1968) and say that "since everything lies open to view there is nothing to explain" (# 126). Furthermore, "the aspects of things that are most important for us [appear to be] hidden because of their simplicity and familiarity. [That is], one is unable to notice something — because it is always before one's eyes" (p. 129).

I want to discuss two areas where I see constructivism playing a major role. The first — on a macro level — deals with one of the muddles faced by the field as a whole, and I want to suggest a way to get out of that muddle (by simply getting to the surface of the problem). And the second — on a micro level — deals with doing therapy by getting to, and staying on, the surface of the problem.

PART ONE

> "The classifications made by philosophers and psychologists are like those that someone would give who tried to classify clouds by their shapes."
>
> — Ludwig Wittgenstein (1968, # 154)

For most traditionalists, a diagnosis is the name of something that is "objectively real" for them. Although they may have long and unresolved conflicts over definitions, nonetheless they would agree that people can be divided and classified into various categories. For example, a person is either an alcoholic or is not. (Of course, this so-called diagnosis cannot be determined by a blood test or an X-ray or anything that trustworthy.) While the category of alcoholic might involve a continuum from "mild" to "severe," there is no such thing as a person's being just "a little bit alcoholic." At least most, if not all, traditionalists hold that there is no cure for the (so-called) disease of alcoholism, and thus a person so diagnosed is still an alcoholic even if he or she had not had a drink in the past 30 years. Not drinking, which is called "abstinence," is seen as the only possible way to deal with or treat this (so-called) disease. In fact, unsuccessful attempts to stop drinking are frequently used to confirm the diagnosis.

Dealing effectively with alcoholism has long been seen by traditionalists as extremely difficult: some research shows that four years after traditional treatment — where abstinence is the only acceptable, positive outcome — only 7% (of 3,000) are successful at being abstinent[2] (Polich, Armor, & Braiker, 1980)! The belief that abstinence is the only approach to treating this "disease," and the finding that only a very few people succeed at being abstinent, suggests that treating alcoholism is frequently going to be at least a hopeless task, if not an impossible one. It is made even more difficult by the related belief that an alcoholic can never become a "normal drinker" (even though there is research that suggests differently[3]). Regardless of the research, this nearly impossible approach of becoming abstinent is still seen as the *only* approach. Thus, the concept of alcoholism, as held by many traditionalists, leads to (and constructs) a problem for the field: The one and only approach to dealing with alcoholism fails as much as 93% of the time. However, since it is seen as the *only* approach, it must continue to be used.[4]

Obviously, when a problem is so constructed as to have only one approach to dealing with it or resolving it, then failure in an attempt at using that approach necessarily becomes construed by the individual as the individual's fault. (The failure is never seen as a result of the difficult task set by the concept of alcoholism. Most individual clients/patients, and most traditionalists, do not see this structural, conceptual problem as an integral part of the construction of the concept of alcoholism. That is, traditionalists see "alcoholism" as a fact, not as a construction.) Each repeated failure both reinforces and confirms the diagnosis, and increases

[2] These results are far worse than chance. How is this to be understood, particularly in light of some research that tells us that as many as 82% of those people who stop drinking for at least one year do so without any treatment! (Sobell, Sobell, Toneatto, & Leo, 1993).

[3] Of course, given the mythological nature of the concept of alcoholism, any "alcoholic" who can resume "normal drinking" was not a real "alcoholic." Rather, the individual was the recipient of a misdiagnosis. Thus, the "theory" is preserved in spite of the evidence.

[4] The traditionalists' view (of alcoholism) seems to be more mythology than science. A myth, according to Vincent Descombes (1995), can be recognized "above all by its encompassing and imperious qualities: it is imposing, it elicits unconditional adherence and rejects in advance all possibility of disagreement on the basis of experiment. It persuades the mind that things must happen in a particular way, even if things seem to happen quite differently" (p. xiii).

the demands that the individual increase his or her efforts in applying the approach. That is, the individual *only* can do more of something that is not working, which is exactly how problems are defined in the brief therapy section of the world.

Each failure naturally leads to greater pessimism and guilt. Family members become more and more disappointed and blaming with each episode of failure. This sets up an interactional situation that further increases hopelessness in both the individual and the others involved. Naturally, these questions arise: Is success possible for me? Is failure inevitable for me? Eventually, many individuals are forced to conclude that for them abstinence is not possible. Therefore, it is perfectly reasonable to stop attempting to use the approach and to continue drinking.

From my point of view (a social constructivist point of view), "alcoholism" is a construction with some very serious and undesirable consequences (and, if the world were rational, the concept would be discarded immediately). The everyday grammar around the concept of alcoholism is permanently fixed, leaving us with no other way to talk about alcoholism and, therefore, no other way to think about it. At least in part, these consequences can be seen logically as a result of a trap set for us by language and how we use it. According to Wittgenstein (1980):

> Language sets everyone the same traps; it is an immense network of easily accessible wrong turnings. And so we watch one person after another walking down the same paths and we know in advance where that person will branch off, where walk straight on without noticing the side turning, etc. What I have to do then is erect signposts at all the junctions where there are wrong turnings so as to help people past the danger points. (p. 18e)

THE VERB "TO BE"

The verb "to be" can be one of the trickiest of language's traps. Here, I want to borrow a technique from Wittgenstein. So, let's compare these sentences:

1. I am a male.
2. I am an American.
3. I am a good cook.

I can say that "I am a male," "I am an American," and "I am a good cook" because I know that I am a male, an American, and a good cook. But none of these are statements of knowledge, and may or may not be based on empirical criteria. We all know that being a male, an American, and a good cook are all (normally) enduring attributes. (I will not suddenly cease being a good cook.) This is the way the verb "to be" is used. Even though occasionally my cooking will be a disaster, as I see it, these beliefs are not subject to change.

The situation changes when we shift from the first person present to the third person present. My use of the words "I am" leads you to seek verification, and there are clues and criteria available to you. These allow you, as an observer, to say: "He is a male." "He is an American." No problem. People I've cooked for can, and most do, say, "He is a good cook." As Wittgenstein (1967) points out: "Sentences in the third person of the present: *information*. In the first person present: *expression*" (# 472).

Next, let's add a fourth pair of sentences.

1. I am a malc. || He is a male.
2. I am an American. || He is an American.
3. I am a good cook. || He is a good cook.
4. I am an alcoholic. || He is an alcoholic.

What happens in this fourth pair of sentences? The form of the verb "to be" is the same in all four first-person-present verbs (I am an *X*), and it is also the same in each of the third-person-present verbs (He is an *X*). The third person singular, in each case, involves the same grammatical form. This is a very seductive trap that leads us automatically to process the sentences in the same way, and it leads us inevitably to the conclusion that being an alcoholic is similar to being a male, an American, and a good cook in that all four are permanent and enduring attributes of the individual. Otherwise, we would not use the same verb when talking about these things. We do not need psychiatry, Alcoholics Anonymous, or even theory to build this trap: all we need is our everyday grammar. Of course, many people whom traditionalists would diagnose as "alcoholic" intuitively "see" this trap, disagree, and argue with the diagnostician. They want to be able to drink, just like other, normal people.

ON THE SURFACE

Constructing a way out of the trap, a way to solve the "alcoholism" problem, is not easy. Our grammar gets in the way: It is very difficult, because it is "unnatural," to use a different verb artificially, such as "he does alcoholism" or "he is caught by alcoholism," because, as Ferdinand de Saussure says, "You cannot legislate changes in language." Therefore, the problem needs to get a new name, a new construction, such as "problematic drinking," and a whole new conceptualization will follow. (The term "problematic drinking" doesn't mean that the drinking is a problem, but rather that how the drinker goes about drinking leads to and/or is associated with problems.) If we simply were to describe our observations (cues and criteria) — that is, just describe the surface of the problem — that would lead to the traditional diagnosis of alcoholism: it is clear that the individuals (1) drink too much, and/or (2) too often, and that (3) they usually say, for instance, that if they have a bottle of beer in front of them, then they feel they *must* drink it. They do not see that they have a choice in the matter.

If the situation were constructed as "problematic drinking," then alternative approaches could readily be developed to help the clients (1) drink less, and/or (2) drink less often, and (3) drink if and when they choose, that is, if there is a bottle of beer in front of them, they may or may not decide to drink it. It is a matter of choice. The situation is entirely changed once a second possible approach to the problem is introduced. With two ways to approach problematic drinking, failure at one only means that, logically, the person should try the other approach. Perhaps that will work. It is important to note that with two approaches, the individual is not forced to try to become abstinent. He or she is not trapped in a situation in which there is no choice. Once there is a second approach, trying to become abstinent is only one option. Within the context of choice, even continuing to drink is an option, since there is a big difference between choosing to drink and believing that you have no choice but to drink.

For about 10 years now, this new approach to problematic drinking has been used at the Department of Psychiatry and Psychosomatics at St. John's Hospital in Bruges, Belgium (de Shazer & Isebaert, 1998). Here the patients have a choice of ways in which to deal with their problematic drinking: (1) they can attempt what is called "controlled drinking" or "normal drinking" (which the World Health Organization defines as three beers per day with two days "off" per week) or (2) they can attempt to become abstinent. At any point during treatment (or after), the individual can change his or her mind and decide to try the other approach. The therapists involved in the program accept an individual's choice of approach, which the patient usually makes in consultation with the family.

Furthermore, after one day as inpatients, patients can choose to continue as inpatients, switch to the day-hospital program, switch to being outpatients, or leave the program.[5] In general, most clients remain as inpatients for about two weeks and then switch to the day hospital. Patients can change their minds at any point and make a different choice. Although there is no time limit, people usually remain in the program no longer than four weeks.

A recently completed five-year follow-up with 250 patients (out of 250) shows the success of this approach:

1. Of the 250, 123 (49.2%) are abstinent.
2. Of the 250, 62 (24.8%) are controlling their drinking.
3. Another 25 (10%), although still drinking "too much" and/or "too often," are drinking significantly less than they were before treatment.

Interestingly, 10% of those who originally had decided to use the controlled-drinking approach and then switched to trying to become abstinent were still abstinent (for at least 4.5 years) at follow-up (de Shazer & Isebaert, 1998). Choosing controlled drinking — and deciding it was not the right approach — can be constructed as a step on the way to abstinence.

For 80% of those still drinking, neither the patients nor the families nor their primary physicians thought that their drinking was still a problem, however 12% reported that they or their families sometimes thought their drinking was still a problem, but was far less of a problem than it had been before; 25% of the controlled drinkers only drink on weekends.

When asked about how they felt most of the time, 223 (88.8%) reported doing well, or feeling good, or even feeling very good. In addition, 179 (69.4%) reported that their family relationships had improved in the five years since their hospitalization. Furthermore, 198 (79.2%) reported that they had received no further treatment since discharge — after a typical

[5] About one-third of the patients are initially involuntary, that is, referred by someone, such as the police. This initial status has no effect on outcomes.

two-week stay as an inpatient, and then another two weeks either as an outpatient or in the day-hospital part of the program.

Pragmatically, treatment based on the construction of "problematic drinking" is better at promoting abstinence than is treatment based on the traditional construction of "alcoholism." That is, treatment based on abstinence as a *choice* is about seven times as effective as treatment based on demanded abstinence. Will these results influence the traditional view? Probably not very much, if at all. Will they influence therapists who use the traditional approach? A few, perhaps. Worldviews do not change easily.

PART TWO

In my little part of the field, unless it is totally rejected as unmitigated nonsense, as it is by the majority of (traditional) psychotherapists, the idea that (so-called) reality is constructed is most frequently used as though it were an established "truth." Everybody *knows* that "reality is constructed." Since it is something "everybody knows," this phrase has lost its radical meaning(s) and has become a slogan or rallying cry, a ticket or "password of acceptability" — as Ludwig Fleck put it (1979, p. 43) — that either gets you instant admission to a select circle or gets you instantly rejected. Believing that this is an established truth tends to prevent the user from wondering about, or thinking about, just exactly what this phrase means. At times, it seems to mean that a client constructs problematic realities and it is the therapist's job somehow to fix the client's reality so that it works better. Thus, the status quo is maintained: the therapist is able to maintain his or her position as expert. At other times, it means other things, but — being a generalization and an interpretation — it is a $1,000 word that hides each of the 1,000 little $1 words that go into composing the meanings and usage of the big one. The idea that reality is constructed has become an answer when instead what is wanted are questions, such as: How is "reality constructed?" What materials are used to construct reality? What are the processes involved? Who constructs reality? What are the bricks? What is the mortar? As a result of accepting this phrase as accepted truth, a concept useful for thinking, it has become a substitute for thinking (Weakland, 1993, p. 139). "Words which formerly were simple terms become slogans; sentences which once were simple statements become calls to battle" (Fleck, 1979, p. 43).

§

It is easy for me to say that "I construct reality" because I know that I construct reality. And I really believe this. But this is not a statement of knowledge; it may or may not be based on some (empirical) criterion. Simply put, it is a statement about what I believe. That is, I really have no good reason for this statement except that when I first heard this phrase, my response was, "Of course." Interestingly, as Ludwig Wittgenstein (1967) points out about such beliefs and various other first-person-singular statements, I cannot be wrong about this. "He has got to know that he knows: for knowing is a state of his own mind; he cannot be in doubt or error about it" (# 408). Of course, I might be lying, but I cannot be mistaken. You see how this sort of thing can easily become a matter of faith and an established truth! All too often, we forget that if there is no opportunity for me to be wrong, then I also cannot be right: it is not a statement of knowledge.

INVESTIGATING CONSTRUCTIVISM

> Conversation flows on, the application and interpretation of words, and only in its course do words have their meaning
>
> — *Ludwig Wittgenstein* (1967, p. 24e)

The situation changes when I attempt to attribute this constructive activity to other people, that is, when I say, "He constructs reality." As Wittgenstein (1967) put it, "Psychological verbs [are] characterized by the fact that the third person of the present is to be verified by observation, the first person not. Sentences in the third person of the present: information. In the first person present: expression" (# 472). How can I know whether or not he constructs reality? What information should I look for? Suppose he has never heard of this idea and I ask him, "Do you construct reality?" He might think I am crazy and get the idea that I think he might be God — since God made the world in seven days! But suppose that he says, as I did, "Of course I construct reality." Am I any further ahead? Is this information or an expression? How can I know what it is he knows and/or believes? Of course, I cannot assume that what goes on inside his head is similar to what goes on in mine. I might be unique, he might be unique; everybody might be different from either or both of us. Do I now know something more than he now says that he constructs reality? Do I have any idea what he might mean by that?

Suppose instead I want to be more of an investigator, to do some research, and, therefore, I decide just to observe his behavior without asking such a leading question. What criteria would I need to use for *me* to know that he believes that he constructs reality? This investigation is rather complicated since I have to include myself, the observer, in the description because I cannot know that he would behave in the same ways with other observers or in other contexts with or without an observer. Of course, there is always the danger that my description may be too interpretive, particularly since I have this goal of figuring out whether or not he constructs reality. I have to be extremely careful to exclude anything hypothetical and just to describe what is readily observable.

> He is a poor observer who does not notice that a stimulating conversation between two persons soon creates a condition in which each utters thoughts he would not have been able to produce by himself or in different company.
>
> — *Ludwig Fleck* (1979, p. 44)

Fortunately, doing therapy is one of the contexts in which two or more people have a conversation that can be observed. Sitting attentively behind the mirror and/or carefully watching videotapes and/or closely reading transcripts of sessions allows us to watch the conversation and we can describe what we see. Certainly, therapists hope their work will lead to the client's uttering thoughts that he or she had not been able to produce by himself or herself. Directly observing these conversations allows us to avoid being either hypothetical or speculative. We can ask ourselves: Can what we see and hear be described as "creating reality"?

The Bricks

If you watch session after session of Solution-Focused Brief Therapy (SFBT), it will become obvious that the therapist's primary activity is asking questions and that, across sessions, these questions remain pretty much the same. In fact, the role of the therapist often appears to outsiders to be very, very boring indeed. (I hear this in seminar after seminar. This puzzles me, since I never would think of describing doing therapy using a "boring/exciting" yardstick. It is just a job to be done and entertaining the therapist is not one of the tasks involved.)

In almost every first session, solution-focused therapists ask the miracle question, using pretty much the same words time after time, and at least one scaling question, again, using pretty much the same words. (I'm going into some detail here because all too often people have misunderstood the miracle question and ask it in not very useful ways.) Usually, I introduce the miracle question by telling the client that I have an unusual, and perhaps difficult, question to ask, one that takes some imagination. I then pause, waiting for some signal to go ahead. Then I begin to ask in this way:

Suppose ... [A pause always follows this word. "Suppose" is a nice, harmless, but useful little word. The pause allows clients to wonder what strange and difficult thing I might ask them to suppose.]

after we finish here, you go home tonight, watch TV, do your usual chores, etc., and then go to bed and to sleep ... [A pause here. So far, what I am asking the client to suppose is very normal, everyday stuff. Not so strange after all.]

and, while you are sleeping, a miracle happens ... [Pause. The context for this miracle is the client's normal, everyday life. Thus, it is a "normal miracle" and not something too out of the ordinary. However, this construction does allow for any kind of fantastic wishing on the client's part. But this pause should not be too long since — if it is too long — the client is likely to interrupt and say that he or she does not believe in miracles. If the client should say that he or she does not believe in miracles, it is frequently enough to say something like this: Me neither (which is true), but pretend — for the moment — that you do."]

and, the problem that brought you here is solved, just like that! ... [Pause. Now the focus is on one particular, everyday or garden variety miracle that is in line with his or her coming to see a therapist. Failure to include this focal point will often lead to the client's giving a response that is vague, general, and so nonspecific as to be almost useless.]

But, this happens while you are sleeping, so you cannot know that it has happened ... [Pause. This is designed to allow the client to construct his or her miracle without any consideration of the problem and without any consideration of the steps that might be or might have been involved.]

Once you wake up in the morning, how will you go about discovering that this miracle has happened to you? ... [Pause. This is the point when the client has his or her most difficult work to do. Therefore, I am prepared for what often seems like a long silence. I have learned not to interrupt this silence; it is the client's turn to talk, to answer the question.]

After the client's response has been explored, I will inevitably use at least one scaling question in every first session and in most subsequent ones, a scale that can loosely be called "the progress scale." It goes like this: "On a scale from '0' to '10,' with '10' standing for how things are the day after the miracle and '0' for how things were at the point you called and arranged for this appointment, where between '0' and '10' (with a rising hand gesture) would you say things are right at this moment?"

Constructing "Better" Using a Yardstick

Scaling questions have been part of my practice since I learned about clients' spontaneous use of such ratings in the early 1970s. (In a Chinese restaurant, I was recently asked how hot I wanted my main course. The waiter used a 0 to 10 scale. It was easy: 7.) At first, I used scales to attempt to get some sort of way to describe vague things that are very difficult to describe, such as "(degrees of) depression," "(degrees of) anxiety," "(degrees of) satisfaction," and "(degrees of) effective communication between people," helping clients to access their situations and to shift from general black-and-white constructions, that is, either depressed or not depressed, to something more discrete and descriptive, that is, sometimes more or less depressed. Over the years, my use of scales has increased in both frequency and importance. Now clients will frequently report — when asked — that they found the scales to be the most useful and important part of the therapy because the scales give them a way to assess their own situation and to measure their own progress. Some clients will begin a session by announcing where they are on the scale.

Of course, this kind of "better yardstick" is a system. A "6" is simultaneously a "6" and not a 0, not a 1, not a 7, not a 13, and so on. Furthermore, this sort of a yardstick/system implies the various ratings above "10" and the ratings below "0." A "10" is not constructed as "good," but rather as "better than 9, 8, 7, and so on. Below "0" ratings are not constructed as "bad," but rather as "better" in this way: If the client says that things are "-2," this rating is, obviously, "better" than a rating of "-3"! This implies that even though things are "worse" right now, getting "better" remains possible; if things get "worse," the situation is always better than something still worse. Thus, "better" is constructed in such a way that "good" and "bad" are not mentioned. They are not part of this scale/system.

I could go on listing "standard" question after "standard" question, which would be boring. All our questions, like bricks, are pretty much the same. But one cannot build much just by piling one loose brick on top of another. (To me, this proves that the approach is not just a collection of techniques.) We need some mortar to hold these bricks together and the mortar — which holds things together — is the clients' responses, which we will look at soon.

PART THREE

At St. John's Hospital, they go even further in destructing the old concept of alcoholism than just giving the problem a new name: problematic drinking. The therapists there use SFBT, including the miracle question (to find out what it is that the client wants from therapy) and scales (to help the client figure out where he or she stands) to access progress. Usually, the result is that neither abstinence nor controlled drinking is the goal of the therapy. The client's responses to the miracle question are used to develop the goal for therapy, and these responses usually deal with the *consequences* of significantly changing the problematic drinking. Thus, from an Ericksonian perspective, the therapy deals with problematic drinking indirectly and the choice of approach that the client wants to take to changing his or her drinking pattern usually is not discussed as part of a therapy session.

THE MORTAR

Case Example

Franz, 42, has been a secret beer drinker for many years (I never had a chance to ask about his technique). He had tried many times to stop drinking on his own, but with limited success. He had been laid off from his job five months before coming into the hospital. During these five months, his wife and two sons (15 and 17) had learned about his drinking. In a therapy session one day and a half after entering the hospital, he talked about wanting to be a good father and a good husband again.

The miracle question prompted his talking about keeping what he had already achieved in life: a family and a home. He said he really would not want a miracle to happen because he would want "to know what I had done to make the miracle happen." He saw himself, after the miracle, as again being a good father who "would discuss things with my boys and not avoid answering questions that they asked me." This, he thought, would lead him to taking more initiative with them. He would also take more interest in his wife, which he would show by "going to sit next to her" without an invitation. In this way, she would also know that he was more interested.

(Notice that there is no direct mention of either drinking or not drinking. These consequences of the miracle that Franz describes do not in the least depend on his eliminating his problematic drinking. The type of problem the individual has will not allow us to predict the details of his construction of the day after the miracle. Furthermore, the construction of the day after the miracle will not allow us to figure out what the problem might have been. The miracle question permits him to begin to construct a more desirable future for himself and his family. That future is probably different from the future he would have imagined without the therapist's asking the miracle question.)

On the progress scale, he said that he was at "6," with the major difference between "0" and "6" being that he was "interested in contact with other people." He felt more energy, "almost a lust for life." Furthermore, he was looking forward to visiting with his family in the evening. He thought that his wife, if she were there, would rate him at "7" and that his sons would rate him at "7 or 8." Asked how he would know he had moved up to "7," he said that his wife "would notice that I love her" by the way he hugged her and held her hand. He said, however, that it would take some time before she would really believe. When she did believe, he would surely be at "10."

(The scale allowed Franz to construct his current situation, "6," as an improvement from "0" on the way to "10," a situation that subsequently he constructs as even better when he tells the therapist that his wife and children would give the situation a "7," or even an "8" — clearly not something he would have described if the therapist had not asked the questions in the way he did.)

When asked in the corridor after the session, he said that he wanted to talk to his wife and sons that evening about which approach to take (abstinence or controlled drinking). He did not want to do anything without consulting them.

(He reported later that they decided to try the controlled-drinking approach. Obviously, "controlled drinking" was a vastly different construction for them. It changed the context from "secret drinking" to "public drinking," and thus was likely to lead to both different thinking and different behaviors. Subsequently, they decided that his controlled drinking should be done in front of one or more of the members of his family. Thus, his controlled drinking was constructed as part of his being more involved with his family, which was part of his construction of the day after the miracle.

(This reminds me of the kind of intervention that brief therapists, such as Milton Erickson, John Weakland, and Jay Haley, are famous for designing. But, in this case, it was designed by the family without the help of any therapist.)

So far, Franz has been successful doing controlled drinking, but we still have to wait 3.5 years until follow-up.

CONCLUSION

Getting to the surface of the problem and simply describing what is going on (who?, what?, when?, where?), such as with problematic drinking, allows us to avoid the traps inherent in the concept of alcoholism and the grammar involved in our talking about it. Moving to the surface, and staying on the surface, allows us to see what it is that is going on in a particular case, and forces us to pay attention to details and not to generalize. Although it is a relatively simple move, it is not an easy one, because it requires some discipline to avoid talking about things using the standard vocabulary and concepts.

References

Descombes, V. (1995). Foreword. In J. Bouveresse, *Wittgenstein reads Freud: The myth of the unconscious* (trans. C. Cosman). Princeton, NJ: Princeton University Press.

de Shazer, S., & Isebaert, L. (1998). A solution-focused approach to the treatment of problematic drinking: The Bruges model. (Unpublished manuscript.)

Fleck, L. (1979). *Genesis and development of a scientific fact* (trans. F. Bradley & R. Merton). Chicago: University of Chicago Press.

Polich, J. M., Armor, D. J., & Braiker, H. B. (1980). *The course of alcoholism: Four years after treatment.* Santa Monica, CA: Rand Corp.

Sobell, L. C., Sobell, M. B., Toneatto, T., & Leo, G. I. (1993). What triggers the resolution of alcohol problems without treatment? *Alcoholism: Clinical and Experimental Research, 17*(2), 217–224.

Weakland, J. H. (1993). Conversation — but what kind? In S. Gilligan & R. Price (Eds.), *Therapeutic conversations.* New York: Norton.

White, M. (1993). Commentary: The histories of the present. In S. Gilligan & R. Price (Eds.), *Therapeutic conversations.* New York: Norton.

Wittgenstein, L. (1967). *Zettel* (trans. G. E. M. Anscombe). In G. E. M. Anscombe & G. H. von Wright. (Eds.). Berkeley, CA: University of California Press.

Wittgenstein, L. (1968). *Philosophical investigations* (trans. G. E. M. Anscombe) (3rd ed.). New York: Macmillan.

Wittgenstein, L. (1980). *Culture and value* (trans. P. Winch). Chicago: University of Chicago Press.

15

Better, Deeper, and More Enduring Brief Therapy

Albert Ellis

I had better, right at the start, give my definition of better, deeper, and more enduring psychotherapy. I hinted at what it is in my first major book on Rational Emotive Behavior Therapy (REBT), in 1962, *Reason and Emotion in Psychotherapy.* Then I was more specific in a 1972 paper, "Helping People Get Better Rather Than Merely Feel Better." I finally went into more details about what I call the "elegant" solution in psychotherapy in several more recent articles and books (Ellis, 1991, 1992, 1996, 1997; Ellis & Dryden, 1997; Ellis, Gordon, Neenan, & Palmer, 1997; Ellis & Harper, 1997).

As I have noted in these writings, helping people to feel better is relatively easy, and many different kinds of therapy do so (Beutler, 1991; Frank, 1985; Luborsky, McLellan, Woody, O'Brien, & Auerbach, 1985). This is probably true because, as Frank (1985) has noted, therapists maintain a close relationship with clients, show that they are definitely on their side, give them a plausible explanation for their symptoms, and establish a procedure or series of tasks that both they and the clients believe will restore client functioning. These common methods help many, although not all, clients feel better, sometimes in a short time. So psychotherapy, as a recent *Consumers Reports* survey shows, works pretty well.

Not so fast, please! Do most people in therapy actually *get* better? I am highly skeptical that they do. To get better, rather than merely feel better, involves clients' making several important changes by: (1) minimizing their presenting symptoms, (2) acknowledging and reducing other emotional-behavioral problems, (3) maintaining their progress and rarely experiencing their symptoms again, and (4) thereafter, seldom making themselves seriously disturbed even when encountering severe failures, losses, and other adversities.

Have any of the thousands of studies of the effectiveness of psychotherapy that have been done evaluated their results according to these strict criteria? Very few. Consequently, we partly know how to help people feel better in psychotherapy — but as yet we know little about helping them get better.

REBT is one of the few systems specifically designed to help people make the "elegant" kind of transformation just described. It practically always attempts to show clients how to make a profound philosophical change that includes intense emotional and habitual behavioral aspects. I established it in 1955 as the first of the major cognitive-behavioral therapies, and soon added many emotive-evocative and experiential techniques to its procedures — because, as I said in my first major paper on the topic at the Annual Convention of the American Psychological Association in Chicago (Ellis, 1958), it sees thinking, emotion, and behavior as connected and integrated, not as disparate.

REBT's central thesis is that humans are natural constructivists and that, in addition to their creative and problem-solving abilities, they also construct self-defeating musts and demands out of their learned and innate desires and preferences. They thereby get themselves into cognitive-emotional-behavioral trouble. Thus, they take their wishes (which are cognitive, affective, and action tendencies) and raise them to commands (which are a different kind of cognitive, affective, and action tendency). Their absolutistic musts are often unrealistic, illogical, and impractical, but they nevertheless tend to think them intensely, feel them strongly, and act rigidly — to their neurotic detriment.

Anxious, depressed, and enraged people, REBT hypothesizes, frequently construct three major absolutistic shoulds and musts out of their healthy preferences: (1) "I *absolutely must* succeed at important projects and relationships," which leads to anxiety and depression when not fulfilled. (2) "Other people *absolutely must* treat me considerately and fairly," which results in anger, rage, and violence when not experienced. (3) "Conditions *absolutely must* be the way I want and must not seriously frustrate me," which results in low frustration tolerance, anger, and depression. These grandiose musts usually accompany such core self-defeating conclusions as: "I am an inadequate person, when I don't do as well as I *must*!" "You are a thoroughly rotten individual, when you don't act as well as you *must*!" And "Conditions are awful and terrible, and I can't stand them when they aren't as good as they must be!"

If therapists use REBT, the theory just outlined gives them unusual double advantages. First, they can zero in very quickly on one, two, or three of their clients' major musturbatory beliefs, find them almost immediately, and show clients how to dispute them. In other words, they can demonstrate the ABCs of REBT to the clients, using the clients' own presenting problems. **A** stands for adversity — meaning that the client has failed, been rejected, been afflicted with a disease, or suffered from some other adversity. **C** is the emotional-behavioral consequence, the symptom the client is suffering, such as anxiety or depression. **B** is the client's beliefs about A, particularly his or her irrational beliefs, such as musts, damning of himself or herself, damning other people, and damning world conditions for not being absolutely as good as they *absolutely should* be.

When therapists, with the help of REBT theory, zero in on the client's few core irrational beliefs, rather than on a host of automatic negative thoughts and inferences that stem from these central irrational beliefs, not only do they cut through quickly to more relevant cognitive-emotive "reasons" for their disturbances (including so-called psychodynamic reasons) and thereby save much time for themselves and their clients, but they may get to the main philosophic underpinnings of the clients' symptoms and so help them make the unique kind of changes that promote their getting better rather than feeling better.

In other words, if a client is depressed because he or she strongly has the irrational belief that he or she absolutely must be loved by significant others, and the client is helped by REBT to clearly surrender this demand and change it back to a preference, he or she will tend to change many corollary automatic beliefs, such as, "People who criticize my behavior thoroughly hate me," "If one significant person dislikes me, that means I am unlovable," and "I cannot have any joy in life whatever if so-and-so doesn't like me."

Moreover, if clients who have a dire need for love and approval see with the help of REBT that their demands largely lead them to become depressed when they are or think they are disapproved, they will also tend to dispute and surrender some of their other grandiose demandingness, such as the dire need to excel in school, at public speaking, or in sports, and their insistence that they absolutely must not be frustrated at home or at work. They will, therefore, be able to cope with their feelings of anxiety and depression about many things, in addition to approval, and will tend to become less generally disturbed about almost anything.

REBT, then, not only tackles clients' symptoms or disturbances, but also their future disturbability. It enables people to give up the specific musts and demands that largely brought them to therapy. But it also teaches them the harm of all kinds of pervasive musturbatory thinking–feeling–behaving and thereby encourages them to be significantly less disturbed and less disturbable. Once again, I hypothesize that the achievement of less disturbability is probably the most important aspect of clients' getting rather than merely feeling better.

Can REBT's emphasis on changing people's core musts and demands actually be carried out in brief therapy? Assuming that it can be achieved and can lead to personality change that is lasting and pervasive, can it be accomplished in relatively few sessions, especially with clients who have severe personality disorders?

Yes and no. With some clients, definitely yes. Although they may be seriously disturbed and have lifetime diagnoses of severe depression or borderline personality disorder, they take to REBT in 10 or 15 sessions, use it forcefully and persistently, and not only overcome most of their rage at themselves and others, but remain much less prone to being disturbed for years to come. They really see that they don't absolutely need to perform well, be approved by others, or get what they want when they want it; and when they fall back to anxiety, depression, or rage, they observe their contributory shoulds, and musts, change them back to preferences, and stop their disturbances in their tracks. They also become much less upset about adversities than they previously did, so they are significantly less disturbable. They still may have biological and learned tendencies to overreact or underreact to adversities — especially if they have borderline personality disorders. But, with some exceptions, they deal with these tendencies and lead much happier lives.

But watch it! Yes, severely disturbed individuals — including some with psychosis — sometimes can use REBT to make a quick and profound cognitive-emotional change, but not too many of them do. First, they have to work hard not only to see, but also to use, the many cognitive, emotive, and behavioral methods that REBT includes. Second, they have to keep doing some of this work for the rest of their lives — just as all of us have to continue to eat healthy foods and to exercise regularly if we are to remain in good shape. Unfortunately, even those I call the "nice neurotics" who benefit from psychotherapy often fail to do the initial and continuing work it requires. And this is more true, for several reasons, of clients with severe personality disorders.

The human condition, moreover, is to change yourself constructively — for example, to make yourself less anxious, depressed, and enraged — and to keep going back to your musturbatory thinking and feeling, even after your crazy-making leads to very bad results. Moreover, like most humans, you have a tendency to tell yourself, "I must not be anxious! I must not feel depressed!" Then you make yourself anxious about your anxiety, depressed about your depression! REBT, therefore, says that only work and practice in this respect are likely to be effective. So REBT brief therapy definitely works, as scores of studies have shown (Hajzler & Bernard, 1991; Lyons & Woods, 1991). But almost always it and other brief therapies work because the clients learn in a few sessions to continue on their own to make efforts and to use what they have learned. In this sense, just about all effective brief therapy really includes a steadily repeated self-help process.

REBT offers a number of cognitive, emotive, and behavioral methods to clients — both "nice neurotics" and those with severe personality disorders — who want to benefit from brief therapy. I don't have enough room in this chapter to describe most of them. Here are some of its main thinking–feeling–acting techniques that you can use to help your clients — not to mention yourself — become less disturbed and less disturbable.

- *Unconditional self-acceptance (USA)*: Believing, feeling, and acting on the philosophy that they will try to perform well at chosen goals and try to win the approval of significant people they select, but that they don't absolutely have to do so and can accept themselves, their being, and their personhood whether or not they succeed.
- *Unconditional other-acceptance (UOA)*: Believing, feeling, and acting on the philosophy of being disapproving of other people's ideas and actions, when they think these others act wrongly or unfairly, but

refusing to condemn or damn people as a whole by demanding that they absolutely must act fairly.

- *High frustration tolerance (HFT)*: Believing, feeling, and acting on the philosophy that many life conditions are aversive and frustrating, and that they should do their best to improve them or avoid them, but that they will fully accept poor conditions that can't be changed and stop whining and demanding that they absolutely must not exist.
- *Anti-overgeneralization*: Believing, feeling, and acting on the philosophy of evaluating specific adversities and their consequences as bad but refusing to overgeneralize about them and to resort to all-or-none thinking. Sticking to probabilistic and flexible conclusions and avoiding hypothesizing that because they failed a few times, they will always fail, and that because they were rejected by several important people, they will never gain the desired approval.

As my language implies, all these fundamental philosophies, which REBT considers healthy and prophylactic for maintained emotional disturbance, are cognitive, emotive, and behavioral, and are usually achieved and steadily held by using a number of REBT techniques. Individual clients, however, are unique and also distinctly vary from time to time. Therefore, what works with one or what works at one time hardly is effective with other clients or with the same client at all times. Consequently, REBT includes about 20 often-used cognitive, 20 emotive, and 20 behavioral methods. It is also free to use other methods from other therapies when its own favorite techniques do not seem to be effective with a particular client at a particular time. So it is multimodal — to use Lazarus' (1989) term — and integrative, in that even it at times uses "irrational" methods to get "rational" or self-helping results.

Rational Emotive Behavior Therapy is one of the few major therapies specifically designed to be brief (Ellis, 1992, 1996, 1997a, 1997b, 1998). But it also is designed to help people *get* better and not merely to *feel* better, and, therefore, aims to be deep and enduring. It hypothesizes that clients who are helped to use it can make themselves significantly less disturbed and less disturb*able*. Let us have considerable research to test this hypothesis.

References

Beutler, L. E. (1991). Have all won and must have prizes. Revisiting Luborsky et al.'s verdict. *Journal of Counseling and Clinical Psychology, 59*, 226–232.

Ellis, A. (1958). Rational psychotherapy. *Journal of General Psychology, 59*, 35–49.

Ellis, A. (1962). *Reason and emotion in psychotherapy*. Secaucus, NJ: Citadel. Revised ed. Secaucus, NJ: Carol Publishing Group, 1994.

Ellis, A. (1972). Helping people get better rather than merely feel better. *Rational Living, 7*(2), 2–9.

Ellis, A. (1991). Are all methods of counseling equally effective? *New York State Journal for Counseling and Development, 6*(2), 9–13.

Ellis, A. (1992). Brief therapy: The rational-emotive method. In S. H. Budman, M. F. Hoyt, & S. Friedman (Eds.), *The first session in brief therapy* (pp. 36–58). New York: Guilford.

Ellis, A. (1996). *Better, deeper, and more enduring brief therapy.* New York: Brunner/Mazel.

Ellis, A. (1997a). Extending the goals of behavior therapy and of cognitive behavior therapy. *Behavior Therapy, 28*, 333–339.

Ellis, A. (1997b). Postmodern ethics for active-directive counseling and psychotherapy. *Journal of Mental Health Counseling, 10*, 211–225.

Ellis, A. (1998). *How to control your anxiety before it controls you*. Secaucus, NJ: Carol Publishing Group.

Ellis, A., & Dryden, W. (1997). *The practice of rational emotive behavior therapy*. New York: Springer.

Ellis, A., Gordon, J., Neenan, M., & Palmer, S. (1997). *Stress counseling: A rational emotive behavior therapy approach*. New York: Springer.

Ellis, A., & Harper, R. A. (1997). *A guide to rational living*. North Hollywood, CA: Melvin Powers.

Frank, J. (1985). Therapeutic components shared by all psychotherapies. In M. Mahoney & A. Freeman (Eds.), *Cognition and psychotherapy* (pp. 49–79). New York: Plenum.

Hajzler, D., & Bernard, M. E. (1991). A review of rational-emotive outcome studies. *School Psychology Quarterly, 6*(1), 27–49.

Lazarus, A. (1989). *The practice of multimodel therapy*. Baltimore: Johns Hopkins.

Luborsky, L., McLellan, A. T., Woody, G. E., O'Brien, C. P., & Auerbach, A. (1985). Therapist success and its determinants. *Archives of General Psychiatry, 32*, 995–1008.

Lyons, L. C., & Woods, P. J. (1991). The efficacy of rational-emotive therapy: A quantitative review of the outcome research. *Clinical Psychology Review, 11*, 357–369.

16

Gender Differences in Depression

Peggy Papp

Depression is one of the most difficult conditions to treat because of the vast range of factors that may be creating and maintaining it and also because of the current conflicting and contradictory theories regarding its cause and cure. Therapists are left wondering is this person depressed because of a biological disorder, an unhappy marriage, the loss of a job, business failure, a death in the family, divorce, separation, a traumatic life event?

The fact is it is never just one thing. Depression is multidetermined, having to do with a complex combination of biological, psychological, interpersonal, social, and cultural factors. It, therefore, requires a multidimensional approach that takes into account a person's total life situation.

During the last decade a spotlight has been thrown on depression in both the mental health field and the mass media with anti-depressants being hailed as a great pharmacological breakthrough. Prozac has been featured on the front pages of *Time* and *Newsweek* with stories of instant transformation. Peter Kramer's book *Listening to Prozac* became a best-seller and prozac anonymous groups sprang up around the country. People came together in groups to discuss their dosages, side-effects, and moods. I often think our age will be remembered as the age of prozac.

Nearly all of the research over the past decade has been biologically oriented with an emphasis on medical solutions and a devaluation of interpersonal therapy. This is despite the fact that the most biologically oriented researchers agree that depression occurs in an interpersonal context and is profoundly affected by the quality of intimate relationships.

A break in this biological climate came in a 1995 *Consumer's Report* study that showed that cognitive psychotherapy was as effective or more effective than anti-depressants with lower rates of relapse. As a result, our field now has a more realistic appraisal of anti-depressants and what they can and cannot do. While they can be enormously helpful in alleviating the most severe symptoms of depression and enabling people to begin to face life's problems, they don't solve life's problems.

Several recent books present interpersonal approaches to depression. Michael Yapko's *Hand-me-down Blues* presents a family systems approach, Terry Real's *I Don't Want to Talk About It* deals with the treatment of depressed men and their families, and Dana Crowley Jack's *Silencing the Self* is about depressed women who are disconnected from personal relationships.

The work I am going to present to you is from the Depression Project of the Ackerman Institute, which was set up to develop a multidimensional approach to treating depression with a particular focus on understanding gender differences in depression.

We became interested in gender differences because of the following statistics:

1. Twice as many women as men are diagnosed with depression worldwide.
2. The most stressful life event that precipitates depression is marital conflict.
3. Marital conflict is the single most predictable indicator of relapse.
4. Marriage has a protective effect for men but is detrimental to women in terms of depression; married men are the least subject to depression as compared to single men or married women.
5. When a couple with a depressed spouse reverses stereotypical gender roles, the quality of their relationship improves.

We believe these statistics have profound implications for the diagnosis and treatment of depression, yet until recently they have been largely ignored by the mental health profession. We began the work of the depression project by addressing the following questions: Do women and men become depressed for different reasons? Do they react differently when they are depressed? Is the adaptive behavior of husbands and wives to a depressed spouse different? How does this affect their marital interactions? How do their personal gender beliefs and practices effect their depression?

We decided these questions could best be explored by treating couples in marital therapy in which one spouse has been hospitalized for depression. Marriage is the place where the personal and cultural meet, where one's image of oneself as a man or women comes into sharp focus and where gender beliefs and expectations are played out on a daily basis. We chose couples in which one spouse had been hospitalized with a clinical diagnosis for depression as this provided a base line for the degree of depression.

Besides being the dominant factor in a marriage, gender is directly connected with depressive symptoms. Depression is universally described as a profound disturbance of mood connected with a negative view of one's self-image. Terms such as "lack of self-esteem," "low self image," and "feelings of worthlessness and failure" are used over and over in the literature on depression. Self-esteem does not exist in a vacuum but in a relational and social context. This context includes constraining gender norms and expectations for men and women. Does failure to live up to these norms and expectations predispose both men and women to depression? For women, the prohibition against self-assertion and independence, the need to please others, to inhibit their anger, to put their own needs second, and the propensity to accept blame are all characteristics associated with depression. Women are at risk for depression when the quality or continuity of their relationships are disrupted or if they fail in their caretaking.

Men's self-esteem is highly performance oriented having to do with work, achievement, money, status, and competition. They are at risk for depression when their experience of their performance fails to live up to their ideal and when their relationship needs are not acknowledged.

PROJECT STRUCTURE

Our treatment team consists of Jeffrey Geibel, Gloria Klein, Paul Feinberg, and myself, working in female/male co-therapy teams. While the primary team interviews the couple, the other two therapists observe from behind the one-way mirror and serve as a consultation team.

Referrals come primarily from psychiatric hospitals and all of the depressed spouses are on anti-depressants when they are referred to us. Medication continues to be monitored by the outside psychiatrists with whom we maintain a collaborative relationship. All of the depressed spouses had been on a variety of anti-depressants for many years prior to their hospitalized and some were on antidepressants when they attempted suicide. Most had been in and out of individual therapy, which had no or little effect on their marital problems.

I will now talk about some of our observations. First, we observed there was a difference in the ability of men and women to recognize and acknowledge depression. The women were quicker to recognize their feelings and seek help and were better able to connect their depression with certain events or relationships in their lives. They were finely attuned to the emotional distance in their marriages and had made many attempts to reach out and bridge the distance. We repeatedly heard statements such as, "I feel I'm living on an emotional desert," "We never talk to each other," or "He's not interested in my feelings."

The men's experience of being depressed was described differently. They were often surprised to find themselves in the hospital and had little awareness of what led up to the breakdown in their functioning. They spoke most often of work-related pressures, business failure, poor job performance, competition, or lack of status. Their statements reflected feeling over-burdened and frightened by the responsibilities and pressure of the outside world: "I failed to achieve what I set out to do," "I'm being replaced by younger guys," "My boss is always putting me down."

The depressed husbands rarely connected their depression with any aspect of their marriage. They seemed unaware of their need for intimacy and seldom reached out to their wives for more contact. Because their identity was mainly tied up in the workplace and they had not developed close relationships at home, when their professional pillars crumbled, they found themselves in a void with nothing to sustain them. The idea of sharing their disappointments and frustrations with their wives was foreign to them. "I've always handled my problems alone," "I like to keep my work and family life separate," "what good would it do to talk about my problems?" were familiar statements. The wives felt excluded from the husband's inner and outer lives, and the husband's were left without the comfort and support of a sustaining relationship.

DIFFERENCES IN CARETAKING

We noted a marked difference in the caretaking practices of husbands and wives, which again fell into stereotypical gender patterns. When wives were depressed, the husbands typically tried an instrumental problem-solving approach replete with "fixing it," "analyzing the situation," "coming up with a constructive solution," "mapping out a plan of action."

The husbands showed less tolerance than the wives for any kind of mental or physical disability either in themselves or others, and they became impatient when their wives did not follow their advice. They took it as a personal affront and often became verbally abusive or withdrew into a cold distance.

Wives reacted differently when their husbands were depressed. They tended to protect, placate, and appease. They monitored their husband's moods, shielded them from telephone calls, kept the children away, and were careful not to make too many demands. They blamed themselves for not being good enough wives and put their own needs second. However, underneath their dutiful exterior they harbored a smoldering resentment at never receiving any appreciation or acknowledgment for their efforts. The husbands sensed the covert resentment, which added to their depression.

TREATMENT APPROACH

We cast a wide net in our treatment approach, focusing on the triggers that might set off the depression in the marital relationship, extended family, work or social situations. We then looked at the beliefs, attitudes, and interactions that activated the depressive response and for the hidden strengths and resources available for changing these. Essential to this approach is the view of the marital relationship as a primary source of recovery and future prevention.

At some point in the therapy, the couples were informed of our curiosity concerning the possible connection between stereotypical gender beliefs and depression, and they were asked to participate in our exploration of this uncharted territory by filling out a gender questionnaire. The questions on the questionnaire concern the messages each spouse received from family, peers, and the mass media that formed their ideas about how they should function as a man or woman and how these messages are currently effecting their lives and relationships. The couple was then asked to bring the filled-out questionnaires to the session and discuss their answers with each other. These discussions often throw new light on sensitive closed-off areas such as sex, money, power, and responsibility.

We asked the couples for their feedback regarding the usefulness of the questions in raising their awareness of their gender beliefs and then revised them according to their suggestions. This gives the couples the opportunity to collaborate with us in exploring this new territory and connects them with the wider community. Occasionally, we invite the couples to go behind the one-way mirror and listen to the four therapists discuss their own personal struggles with gender constraints.

Each partner's functioning, not only as a marital partner but in other gender roles — as a daughter, son, mother, or father — was examined when it seemed to have a direct bearing on their depression. This is based on our observation that conflictual relationships with parents or children can contribute substantially to depression. Chronic conflicts in the nuclear as well as the extended family that are contributing to the depression are addressed.

Silencing the Self

We discovered that the most important first step in working with depressed wives was to create a safe context in which they could be "heard" without having their thoughts and feelings dismissed or invalidated by their husbands. The wives had silenced their voices not because they were "passive and dependent" as they are so often described in the professional literature, but because they didn't trust their perceptions and feelings and were afraid of isolation or reprisal if they expressed them openly. In *Silencing the Self*, the depressed women the author interviews speak over and over again of having lost their voices in their marriages.

The husbands, although highly motivated to help their wives, had great difficulty understanding what it was they were asking for. We discovered that the simple question, "What does your spouse do that is helpful or unhelpful when you are depressed," brought forth each partner's different perceptions of "help." These perceptions fall into stereotypical gender divisions with the depressed wives asking for relatedness and communication while their husbands connected help with action and advice.

A typical exchange was the husband, who after failing to cheer up his wife with a weekend of planned physical activities, exclaimed in exasperation, "I took you boating didn't I?" To this, the depressed wife responded, "Yes, but you never talked to me." For the wife, help meant sharing feelings and exchanging experiences, for the husband it meant teaching her how to row.

When the husbands were able to "hear" their wives and respond to their feelings, the wives invariably became more expressive and less depressed. After the wives felt more secure in their relationships with their husbands, we addressed other neglected aspects of their lives such as career opportunities, further education, family of origin issues, or developing new social relationships. Their depression lifted as they changed their image of themselves from helpless victims, powerless to influence events and relationships, to assertive woman, capable of expressing themselves and taking charge of their lives.

Establishing a Connection

Generally the first phase of therapy with the depressed husbands involved helping them to become connected with their wives as a way out of their emotional void. Contrary to the prevalent practice in our field of helping men to get in touch with their feelings and expressing them, we found probing their psyches only made them feel more inadequate and depressed. In our experience, it was more important to help them get in touch, not with their own feelings, but with those of their wives and respond to them. This activated the emotional part of them they had shut down. It gave them a way to become involved that was tolerable as they felt needed and competent in an area in which they generally felt incompetent. As a result of developing more open and supportive relationships with their wives, the men were better able to handle the stress and combativeness of the workplace.

CASES

To illustrate some of these concepts, I am going to describe a case with a depressed wife. Sonya, aged 53, had requested marital therapy after having been hospitalized for depression and suicidal ideation. Upon her release, the hospital staff insisted she needed individual psychiatric treatment and she saw a psychiatrist for the next six months. However, she continued to believe that the ongoing conflict in her marriage, which predated the hospitalization, was intimately related to her depression. Eventually she contacted the Ackerman Institute for marital therapy.

What became apparent in the first session was how much Sonya depended upon her husband, Tom, for approval and validation, which she constantly sought but failed to attain as he was extremely critical of her. Tom saw his mission in life as keeping his wife from "going down the tubes" and he did this in the only way he knew how — by constantly criticizing her and giving her what he considered to be "helpful advice."

Much of Tom's criticism centered around Sonya's attempts to re-establish her own small business, which had lapsed since her hospitalization. As a retired business executive, he believed she should benefit from his superior knowledge and expertise.

Although his constant criticism had a devastating effect on Sonya, she was afraid to challenge him for fear of losing the marriage. Instead she swallowed her anger and withdrew to her room, where feeling totally helpless and defeated she would sink into a profound depression. In the first two sessions we focused on helping Sonya to react to Tom's criticism differently and instead of withdrawing to assert herself, trust her own judgment, and speak with her own voice.

In the following dialogue, Tom reveals his deeply embedded belief concerning his role as a husband. He recently made a mistake in assuming a brochure Sonya had put together was the final copy rather than a rough draft. He screamed at her for her presumed carelessness but refused to apologize when he realized his mistake. The therapists uncovered and challenged his gendered belief around weakness and strength.

THERAPIST: You knew you made a mistake?

TOM: Yes, I knew I made a mistake but there was nothing I could do at that point.

THERAPIST: You didn't apologize?

TOM: No, that's not my nature.

SONYA: He never says he's sorry.

THERAPIST: But you felt that way? You thought you'd made a mistake?

TOM: I knew I'd made a mistake.

THERAPIST: But you would never apologize?

TOM: Not if I'm going to help her. Because then she's going to think I'm weak and not capable of taking care of her.

THERAPIST: I see. You think if you apologize then you —

TOM: She would not accept my criticism then.

THERAPIST: So you feel you have to remain very stern and —

TOM: I have to remain very stern —

THERAPIST: Like a father and —

SONYA: Are you serious?

TOM: Yes.

SONYA: Wow! I never knew that.

TOM: If I weaken she's going to go ahead and do all this stuff.

THERAPIST (*to Sonya*): What do you think? If he had said he was sorry would you —

SONYA: I would have cried out of happiness realizing how strong he is that he has grown to understand how to relate to a woman.

THERAPIST: I see — so you would think he was strong if he did that?

SONYA: Of course!

THERAPIST (*to Tom*): You thought she would think you were weak?

SONYA: It takes strength to admit something that didn't go quite right.

THERAPIST: Did that ever occur to you that she might think you were strong to do that?

TOM (*after a long pause*): No.

THERAPIST: How does that sound to you now?

TOM: Would you accept my criticism if I apologized?

SONYA: I wasn't asking for criticism.

THERAPIST: Do you think she needs your criticism or your support?

TOM: She needs my help. I think it's support. I don't see anything wrong with it.

THERAPIST (*to Sonya*): What do you think is wrong with it? What would you rather have him do?

SONYA: I'd like to have an adult discussion with him person to person. I don't want a father figure. I don't want a police figure. I don't want a superior figure talking to me.

Sonya was now able to state clearly and calmly her need for an "adult" relationship involving support, equality, and understanding. This conflicted with Tom's masculine belief that coercion and criticism equal strength while support and empathy equal weakness. He was reluctant to relinquish his expert position for fear he would lose Sonya's respect and, therefore, his control over her. The idea that she could respect him as anything but a stern authoritarian father figure was new to him.

Changing this idea was pivotal to the course of therapy. In future sessions, Tom learned to tolerate the anxiety that accompanied his letting go of his authoritarian stance as he experienced the rewards of a closer relationship with Sonya.

GENERATIONAL GENDER BELIEFS

Tom's practice of using intimidation to exert control was learned early in his life. As the eldest son, he felt compelled to control a "crazy and chaotic" family. The only option that seemed open to him was to use strong-arm tactics. This practice served him well as a teenager growing up in a tough macho neighborhood and was later reinforced in the business world where it brought him status and money.

Sonya's desire for an "adult" relationship required a continuing effort on her part to avoid lapsing into the helpless victim position and instead to take charge of her life and relationships. This was difficult for her as she had no model of an assertive woman. She saw her mother as weak and passive, succumbing to her father's abusive and domineering behavior. She blamed her mother for not saving her from her father's physical abuse, and she favored her father in spite of his abuse.

It is not uncommon for depressed women to have contempt for their mothers, seeing them as disempowered second-class citizens, while respecting the power and authority of their fathers even when it is turned against them. This gender-biased view is bound to effect their feelings about themselves as well as their relationship with the opposite sex. Sonya's contempt for her mother was mirrored in her contempt for herself and led to feelings of despair whenever she experienced the inevitability of following in her footsteps. An important part of our work lay in helping Sonya to perceive her mother differently and reconnect with her on a new basis. This was accomplished by exploring the social and cultural conditions of her mother's life and the oppressive gender beliefs that limited her going beyond them. Sonya concluded, "I have not given her enough credit." Through the exchange of letters, she was able to forge a new relationship with her mother and develop a kinder, more forgiving, attitude toward her and thus toward herself. She stated tearfully, "For years I have had this nightmare of standing over my mother's grave and feeling sad and guilty. Now I know I won't have to do that and it is such a relief!"

As a result of no longer feeling cut off from her husband and mother, Sonya was able to turn her attention and energy to her business pursuits. The major thrust of our therapy with Sonya lay in enabling her to overcome her image of herself as a helpless victimized woman, destined to be dominated and controlled by an authoritarian father figure, and instead to experience herself as an assertive woman capable of relying on her own judgment and values rather than those of her husband.

In a two-year follow-up, Tom opened the session by praising Sonya's accomplishments and extolling her many talents. She was successfully managing her own business and Tom's former critical attitude was replaced with one of admiration, affection, and respect. Sonya had stopped all medication and spoke of feeling "a light inside."

This is just one example of how we helped a couple to examine the gender beliefs, expectations, and behavior that were impoverishing and depressing, and to change them to ones that promoted a feeling of harmony and well-being.

References

Jack, D. C. (1991). *Silencing the self.* Cambridge, MA: Harvard University Press.

Real, T. (1997). *I don't want to talk about it.* New York: Scribner Publishing.

Yapko, M. (1999). *Hand-me-down blues: Overcoming depression in families.* New York: Golden Books.

17

Ericksonian, Cognitive, Behavioral, Strategic, or All Four?

Betty Alice Erickson

When I read about the different schools of psychotherapy or hear addresses by leaders in various methods of therapy, I often have difficulty sorting out what is Ericksonian and what is better named strategic or brief or cognitive or behavioral therapy. Sometimes, it all seems to be the same. And most of the time, it doesn't matter what the method is called as long as the client receives the needed help.

I do think, however, that understanding the basics of Ericksonian psychotherapy and seeing their connections to the multiplicity of current therapies gives modern therapists clarity to define their own stances and philosophical frameworks. We all want to give our clients what they need in ways that are most palatable and understandable to them. Picking and choosing conceptualizations, approaches, and interventions from the various schools, becoming truly eclectic, is one way to do that.

Before Milton H. Erickson, M.D., there were just a few somewhat rigid theories, sweeping generalizations, and only a few "right" ways to do therapy. Therapy, once began, often became part of a person's life essentially forever. It was not uncommon for a patient to see a therapist multiple times a week for years and years.

The patient's personal history and recollection of past events were deemed of paramount importance. They were examined in great detail for reasons and understanding. Insight was a requirement for change. Change without insight was considered superficial and not long lasting; it was not really change at all.

Symptoms were regarded as entities in themselves — a behavior that was "needed" or required for the level of functionality that the patient displayed. "Curing" or altering a symptom was foolhardy. It was thought that the symptom well might reappear in a different, and probably more harmful, manifestation.

Psychotherapy, necessarily, became limited to those people who had the time, money, and energy to spend years examining themselves and their remembered past, and coming to insightful understanding about their present lives. Obviously, great numbers of people who had troubles and who were struggling to make better lives could not get psychotherapeutic help.

Erickson played a very large part in revolutionizing this way of doing therapy. He built a bridge between that kind of psychotherapy, the psychotherapy of his time, and his own conceptualizations and ideas. These ideas, these bridges, have helped create many of the modern schools of therapy.

Erickson believed that theories were too restrictive for the infinite variety and variations of the human race and the infinite creativity of human thinking and behavior. So Ericksonian psychotherapy has remained atheoretical. That may be good for the client, but it is not so good for ease of understanding by students. There is simply no way to fit what is done in Ericksonian psychotherapy into a neat tidy theory.

Nothing in Erickson's life altered his fundamental belief about the inadequacy of a single theory of human function and dysfunction. His work in prisons and mental hospitals, the psychiatric examination of thousands of military inductees during World War II, his work with the courts and the legal system, his private practice, and his work with students all emphasized that people are different. People live functional, productive, and happy lives in an infinite variety of ways, and they think and behave in infinitely creative ways. Creativity and problem-solving abilities are the frameworks of human behavior.

In 1990, at the second Evolution of Psychotherapy Conference, Arnold Lazarus, who is clearly identified as a noted cognitive-behavioral therapist, alluded to that thought when he advocated a "flexible personal therapeutic stance that tries to calibrate the goodness-of-fit of the treatment to the client's basic style." He continues with the quotation from Erickson that Jeffrey Zeig and Stephen Gilligan use to preface the front of their edited book, *Brief Therapy*. "Each person is a unique individual. Hence psychotherapy should be formulated to meet the uniqueness of the individual needs, rather than to tailor the person to fit the procrustean bed of a hypothetical theory of human behavior" (1990, p. 103). (Zeig, in a footnote to Lazarus' comment, explains the history of that quotation. Erickson selected it when asked for a statement for the promotional literature for the first International Congress on Ericksonian Hypnosis and Psychotherapy held in 1980.)

Erickson believed insight was not always important. He focused on productive change, with or without understanding and insight. The future was truly "yet to be" and was rarely ordained by the past. A person's past was just that — past, even though personal perceptions of that past were highly changeable.

Therapy could often be very brief. There is a story Erickson used to tell. When he was growing up, there was a young man in his small hometown who was well known as a troublemaker. That young man's life was changed completely by just one moment of meaningful interaction. He asked the prettiest girl in town if he could take her to a Friday night dance. According to Erickson, she looked the young man up and down and said, "If you're a gentleman, you can." And so he became a gentleman. He turned his dysfunctional behaviors into ways of productive living. Was that really therapy? I am not sure. But I am sure that, without insight, and without examining his past, this young man rebuilt his life in wholesome ways that earned him more pleasure and rewards.

Understanding the concepts of how and why the man was able to change and move forward with his life, as well as concepts of Ericksonian psychotherapy overall, is central to comprehending the wide variety of therapeutic approaches competing for our attention today, including Strategic, Brief, Cognitive, Solution-Focused, and Behaviorial therapy, among others. Many of these concepts, Erickson helped to create. Some of these ideas provided a foundation for changes and the current proliferation of a broad range of different orientations. And more important, many of these changes have become standards of modern therapy.

There are all kinds of ways to do therapy, but they include very few "right," rigidly structured methods. Theories mostly have taken second place to practicalities, and people are recognized for their individualism and differences. Therapy is "supposed" to be quick, brief, goal directed, future focused, and aimed at returning the clients to more productive, and happier lives. Much of the time it is not necessary to understand the reasons for behavior; change is what counts. And all of these ideas were pioneered by Erickson.

With the pace of life becoming faster and faster, and the increasing emphasis on immediate gratification, psychotherapy is almost certain to continue to move, in fact, to gallop, in the direction of brief, strategic, practical, reality-based, and future- and goal-focused work. Insight and the understanding of patterns, systems, and theories will probably become less and less important, although they will still be relevant. Managed care certainly approves of this trend, and will do its best to continue and promote it.

Any number of people and events have taken part in the inventing and reinventing of psychotherapy. Any number of dedicated professionals have been working, studying, and experimenting with the human condition for countless years. There has always been available a community warehouse and wealth of knowledge about human psychology. Therapists, known and unknown, have played significant roles in the creation and promotion of very important advances in psychotherapy.

Erickson was fortunate in that his work was studied by some very bright hardworking students who were able to take some of what he taught them and teach it to others. I do not mean to imply that Erickson was the sole originator of some of the ideas and techniques for which he has become so famous. But this chapter is about understanding the underpinnings of Ericksonian psychotherapy.

All good and effective therapies have commonalities. Respect for the individual, plans for a productive future, enjoyment of life, the overcoming of obstacles, the promotion of self-responsibility are all hallmarks of a wholesome and responsible life and are all parts of good therapy. Certainly Erickson did not invent this!

His methods of achieving these goals were often very different from other methods. He understood the unconscious to be a storehouse of resources and abilities, he relied on the strengths of the individual, and he used the client's own world, own resistance, as a tool for change. That, and his careful observation of and attention to details and language, created a framework of therapy so flexible, and yet so individualistic, that it is timeless.

There are inherent limitations in attempting to encapsulate an entire psychotherapeutic theory in a sentence or two. This is certainly true for Erickson's multileveled and apparently simplistic, yet complex, work. It is just as unfair to pull a sentence or two from other schools of therapy, and through these sentences show a connection to Erickson's work. Additionally, much good therapy overlaps. Should a particular approach be identified as Cognitive? Solution-Focused? Behavioral? Strategic? Narrative? The subtleties between the different names are virtually impossible to sort out.

Here is where the one of the real gifts of Erickson's works lies. His framework for psychotherapy was so flexible that many of his ideas and methods have been incorporated into other schools. Understanding the versatility and applicability of his work as a source for some of these conceptualizations and methods broadens perspectives and allows each of us to become just a little more knowledgeable about psychotherapy. Familiarity with his work, and with the work of those who studied with him, heightens our ability to view other branches of psychotherapy more clearly.

Casework done from an Ericksonian point of view blends with, and supports, other types of more "modern" psychotherapy. This is true even when at the surface the problem and the intervention are strictly Ericksonian. Hypnosis, for example, is inextricably linked with Erickson's work. The underlying principles of much of the use of hypnosis, however, are the same principles that underlie other schools of therapy. Hypnosis is, after all, a technique for communication and for accessing the client's own resources.

In an article in the Milton H. Erickson Foundation *Newsletter* (vol. 16, no. 2), I described a client with whom I had worked who had been referred to me for hypnosis to help him learn to swallow pills. He had always found it difficult to take them, and, in childhood, his mother had accommodated him by crushing the pill and mixing it with applesauce. Later, he simply tried to avoid pills. And when he really needed to take one, he would grit his teeth and chew it no matter how bad the taste.

He now has a serious illness and must take up to 30 pills a day. Avoiding pills not only no longer is an option, but some of the tablets must be swallowed intact if they are to work effectively.

He knew he was being illogical. He had no trouble eating, and realized that pieces of food he swallowed were often larger than tablets. He also could swallow gum. But he gagged if he tried to swallow pills.

I could have worked with this client about possibly unresolved issues with his mother. Perhaps he had a fear of self-responsible adulthood, and this was a symptom of deeper underlying issues. Perhaps his illness was so frightening that a part of him wanted to avoid medication, and this was one way to do it. Perhaps his habitual behavior precluded open and flexible thinking. I didn't know, and I didn't think it was important.

From an Ericksonian standpoint, the therapist works with the world of the client. This client's world was simply that he wanted to learn to swallow pills — briefly, quickly, and without trying to know the unknowable reasons "why" he couldn't.

Ericksonian therapists also have a penchant for dealing with the simplest symptoms first. Changing one small part of a person's thought pattern or behavior often creates an unexpected number of other changes. Also, it is more respectful to the client to address issues from the "top down," so to speak. Finding pathology from a particular symptom usually isn't respectful or helpful.

My client wanted to be hypnotized into swallowing pills. I could have helped him achieve that goal by relying strictly on his definition. I could have used my authority as the hypnotist to command — or I could have given a posthypnotic suggestion.

I also could use his world to teach him about his unconscious and underutilized resources. When I teach hypnosis, I talk about how we all have such resources. Most of us do not consciously realize that we can manipulate blood-circulation patterns; he didn't believe he could. I told him that if I were to say just a few words, he would know he could manipulate part of his circulatory pattern. He would blush. I waited a moment while he thought of the words I might say, and he blushed, just as I did when Erickson used that example with me when I was learning formal hypnosis.

I pointed out that I hadn't even said those words. He had manipulated the circulatory pattern in his face all by himself, and simply by the power of his unconscious resources.

The next week, he told me had thought a great deal about how he could manipulate his blood flow. He had spent hours thinking about how he did it and blushing again and again until he could blush whenever he wanted. He demonstrated.

He had decided, he then said, that if he could do that seemingly impossible feat, controlling his gag reflex in order to swallow a few pills had to be simple. He had imagined the pills going down his throat smoothly, without triggering his gag reflex, until he could take his pills easily. He proudly demonstrated his newly recognized abilities.

Erickson said, in 1976, that if you really want to prove something to a client, let that proof come from within the client. Cognitive therapy points out that one of its goals is to help the client become his or her own therapist. Therapists do not need to confront or challenge the client's beliefs head on to produce change. It seems to me that my client proved something to himself — that he became his own therapist (Meichenbaum, 1992).

Behavioral therapy, which has a great deal of empirical research substantiating it, recognizes that imagery is a powerful conditioning and reconditioning tool. Calmness of relaxation is often juxtaposed against anxiety as clients learn to overcome their stress with regard to a particular situation (Wolpe, 1997). As that young man imaged pills moving smoothly down his throat, I don't know if he was in a self-hypnotic trance, or merely imaging comfort and relaxation. But I do know he changed, without having to receive any new information, and without my confronting and dealing with his illogical beliefs. He didn't need insight or self-understanding. Perhaps he "desensitized" himself by the imagery, perhaps he corrected his faulty thinking, perhaps he gained flexibility in thinking, perhaps ... who knows? I don't even know if I, an Ericksonian therapist, can declare this a therapeutic success, let alone put it in the column of Ericksonian psychotherapy.

Strategic therapy aims to be quick and dynamic therapy, finding ways to solve problems and recognizing that changing one part of a dynamic system necessarily affects the rest of the system. Erickson called this method of change "the snowball effect," comparing it to a snowball rolling down a hill, gathering snow and bits of grass and leaves while changing its size and appearance.

In 1964, one of my friends saw Erickson for one lengthy session. She had a three-year-old daughter diagnosed as borderline microcephalic — the child's brain was going to remain small and poorly developed. The little girl's abilities and disabilities were oddly scattered. She had never uttered an intelligible sound, but she understood rather complex sentences and sequencing. She lacked certain abilities usually found in children her age, but she was able to perform beyond her years in other areas.

The mother had been advised to institutionalize her. The girl would take time from the family's other children, she would not develop further mentally, and, as she got older, she would probably become rageful and difficult to control physically. The mother came to see Erickson, tearful and frightened.

Afterwards, she told me only that Erickson had asked her questions that made her think. Over the ensuing years, we both moved several times and lost track of each other.

When Erickson died, almost 15 years after her only visit with him, she called me. She said she wanted to tell me what had happened in that session. She said she had cried very hard as she told Erickson about her fears for the future and the dismal outcomes the other doctors had predicted. When her tears finally ceased, Erickson told her one thing that changed her life. "No one knows the future," he said. "No one. But you can prepare for a future that may be possible."

She said he then began asking questions. What did my friend really want for her child? How could she use her daughter's attributes as a foundation for her life? By the time the session was over, my friend felt hopeful. She knew her daughter's life would be difficult, but she knew she could prepare for a possible future. She had gone from "problem talk" to "solution talk" my friend said, using the language of Solution-Focused Therapy even though she knew nothing about that psychotherapeutic orientation (deShazer, 1988).

My friend told me that her daughter, now a young woman, was happy and busily raising show rabbits that had won numerous prizes throughout the country. She even earned a modest income through the sale of her animals. The daughter needed help in keeping records, her mother acknowledged, but she did all the other work. "You don't need words to communicate with rabbits," my friend told me. "You don't even need words to communicate to other rabbit fanciers — the animal speaks for itself."

I know Erickson didn't plan this life for my friend's daughter. After all, no one knows the future. But his statement opened new doors in her mother's thinking.

The constructivist narrative perspective of Cognitive Therapy, as described by Don Meichenbaum (1997) at the third Evolution of Psychotherapy Conference, conceptualizes this dynamic way of working with patients. Patients are viewed as "meaning-making agents who proactively create their own personal realities" (p. 100). This type of therapy, he says, is both exploratory and discovery oriented, with the therapists helping the clients to see how their personal realities are created and the consequences, both good and bad, that are a result of those created realities. Sounds exactly like what Erickson did with my friend.

Almost all formal definitions of psychotherapy include mention of some sort of client education. Cognitive therapist Aaron Beck (1997) defines it as "modification of dysfunctional thinking" (p. 56). Multimodal therapist Arnold Lazarus (1997) says education in therapy deals with missing information.

Erickson's (1980) view of education fits well within his definition of therapy — that is, helping the "patient achieve a legitimate personal goal as advantageously as is possible" (p. 382). His way of teaching included two often overlooked, but vitally important, parts of Ericksonian psychotherapy — utilization and seeding.

Utilization is using whatever the client presents, whenever the opportunity presents itself, to reach the goal of therapy. "Whatever the patient presents to you ... you really ought to use" (Erickson & Rossi, 1981, p. 16). Because the therapist is using what is brought by the client, the client's world, it ensures that the therapy, the information, is given in ways meaningful to the client.

Erickson would frequently use a necessary part of life to teach people to expand their lives, as well as to provide them with a way of thinking that would help them learn the enjoyment-seeking alternatives and options. In that way, the learner, be that learner a patient or a student or Erickson's own child, would become more flexible and creative in the personal search for betterment.

At the 1990 Evolution of Psychotherapy Conference, Albert Ellis (1992) talked about the importance of flexible, open-ended thinking. At that same event, Meichenbaum (1992) discussed schemata, the cognitive representations of past experiences that assist and influence the construction of current experiences and the organization of new information, or how people create data that confirm views. Sounds like what Erickson was doing.

Erickson used virtually everything as a teaching tool. He appreciated hard work; most of those associated with him learned to value work on many levels. When he assigned tasks to us children, which he never hesitated to do, he often used that work to help us learn to think creatively. I don't think that mowing the lawn in Phoenix, Arizona, in the summer could ever be classified as real fun. However, even as we were complainingly lugging out the lawn mower, Erickson would ask, in an interested way, if we thought we could get the job done faster if we mowed in circles, or maybe in diagonal lines. Perhaps if we mowed a strip on the part close to the end and then "forgot to remember" that strip, the welcome, almost surprise, sight of that already mowed part would make it seem as though the job were moving faster. In other words, he was teaching us to approach life with creativeness and curiosity, to utilize what was in our life as a way of enhancing it. To this day, if I have a repetitive task, I figure out different ways to do it and how to do parts in the middle so I can have a pleasant "surprise" as I come upon a completed bit.

My brother, Lance, in the keynote panel address for the 1983 International Congress on Ericksonian Psychotherapy, talked about sweeping the basement when he was a youngster in the 1940s. Lance was interested in the Civil War, and Erickson discussed with him how the cracks and lines on the concrete floor could be seen as boundaries between countries. The dust and debris could be seen as armies. Then Erickson asked Lance if he thought that if the armies fought battles over and through the boundaries, the results would be the same each time. With that careful setup and the curious question, Erickson invited his young son to construct the reality of sweeping the basement floor in a more pleasurable way (Erickson, 1985).

The same framework for thinking was provided in many different ways. All of the Erickson children walked at least a mile to and from their various schools. We don't remember those daily walks as drudgery. We remember some of the things we learned from what I now realize was Erickson's carefully constructed paradigm. Did the flowers on the north side of the street bloom before those on the south side? How many shortcuts could we find, and how much shorter were they really? Did some longer ways actually take less time because the environment was different? How much of our homework could we get done in our heads on the way home?

Erickson obviously was not doing therapy on us. However, the concept is the same. He was helping us to create a flexible view of the realities of life that, in turn, would create a flexible way of constructing data for the rest of our lives. Our personal schemata of our tasks just as easily could have been created so that there was no creative pleasure or intellectual curiosity in the drudgery. But Erickson carefully structured and seeded a way of constructing reality, using natural curiosity and the inclination to find "easier" ways of doing work. He utilized what we brought in to seed more productive ways to achieve goals.

Erickson looked at this type of seeding as a farmer looks at seeding crops. If you sow enough seeds, some of them will take root and grow — especially if you are wise enough not to keep going back and pulling them up to see if they have sprouted.

Even in the autographing of books, Erickson sought to seed information. My son, at age 10, was noted for his carefree, nonchalant attitude. Erickson's inscription in one of his books to Michael referred to a time when Michael had thoughtfully planned for the future of his pet birds, which had to be left behind when our family moved back to the United States from overseas. My son cherished what was written; he quoted it many times during his growing up, usually when he was being chastised for some impulsive behavior. As an adult, he still credits Erickson for being the first to recognize his "foresight in planning for the future."

I don't know for certain that the inscription helped him mature. I do know he thinks it influenced him. His personal reality, his schema for life, began to incorporate planning for the future as a counterpoint to his inclination to impulsivity.

Deliberately creating interventions that invited a client to provide his or her own meaning, to become his or her own therapist, was a strong point in Erickson's methods and is a goal of Cognitive Behavioral Therapy (Meichenbaum, 1997). Resistance is side-stepped as the clients truly become the experts on themselves, and independence is fostered.

I don't have to go too far to find ways in which Erickson did that. He advised hundreds of people to climb Squaw Peak, but rarely told them what he expected them to get out of the hike. Because people could create their own meanings, the hike meant whatever the person needed it to mean.

Sometimes he structured the event for a positive interpretation, knowing that this would help the client's overall sense of self. He knew, as the late Viktor Frankl espoused so poignantly and meaningfully, that people always search for meaning. He believed that if a positive meaning is implied, people are likely to adopt that positive definition.

I recently talked with a patient who had seen Erickson in the mid-1950s. While working with him, she had learned Origami — the Japanese art of creating objects by folding paper in specific and careful ways. Right there, I could see the opportunity for a multiplicity of meanings. At her last session, she said, she gave Erickson a small Origami box she had made. He examined it carefully and admiringly, then handed it back to her, and told her that she could keep it as a reverse Pandora's box. "Badness" would be safely locked in the closed box. She could continue to feel control and self determination in life.

She showed me the little blue-and-white paper box. She has kept it for more than 40 years, through countless moves and upheavals in her life. The box she had made so long ago has continued to be a symbol to her of empowerment in her life. The sole purpose of her visit to me was to show me how her cherished reverse Pandora's box was still working for her. She was still managing her life well, she said. When I reflected that to her, she smiled. She already knew. She wanted to be sure that I, as Erickson's representative, knew it too.

Erickson's ability to incorporate a vision of the future in the present is one part of his framework that is difficult to quantify and teach. It does not seem to have yet become a regular component of other theoretical positions. The future was very real in a great deal of his therapeutic work, and even in casual conversation. People were given permission and the empowerment they felt they needed to do things in the present so that, in the future, they would be able to look back at their accomplishments. It might be hard work now, he would indicate, but it will be so fulfilling in the future to look back at it.

In this chapter, I have barely addressed the use of hypnosis, which was an important and integral part of his work. I do not believe Erickson's therapeutic methods can be well understood without a basic understanding of hypnosis.

I have also barely addressed his use of metaphors and his storytelling, about which entire books have been written. This method of teaching, of providing options, of creating new and flexible thinking, is so strongly identified with Erickson that some think it constitutes the major part of his psychotherapeutic orientation. But Erickson knew that a story is just another way of helping a client to rely on internal resources and to learn how to think flexibly and creatively. It was a small part of his repertoire, but part of his lasting legacy. We all need to learn to tell stories — what a delightful way to evoke curiosity and concentration, to teach, to normalize, to give humor, and to promote independence.

If Erickson were reading this, I know he would be shaking his head at me. I have not even mentioned two integral parts of his orientation that he emphasized to others over and over. One is observation. "Observe,

observe, observe," he would say. The therapist must learn to set aside personal perspectives and really see and hear from the client's point of view.

The other is the careful choice of words. Words have multiple meanings, not only to different individuals, but within the context of the moment. Pop psyche says it all — men are from Mars, women are from Venus. We are all unique with different experiences upon which we build meanings. But words are a primary pathway to thoughts, as well as to manipulating and changing personal thoughts and schemata.

I almost always ask clients, at the end of therapy, to tell me what was most valuable to them. One, a young man I'll call Tommy, answered immediately. "That's easy," he said. "You told me, 'Be fearless, Tommy. Write it on your hand if you have to, but be fearless.' So I did. Every time I had to do something that was scary, I'd take a deep breath, read the imaginary writing on my hand — be fearless — and go for it."

I told that story to a little girl named Beatrice. She listened intently and said she was going to do that too. But she was going to write 'Be scaredless."

I smiled, thinking she was misusing a word, as children do. "No," she explained. "You don't understand. I am writing 'Be scaredless' because my name is Bea, and every time I do something hard, I will be scared less."

Bea reorganized her understanding of her world by using words to help create new internal experiences. She manipulated her thoughts by words. She created her own scheme for her future. She also re-reminded me of the importance of remembering that the meanings of words are created, in part, by the uniqueness of the individual's perspective.

In this chapter, I have focused primarily on some of Erickson's methods that have become part of the larger therapeutic world. Sometimes his ideas and thoughts have been incorporated into other therapies, sometimes they overlap the good therapeutic methods developed from different roots, and sometimes they have been altered to fit the culture of today.

So where are we going now? What is the future of Ericksonian psychotherapeutic methodology? I don't know for sure. No one knows the future. But I would bet that the foundation of Erickson's work will still enrich and be part of therapy as it continues to develop. As therapists search for the best, most efficient, most respectful ways of doing therapy, the work that Erickson did and taught will remain a part of their base.

Perhaps refusing to define a theory was one of Erickson's greatest gifts to modern therapies. As humans, we all are unique, and so individualistic that each of us should choose wisely from the vast buffet of psychotherapeutic methods available according to our tastes. To benefit the most, each of us should come to that plethora with an appetite to learn and an understanding of the ingredients of each offering.

Studying the original work of Erickson, along with the work of those who studied with him directly does that. It gives today's therapists a deeper understanding of the ingredients, of the complexities and nuances, of many therapeutic stances. This, in turn, allows all of us to become even more effective. We can pick and choose among the ways of doing therapy or of giving information those that are best for a particular client on a particular day. We can help to create a possible future. And we fulfill the real goal of therapy — to help our clients achieve legitimate personal goals as advantageously as possible.

References

Beck, A. T. (1997). Cognitive therapy reflections. In J. K. Zeig (Ed.), *The evolution of psychotherapy: The third conference*. New York: Norton.

de Shazer, S. (1988). *Keys to solutions in brief therapy*. New York: Norton.

Erickson, L., et al. (1985). Keynote address: Special (family) panel on Milton Erickson. In J. K. Zeig (Ed.), *Ericksonian psychotherapy, Volume I: Structures*. New York: Brunner/Mazel.

Erickson, M. H. (1980). *The collected papers of Milton H. Erickson on hypnosis. Vol IV.* E. L. Rossi, (Ed.) New York: Irvington.

Erickson, M. H., & Rossi, E. (1981). *Experiencing hypnosis*. New York: Irvington.

Erickson, M. H., Rossi, E. L., & Rossi, S. I. (1976). *Hypnotic realities*. New York: Irvington.

Lazarus, A. (1992). Clinical/therapeutic effectiveness. In J. K. Zeig (Ed.), *The evolution of psychotherapy: The second conference*. New York: Brunner/Mazel.

Lazarus, A. (1997). Can psychotherapy be brief, focused, solution-focused and yet comprehensive? In J. K. Zeig (Ed.), *The evolution of psychotherapy: The third conference*. New York: Brunner/Mazel.

Meichenbaum, D. (1992). Evolution of cognitive behavior therapy. In J. K. Zeig (Ed.), *The evolution of psychotherapy: The second conference*. New York: Brunner/ Mazel.

Meichenbaum, D. (1997). The evolution of a cognitive-behavior therapist. In J. K. Zeig (Ed.), *The evolution of psychotherapy: The third conference*. New York: Brunner/Mazel.

Wolpe, J. (1997). From psychoanalytic to behavioral methods in anxiety disorders. In J. K. Zeig (Ed.), *The evolution of psychotherapy: The third conference*. New York: Brunner/Mazel.

Zeig, J. K., & Gilligan, S. G. (Eds.). (1990). *Brief therapy: Myths, methods, and metaphors*. New York: Brunner/Mazel.

18

The Therapeutic Honoring of Emotions in Brief Therapy

Mary McClure Goulding

Emotional health doesn't mean perpetual happiness. What it does mean is the ability to respond to internal and external stimuli with a full range of emotions, to be willing to accept one's own emotions, experience them, let them go, and accept them again.

People differ in their natural emotional responsiveness. Some feel very strongly; other people have milder emotional reactions. In essence, every person is born with a unique set of affective ranges and capabilities, a personal affective quotient, if you will.

Some people seem to be naturally joyous. Others are naturally placid or content; nothing bothers them much. Still others easily become irritated or agitated. And many of our patients spend a lifetime fighting mild to severe depression, even though their current lives appear to be successful and trauma-free.

We all know that each infant is different. There are healthy babies who cry every time they are put down, and there are those who almost never cry. Some are eager for contact, and others spurn it.

Children and parents, with all their differing affective responses, have to figure out how to live together, and that may not be easy. It may be difficult for type A parents to appreciate a type B child. The child is so laid back and seemingly uninvolved. This is not a family that welcomes a Buddha. On the other hand, an overworked and overstressed single parent longs for a calm, easy child. Thus, each person's innate affective abilities also are both enhanced and suppressed by life experiences.

Children learn to repress certain emotions and to substitute others that are safer or more acceptable at home and at school. Anger may replace tears, or vice versa. Children learn to hide sadness, fear, jealousy, shame, pride, and all the various wonderful manifestations of happiness. People who learned in childhood that their feelings were intolerable to their parents may spend their lives muting or discounting their own feelings. Emotional responsiveness, then, is based on both nature and nurture.

But although, as I will stress, it is important to honor all of a client's emotions throughout the therapeutic process, some brief-therapy techniques disregard those aspects of a patient's life. These therapists, trying to accomplish the most in the fewest number of sessions, tend to overlook their patients' feelings as they fine-tune their problem-solving techniques.

In a skit satirizing the effects of HMOs on therapy, presented at a meeting of the American Academy of Psychotherapists, the "Phantom of the HMO" sang:

> Help your patients feel that their problems are not real
> And they're taking too much time to reach their goals.
> And always treat their symptoms, not their souls.

The fact of the matter is that in brief therapy, we therapists can, and must, find the time to address both our patients' symptoms and their souls.

In my early years as a transactional analyst, my objective was to teach everyone to be happy as fast as I possibly could. The advantage of this approach was that I learned how to be an effective brief therapist. The disadvantage was that I tended to see unhappiness as pathology. I now believe that the acceptance, by therapist and clients, of all emotions leads to a more profound therapy and results in both self-acceptance and an increased capacity for intimacy. I want to provide clients with an experience that enhances emotional growth. My goal is for our work together to be as positive and emotionally intimate as is possible within even the briefest time frame.

Although I still utilize much of the theory of Transactional Analysis,

I am a redecision therapist. Redecision therapy (which was developed by my late husband, Robert L. Goulding, M.D., and myself) involves three basic elements, or steps: (1) therapeutic contract, (2) redecision, and (3) implementation and reinforcement.

THE CONTRACT

The contract spells out what the client wants to change about himself or herself during the course of the therapy. The client and the therapist agree that the contract is viable; that is, that it is understandable, doable in therapy, potentially beneficial for the client, and not harmful to others.

Sometimes it not possible to begin immediately with, "What do you want to change about yourself today?" (which was Bob's favorite opener). Although clients come to psychotherapists for relief from symptoms and for the resolution of problems, their first, almost overwhelming, need is to experience positive contact with the therapist, to feel validated. Their hidden, sometimes immense, fear is that instead of validation, they will be shamed. What the therapist first sees in a client may be defense against potential shame. To avoid shaming clients, a therapist offers interest and respect rather than judgment. We recognize their uniqueness and worth, even if they themselves don't, and we let them know that we care about their lives.

The easiest way to accomplish this is to focus on their emotions with kindness. Accepting the client's feelings sets the tone for truthful, tender contact, a coming together of therapist and client. This is what I mean by validation. I'll respond to a client's words with: "That is sad." Or, simply, as a client fights tears, "It's okay to cry." I might say, "This is hard to talk about, isn't it?" Or, "Do you give yourself credit for being courageous?" By my tone of voice, posture, and words, I want to convey to clients that I honor their emotions and, also, that they can be proud, rather than ashamed, for admitting that they need help with their lives.

Usually, a client begins with vague generalities. "I seem to have trouble at home (at work, with my son, etc.)" Immediately, I ask the client to describe a scene that explains the problem. "Give a 'for instance.' Tell me about a specific scene ... a recent one, when you were having this trouble."

When the client starts to report a recent scene, I say, "Tell it as if it's happening right now. Where are you and what's going on?" I draw up a second chair, and say, "So that I can understand better, sit in this other chair when you are being your wife" (or mother, son, teacher, supervisor) "and stay in your own seat when you are being yourself. Okay?"

Again, I focus on the client's feelings in the current scene. "That is sad." Or, "How frightening!" Or, "I'm impressed with your honesty ... it isn't easy to admit your part in this scene." If the client does not express feelings, I might say, "Test out saying, 'I'm angry'! and see if it fits." Or, "You've been enduring a lot these days and you sound so stoical. In this scene, if you were to let yourself feel, what would you be feeling?"

If the client is the victim, I empathize, and later the client will probably frame a therapeutic contract, "I want to stop being a victim." If the client is the villain in the scene, I empathize with the hurt, fear, loneliness, awkwardness, or passion that precipitated the villainy, and later look for a contract for the client to stop being the villain.

I want the client to relive a recent scene for three reasons.

1. Reliving a scene rather than just talking about it makes the problem understandable to both the therapist and client.
2. Reliving a scene draws forth its emotional as well as factual content, making the problem come alive in a way that "talking about it" never would.
3. Recreating a scene sets the stage for the next step, redecision work.

After the client finishes reliving the recent scene, we think about it and discuss it. We look at the problems that the scene illustrates: What are possible solutions? We'll discuss these solutions. We'll talk about how the client has solved similar problems, and focus on what abilities the client used to solve them. Can these same abilities be used to solve the problems depicted in this scene? What might the client have to change about herself or himself in order to resolve the issues in the scene, to solve the problems? The client's answer, what the client is willing to change about self, becomes the therapy contract, the goal of the therapy.

Examples of Contracts

A contract to change a feeling reaction might be to stop becoming depressed over the behavior of others. A thinking contract might be to learn the difference between problem solving and obsessing — to stop obsessing and to plan how to solve a problem. A behavioral contract might be to carry out the planned action. A behavioral-control contract might be to permit oneself to be angry, to state one's anger, and not to abuse oneself or others.

In the contract phase of therapy, I am careful to emphasize the client's personal autonomy. The client, and only the client, is responsible for his or her thoughts, beliefs, emotions, and behavior, and only the client is responsible for making contractual changes. The following example of what I mean by emotional autonomy is from a paper I presented at the third Evolution of Psychotherapy conference, "Coping with Loss — A Personal and Professional Perspective" (Goulding, 1997). I wrote this about my reactions to Bob Goulding's death:

> My emotional life was chaotic. I veered back and forth between sadness, loneliness, bursts of happiness and laughter, guilt, numbness, vulnerability, and despair. I was bereft. There was no pattern to my grieving, in spite of the patterns that the "how to" books suggest. I lost my heart when I lost Bob. Bob and I taught the importance of personal autonomy. By this we meant that each person chooses his or her own emotions, beliefs, thoughts, and actions. Although I have felt, since his death, as if I have not been choosing my feelings, I do choose them. I respond emotionally to a song, a memory, a physical sensation, a day with family or friends, an evening alone. My emotions are my own responses to the stimuli I choose to perceive. I choose the stimuli and the responses, and I contaminate both by my constant awareness that Bob is dead.

I urge therapists to learn to understand personal autonomy and not to confuse it with self-control. The fact that a person "chooses" grief, for example, does not mean that the person should change from grief to happiness. A therapist can offer a real gift to clients by understanding the concept of autonomy while believing that all emotions are natural and acceptable, and that there is no automatic time limit for any feeling.

As clients formulate their contracts, I encourage them to take pride in their problem-solving abilities by saying, "Good thinking," "Great idea," or "You've got it!" Throughout the therapy process, therapists need to help clients to be proud of themselves. Pride is the antithesis of shame, and is a positive emotion that therapists need to promote in themselves, as well as in their clients.

The contract establishes the focus of the redecision work, which I like to begin during the first session, so that there is a tie-in between the contract and redecision.

THE REDECISION

Sometimes, a client and I may do only problem-solving work, without redecisions, although this is rarely my preference. To me, it seems shallow. Here I am emphasizing redecision work within childhood scenes, in which the client brings the past into the present in order to resolve current problems.

How do we find a scene to use for redecision work? There are many ways, including the following.

1. A client says, "This feels like what happened to me with my father when I was just a kid." I suggest that the client choose a specific scene with his or her father.
2. I ask, "Did you have a similar problem when you were a child?" If the answer is Yes, the client chooses a specific scene.
3. I guess. "You're saying that you don't speak up for yourself, that you don't consider yourself important. I wonder how important you were at the family dinner table when you were a child." I choose the scene.
4. Most commonly, a client's words and body language lead to a childhood scene. For example:

   - "Hold your hands against your mouth the way you were doing a moment ago ... that's it. You said you felt anxious, so let yourself experience your anxiousness, and say your words again, 'I'm no good at asking for what I want.' Now move back in time and perhaps you'll find a scene ..."
   - "Double your fist again, and say again, 'I get so frustrated! I just want to walk out on him.' How does that fit with when you were a little kid?"
   - "You said, 'He expects more than I can give,' and you are sad, and you are rubbing your hands together. Shut your eyes, if you like, rub your hands together, say again sadly, 'He expects more than I can give,' and feel your sadness. Does that fit a time when you were a child?"
   - "You are really angry because they won't listen, but you bite

> your lip and don't show your anger. Do you remember a time like that when you were a child, angry, not heard, and having to bite your lip to hide your anger?"

Most clients have no trouble in finding a relevant scene. The client then enters the specific remembered scene in fantasy and relives it. Although the client is a child in the scene, the client also has access to his or her own adult knowledge and strengths that were unavailable in childhood. The redecision occurs within the scene, when the client forcefully experiences new insights and new ways of behaving, thinking, or feeling.

For example:

"I wonder how important you were at the family dinner table." The redecision, acted out at the imaginary dinner table: "Okay, all of you ... you don't listen to me, don't care what I have to say. You're too busy drinking and arguing. Well, I'm talking up even though you don't listen. I am important to myself!" Later, the client practices being important at current dinner tables and business meetings.

"Hold your hands against your mouth the way you were doing a moment ago, let yourself experience your anxiety, and say your words again: 'I'm no good at asking for what I want.' The childhood scene turns out to be a tragic one, in which the mother is dying and the child is being taken to live with foster parents. In this childhood scene, the client concentrates on mourning her mother's death. This takes several sessions. Her redecision comes with the recognition, within the childhood scene, of the child's bravery and strength. She reenters the scene to be a new mother for this orphaned child. She then begins to separate her tragic past from her potentially fulfilling present. As homework between sessions, she makes lists of what she wants, and practices praising herself whenever she asks for something from the list. Then, as she is successful in therapy, her basic problem emerges, her fear of being intimate, and she struggles with this, both in her relationship with her therapist and in other childhood scenes. She begins to practice what she terms "tiny bits of closeness" with two co-workers. Her therapy consisted of about 30 sessions, so it was not brief therapy according to my definition of the term.

"I get so frustrated! I just want to walk out ..." The childhood scene is one in which the client, a little princess, is making demands and becoming very frustrated at not getting her way. It takes several sessions for her to recognize that she is a frustrator as well as a frustratee, and that she ignores the rights of others. Fortunately, she has a sense of humor that the therapist appreciates, and she uses her humor to make the scene comic rather than tragic. Her redecision, stated in the scene, was: "I am asking for what I want, but I don't have to win every round. And if what I want is important, I'll use my own ingenuity to get it for myself."

"He expects more than I can give ..." In a childhood scene with her father, the client recognizes that it was her father, rather than her husband, who was never satisfied with her. She removes her father's face from her husband, and recognizes that her husband and her father are very different people. She explores ways in which she, like her father, is never satisfied, and then decides that she is satisfied with what she has done in this single session of therapy. She leaves happily, and later she and her husband ask to have two or three sessions together in order to resolve some minor difficulties. In this case, although she made no changes in herself within the childhood scene, she redecided by recognizing differences between the past and the present.

"I'm so angry ... I bite my lip ..." The scene is a clear example of a father's abuse of a child, the client. The client recognizes his vulnerability and knows that biting his lip was the best thing he could do to prevent being beaten. He imagines his favorite football players immobilizing his father while he yells his fury at the way he was treated. He allows himself to throw pillows and to imagine beating his father with them. Then he enters the scene as himself, an adult, and takes the child away. "I am now your parent, and I will never let anyone beat you again," he tells the boy. He has permitted himself to express rage and has agreed to protect himself, and then he recognizes the vast difference between the present and past scenes.

During these redecision dramas, the therapist listens, and, in a sense, is assistant director and stage manager. The therapist is also an enthusiastic audience. One of the reasons I prefer group to individual therapy is that a larger audience is more exhilarating for the individual who is creating the drama.

A redecision takes place when the client experiences a new way of thinking, feeling, or behaving within the scene. Often the client creates a new ending, substituting autonomy for victimization. Clients redecide to live in spite of life's difficulties, to be important to themselves, to allow others into their emotional lives, to be playful, self-protective, mature.

As another example I'll quote a piece of work by Bob Goulding, done at a one-week workshop for therapists that he and I co-led a few months before he died. There are no overt expressions of empathy from Bob in this work, but his love and acceptance are obvious. I included this segment of therapy in my book about Bob, *Sweet Love Remembered* (Goulding, 1992, pp. 147–150).

JOE: My contract was ... is ... what I want is not to be guilty when I haven't done anything.

BOB: Say more.

JOE: My girlfriend is ... I mean, she gives me all her love and that's good, but sometimes I feel guilty because, I don't know, I guess somehow I'd be more comfortable if she gave me less, somehow.

BOB: You say, "I don't know" and "I guess" and "somehow." Say what you know.

JOE: What I know is that she loves me and ... I know that. I also know that she makes demands that are not comfortable. And then I feel guilty, even though I haven't done anything wrong, and neither has she.

BOB (plays back the videotape): I want you to see yourself. When you said you didn't know, notice how your head is cocked to one side and your feet are twisted together. When you said what you did know, you uncrossed your feet and held your head straight.

JOE: Amazing. The first time I look like a nervous kid. The second time I look my age. Thank you.

BOB: You're welcome. Say more. Give an example of a scene with you and your girlfriend. Actually, woman friend.

JOE: Sure. Coming here. I offered to bring her, but she couldn't get away from her work. So, she didn't want me to come. I know she loves me, and she trusts me, and yet she didn't really want me to come. That may not be fair. She made a flip comment about who I might be meeting here, and I feel very guilty being here without her.

BOB: Okay, that's the present scene. You decide to come here, she makes a flip comment, whatever that means, and you are guilty. Now, put your feet back in the twisted position. That's it. Cock your head to the right side, like that. That's it. Try out the words, "I'm guilty ... I shouldn't leave her. I ..."

JOE: Good God! ... You were going to ask for a past scene, right?

Bob nods.

JOE: I hadn't thought of this. In years. My girlfriend is nothing like my mother, really. But I made the scene the same. I was about 12 . . ."

MARY: Be there. I am about 12 . . .

JOE: I have a chance to go to summer camp for a whole month. My grandparents are going to pay for it. These are my father's parents. My father left before I was born and I hardly ever even saw him. Anyway, they offered to pay and I wanted to go so much. It was a sort of wilderness camp. With canoeing. (*Starts to weep, shakes his head.*) It still gets to me. My mother calls me into her bedroom. She tells me I am all she has. I know that. She says a month is too long, and she is very upset. (*Joe is weeping openly. Long pause.*) I am overcome with guilt because I want to go so much.

BOB (*very gently*): Do you go?

JOE: No. I tell her I didn't want to go anyway.

BOB: Now uncross your legs, keep your head straight, and tell her the truth.

JOE: The truth is, I'm growing up. It won't hurt you for me to go to camp. It's only a month and then . . .

BOB: I want to go to camp!

JOE: Yeah, that is the truth. I want to go to camp. I want to stop taking care of your feelings. If she feels bad, am I'm guilty? No, I am not guilty! (*Goes on talking to her in fantasy about the difficulty he had separating from her, and repeats that he is not responsible for her. She had many options, such as finding friends and building her own interests.*) I am not your only joy in life! (*Pause.*) I believe this is a crucial piece of work for me.

MARY: Yes, I agree. You aren't quite done. Take your mother off the chair and put your woman friend on the chair. What do you want to say to her?

JOE: I think we've had some problems because I put my mother's face on you. You have a right to be ambivalent about my coming here. You weren't trying to stop me. I see that. I was reacting in a panic, as if you were my mother, and I'd be guilty if I came. I did come here, but I felt guilty and resentful. Hey, I love you and we are two separate human beings. I have been afraid to marry because I didn't know how to stay separate. It was so hard with Mom. (*Turns to Mary.*) But now I think I've got it.

BOB: Tell her what you told your mother, 'I am not your only joy in life.'

JOE: That's true. Besides, you run your own show very well. Yeah. This is my problem, not yours. I am not your only joy in life. (*Big smile.*) I'm done.

Each piece of redecision work is unique. The following final example accents the "nature and nurture" aspects of emotions. I reported this work in *The Journal of Redecision Therapy* (Goulding, 1998).

A chronically unhappy patient read *Changing Lives* (Goulding & Goulding, 1979) and came to a workshops loaded with childhood scenes that explained his inability to find joy in life. He relived several scenes, none of which seemed particularly traumatic, although he thought they accounted for his unhappiness.

Finally, the therapist said, "You know about diabetes ... lack of production or utilization of body insulin. Well, perhaps you lack some body chemical that is responsible for natural happiness. You could take antidepressants, or perhaps you could learn to make yourself happy even though you were cheated out of whatever chemicals or genetic structure makes for easy happiness. I've got an idea ..." The therapist suggested that the patient return to the childhood scenes in which he'd worked previously. This time, he was to pretend that he was born with an incredible abundance of happiness genes. He would enter and leave each scene as a chronically happy little boy.

The first scene was the birth of his sister. Instead of his previous bitter unhappiness at being pushed out of the limelight, he imagined himself playing with his toys in a very sunny room and scarcely noticing that a new baby had come into his life. With a little help from his therapist, he imagined himself happy with his parents and imperturbable with his sister. He was astonished. "I think we've got something here! It's true ... It's like I was predestined for unhappiness." He did several other scenes, to wild applause from the other participants. After the workshop, he worked hard toward achieving the goal of being happy. He didn't experience a natural joy, although he certainly began being nicer to himself and others and finding more entertaining activities. He reported that whenever he had a problem in life, he would ask himself, "How would a chronically happy man handle this?"

IMPLEMENTATION AND REENFORCEMENT

The objective of all therapy is the attainment of a richer, more desirable life. The past is memory, sometimes to be cherished and sometimes to be discarded, and always to be dealt with in therapy as quickly as possible. What is important is the present, not the past.

Implementation of a redecision means practicing the new way of being. For example, after conquering a snake phobia in fantasy, a client has to visit a pet shop and meet a real snake. A person who is afraid of intimacy faces a tougher, but perhaps more exciting, challenge in learning to share thoughts and feelings with other humans, to enjoy rather than fear human contact.

Most clients will move, within the same therapy session, from the childhood scene to the current scene, as Joe did. Using the new insights from the scene with his mother, he redoes the current scene as he imagines explaining to his woman friend, "I think we've had some problems because I put my mother's face on you," and finishes by repeating, "I am not your only joy in life." The next step, of course, is to show her (and himself) what he has accomplished. He will do this at home by behaving, feeling, and thinking in new ways. Many clients believe they have to explain their redecisions to others. They may do this if they wish, but they need to know that what is most important is that they live their changes rather than talk about them.

As clients grow and make changes, they need reinforcement from important people in their lives. They are fortunate if they have already surrounded themselves with friends and family members who are supportive. If not, homework assignments will include finding such people and asking for support.

Clients also need internal reinforcement. They need to learn to treat themselves in positive, loving, nurturing ways. Many people, including many therapists, parent others well but parent themselves very harshly. In therapy, they learn to treat themselves as they treat others. If they don't have a good internal parent, they need to develop one.

To practice parenting themselves well, clients return to the redecision scene and speak to the hurting child. "I am taking you out of this scene forever, and from now on I will protect you." "I will not ridicule you the way others have." "I admire you." "I will never shame you." "I value you and love you." The client alternates between being the child in the redecision scene and being the new parent, to experience both being accepted and accepting.

A hurting child is comforted. Grieving children are encouraged to speak of their loss as often as they choose. A wise internal parent knows that there is not a mandatory time limit on grief. Angry children are understood by the new, wiser parents, and are allowed to express their fury. All children are encouraged to have pride in themselves. They are not expected to be perfect.

After parenting the child, clients practice parenting themselves as they are today. They speak the same words of encouragement to themselves, "I love you." "I will take good care of you." "I admire you."

CONCLUSION

Clients learn kinder, more empathic ways of treating themselves and others by incorporating within themselves their experiences of the positive ways their therapists have treated them. The following is from the tape of a question-and-answer session with Bob Goulding, taped a week before Bob died (Goulding, 1992). Bob responded to questions about transference, and then said, "A lot goes on in therapy between patients and therapist. We come to esteem each other. That is not transference or countertransference. Friendship and regard and mutual appreciation in a true sense are not transference. It is the intimacy that develops from caring and working together. I believe in the basic goodness of people. Sometimes people try hard to prove me wrong, but I'll hang in there" (p. 163).

References

Goulding, M. M. (1992). *Sweet love remembered*. San Francisco: TA Press.

Goulding, M. M. (1997). Coping with loss in later years. In J. K. Zeig (Ed.), *The evolution of psychotherapy: The third conference* (p. 218). New York: Brunner/Mazel.

Goulding, M. M. (Spring, 1998). Nature and nurture. *The Journal of Redectision Therapy*, pp. 25–26.

Goulding, M. M., & Goulding, R. L. (1979; revised and updated 1997). *Changing lives through redecision therapy*. New York: Grove Press.

Lennox, C. E. (Ed.). (1997). *Redecision therapy*. Northvale, NJ: Jason Aronson.

19

Family Therapy: A Braided Challah

Lynn Hoffman

This chapter can be divided into three main topics. The first is the present situation of family therapy. The second is my own take on the succession of approaches in the field, and the third is the story of my deepening appreciation for the collaborative style of work that was pioneered by the late Harry Goolishian, together with Harlene Anderson, Tom Andersen, Peggy Penn, and myself, among many others. This work leaves the essentialist framework of traditional family therapy to move toward one that relies on a more communal perspective. The idea of a therapist's operating on a unit in trouble disappears. In its place, we find a new kind of social weaving that is jointly produced and has surprising, unexpected outcomes.

THE BRAIDED CHALLAH

To begin, then, I have been wondering whether or not our specialty might be facing extinction. Managed care, with its demands for accountability, has pushed the field of family therapy to the limits. Many of us are asking what, if anything, backs up our claims. Research results are not outstanding, in part because many of our approaches don't emphasize outcomes. Worse yet, we don't even agree on what kind of issues should be dealt with in family therapy. In a kind of creep, each approach has added a rich new bank of problems to the roster. Starting modestly with schizophrenia, we moved on to parent/child problems, marital woes, developmental traumas, life-stage inertia, gender discrimination, sexual abuse, violence, addiction, poverty, and all the injustices engendered by class, ethnicity, and race. Our increasingly medical/behavioral vocabulary for describing unexplained suffering turns every woe into a disease or a disorder.

At the same time, the competition between the "helping professions" for the right to treat these woes intensifies. A community college near my home offers degrees in art therapy, mental health counseling, social work, and marriage and family therapy. This competition has been intensified by the appearance of new medications that have been amazingly successful in ameliorating problems that used to belong to counseling alone.

This seemed like a good time to assess the field. Using an analogy from a simple cardgame of my childhood, I used to think that family outranks individual, systemic outranks family, gender outranks systemic, culture and race outrank gender, and, at a paradigm level, postmodern outranks everything that has gone before. But this formulation implies an upward and onward progression, which I do not believe exists.

An alternative was to look at practice ideas unrelated to model or rationale. I asked myself: "What are the biggest hits of family therapy?" This was all too easy. My list included triangles, genograms, boundaries, paradoxes, secrets, reflexive questions, reflecting teams, and "as if" exercises, and kept getting longer until it began to resemble a scenario for a Tower of Babel. There was no way to translate these disparate therapeutic tongues.

Then I had a rescuing thought: perhaps the real "biggest hit" of the family-therapy movement was its power to fold back upon itself and change in a reflexive way. An evolutionary image came to mind. I began to think of family therapy as a braided challah bread, with early strands disappearing and then reappearing in a changed position or on another side. Each new strand suggested an answer to a question that had been brought to the fore by a previous strand, and a later strand would compensate for a deficiency in the one before. And it was the conversation between the strands, so to speak, that made the entire braid so special.

The Etiological Strand

I found inspiration for this idea in an article by psychologist Margaret Singer (1996) that described the shift in the mental health field from a rehabilitative to an etiological framework. Singer says that the work of the German psychologist Adolf Meyer, which was widely influential in the United States in the first half of the century, set the tone for a rehabilitation approach to psychiatric problems. For Meyer's followers, finding a cause was less important than returning the person to better functioning. After World War II, Singer says, owing to the influence of theories that addressed the psychological and developmental causes of emotional distress, an etiological view took over.

This causal bias has informed psychotherapists from Freud to the present day. Repression theory held that symptoms result from developmental traumas that must be recalled and "worked through" for healing to take place. Singer has called this general view, which pervades popular psychology, the "blame and change game." If you can find someone or something to blame, such as your parents, then you can change. This prescription was eventually enlarged to include confronting the offending persons, and even taking them to court or jailing them. Singer points to the excesses of the recovered-memory movement for examples of the harm this rationale can do.

It was only natural that early family therapy schools would develop a "family repression theory" of their own. Throughout the history of the field, much has been written about covert coalitions, family secrets, buried myths, and unacknowleged grief. These areas, it was thought, needed to be exposed and addressed before any change could take place. The key example was the idea that the symptomatic child masked a hidden conflict between the parents. Once the therapist focused on the unhappy marriage, it was thought that the child's symptoms would dissipate.

As a result, the question of "who done it?" has characterized the family therapy movement, which has had a chilling effect on families and practitioners alike. In early family research, it seemed that mothers were the problem. Then therapists went after the nuclear family. Systemic approaches added agency persons who had been inducted into the "family system." With the advent of feminist therapies, the focus shifted to domestic violence, implicating fathers and husbands. As this perspective evolved, it seemed that anybody in a position of power over another person could be seen as a perpetrator, including colleagues and other professionals.

The Rhetorical Strand

The one exception to this etiological framework was the interactional view of the Mental Research Institute (MRI) (Watzlawick, Weakland, & Fisch, 1974). From early on, the MRI had replaced insight about causes with a rhetorical approach. In line with Milton Erickson's work, the MRI bypassed casual questions in favor of the idea that reality is constructed and that it was the therapist's job to shape it differently. This new strand was a welcome corrective to the tendency to blame the family built into the early family approach. Parents occasionally rose up in self-defense against structural or strategic therapies, but no client ever attacked the interactional view; the motto of the MRI was "No Blame."

The down side of the approach was its condescending attitude toward the client. Family therapy was likened to a game of chess. The therapist, who knew the rules of the game, was the master player, whereas the family members were the pieces on the board. Such an approach, of course, would tend to hide the thinking behind the moves. If the client knew the reason for the use of such maneuvers as paradoxical interventions, this could undermine their success. As a result, one had an extraordinary sense of a band of therapists conducting guerilla warfare, not only against a psychotherapy estalishment of which they disapproved, but also against the families they were trying to help.

At this time, a strand appeared that widened the scope of the movement and blended elements from both the etiological and the rhetorical camps. The Milan systemic group (Selvini-Palazzoli, Boscolo, Prata, & Cecchin, 1978) went in search of a relationship constellation they associated with psychosis in children, but used a rhetorical means to expose it: the famous counterparadox. As in the MRI approach, the family was treated as a clever enemy and the therapy armamentarium was formally expanded to include a team behind the mirror. This outlook, while much enjoyed by the therapists, created a huge distance between them and their clients and turned the one-way mirror into a one-way street.

This emphasis of the systemic approach changed when Boscolo and Cecchin separated from Selvini and Prata and started their own training center. The invention of "circular questioning" (Selvini-Palazzoli et al., 1980) had given Milan-style therapists a tool for placing family members outside their accustomed positions, thus allowing them to take a larger view of the system in which they were caught. Cecchin (1991), in particular, moved off in this direction, along with other systemic practitioners, such as Karl Tomm (1987). Owing to this shift, the pejorative "systemic hypothesis" began to be replaced by reflexive formats that created openings for families and included them in a more user-friendly way.

The brief therapy of the MRI also mutated in this direction in the form of the new solution-focused approach formalized by Steve de Shazer (1985) and Insoo Berg (1994). These therapists took the strategic idea of resistance and turned it on its head. What therapists experienced as resistance from families, they said, was merely their unique way of cooperating. With help from other innovators, including Eve Lipchik (1993), Ben Furman (Furman & Tappi, 1992), and William O'Hanlon (1989), they moved the emphasis of family therapy from problems to solutions. "Solution talk," despite being just as rhetorical as the "problem talk" of the MRI, emphasized possibility rather than pathology, and had a vastly more sympathetic feel.

You could say that this shift was merely more of Milton Erickson's "utilization" idea, but the solution-focused therapists offered some simple and elegant methods for covering the grit in the oyster with pearl. "Exception questions" were used to look for the smallest proof that things had already changed for the better, and the "miracle question" was designed to get people to imagine what would be different if the problem no longer were there. As a result of this optimism, the client was no longer an opponent, but an ally.

The Narrative Strand

The reflexive trend in systemic therapy and the solution-focused development in strategic therapy counteracted the negative labeling of earlier etiological views, while adding more humanity to rhetorical ones. However, there was a greater difficulty that was found in all family therapy schools to date. Where was any awareness of political or cultural constraints? Is family therapy, as Rachel Hare-Mustin (1994) has asked, merely an exercise in the mirrored rooms? Out of postmodern feminist critiques like this one, and the general movement known as identity politics, came yet another strand in the braid, one that pointed to the new "postmodern" paradigm and called itself a narrative approach.

The originators of this approach, Michael White and David Epston (1990), abandoned the idea of the family, or even family-plus-wider-systems, as the treatment unit. Postmodern theorists that they were, they challenged the premises of the etiological approaches by casting doubt on the validity of diagnostic categories for individual dysfunction. At the same time, they challenged the insensitivity of rhetorical models to issues of gender, ethnicity, and race.

In one way, the inventors of Narrative Therapy stayed traditionally etiological. Like the rings around the pebble in the pond, the emphasis of therapy had now widened to the ring of social beliefs and habits known as "culture." This shift obliterated the innovations of traditional family therapy. The family ring, unseen by individual-oriented therapists of the past, became invisible once more. We moved directly from an individual location to a cultural location, totally bypassing the family, to look for the villains of the piece.

This more anthropological emphasis was attributable to a philosophical voice new to family therapy. White and Epston were greatly influenced by cognitive psychologist Jerome Bruner's (1990) invention of the new field of cultural psychology. Bruner says that cultural psychology "will not be preoccupied with 'behavior' but with 'action,' its intentionally based counterpart — action situated in a cultural setting, and in the mutually interacting intentional states of the participants" (p. 19).

Taking Bruner's perspective meant challenging one's own cultural blind spots. A typical Bruner anecdote goes as follows: The anthropologist Edward Evans-Pritchard is talking to some people from the Nilotic Nuer tribe of Africa about their religious beliefs. When he asks if they want to question him in turn, one informant asks him about the divinity he wears on his wrist, which he consults each time he seems to make a decision. The interest in uncovering therapist bias fitted well with the growing sensitivity to multicultural issues of the 1990s.

To Bruner's views, White and Epston added French philosopher Michel Foucault's (1972) emphasis on the hidden feelings about domination that pervade everyday life. Their therapy model sought to expose the unjust cultural attitudes we unconsciously hold: whites' belief in their superiority over those who are not white; men's belief in their right to dominate women; heterosexuals' belief that they are more normal than homosexuals; professionals' belief that their knowledge is superior to that of laypersons; and so forth.

For White, the complaints of the persons who consulted with him were linked to issues of oppression and abuse. This view was a powerful message that exonerated victims of family violence, particularly women. And by "externalizing" the violence, or some aspect of it, White sought to persuade the persons caught up in it — perpetrators and victims both — to join with him in defeating it. Many therapists were glad that White put moral agency back into family therapy after the neutral stance of the systemic years, and warmed to the heroic implications for therapists.

One drawback — although some would deem it a plus — is that, in White's writings, a world is evoked like the one in Margaret Atwood's (1992) *The Handmaid's Tale*. Its defining parameters are imprisonment, surveillance, and the fight for freedom. This view, while seductively romantic, imposes its own constraints. Family therapist Randall Ryle (1997) feels that White should move beyond the polarity of "dominating" versus "subjugated" discourses. He quotes philosopher Paul Ricoeur (1996), who speaks of "an economy of the gift whose logic of superabundance exceeds the logic of reciprocity."

Chris Kinman (1996), a communal therapist in Vancouver, Canada, who works with First Nations youth and their families, focuses very consciously on the language of gift. On his Case Assessment forms, one finds such phrases as "gifts and potentials," "roadblocks," "connections," and "chosen goals." His group puts out a grass roots newsletter called *Local Wisdom*, featuring such titles as "The Wisdom of the Mothers," "The Wisdom of Indo-Canadian Youth," and "The Gifts of Community." By acting as collector and editor of these voices, he amplifies their power in the service of healing and change.

White also has adopted the language of gift. He tells his reflecting groups to think of their comments as gifts for the people who consult with him. And his style has softened. His initial way of asking questions could be likened to that of sheep dogs herding their charges into a little corral. Now it does not. Taking seriously his own advice to "stay one step behind," he has become careful to keep close to the experience of the person he is with, checking back often to be sure that he is not going too fast or imposing his own point of view. In so doing, he has brought an unprecedented tenderness to his work.

The Collaborative Strand

In this respect, the narrative approach has now come close to another emerging strand, which bills itself as constructionist. This strand, although it puts itself under the same postmodern banner as narrative, selects a different group of thinkers: from the past, the linguistic philosophers Ludwig Wittgenstein (1963), Mikhail Bakhtin (1981), and Lev

Vigotsky (1986); from the present, social philosophers Kenneth Gergen (1994), John Shotter (1993) and Paul Ricoeur (1996). Harlene Anderson's (1997) *Language, Conversation and Possibilities* is a wonderfully clear presentation of the relevance of their ideas to practice.

For me, the reason that these particular writers are important is their challenge to two of the therapy world's most misleading premises: (1) the belief in objective pathology, and (2), the belief that behavior can be explained within the scientific paradigm. In *Unscientific Psychology*, social philosophers Fred Newman and Lois Holzman (1996) use the arguments of the linguistic constructionists to make a convincing attack on modernist psychology and the schools of psychotherapy that derive from it. Falling back on Vigotsky's (1986) theories of proximal development, they offer a "creatively emergent, social action format" that they call "social therapy."

For Newman and Holzman, narrative therapy is not postmodern enough. Insofar as narrative reconstruction pushes people to construct a "better story" so as to live a "better life," they believe it reifies the story and buys into essentialist ideas of identity and self. In contrast, they say, language in a constructionist sense is a matter of *activity*. As Wittgenstein (1963) points out: "The term 'language-game' is meant to bring into prominence the fact that the speaking of language is part of an activity, or of a *form of life*" (italics added).

And here I want to make a claim for the genius of my braided challah: in its fitful, self-revising wander across the landscape of psychology, it has evolved to the point of being able to critique itself *at the level of its own premises*. The thrust of postmodernism is to help us to realize that human life cannot be understood through the recipe-bound precepts of modern science. Scientific psychology is like a cook who claims to have a superior method for making baking-powder bread: combine the materials in the right way and the same result will appear every time. The work of postmodern therapies comes closer to the mysterious activity of kneading bread dough.

When I was a faculty wife in the early 1950s and living in the country, a neighbor taught me how to make bread. You put these inert elements — flour, water, yeast, salt — into a bowl and mix them into a sticky ball. Then, with the help of more flour, you begin to turn the edges over toward the center. After a while, my teacher told me, the dough will come alive. "How will I know that?" I asked. She said, "When you feel it resist your hands."

She was right. After 5 or 10 minutes of folding it over and over, the bread no longer obeyed me. When I poked my finger into it, the hole filled up. Was this magic? No. But the folding action that brought layers and lightness into the final product was only part of it. The crucial element in causing the dough to rise was the warmth of the human hand.

The reason I like this metaphor is that it expresses an "activity," and even more a "life form." To explain therapy, you must "do" therapy. The practice itself becomes the source of your philosophy about it. If you move to examples of what therapists such as Harlene Anderson, Harry Goolishian, Peggy Penn, and Tom Andersen do, you see that their interviewing styles contrast sharply with that of most other approaches, except perhaps that of Carl Rogers. Most therapeutic styles are based on a belief in the planfulness of the therapeutic process. Their proponents have their favorite lists of questions, their favorite interviewing schedules, their favorite interventions.

The constructionists are not planful in these ways. As Anderson and Goolishian say (1988), they seek "to come from a place of not knowing." They prefer to follow the openings in the conversation as it develops, believing that new thoughts or stories are inspired by what happens within the exchange rather than being imposed from outside. And this is logical. If therapy is about changing a behavior, altering a structure, creating a new reality, or finding a better story, it is instrumental. Only the therapist knows what must be changed, altered, created, or found. On the other hand, if therapy is about the characteristically human activity that Nelson Goodman (1978) calls "worldmaking," then it is something that can only be arrived at serendipitously. And not just any old world will qualify. It has to offer an environment in which we can all, temporarily at least, feel safer, freer, and more alive.

A COMMUNAL PERSPECTIVE

What was it about this constructionist way of working that attracted me? Perhaps I should start with a conference I attended at which Harlene Anderson showed a taped interview in which "nothing" happened. She sat and listened to an adolescent daughter for almost the entire session while everyone else sat back.

Up until then, I had taken on faith this perplexing kind of interview that she and Goolishian had persisted in doing, but now I decided to speak up. I waited for a private moment when nobody would hear us and asked her what she was up to. She was thoughtful, and then said that when she listened carefully to one person in that way, she felt that the others who were there listened to that person differently.

A light went off in my head. Harlene was not concentrating so much on the act of speaking as on the act of hearing. By offering an experience of indirect listening, she gave those present a chance to overhear the speaker's story without having to be defensive or to respond immediately. I saw that the context of listening could act as a solvent that altered the feelings and attitudes, or what I began to call the "cloud of perceptions," usually not very happy ones, that had come in the door.

Oddly enough, what came to mind at the time was the work of Virginia Satir. I had just rediscovered a paper I had written 35 years earlier when I was helping Satir (1964) with her book *Conjoint Family Therapy*. I was trying to look at what she did from an eyewitness point of view rather than through her own odd version of communication theory. And what came through most strongly was a general stance that was very similar to the one I saw when I watched Anderson work. Satir acted as a screen through which blaming ideas penetrated at their peril. Everything she said or did transmuted even the most dreadful events into possibilities for good.

For an example, I always return to the interview she did with the family of a high-school boy who had impregnated two classmates. His father was a minister, and the first thing Satir (1967) did was to address the boy, saying, "Well, we know one thing, God gave you good seed." This was called, in the strategic parlance of the time, "positive reframing," and was seen as a technique to counteract resistance. But I now saw it differently. What Satir did resembled what Anderson did: she acted to influence the community of perceptions around her. As an early social constructionist, working to build hopeful local worlds, she was without peer.

Another parallel with Anderson's work was the idea of helping people listen to each other. Satir would suggest that when at home, people should make sure that whomever they were talking to heard them, by touching the person and then asking, "Are you feeling the touch?" Or she would explain that she had a "paper eardrum," a hearing device she wore, and would ask someone to speak louder. People could say all sorts of things and not be afraid because Satir was protecting them like a human dialysis machine.

At about the same time that I was noticing Anderson and Goolishian's different voices as therapists, I became enchanted by Tom Andersen's (1990) invention of the reflecting team. This format gave a concrete form to the overhearing position, differentiating it from the observing position of most models in the field. It encouraged the therapist to move away from causal theories about dysfunction and toward the not-knowing stance. The reflecting process, as Andersen came to call it, became another medium for creating spaces where the possible could come to life.

This brings me to the work of Peggy Penn (Penn & Frankfurt, 1994), which I have followed and loved for a long time. Penn gives us another example of an approach that follows rather than leads. Herself a poet, she has turned the tables in her consultations and gives the job of writing over to her clients. They write all kinds of things: journals, commentaries, poetry, letters to persons dead or alive. Somehow this "sheds power" on them, so that they, rather than the therapist, become central. Peggy has some very moving tapes of her work, and in them one often finds tears. However, unlike the days when getting out the tissue box was a sign that the client was "working through" the pain, these tears may only mean that messages from the angels are coming through.

In individual therapy, encouraging "affect" was supposed to help clients relive repressed emotions. Family therapists, in line with their distrust of all things touchy-feeley, have mostly avoided this whole area but the newer practitioners seem to believe that emotions are not a tool, but a language as important as words. At a conference in Europe, Peggy Penn, Tom Andersen, and Harlene Anderson presented their work, and were surprised by the viewers' objections to the fact that people in the tapes, not just clients, but also the therapists, occasionally wept. Their approach was quickly entitled "crying therapy."

In general, I discern a more compassionate tone in our work. White's more recent emphasis on what he calls the "community of concern," and I call an "attending community," seems to be part of this trend. First White began to use reflecting groups as sympathetic witnesses. Then he began to look for inspiring presences, dead or alive, imaginary or real, to make up what he called "the club of your life." Then it was a short step to activating whatever affirming community might be coaxed from a person's own life situation and included as a primary unit of help.

I am convinced that encouraging this kind of community, particularly one that persists through time, is one of the most important things a therapist can do. As a result, I was happy when Tom Andersen offered the following theme for an upcoming discussion in Norway to which he had invited me: "Toward a Communal Perspective." The word "communal" is close to the meaning of "collaborative," and, at the same time, expresses the constructionist view that our job is the weaving together of new social worlds. So it puts the two ideas together in one bag.

What seems clear to me about my braided challah is that it has an enchanted life. One promising pathway may turn out to be a blind alley, but another twist takes it out on the high road and we are once more on our way. When I look back on all these groupings — the etiological, the rhetorical, the systemic, the solution focused, the narrative and the constructionist — I realize that they are all precious to me. It is not important whether or not I agree with their stated rationales; I can still pick and choose among my list of "biggest hits." And thanks to the tradition of recording our work, we can continue to go back to the past to be inspired.

But there is one irreversible advance for our field that the postmodern position has given us: its scepticism with regard to a science of human behavior. In an unpublished paper, Newman describes postmodern therapy as a study of the unknowable, meaning the domain of things that cannot be "discovered" in the same way that things in the physical universe can. For the same reason, he states, storytelling should not be turned into a kind of explanation, but should be seen as "a nonexplanatory way of understanding the activity of human life."

I like that idea. I want to continue to be "not knowing" at the level of the road map, while still exploring the road. If you are like me, you will remember the sand tunnels we used to dig at the beach as children, and that delicious moment when our fingers met.

References

Andersen, T. (Ed.). (1990). *The reflecting team: Dialogues and dialogues about the dialogues.* Broadstairs, Kent, England: Borgmann.

Anderson, H. (1997). *Language, conversation and possibilities.* New York: Basic Books.

Anderson, H., & Goolishian, H. (1988). Human systems as linguistic systems. *Family Process*, *27*, 3–12.

Atwood, M. (1992). *The handmaid's tale.* New York: Doubleday.

Bakhtin, M. (1981). *The fialogical imagination*, C. Emerson, trans. In M. Holquist (Ed.). Minneapolis: University of Minneapolis Press.

Berg, I. K. (1994). *Family based services: A solution-focused approach.* New York: Norton.

Bruner, J. (1990). *Acts of meaning* (p. 37). Cambridge, MA: Harvard University Press.

Cecchin, G., & Lane, G. (1991). *Irreverence: A strategy for therapist survival.* London: Karnac.

de Shazer, S. (1985). *Keys to solution in brief therapy.* New York: Norton.

Foucault, M. (1972). *The archeology of knowledge.* New York: Pantheon.

Furman, B., & Tappi, A. (1992). *Solution talk.* New York: Norton.

Gergen, K. (1994). *Realities and relationships.* Cambridge, MA: Harvard University Press.

Goodman, N. (1978). *Ways of worldmaking.* New York: Hackett.

Hare-Mustin, R. (1994). Discourses in the mirrored room. *Family Process, 33,* 19–35.

Kinman, C. (1996). *Honouring community.* Abbotsford, Canada: Fraser Valley Education & Therapy Services.

Lipchik, E. (1993). Both/and solutions. In S. Friedman (Ed.), *The new language of change.* New York: Guilford.

Newman, F., & Holzman, L. (1996). *Unscientific psychology: A cultural-performatory approach to understanding human life* (p. 35). Westport, CT: Praeger.

Penn, P., & Frankfurt, M. (1994). Creating a participant text: Writing, multiple voices, narrative multiplicity. *Family Process, 33,* 217–231

Ricoeur, P. (1996). Reflections on a new ethos for Europe. In R. Kearney (Ed.), *Paul Ricoeur: The hermeneutics of action.* Thousand Oaks, CA: Sage.

Ryle, R. (1997). The narrative of ethics and the ethics of narrative. In *Food for thought and dialogue,* a collection distributed for the Galveston VII Symposium in 1998.

Satir, V. (1964). *Conjoint family therapy.* Palo Alto, CA: Science & Behavior Books.

Satir, V. (1967). A Family of Angels. In J. Haley & L. Hoffman, (Eds.), *Techniques of family therapy.* New York: Basic Books.

Selvini-Palazzoli, M., Boscolo, L., Prata, G., & Cecchin, G. (1978). *Paradox and counterparadox.* New York: Jason Aronson

Selvini-Palazzoli, M., et al. (1980). Hypothesizing–circularity–neutrality. *Family Process, 19,* 3–12.

Shotter, J. (1993). *Cultural politics of everyday life.* Milton Keynes, England: Open University Press.

Singer, M. (1996). From rehabilitation to etiology: Progress and pitfalls. In J. Zeig (Ed.), *The evolution of psychotherapy: The third conference.* New York: Brunner/Mazel.

Tomm, K. (1987). Interventive interviewing: Part II: Reflexive questioning as a means to enable self-healing. *Family Process, 26,* 167–183.

Vigotsky, L. (1986). *Thought and language* (A. Kozulin, trans.). Cambridge, MA: MIT Press.

Watzlawick, P., Weakland, J., & Fisch, R. (1974). *Change: Principles of problem formation and problem resolution*. New York: Norton.

White, M. (1995). Reflecting teamwork as definitional ceremony. In *Re-authoring lives*. Adelaide, Australia: Dulwich Centre Publications.

White, M., & Epston, D. (1990). *Narrative means to therapeutic ends*. New York: Norton.

Wittgenstein, L. (1963). *Philosophical investigations* (G. Anscombe, trans.). New York: Macmillan.

20

Sprouting Wings: Four Catalysts for Accelerating Change in Brief(er) Prescriptive Therapy

John C. Norcross

A woman suffering from depression, let's call her Penelope, consulted me a few months ago on the referral of her cousin, whom I had seen several years earlier for seven or eight psychotherapy sessions. As Penelope described the transformation of her depressed cousin, it was a miracle: "She sprouted wings overnight!" Penelope was sufficiently impressed by her cousin's positive and maintained changes that she was inspired to attempt psychotherapy herself after years of reluctancy, although still with some misgivings. Part of her reticence was embodied in the fear that she would develop "strong, huge wings too quickly," like her cousin, who had transformed herself from a tired plow horse into a vibrant Pegasus within a few short months. Penelope was afraid that she, too, would change rapidly if I were to give her the wings. After we explored her fear, she modified her metaphor in several substantial ways: Penelope would sprout small, delicate wings that would gently accelerate her movement, allowing her to skim the ground with her feet, instead of being taken high above the earth; and further, rather than my somehow magically granting her wings, she would grow the wings herself.

The general case of Penelope and the specific ways in which we worked together so that she might sprout wings communicate the essence of how I have learned to accelerate change collaboratively in briefer prescriptive therapy. This chapter highlights four empirically supported catalysts for tailoring psychological treatments to individual clients: (1) customizing therapeutic relationships; (2) matching interventions to stages of change; (3) incorporating self-help resources; and (4) mobilizing a client's own strengths. But first a brief introduction to my way of conceptualizing and conducting psychotherapy, known as *prescriptive eclecticism.*

A PRIMER ON PRESCRIPTIVE ECLECTICISM

The rapid evolution of health-care delivery and the encroaching dominance of managed care have lent increased urgency to the task of tailoring psychological interventions to the client and his or her unique situation. Brief therapies demand integrative, explicit, and empirically based treatment selection (Norcross & Goldfried, 1992). Within 6 or 16 sessions, the practitioner is expected to create a therapeutic alliance, to diagnose psychosocial or mental disorders, to select specific technical and interpersonal methods to remediate those disorders, to apply those methods in sequences or stages over the course of treatment, and then rapidly to terminate the efficacious psychotherapy while preventing relapse (Norcross & Beutler, 1997). An audacious challenge!

My particular form of integrative psychotherapy attempts to customize psychological treatments and therapeutic relationships to the specific and varied needs of individual patients. It does so by drawing on effective methods from across theoretical camps — eclecticism — and by matching those methods to particular cases on the basis of empirically supported guidelines — prescriptionism (Norcross, 1994). The result is a more efficient and effective therapy that fits both the client and the clinician.

Of course, on the face of it, virtually every psychotherapist endorses prescriptive eclecticism. After all, who can seriously dispute the notion that psychological treatment should be tailored to fit the needs of the individual patient in order to improve the outcome of psychotherapy?

However, prescriptive eclecticism goes beyond this simple acknowledgment in at least four ways (Norcross & Beutler, 1997). (1) Our basis of prescriptive matching is derived directly from outcome research, rather than from the typical theoretical basis. (2) We adopt an integrative or transtheoretical basis that acknowledges the contributions of multiple systems of psychotherapy, rather than working from within a single theoretical system. (3) The guidelines are culled from multiple diagnostic and nondiagnostic client variables, in contrast to the typical reliance on the single, static variable of patient diagnosis. (4) Our aim is the research-informed and practice-tested selection of technical interventions *and* interpersonal stances, whereas most previous prescriptive efforts focused narrowly on the selection of disembodied techniques. Prescriptive eclecticism, then, applies empirical research and clinical wisdom from multiple theoretical orientations on both diagnostic and nondiagnostic variables to the task of selecting psychological treatments and therapeutic relationships that best fit individual patients.

CATALYST 1: CUSTOMIZING THERAPEUTIC RELATIONSHIPS

Within this context, let us turn to the first catalyst. The term "catalyst" is employed here in the dictionary meaning of an agent that provokes or speeds significant change. So it is an especially appropriate metaphor for the interpersonal chemistry of the therapeutic relationship.

The traditional process of prescriptive matching, as previously mentioned, was to diagnose the patient and then to select appropriate techniques. This was the classical definition of eclecticism, which is now recognized as seriously incomplete (Lazarus, Beutler, & Norcross, 1992).

Psychotherapy will never be so technical and impersonal as to overshadow the power of the therapist's ability to form a therapeutic relationship. The historical neglect of interpersonal stances customized to particular clients is all the more serious in that, with most disorders, the therapeutic relationship accounts for as much, if not more, of the psychotherapy outcome variance than does clinical technique (Lambert & Bergin, 1994; Norcross, 1993). One way to conceptualize the matter, paralleling the notion of "treatments of choice" in terms of techniques, is how clinicians determine "therapeutic relationships of choice" in terms of interpersonal stances (Lazarus, 1993, 1997; Norcross, 2002).

What is the relationship of choice for Penelope? She preferred a reasonably active and talkative therapist of medium formality. From her expressed fears, we may safely surmise that she preferred a collaborative approach. Her low reactance level indicated a fair degree of directiveness on my part, but she "never wanted to be pushed," in her words. Penelope expressed a strong dislike for a continual string of empathic reflections, which she characterized as "empty parroting" in her prior, unsuccessful, therapy some 10 years earlier. The simple act of soliciting her relationship preferences demonstrates collaboration, enlists her strengths, and co-creates therapeutic goals.

Research has identified a few, readily assessed client features that are reliably associated with differential responses to various styles of therapeutic relating. Patient preferences, for example, can guide the degree of warmth, formality, and activity; the stages of change guide the evolution of therapist posture over the course of treatment; reactance level guides the degree of therapist directiveness; and so forth. All these, and other, client characteristics can guide the practitioner in customizing his or her interpersonal stance, and thus accelerate psychological treatment (Beutler & Clarkin, 1990; Norcross & Beutler, 1997).

Acceding to the preferences of the patient is not always ethically or clinically indicated; nonetheless, if clinicians had more respect for the notion that their clients often sense how they can best be served, fewer relational mismatches might result, and therapists would be better able to adapt interventions to accommodate the changing expectations of patients. Salutary outcomes are likely to be achieved with increased regularity if we customize the therapeutic relationship (Lazarus, 1993; Mahoney & Norcross, 1993; Norcross, 2002).

Prescriptive eclecticism posits that many interpersonal stances have a place, a specific and differential place, in the relational repertoire of the brief therapist. Different folks need different types of interpersonal strokes, and psychotherapy can be enhanced and expedited by thoughtfully selecting among interpersonal processes in specific circumstances. Demonstrating deep caring and nonpossessive love may be indicated for all patients, but how we demonstrate that love will vary from patient to patient, from session to session, and indeed, from moment to moment in psychotherapy.

CATALYST 2: MATCHING INTERVENTIONS TO STAGES OF CHANGE

The optimal tailoring of psychotherapy also entails understanding the stages of change through which people progress. As every practitioner knows, change is a phenomenon that unfolds over time. In the transtheoretical model, change takes place over a series of five stages: precontemplation, contemplation, preparation, action, and maintenance (Prochaska, DiClemente, & Norcross, 1992; Prochaska, Norcross, & DiClemente, 1995).

Precontemplation is the stage in which there is no intention to change behavior in the foreseeable future. Many individuals in this stage are unaware or underaware of their problems. As G. K. Chesterton once said, "It isn't that they can't see the solution. It is that they can't see the problem." Families, friends, neighbors, or employees, however, are often well aware that the precontemplator has problems. When precontemplators present for psychotherapy, they often do so because of pressure from others. Usually, they feel coerced into changing by a spouse who threatens to leave, an employer who threatens to dismiss them, parents who threaten to disown them, or judges who threaten to punish them.

Contemplation is the stage in which people are aware that a problem exists and are seriously thinking about overcoming it but have not yet made a commitment to take action. People can remain stuck in the contemplation stage for long periods. In one of our self-change studies, we followed a group of 200 contemplators for two years. The modal response of this group was to remain in the contemplation stage for the entire two years without ever moving to action.

Preparation is the stage that combines intention and behavioral criteria. Patients in this stage are intending to take action immediately and are reporting some small behavioral changes. They are, literally and figuratively, taking "baby steps" toward action. Although they have reduced their problem behaviors somewhat, they have not yet achieved a criterion for effective action, such as abstinence. They are intending, however, to take such action in the very near future.

Action is the stage in which individuals modify their behavior, experiences, and environments in order to overcome their problems. Action involves the most overt behavioral changes and requires a considerable commitment of time and energy. Modifications of a problem behavior that are made in the action stage tend to be most visible and receive the greatest external recognition. People, including professionals, often erroneously equate action with change. As a consequence, they overlook the requisite work that prepares changers for action and the important efforts necessary to maintain the changes following action. Modification of the target behavior to meet an acceptable criterion and significant overt efforts to change are the hallmarks of action.

Maintenance is the final stage, in which people work to prevent relapse and to consolidate the gains attained during action. Traditionally, maintenance has been viewed as a static stage, but over the past 20 years, we have come to the realization that it is a continuation, not an absence, of change. For chronic problems, this stage extends from six months to an indeterminate period past the initial action. For some behaviors, maintenance can be considered to last a lifetime.

A number of research studies attest to the clinical utility and predictive validity of the stages of change. Suffice it to say that a patient's pretreatment stage of change is an important determinant of the optimal treatment and the eventual prognosis (see Prochaska, Norcross, & DiClemente, 1995, for a review). One of the most useful findings to emerge from our research is that particular processes of change are differentially effective during particular stages of change. That is, the patient's stage of change provides prescriptive and proscriptive guidance to the psychotherapist. Once a patient's stage is evident, the therapist knows which processes to apply in order to help that patient progress to the next stage. This reduces the haphazard or trial-and-error application; we can employ a more systematic and efficient style.

Table 1 demonstrates the integration between the stages and processes of change. Specifically, the table shows the change processes used most often during the five stages of change. During precontemplation, quite predictably, patients use change processes significantly less than do people in any other stage. Precontemplators process less information about their problems, spend less time and energy reevaluating themselves, experience fewer emotional reactions to the negative aspects of their problems, and do little to shift their attention or their environment in the direction of overcoming their problems. In treatment, these patients are labeled as resistant or defensive.

Several pivotal processes are most effective in helping the transition from precontemplation to contemplation. First, *consciousness-raising* interventions, such as observations, confrontations, and interpretations, can help clients become more aware of the causes, consequences, and cures of their problems. Clients become more aware of the negative consequences of their behavior and, often, they become more aware of their defenses. Second, the process of *dramatic relief* (or catharsis) provides clients with potent affective experiences, such as those used in Gestalt interventions, like the empty chair. These experiences can release emotions related to

Table 1. Stages of Change in Which Change Processes Are Most Effective

Stages of Change

Precontemplation	*Contemplation*	*Preparation*	*Action*	*Maintenance*
Consciousness raising				
Dramatic relief				
	Self-reevaluation			
		Self-liberation		
			Contingency management	
			Counterconditioning	
			Stimulus control	

Source: Prochaska, J. O., & Norcross, J. C. (2002). *Systems of psychotherapy: A transtheoretical analysis* (5th edition). Pacific Grove, CA: Brooks/Cole.

problem behaviors. Third, as clients become increasingly more aware of themselves and the nature of their problems, they are freer to reevaluate themselves both affectively and cognitively. The *self-reevaluation* process includes an assessment of which values clients will try to actualize, act upon, and make real, and which they will let die. The more central the problems are to their core values, the more their reevaluation will involve changes in their sense of self and the impact of those changes on the people about whom they care most.

Like anyone on the verge or cusp of momentous actions, Penelope and other individuals in the preparation stage are developing willpower and setting priorities. As she prepared for action, she developed a stranger sense of *self-liberation*. She knew in her gut that she possessed the autonomy to change her life; she discovered that she held the keys. She quickly set goals, and then dedicated herself to a specific action plan.

In taking action, Penelope, like others, also became effective with behavioral processes, such as counterconditioning, contingency management, and stimulus control. Her *counterconditioning* entailed cognitive restructuring and assertion training — healthy substitutes for avoidance and passivity. *Stimulus control* entailed rearranging her environment. Here, Penelope was a marvel to behold. She stuck at least 50 yellow post-it notes with reminders and encouragers around her home, at the office, and inside her car. Additionally, Penelope restructured her interpersonal environment so as to allow her to interrelate more frequently with positive, caring people, as opposed to "old, depressed nags like me." She abhorred the notion of contingent reward — in fact, she briefly lectured me on the evils of dehumanizing behaviorism — but gratefully accepted practice and materials on the fine arts of self-soothing and self-congratulation.

Successful maintenance builds on each of the change processes that came before and entails a candid assessment of relapse potential. Penelope continued to employ her cognitive restructuring and assertion (counterconditioning), reminder post-its and involvement with caring friends (stimulus control), and self-congratulation (contingency management) methods for several months, but less frequently and with less intensity. She also assessed the alternatives she had to relapse without resorting to self-defeating defenses and depressive responses. During our last session, she proudly presented me with a copy of her "relapse-buster" tips, written on one of her ubiquitous yellow post-it notes.

We have determined that efficient behavior change depends on doing the right things (processes) at the right times (stages). We have observed two frequent mismatches in this respect. First, some clients (and clinicians) appear to rely primarily on change processes most indicated for the contemplation stage — consciousness raising, self-reevaluation — while they are moving to the action stage. They try to modify behaviors by becoming more aware, a common criticism of classical psychoanalysis: insight alone does not necessarily bring about behavior change. Second, other clients (and clinicians) rely primarily on change processes most indicated for the action stage — contingency management, stimulus control, counterconditioning — without the requisite awareness, decision making, and readiness provided in the contemplation and preparation stages. They try to modify behavior without awareness, a common criticism of radical behaviorism: overt action without awareness is likely to lead only to temporary change (Prochaska, DiClemente, & Norcross, 1992).

To sum up: Penelope entered psychotherapy in the preparation stage, accomplished much of her work in action, and then terminated treatment in the maintenance stage. My task was to accommodate her stages and match my interventions to them as they evolved. In doing so, we accelerated the journey to her destination with a minimum of mismatches.

Theoretical complementarity is the key to synthesizing the major systems of psychotherapy. Table 2 illustrates where leading systems of therapy fit best within the integrative framework of the transtheoretical model. Depending on the stage of change, different therapy systems will play a more or less prominent role. Each psychotherapy system has a contribution to make; the catalyst is finding that contribution for each client.

CATALYST 3: INCORPORATING SELF-HELP RESOURCES

People in their natural environments and psychotherapists in their consulting rooms routinely employ self-help resources, which include, *inter alia*, self-change methods, support groups, self-help books, and autobiographies written by people who have conquered a disorder. Results from one of our recent studies, as summarized in Table 3, demonstrate the frequency with which psychotherapists recommended self-help materials to their clients. Specifically, in the past 12 months, 87% recommended a self-help group to their patients, 85% a self-help book, and 73% a personal journal of their experience in psychotherapy. A smaller proportion, a third, rec-

Table 2. Integration of Psychotherapy Systems Within the Transtheoretical Model

	Stages of Change				
Levels	*Precontemplation*	*Contemplation*	*Preparation*	*Action*	*Maintenance*
Symptom/situational	Motivational interviewing			Behavior therapy EMDR and exposure	
Maladaptive cognitions		Adlerian therapy	Rational-emotive therapy Cognitive therapy		
Interpersonal conflicts	Sullivanian therapy	Transactional analysis	Interpersonal therapy (IPT)		
Family/systems conflicts	Strategic therapy	Bowenian therapy		Structural therapy	
Intrapersonal conflicts	Psychoanalytic therapy	Existential therapy	Gestalt therapy		

Source: Prochaska, J. O., & Norcross, J. C. (2002). *Systems of psychotherapy: A transtheoretical analysis* (5th edition). Pacific Grove, CA: Brooks/Cole.

ommended an autobiography. Psychotherapists realize that incorporating these materials into psychotherapy constitutes a central, cost-effective catalyst: 95% report the effects of doing so as "very helpful" or "somewhat helpful" (Clifford, Norcross, & Sommer, 1999).

Table 3. Frequency of Recommending Self-Help to Psychotherapy Patients

Type of Material	% of psychologists recommending	% of patients recommended to *M*	SD
Support group	87	15.5	17.1
Self-help book	85	24.6	26.1
Autobiography written by client	33	3.8	10.3
Autobiographical film	26	3.2	10.4
Personal journal	73	21.6	26.9

Source: Clifford, J. S., Norcross, J. C., & Sommer, R. (1999). Autobiographies of mental patients: Psychologists' uses and recommendations. *Professional Psychology: Research and Practice, 30,* 56–59.

The success of these self-help methods has been reasonably well established by controlled research, as well. Several meta-analyses have determined the effectiveness of self-help programs as compared with no-treatment controls (Scogin, Bynum, & Calhoun, 1990). Gould and Clum (1993), for example, conducted a meta-analysis on the effectiveness of 40 self-help studies that used no-treatment, waiting-list, or placebo comparisons as control groups. The effect sizes for self-help interventions (.76 at posttreatment and .53 at follow-up) were nearly as large as for therapist-assisted interventions in the same studies. Fears, depression, headache, and sleep disturbance were especially amenable to self-help approaches.

Support or mutual-aid groups have a long and distinguished history in the behavioral disorders. Outcome studies on these groups are infrequent and plagued with methodological problems; nonetheless, the nascent research shows positive results. A meta-analysis (Tonigan, Toscoova, & Miller, 1995) summarizing the findings of Alcoholics Anonymous (AA) affiliation and outcome, for example, found that AA participation and reduction in drinking were positively related, especially in outpatient populations. Several well-controlled evaluations of 12-step programs for addictive disorders show that they generally are as effective as professional treatment, including at follow-up (Morgenstern, Labouvie, McCrady, Kahler, & Frey, 1997; Ouimette, Finney, & Moos, 1997; Project MATCH Research Group, 1997). Similarly, "effectiveness" research on psychotherapy practiced in naturalistic settings, as opposed to "efficacy" research based on randomized controlled studies, has generally found that clients consider 12-step groups as helpful as professional psychotherapists (e.g., Seligman, 1995).

The use of bibliotherapy (self-help books) as an adjunct to psychotherapy can also expedite our clinical work. A recent meta-analysis examined the efficacy of bibliotherapy as compared with control groups and therapist-administered treatments (Marrs, 1995). The mean effect size of bibliotherapy was .56, a moderately powerful effect, and one not different from that of therapist-administered treatments. Another meta-analysis of the effectiveness of bibliotherapy for unipolar depression (Cuijpers, 1997) delivered essentially the same verdict: the mean effect size was .82, a large effect, and one not different from the size of effect obtained by individual and group treatment.

The clinical advantages of recommending autobiographies are similarly encouraging. These include providing phenomenological accounts of disorders, enhancing identification and empathy, generating hope and insight, and explaining treatment strategies and procedures (Norcross et al., 2000). Put another way, the use of autobiographies in psychotherapy can facilitate the accompishment of six clinical purposes, or the six "Es" (Riordan, Mullis, & Nuchow, 1996). That is, they can:

- *E*ducate by filling in psychological knowledge and gaps
- *E*ncourage by provding inspirational readings
- *E*mpower by reviewing goal formation and attainment
- *E*nlighten by increasing self- and other-awareness
- *E*ngage the patient with the social world through modeling and social mentoring
- *E*nhance by reinforcing specific points and lifestyle changes addressed in psychotherapy

In an attempt to identify useful self-help books, Santrock, Minnett, and Campbell (1994) conducted a national survey of psychologists and asked them to rate those books from a list of more than 350 self-help books with which they were familiar. Table 4 lists the 20 books with the highest average ratings in order from highest to lowest. Penelope, to take the case of one client struggling with unipolar depression, thoroughly benefited from reading David Burns' (1980) *Feeling Good*: she identified with the depressive symptoms, found her own "crooked thinking" in the pages, and was eager to try cognitive therapy.

Table 4. Top 20 Self-Help Books

The courage to heal by Ellen Bass and Laura Davis (abuse)
Feeling good by David Burns (depression)
Infants and mothers by T. Berry Brazelton (parenting)
What every baby knows by T. Berry Brazelton (child development)
Dr. Spock's baby and child care by Benjamin Spock and Michael Rothenberg (child development/parenting)
How to curvive the loss of a love by Melba Colgrove, Harold Bloomfield, and Peter McWilliams (death and grief)
To listen to a child by T. Berry Brazelton (child development/parenting)
The boys and girls book about divorce by Richard Gardner (divorce)
The dance of anger by Harriet Lerner (anger)
The feeling good handbook by David Burns (depression)
Toddlers and parents by T. Berry Brazelton (child development/parenting)
Your perfect right by Robert Alberti and Michael Emmons (assertion)
Between parent and teenager by Haim Ginott (teenagers/parenting)
The first three years of life by Burton White (child development)
What color is your parachute? by Richard Bolles (career development)
Between parent and child by Haim Ginott (child development/parenting)
The relaxation response by Herbert Benson (relaxation)
The new aerobics by Kenneth Cooper (exercise)
Learned optimism by Martin Seligman (positive thinking)
Man's search for meaning, by Viktor Frankl (self-fulfillment)

Source: Santrock, J. W., Minnett, A. M., & Campbell, B. D. (1994). *The authoritative guide to self-help books*. New York: Guilford.

Autobiographies written by recovering or recovered patients can also play a curative role in self-change efforts. We recently identified the most useful autobiographies (Clifford, Norcross, & Sommer, 1999) based on psychologists' recommendations. Table 5 presents the dozen autobiographies with the highest average rating, listed in order from highest to lowest.

For Penelope, an avid reader, William Styron's (1990) *Darkness Visible* was a perfect fit: he, like Penelope, began experiencing depression in later life, and he writes movingly of his ordeal. Demonstrating the imperfect success of my recommendations, Penelope found O. H. Mowrer's (1983) *Leaves From Many Seasons* uninspiring and somewhat academic.

Table 5. Top 12 Autobiographies

An unquiet mind, by K. R. Jamison (bipolar disorder)
Darkness visible: A memoir of madness by W. Styron (depression)
Girl interrupted by S. Kaysen (borderline disorder)
Nobody nowhere: The extraordinary autobiography of an autistic by D. Williams (autism)
Out of the depths by A. T. Boisin (schizophrenia)
Welcome silence: My triumph over schizophrenia by C. L. North (schizophrenia)
Too much anger, too many tears by J. Gotkin & P. Gotkin (schizophrenia)
Diary of a fat housewife: A true story of humor, heartbreak and hope by R. Green (eating disorder)
Undercurrents: A therapist's reckoning with her own depression by M. Manning (depression)
A drinking life: A memoir by P. Hamill (substance abuse)
Leaves from many seasons by O. H. Mowrer (depression)
The liar's club: A memoir by M. Karr (family dysfunction)

Source: Clifford, J. S., Norcross, J. C., & Sommer, R. (1999). Autobiographies of mental patients: Psychologists' uses and recommendations. *Professional Psychology: Research and Practice, 30,* 56–59.

My point is this: Empirical research and clinical wisdom converge in advocating that we frequently recommend a myriad of self-help resources to our patients. These resources extend the therapy hour into the 99% of life between appointments, and ideally, into life beyond the end of therapy. Psychotherapy is only one component of psychotherap*eutic* experiences for our patients; we catalyze our one component by systematically encouraging and incorporating self-help materials.

CATALYST 4: MOBILIZING CLIENT STRENGHTS

A dispassionate examination of the history of psychotherapy will convincingly demonstrate a preoccupation with identifying and cataloging psychopathology (Hubble, Duncan, & Miller, 1999). With the recent exception of solution-focused clinicians, and before them, humanistic clinicians, psychotherapists have been very much into dysfunction, disease, disorder, and distress. A recent exercise in my psychopathology class is illustrative: we were able to gather over 125 terms and metaphors for *disorder*, but only a handful for *health*. Our patients have silently, and inevitably, experienced our perverse fascination with their deficiencies at the expense of their strengths.

Hundreds of articles and books have recently generated methods to mobilize our clients' strengths. I have assimilated many of these into my practice, and would urge you to do likewise. In particular, I recommend methods encoded in specific therapist behaviors that invoke complementary client behaviors. These are performance based, not simply exclaiming, "You are stronger than you think."

Mobilizing strengths requires more than words. The objective is to access and reinforce "strong" patient behaviors, both in the therapy hour and between sessions. Such "performance-based methods"of change have generally proved superior to simply talking about or encouraging health (Bandura, 1976).

Here is a sample of performance-based methods to activate client strengths that an intern and I developed while watching videotaped therapy sessions:

- Assessing and respecting patient preferences in the session
- Identifying problems that were successfully changed and maintained in the past (B. F. Skinner once quipped that a disadvantage of psychotherapy is the behavioral demonstration of the patient's helplessness and incompetence!)

- Locating and punctuating exceptions to dysfunctional behavior
- Empowering patient choices in the treatment structure and frequency
- Acknowledging and reinforcing patient successes
- Soliciting and recommending previously effective self-help resources
- Designing performance tasks to be carried out within and between sessions that facilitate self-efficacy
- "Playing to the strength" of patients, instead of addressing their deficiencies
- Validating difficult life experiences and normalizing temporary lapses
- Confronting "selective abstraction" by noting the high probability of adaptive behavior in the session and in vivo
- Demonstrating (instead of merely saying), "This is your therapy!"

The clinical initiative, as Michael Hoyt (1999) has written, should be designed to ignite clients' initiative and resources. Our responsibility is to help them to use their response-ability better.

IN CONCLUSION

Penelope's brief psychotherapy, like that of her cousin, proved effective in the short run and appears promising for the long run. I accept only a modicum of responsibility for her sprouting wings: she gratefully articulated and realized her interpersonal preferences for the therapeutic relationship, clearly profited from stage-matched interventions throughout the course of treatment, readily incorporated several self-help resources, and easily mobilized her considerable strengths. In several respects, my role was to stay *out* of the way of her growth by minimizing the mismatches that all too frequently are imposed on clients.

Not every patient will be as talented as Penelope, and not every brief treatment will be as successful. Indeed, we know that not every psychotherapy can — or should — be brief, but the catalysts can accelerate the pace of treatment and enhance its efficiency. Thoughtfully employing these four catalysts may well produce similar cases of brief therapy with lasting impressions. Or as Penelope would put it: sprouting wings for *all* of us, but different wings for *each* of us.

References

Bandura, A. (1976). *Social learning theory*. Englewood Cliffs, NJ: Prentice-Hall.

Beutler, L. E., & Clarkin, J. F. (1990). *Systematic treatment selection*. New York: Brunner/Mazel.

Burns, D. (1980). *Feeling good: The new mood therapy*. New York: Signet.

Clifford, J. S., Norcross, J. C., & Sommer, R. (1999). Autobiographies of mental patients: Psychologists' uses and recommendations. *Professional Psychology: Research and Practice, 30*, 56–59.

Cuijpers, P. (1997). Bibliotherapy in unipolar depression: A meta-analysis. *Journal of Behavior Therapy & Experimental Psychiatry, 28*, 139–147.

Gould, R., & Clum, G. (1993). Meta-analysis of self-help treatment approaches. *Clinical Psychology Review, 13*, 169–186.

Hoyt, M. F. (1999). It's not my therapy — it's the client's therapy. *Psychotherapy Bulletin, 34*(1).

Hubble, M. A., Duncan, B. L., & Miller, S. D. (1999). Directing attention to what works. In M. A. Hubble, B. L. Duncan, & S. D. Miller (Eds.), *The heart and soul of change*. Washington, DC: American Psychological Association.

Lambert, M. J., & Bergin, A. E. (1994). The effectiveness of psychotherapy. In A. E. Bergin & S. L. Garfield (Eds.), *Handbook of psychotherapy and behavior change* (4th ed.) (pp. 143–189). New York: Wiley.

Lazarus, A. A. (1993). Tailoring the therapeutic relationship, or being an authentic chameleon. *Psychotherapy, 30*, 404–407.

Lazarus, A. A. (1997). *Brief but comprehensive psychotherapy: The multimodal way*. New York: Springer.

Lazarus, A. A., Beutler, L. E., & Norcross, J. C. (1992). The future of technical eclecticism. *Psychotherapy, 29*, 11–20.

Mahoney, M. J., & Norcross, J. C. (1993). Relationship styles and therapeutic choices: A commentary. *Psychotherapy, 30*, 423–426.

Marrs, R. W. (1995). A meta-analysis of bibliotherapy studies. *American Journal of Community Psychology, 23*, 843–870.

Morgenstern, J., Labouvie, E., McCrady, B. S., Kahler, C. W., & Frey, R. M. (1997). Affiliation with Alcoholic Anonymous after treatment: A study of its therapeutic effects and mechanisms of action. *Journal of Consulting and Clinical Psychology, 65*, 768–777.

Mowrer, O. H. (1983). *Leaves from many seasons*. New York: Praeger.

Norcross, J. C. (1993). The relationship of choice: Matching the therapist's stance to individual clients. *Psychotherapy, 30*, 402–403.

Norcross, J. C. (1994). *Prescriptive eclectic therapy*. Videotape in the APA Psychotherapy Videotape Series. Washington, DC: American Psychological Association.

Norcross, J. C. (Ed.). (2002). *Psychotherapy relationships that work*. New York: Oxford University Press.

Norcross, J. C., & Beutler, L. E. (1997). Determining the therapeutic relationship of choice in brief therapy. In J. N. Butcher (Ed.), *Personality assessment in managed health care: A practitioner's guide*. New York: Oxford University Press.

Norcross, J. C., & Goldfried, M. R. (Eds.). (1992). *Handbook of psychotherapy integration*. New York: Basic Books.

Norcross, J. C., Santrock, J. W., Campbell, L. F., Smith, T. P., Sommer, R., & Zuckerman, E. L. (2000). *Authoritative guide to self-help resources in mental health*. New York: Guilford.

Ouimette, P. C., Finney, J. W., & Moos, R. H. (1997). Twelve-step and cognitive-behavioral treatment for substance abuse: A comparison of treatment effectiveness. *Journal of Consulting and Clinical Psychology, 65*, 230–240.

Prochaska, J. C., DiClemente, C. C., & Norcross, J. C. (1992). In search of how people change: Applications to addictive behaviors. *American Psychologist, 47*, 1102–1114.

Prochaska, J. O., & Norcross, J. C. (2002). *Systems of psychotherapy: A transtheoretical analysis* (5th ed.). Pacific Grove, CA: Brooks/Cole.

Prochaska, J. O., Norcross, J. C., & DiClemente, C. C. (1995). *Changing for good*. New York: Avon.

Project MATCH Research Group (1997). Matching alcoholism treatments to client heterogeneity: Project MATCH posttreatment drinking outcomes. *Journal of Studies on Alcohol, 58*, 7–29.

Riordan, R. J., Mullis, F., & Nuchow, L. (1996). Organizing for bibliotherapy: The science in the art. *Individual Psychology, 52*, 169–180.

Santrock, J. W., Minnett, A. M., & Campbell, B. D. (1994). *The authoritative guide to self-help books*. New York: Guilford.

Scogin, F., Bynum, J., & Calhoun, S. (1990). Efficacy of self-administered treatment programs: Meta-analytic review. *Professional Psychology: Research and Practice, 21*, 42–47.

Seligman, M. E. P. (1995). The effectiveness of psychotherapy. *American Psychologist, 50*, 965–974.

Styron, W. (1990). *Darkness visisble*. New York: Random House.

Tonigan, J. S., Toscoova, R., & Miller, W. R. (1995). Meta-analysis of the literature on Alcoholics Anonymous: Sample and study characteristics moderate findings. *Journal of Studies on Alcohol, 57*, 65–72.

21

Moments of Eternity: What Carl Rogers Has to Offer Brief Therapists[1]

Maureen O'Hara

As far back as I can remember, I have been a scientist. In nursery school, I collected bugs and slugs, put them in jars, and lost myself for hours watching them go about their "bugging" and "slugging." This rapt fascination with the world, which I still experience each time I encounter an unknown creature, or listen to my son describe his adventures in molecular genetics, has been a reliable source of pleasure, inspiration, and revelation. But all along, my love of science has been combined with something not usually associated with scientists.

Although I hesitate to articulate it, I have also been something of a mystic. Not an uppercase Mystic, who talks to God, has grand visions, writes inspirational texts, or even professes any particular religious faith. Rather, I have been sort of a street mystic, always taken a little by surprise by glimpses of the divine in the ordinary daily-ness of life. I started my career as a biological researcher, but even from the beginning, there

---

[1] First published in *Women Writing in the Person-Centred Approach*, edited by Irene Fairhurst. Ross-on-Wye, UK: PCCS Books Ltd.

was a difference. The professor (Chair) of my department, Dr. Irene Manton, one of the few women Fellows of the Royal Society, was a world famous microscopist. She took me under her wing and resolved to teach me the basics of being a scientist. I didn't realize until much later that she was no ordinary scientist. She, too, was a mystic.

One day, we were gazing into a very high powered microscope, as she tried to show me the fine structure of a particular sub-cellular organelle that she had identified. For a very long time, I looked desperately at the field of random squiggles, but despite all my efforts, I could make out absolutely nothing. I wanted to give up, cursing the "bloody thing." Finally Professor Manton said gently, "Dear girl, if you don't love it, you won't see it. You cannot force the universe to do your bidding. You have to wait until you are ready for it, and it is ready for you." I took a deep breath, relaxed, and began to look at the specimen with a much softer gaze. A few minutes later, in a blink of an eye, the amorphous puzzle on the screen took shape, and with something approaching bliss, I began to see the structures that no one before her had ever seen, and that a few moments before I had doubted even existed.

As an apprentice in her lab, I came naturally by the notion that the scientific attitude is indistinguishable from the mystical. Both require discipline, self-preparation, an openness to experience, and a willingness to dwell in mystery. And at the center of both the mystic's and the scientist's life is a faith that the universe has implicate order, and a desire to encounter this reality in greater depth and complexity and to be transformed in the encounter. Not all scientists, but certainly a far greater number than will admit, are, like mystics, fired by a spiritual longing to dwell in the mysteries of existence in an attempt to get closer to the divine.

With this kind of early training, it was inevitable that when I shifted careers from biological researcher to educator and psychotherapist, I would be drawn to the work of another scientist-mystic — Carl Ransome Rogers (O'Hara, 1995; Van Belle, 1990; Van Kalmthout, 1995). From my first exposure to his written work, and through 17 years of personal relationship as graduate student, and later as a colleague, I saw his approach to therapy and growth in clients, groups, and communities as another path to deepening my exploration of the enigma of Being — my own, and my clients', and the contexts in which we found ourselves.

THE EVOLVING ROGERIAN TRADITION

Carl Rogers, the inventor of person-centered therapy (first called "nondirective therapy," later "client-centered therapy," and, finally, "the person-centered approach" (although the Rogerian community is not all in agreement on this, in this chapter, I use them synonymously), is arguably the most influential American psychologist, and perhaps the least understood. His work spanned 60 years, from the later 1920s to the late 1980s, and he participated in three radical philosophical shifts that occurred in 20th-century psychology — leading one of them. As a college student, he had first thought he would study agriculture. After that, he entered a seminary to become a Protestant minister. He attended an ecumenical religious gathering in China in the 1920s, and on the six-week sea voyage, immersed himself in Chinese religion and philosophy. He began his studies of psychology at Teachers College, Columbia University, in New York, and at first considered himself, and was acknowledged by his peers as, a positivist empiricist scientist (O'Hara, 1995). His driving passion was to discover the "necessary and sufficient conditions" that, if applied, would lead to psychological healing and growth. During this first phase, he succeeded in establishing the basic tenets of client-centered therapy, which eventually formed the ground rules for almost all species of effective "helping" relationships (see below).

In his middle years — partly as a consequence of his disappointment with the dominant mechanistic paradigm for psychological research, but mostly because of what he was learning about human experience from his clients — his ideal of empirical objectivity in psychological research faded into the background (although he never lost it completely). Instead, he turned to the more subjectivist phenomenological approaches to research that he felt could better grasp the highly nuanced complexity of human experience as it was lived. He was attracted to the American transcendentalist and romantic traditions of Thoreau and Emerson, to the pragmatism of James and Dewey, and to European existentialists, such as Søren Kierkegäard, all of whom sought psychological truth in the deep interior world of individual subjective experience. He was also greatly influenced by the ideas of Otto Rank (Kramer, 1995) and the "uppercase" Jewish Mystic, existential philosopher Martin Buber (Kirschenbaum & Henderson, 1989). He became increasingly interested in the interpersonal dimensions of life, enthusiastically embracing the encounter group movement. At this time, he expanded his goals beyond psychotherapy and aimed at discovering the basic rules governing all healthy human relationships.

During these middle years, he remained, however, strongly attached to what Gergen (1994) has called the romantic–modernist idea of a sovereign inner "real self" to which, in the interest of mental well-being and self-realization, one must "be true." His early research on encounter groups focused on the ways in which groups aid the individual growth of participants. As the work developed, however, pulled once more by his desire to step out into unknown regions of experience, he was drawn out of the therapeutic context altogether, and into the messy waters of large-group community processes, cross-cultural communications, and diplomacy and peacemaking on a global scale. It was during this shift toward larger systems that I joined him in La Jolla.

The large-group work took him and his colleagues to Asia, South Africa, Latin America, the pre-Perestroika Soviet Union, Northern Ireland, and Eastern Europe, and increasingly focused on situations of serious intergroup conflict. In Northern Ireland, he worked with groups of Protestants and Catholics; in South Africa, he led a workshop that included both blacks and whites; and in Rust, Austria, he and the members of the Carl Rogers Institute for Peace facilitated the work of a group of diplomats and politicians from Central America and the United States who came together to discuss the conflict raging in Nicaragua at the time.

Observing the world through the eyes of people from many cultures, and trying to understand the strange, nonlinear emergent processes that take place in these large-group contexts, demanded another paradigmatic shift. Confronted, in these polycultural experiences, by the realization that the "essential self" at the center of Western psychology is an almost exclusively 19th- and early 20th-century male European construct, and that it is the exception rather than the rule among most of the world's cultures (Geertz, 1979; O'Hara, 1996), he was forced into a constructivist world of multiple contextual psychological realities.

In 1974, while meditating on a beach in northern California, he wrote an article, "Do We Need 'A' Reality?" (Rogers, 1980), in which he concluded: "[T]he way of the future must be to base our lives and our education on the assumption that there are as many realities as there are persons" (p. 105). He proposed that the work of therapists and educators must be to nurture the birth of a culture and a psyche where human caring would not be conditional on sameness, but on a celebration of differences. He had also loosened (but not quite abandoned) his moorings in the romantic–modernist view of the self, and was describing what he referred to as "persons of tomorrow" who have sufficiently developed levels of consciousness as to be "at home in a world that consists only of vibrating energy, a world with no solid base, a world of process and change, a world in which the mind, in its larger sense, is both aware of, and creates, the new reality" (p. 352). He spent his last years attempting to put to use his learnings about the conditions that foster psychological growth and healing, trying to facilitate the birth of such a consciousness.

Rogers was among those humanistic psychologists who repudiated the instrumentalist, medical model of psychotherapy. In this model, the person seeking help is seen as suffering from some pathology, or as otherwise defective in some way. The effective therapeutic agent is thought to be the therapist-delivered treatment, applied in prescribed doses and according to predetermined protocols to specific diseases or disorders exhibited by a "patient" (Bohart & Tallman, 1999). In place of this "allopathic" view of "treatment from without," Rogers, along with many others (Milton Erickson among them) saw the client as an active agent in his or her own change, and sought to align himself with the self-healing powers of individuals and groups. More radically, Rogers believed that this capacity for self-healing and creative agency is the human organism's local expression of an intrinsic evolutionary tendency in the universe impelling all of nature — from molecules to galaxies — toward greater complexity and expanded levels of consciousness. To align constructively with the formative tendency (Rogers, 1978) of the universe and with the self-actualizing potential of a particular person or group is a far more ambitious project than the alleviation of psychological symptoms! In Rogers' view, and the view of those of us who worked closely with him on the development of what, in 1975, we renamed the "person-centered approach," to establish the kind of relationship in which people make an experiential shift toward greater awareness and higher orders of consciousness is to participate in some minuscule way in the process of matter becoming conscious of itself.

NECESSARY AND SUFFICIENT?

"Encountering another human being means being kept alive by an enigma."
— *Emmanual Lévinas*

When asked about the place of Carl Rogers' methods in his work, solution-focused brief therapist William O'Hanlon replied, "That's the first five minutes. If you don't do that stuff, I don't think you are going to get anywhere" (O'Hanlon, 1993).

What "stuff" is O'Hanlon talking about?

During the 1940s and early 1950s, Rogers and a large team of co-investigators systematically evaluated the therapeutic conditions under which clients progressed toward wholeness in psychotherapy and counseling. These studies, published in 1954 (Rogers & Dymond, 1954), established what he thought were the six essential conditions for therapeutic growth. He summarized the findings in the now-classic paper, "The Necessary and Sufficient Conditions of Therapeutic Personality Change" (Rogers, 1957), in which he states the following. For constructive personality change to occur, it is necessary that these conditions exist and continue over a period of time:

1. Two persons are in psychological contact.
2. The first, whom we shall call the client, is in a state of incongruence, being vulnerable or anxious.
3. The second person, whom we shall term the therapist, is congruent or integrated in the relationship.
4. The therapist experiences unconditional positive regard for the client.
5. The therapist experiences an empathic understanding of the client's internal frame of reference and endeavors to communicate this experience to the client.
6. The communication to the client of the therapist's empathic understanding and unconditional positive regard is achieved to a minimal degree.

Upon going into the project, which was to last for several years, the researchers had expected to identify key techniques and interventions that seemed to correlate with therapeutic shifts, and they hoped that this would provide a standardized approach to therapy and counseling. This was not to be. The further into their project the team got, the more audiotapes and session transcripts they analyzed, the more objective pre- and posttherapy tests they ran, the more they were forced to admit that what seemed to bring about significant shifts in therapy was not the technical expertise of the therapists, but a certain set of attitudes, values, and personal qualities, which Rogers (1980) later came to call "ways of being," that they bring into their relationships. Central to these attitudes are two major positions: first a faith that "each person has within himself or herself vast resources for self-understanding and for constructive changes in ways of being and behaving" (Rogers & Sanford, 1989, p. 1493), and second, that these resources can be released and realized when the therapist and client are in psychological contact within a relationship with certain definable qualities. These qualities are "realness, caring, and a deeply sensitive nonjudgmental understanding," and the willingness and ability to enter into an experiential empathic connection with clients so as to sense the internal experience, the frames of reference, and the flow of feelings and meanings as if from the point of view of the client.

Although these conditions were identified by Rogers as early as 1942 (Rogers, 1942), over the decades since then, a wealth of outcome and process studies have been conducted by others on a wide spectrum of therapeutic approaches, including some that are conscientiously at odds with person-centered approaches, such as cognitive-behaviorist and psychoanalytic approaches, which have largely confirmed Rogers' discoveries (Luborsky, Singer, & Luborsky, 1975; Seligman, 1995). The preponderance of "common factors" research points to the remarkable stability of Rogers' basic constructs over the decades. Even in non–client-centered therapies, client resourcefulness, agency, and capacity for self-directed growth, in the context of a relationship characterized by warmth, respect, and empathic understanding overpowers any other variables, such as technique, theoretical orientation, diagnosis, or level of experience of the therapist (Bohart & Tallman, 1999).

It is ironic, then, that just as there seems to be a convergence of evidence that would support the person-centered approach as the basic therapeutic stance, the approach has been all but banished from U.S. universities, and is rarely the therapy of choice with HMOs, which appear to prefer any therapy with the word "brief," "short term," "strategic," or "medication" in its name.

BRIEF PERSON-CENTERED THERAPY IN BRIEF

"If we can recognize this [time] limit, and refrain from playing a self-satisfying Jehovah role, we can offer a very definite kind of clarifying help, even in a short space of time."

— *Carl Rogers*, 1942, pp. 247–248

To find out if this neglect of person-centered therapy is justified on the grounds that such nondirective approaches, although effective, are too time consuming and expensive in these cost-conscious days, I conducted my own informal survey of person-centered practitioners around the world, concerning therapy length. I belong to several global electronic listserves of humanistic and person-centered therapists, so I asked participants the typical length of therapy needed to arrive at a successful therapeutic outcome as identified by both client and therapist. I also asked them to share any research on the topic they had conducted or knew about, or any anecdotal evidence that could shed some light on the question of whether person-centered therapies could legitimately be considered "short-term" or "brief" therapy.

The responses, which came from Latin America, Australia, Europe and North America, from younger practitioners and from old hands, revealed that most of the respondents had worked, at least some of the time, in settings where the number of sessions was tightly restricted. These settings included employee assistance programs, college and university counseling centers, on-call emergency psychiatric clinics, residential treatment centers, and HMOs.

Most respondents said that although they did not favor the artificial limits imposed by extratherapeutic factors, they nevertheless felt that, under the right circumstances, and even with externally imposed time limits, it was reasonable to expect positive results in several sessions (8 to 12 was the typical number); some reported significant effects in as few as three sessions (Mearns, 1994); and one reported positive changes after an allotted single assessment interview (Cury, personal communication). Interestingly, others who were under no externally imposed time constraints also reported that their typical number of sessions with clients was in the same range. Some of these therapists, however, did report that sometimes clients remained in therapy for up to 50 sessions and beyond.

Respondents were mixed in their overall assessment of the efficacy of short-term therapy. Several had been much influenced by the radical ideas of Rankian social worker Jessie Taft (Taft, 1933), and saw the presence of an externally imposed time limit as a facilitative factor if it were made to stand for unavoidable existential limits within which we all must live. In a radical challenge to the endless psychoanalytic therapies of her era, social worker Taft (1933/1973) argued that even one hour of therapy can provide the occasion for transformation.

> When he can take it [the therapy hour] and also leave it without denying its value, without trying to escape it completely or keep it forever because of this very value, in so far as he has learned to live, to accept this fragment of time in and for itself, and . . . if he can live this hour he has in his grasp the secret of all hours, he has conquered life and time for the moment and in principle. (p. 17)

From the earliest days, Rogers and his colleagues were interested in time-limited treatment. These were the days of interminable psychoanalysis and years of inpatient sanitarium care, and there was, as now, more readily accessible short-term care. Rogers believed that if the contact were to be short term, nondirective therapy was especially worthwhile, but he did not expect any major personality restructuring. Short-term "clarifying help" can "enable the client to express his problems and feelings freely, and leave with a clearer recognition of the issues with which he is faced" (Rogers, 1942, pp. 247–248).

Early research suggested that the longer the therapy, the greater the gains, with 20 sessions being predictive of significant therapeutic benefits when measured as a function of several outcome dimensions related to psychological progress, such as degree of personal integration of the client, life adjustment of the client, degree of satisfaction of client with the outcome of therapy, and therapist rating of outcome (Seeman, 1954). In another related study, Standal and van der Veen (1957) suggested that increases in the degree of personality integration seemed to be correlated with longer therapy (14 or more meetings), but other personality change variables seemed to be achievable in therapies lasting less than 14 sessions.

Shlien (1957) undertook a major study of time-limited client-centered therapy, and concluded that brief time-limited client-centered therapy facilitated positive outcomes on several measurement scales, but appeared to have some negative effects as well. He speculated, on the basis of deterioration in TAT scores on follow-up, that if clients perceived the termination as arbitrary and unwelcome, and, therefore, experienced it as a blow to their desire for autonomy and self-direction, then actual harm might be done by premature termination. On the basis of his own study, which, in some ways, had set out hoping to validate Rank's and Taft's assertions about the positive effects of time limits, Shlien advised caution before endorsing time limitations more generally.

Since the 1950s and until quite recently, person-centered therapists seem to have been less interested in further evaluating the effects of time limits. The issue recently was raised once again, provoked, as it has been in other therapies, by externally imposed time limits on service. Brian Thorne, a leading person-centered therapist in the United Kingdom, described his own unexpected conversion to short-term therapy, after completing a small pilot study. As director of a university counseling service, he was under pressure to economize. After a census of client records revealed that many clients had arrived at satisfactory conclusions to counseling in as few as three sessions, he decided to experiment with voluntary three-session service. Clients who wished to continue were to be referred to an ongoing group. Thorne concluded that very-short-term person-centered counseling can bring significant results with some self-selected and highly motivated clients (Mearns, 1994). My own experience is similar to Thorne's. With some clients, remarkable progress can be made in one or two meetings (see case material below).

From therapists working with people in all degrees of distress, from chronically psychotic to situational crises, the consensus among person-centered therapists seems to be that the crucial variable is not the length of time in therapy, but rather who makes the determination about the duration of service and the agenda to be addressed. If these decisions are made externally to the therapeutic relationship, this violates one of the fundamental tenets of the approach: client self-determination. When they are made mutually by the client and therapist, and are in terms of the client's understanding of his or her growth needs, then the therapy may be short, 1–6 sessions; middling, 16–25 sessions; or long, 30–70 sessions.

Another set of responses came from therapists who pointed out that in the intensive small- and large-group encounter settings, significant life-changing effects could be experienced in short-term encounters. During the large-community-group phase of Rogers' career, he described several such examples, including some with serious psychological difficulties (Rogers, 1977), and he has described the long-term impact of single sessions done as therapy demonstrations. (Rogers, 1980, pp. 207–234; Rogers & Sanford, 1989). In a study co-authored with Rogers and others, we had reliable, independently corroborated reports of radical life changes that took place for some of the participants in a two-day encounter with several hundred people (Bowen, O'Hara, Rogers, & Wood, 1979). Follow-up reports indicated that the changes persisted over time (Rogers, 1980, p. 316).

It seems quite clear that person-centered therapy in its theory and as it is practiced, legitimately can be considered a brief therapy. So why, in the light of this evidence — some of it anecdotal and some of it gained through exhaustive controlled research — do contemporary person-centered therapists, including myself, not identify with the brief therapy movement? And why are we not busy touting the person-centered approach to the managed-care industry and financially strapped social service agencies as a cost-effective method of delivering short-term "quality care" that research studies show (Seligman, 1995) have the added value of receiving high customer satisfaction ratings?

IT'S THE PARADIGM!

> "The single element that most sets client-centered psychotherapy apart from the other therapies is its insistence that the medical model — involving diagnosis of pathology, specificity of treatment, and desirability of cure — is a totally inadequate model for dealing with psychologically distressed or deviant persons." (Rogers & Sanford, 1989, p. 1483)

Put simply, the reason that person-centered therapists are not lobbying to be recognized as practitioners of one of the brief therapies is that most do not think of their practices in the terms of the contemporary medical discourse, and especially not in the aggressively manipulative expert-focused stance of brief strategic approaches (Cade & O'Hanlon, 1993). In the Kuhnian sense, they inhabit a different paradigm (Kuhn, 1970). The medical model focuses on what's wrong — the client's problems, symptoms, illness, dysfunctions, chemical imbalances — and invests all efforts in preparing therapist "experts" to provide ever-better solutions to these afflictions by refining techniques, strategies, and treatment protocols, where the relationship between the therapist and client is only important insofar as it facilitates the client's compliance with therapist interventions (Bohart, O'Hara, & Leitner, 1998; Bohart & Tallman, 1999). Practitioners of person-centered therapy believe they are doing something rather different.

Although described variously over the years, person-centered therapists are attempting to make a soul connection with their clients. Their goal, as far as possible, is to open themselves to be present to the mysterious enigma of Being, and to join with people called clients in ways that facilitate their achievement of the same kind of openness. They seek to stay close to the edge between the known and the unknown, of the moment between the already been and not yet become, that is so pregnant with possibilities for both constructive and destructive action, and to stay alert to opportunities to be a force for constructive movement.

Rogerian therapy is based in faith. At the core of the tradition, as it has evolved over 60 years from nondirective counseling to client-centered therapy and student-centered teaching, including experiential therapy, and its most recent iteration as the person-centered approach, is an invariant radical faith in a self-organizing emergent vector at work in nature. Rogers (1980) described "an evolutionary tendency towards greater order, greater complexity, greater interrelatedness" (p. 133). This faith leads to trust in the inborn desire and capacity of all human beings to choose relational mutuality over either isolation or relationships of exploitation and domination, to choose growth and wholeness over fear and disintegration, and to participate co-creatively rather than compliantly in the formation of larger groups, such as families and communities. Whether or not one believes that such a faith is warranted (and clearly this moves into the realm of metaphysics), without recognizing the difference in their metaphysics, it is impossible to understand how radical the difference is between the person-centered tradition and mainstream medical-model psychotherapy. A fuller discussion of these differences can be found in O'Hara (1997a).

MOMENTS OF ETERNITY

> "I feel continuous waves taking up every cell of me, transforming me 'forever.' They come as feelings, very pure, without words, as I seem to have forgotten what was said either by you or me or the others at the most significant moments. What is here, and is incredibly vivid, a thing of now, is what resulted in those moments."
>
> — *Participant in a Person-Centered Workshop*

Whereas mainstream psychotherapy trusts a mechanistic world of cause and effect, the person-centered therapist's focus is on developing ways of being in relational encounter with the Other, and by so doing, opening sacred space and time — moments of eternity — within which the self-organizing formative tendency in nature can become manifest and effective in the world. Whether with a single individual, a family, or a group, and whatever the level of disturbance, healing becomes not a matter of what one does, but of what and how one is in relationship to the world, including the world of the Other.

Once this is admitted, the nature of the encounter shifts. No longer I–It, as Buber (1970) would say, but I–Thou, in which a true encounter between Beings of infinite complexity and infinite possibilities can occur. If it does occur, the next moment and all future moments are open. The work the therapist must do shifts from techniques to apply to the client to the development of greater capacities to be open spiritually.

In an interview late in his life, Rogers said he endeavored to be as much as possible in a state of "openness" or, as he described it, "a continuing way of meeting life. This includes openness to the beauty of my fuschias, as well to what is going on in me or what is going on in a relationship" (quoted in Harman, 1990). Openness means adopting a learner's stance, what in Zen is called "beginners mind," in meeting with clients. In this state of openness, all stereotypes and prejudgments, including diagnosis and prescription, are suspended, and in their place is an empty mind waiting to be filled with the possibilities presented in the present moment. For Rogers and other person-centered practitioners, this accepting, nonjudgmental, nondirective attitude is the bedrock of their work, out of which comes the courage to listen deeply, to enter into an empathic attunement with the Other, to surrender separate individual consciousness, and to enter the Other's phenomenal world. In doing so, they attempt to become one with the emergent edge between the known and the unknown. Wood (1997) describes the "mediumistic" quality of Rogers' sessions, from an early stage. Rogers and others eventually came to call the states (after Buber) "presence" (B. Thorne, in a presentation to the Fourth International Conference on Client-Centered and Experiential Psychotherapy, July 7, 1997). Rogers (1980) exquisitely captures this experience as follows:

I find that when I am closest to my inner intuitive self, when I am

> somehow in touch with the unknown in me, when perhaps I am in a slightly altered state of consciousness, then whatever I do seems to be full of healing. Then simply my *presence* is releasing and helpful to the other. There is nothing I can do to force this experience, but when I can relax and be close to the transcendental core of me, then I may behave in strange and impulsive ways in the relationship, ways which I cannot justify rationally, which have nothing to do with my thought processes. But these strange behaviors turn out to be *right*, in some odd way: it seems that my inner spirit has reached out and touched the inner spirit of the other. Our relationship transcends itself and becomes a part of something larger. (p. 129)

When clients or groups sense that they are being received with this kind of openness, they, too are more willing to open up to the greater resources within themselves, within the relationship, and in the greater contexts of their lives. They discover, almost miraculously sometimes, new creative responses to what challenges them.

Moments like these seem regularly to involve altered states of consciousness — altered, that is, from the customary ego-bounded state that is valued in contemporary "professional" Western scientific discourse, but entirely recognizable by shamans, hypnotherapists, ministers, poets, mothers, lovers, and other healers. Attention is diffuse, however, rather than sharp; edges are fuzzy; thoughts are quieted; muscles are relaxed; things come to consciousness as images, patterns, sounds, bodily sensations, and symbols more often than they come as words or ideas. The ordinary sense of time disappears, and in its place is a sense of timelessness. There is a sense of alert patience, of waiting. (The origin of the word "therapy" is to wait.) It is common at such moments to lose the sense of separation between self and Other, and instead to experience oneself and all other existence as the same thing, part of one indivisible and endlessly generative whole. In wisdom traditions, these moments are sought as intimations of enlightenment; in religious traditions, as glimpses of God; and in shamanic traditions, as moments of healing.

Such states of consciousness are by no means passive, but the practitioner is wide awake, aroused, fully there, not thinking, judging, evaluating, diagnosing, but simply available. We wait until the spirit moves us, and move us it will. We move toward or away from, we hear a new note, we sense new symbols, we see an opening, we encounter a boundary, we are filled with pain, we are teased, we are swallowed up, we are seduced, repulsed, encouraged, and plunged into despair.

This kind of openness, especially in relationship with a person or situation that is chaotic or dangerous, is no job for the fainthearted. To encounter another, to be available to be moved by his or her story means opening oneself to all the pain and nastiness that life can hurl at us (Neimeyer & Stewart, 1999). Murder, rage, greed, rape, trickery, madness, terror, despair, loss, confusion, incoherence, numbness and death all move through us as if they were our own — because they are. Rogers describes one experience during his University of Chicago years that was so intolerably painful that he felt forced to abandon the client with whom he was working and take a couple of months away from practicing psychotherapy to regain his perspective and his sanity (Kirschenbaum, 1979; Shlien, 1997).

Therapeutic moments are like love, they catch us by surprise. They cannot be willed or "performed" and cannot be domesticated and controlled. Love swells up from some hidden source and flows through us. We cannot hold onto it, it is beyond will, beyond volition. If we are available to it, it will move us to action that is natural and harmonious with the situation, much in the same way that the winds play music on a quiet harp. We become the instrument.

We are not needed to "fix" anything, to perform, or to intervene. The research data are clear (Bohart, O'Hara, & Leitner, 1998). Whatever "fixing" that will happen as a consequence of the meeting will be done by the client. Our clients need us not for what we do, but for who and how we are and for how we can be with them. They need us to bring to the encounter our hope and courage, energy and love, to accompany them on their journey, which, for the moment, is too hard for them to do alone. Therapist creativity, knowledge of psychological processes, techniques for focusing and reframing experience, relaxation, trance induction, guided imagery, narrative restructuring, and so on, may be of assistance to a client. So may aid in learning to think more critically or expansively. Honest feedback about behavior, even giving advice — handy tricks of the therapist's trade — under the right circumstances, may provide useful assistance to clients. But they also may not. In any case, such resources can be accessed by the motivated client from many other sources — friends, self-help books, self-help groups, TV shows, workshops, spiritual retreats. To what degree the therapist's experience and skills are useful remains up to the client. As Bergin and Garfield (1994) concluded in their volume on psychotherapy research, "It is the client more than the therapist who implements the change process. If the client does not absorb, utilize, and follow through on the facilitative efforts of the therapist, then nothing happens."

Our significance to our clients, particularly those who are very troubled or perplexed, is as constant and loving witness to their existence. They need us to stand beside them as they struggle with the happenings of their lives, to love them, to be at least one significant Other who regards them in return, with all their difficulties and flaws, as a significant — Other. With the recognition of one human being by another comes the possibility of going beyond I–It, and even beyond I–Thou to become a "We" (Schmid, 1997). By being willing to risk, even temporarily, becoming a "We" a new never-before-existent universe is created between therapist and client. Friedman (1985) describes this process as the "concrete unfolding of the 'ontology of the between' " (p. 152). Never-before-encountered or even imagined choices become available; creative understandings and solutions to predicaments become possible. For those who feel separated and alone, cut off from themselves and from fellowship with the rest of the human race, the bridge back from exile, into a world of relationship and of infinite possibility, is what Gilligan calls "sponsorship" or nonpossessive love (Gilligan, 1997).

TRANSFORMATIONAL ANDROGOGY

For hundreds of years, practitioners of consciousness traditions have been studying transformational moments, both the details of how they are experienced and how they can be facilitated. The Hindu yogi disciplines, Zen Buddhism, Tibetan Buddhism, Taoism, Sufism, Judaism, and Christianity boast a history of centuries of accumulated wisdom on how best to help another enter transformational states and on the phenomenology of what happens when one does. Illness, in many of these traditions, is regarded as a sign that people or systems are out of balance with the universal flow of Being. Consciousness disciplines, such as awareness work, prayers, martial arts, calligraphy, poetry, philosophy, and meditation, are considered as educational practices developed to help people regain their balance and to realign with the life force.

Owing partly to the West's obsession with objectivism, and partly to

American psychology's abandonment, early in the last century, of William James' studies in consciousness in favor of experimental behavioral science, the detailed exploration of inner psychological processes has been neglected until recently. The convergence of neuropsychology, mind-body interaction, phenomenology, existential psychology, cognitive psychology, developmental psychology, psychophysiology, epistemology, systems science, and complexity science has revitalized the interest in consciousness. It has also provided new nonreligious (or at least nonsectarian) languages with which to speak about the process of consciousness change and its facilitation.

Whether gradually over a period of time, or apparently in an instant, deep, irreversible, transformational change occurs all through life in the way human beings experience their world, make meaning of it, and act in it. See Alexander & Langer (1990) for a review of more recent studies.

Case Example

(*The biographical details have been altered significantly, although the essential elements of the story are intact, and the quotes are the client's words.*)

When Jenny first came to see me, she was 40 years old. She was suffering from acute debilitating panic attacks of recent onset and complained that "instead of getting more self-confident with age," she was "losing ground." She blamed other people for her difficulties: her father, who had abandoned her and a sister when he divorced their mother; her stepfather for being a "drunk"; her husband for being a "workaholic"; even psychologists for not having diagnosed her dyslexia as a child. Her thinking was one-dimensional and she jumped from topic to topic, never able to reflect on her story, but only to recount it.

She was the mother of two teenagers, a son and his younger sister. The wife of a distant, overworked physician husband, she ran a small, not very successful, jewelry-design business. She admitted that she was often close to despair and told me that she had flirted with a neighbor but backed off at the last minute. She was "disgusted with herself"; was feeling "old, unattractive, and ripped off by life"; and was contemplating divorce.

During the first two sessions, she spoke of her pent-up frustration, of her many attempts to solve her problems herself — self-help books, assertiveness training classes, journaling, Oprah, a women's support group, and of her self-diagnosis as a "chronic underachiever who had married out of her intellectual class." (She had a high-school education.) She disclosed that as an adolescent, she had been molested by her stepfather, and that her dyslexia had made high school a "nightmare." All this, she said, had left her alternately depressed and school phobic throughout high school. She had married Mark as an escape. She was not currently sleeping well, had gained weight, and at times felt hopeless. As her sad story tumbled out, it seemed that we might be at the start of a fairly extensive process of psychotherapy, and at her initiative, we even discussed her husband's suggestion that she take medication for depression. Disapproving of "chemicals," she decided to hold off to see if therapy might "work."

Jenny arrived for the third session in a highly agitated state. She obviously had been crying in the waiting room. She began to cry again as she started to speak. Her tears were angry. She was "livid," "incensed," and she would like to "tear the face off" her son's high school principal. Apparently the principal had just announced a new policy whereby only students with B grades or better could play baseball. Her son, Todd (also dyslexic), whose grade-point average was a B-, had been dropped from the team and he was, in his mother's words, "devastated." This affected the whole family, since she, her husband, and her daughter were heavily involved with Todd's baseball team. Jenny had wanted to storm off to speak with the principal on her son's behalf but he begged her not to. This left her even more furious and impotent. At first she ranted, first blaming herself, then the principal, then her son, then her husband. She felt completely stuck, overwhelmed by emotions, not knowing what to do. "I'm damned if I do, and screwed if I don't."

I simply listened, there was no need (or room) for me to say anything for quite some time. Occasionally I asked for clarification, or expressed surprise, sympathy, or curiosity, as any engaged listener would. Once, in frustration, she demanded angrily that I "earn my fee" and give her some advice. "Should I go see the principal even though Todd told me not to?" she asked. "Shouldn't a mother intervene for her son when an injustice has been done?" "Won't he be scarred by being rejected like this?" I responded quite honestly to Jenny's legitimate request for "expert" advice by saying that I had more faith in her ability to work this through than I had in any counsel I might offer. Once or twice, I expressed my confidence in her and my admiration of her fierce support for her son. But mostly I just listened attentively and appreciatively as she explored the multiple dimensions and meanings of her predicament. Gradually, she developed a deeper and more nuanced understanding of the complex basis for her rage. She saw the way it related to her own childhood experiences, separating these transferred feelings from the problem for her son, his need not to be seen as a "mama's boy," her own feelings that baseball had been the reason her son was willing to try to succeed in school and her fear that he would now withdraw his efforts the way she had, her anger at her husband because "as usual, he won't do anything," her anger at male authority, and so on.

Eventually the flow of her words slowed down. She began to listen to herself, and to correct herself as she did so.

JENNY: The principal's a fucking asshole. He's on a big power trip. (*Pause.*) No, that's not really true, it isn't all the principal's fault, he has a job to do and he's probably under pressure to improve kids' grades so they can go to college. I seem to be looking for a villain. I am noticing now that I do that when I don't know what to do. That's what Mark always says I do. It really pisses me off when he says it, but he may be right. (*She smiles, I smile back.*) (*Pause.*) Hmmm.

Sometimes there isn't an answer, right? No easy answers? Somehow that doesn't seem so scary at this moment. (*Pause.*) This seems like a big deal, to be getting this after all these years of knocking my head against a wall.

THERAPIST: You are beginning to see just how complicated the situation is. It's not so easy to see what to do, but now that you have noticed this pattern, you seem to be willing to go beyond your usual search for someone to blame. That seems like something important!

JENNY: Yeah, it does. Finding a villain only makes me feel like a victim. It's even worse when I decide that the villain is me, then I just want to go away and shoot myself. It's like right now I can see it in bigger perspective, somehow. You know, when Mark would say, "You're losing perspective," I didn't really know what he meant, like there was right and there was wrong, and you had do what was right. But it's not so clear, is it?

As Jenny's exploration of the issues continued, what began as a one-dimensional victim story gradually became elaborated into an entirely new, and much more complex, grasp of the situation. This understanding extended beyond herself to include empathy with all the participants, including the principal. As we approached the end of the session, she seemed different. She was more relaxed; she sat quietly, her face calm and her eyes wide. She sat silently for several moments (the first long silence of the session), and then said:

JENNY: Something incredible has just happened. I don't feel angry anymore, I don't feel afraid, I don't feel inadequate. It's as if I am seeing all of this in a new way — like instead of it's all happening to me, I am part of a whole lot of other people's lives and they're part of mine, and what I do affects them and what they do affects me. I suddenly feel a sense of confidence in my own position on this baseball-and-grades thing, I feel like I am a part of it all somehow, not just a bystander. I feel like an adult, like I understand why the principal thought it was a good idea. I just don't agree. And maybe Todd needs his friends' respect more than he needs baseball, and maybe he needs baseball so much because he thought it meant so much to his dad and me. I don't know, but I am going to talk all this over with him.

Between that session and the next, as I was to learn, Jenny had conversations with her family and with Todd alone. With Todd's blessing, she paid a (calm) visit to the principal at which she expressed her disagreement with his educational strategy while affirming his responsibility to "call 'em as he sees 'em." She shared with me that her entire family seemed to be taking her more seriously and that her customary sense of dread had evaporated. She was laughing a lot more.

JENNY: In that last session, it was as if all these years of struggling to come to terms with my shitty life had come to a head over this one issue. I just couldn't hide behind the molest thing anymore, making excuses for not standing up for myself. Even as I talked, part of me knew that more was at stake than Todd's baseball. I think that's why I came. I could either walk away from it and say it's too hard, like I have a thousand and one times, or I could face it and do something else. But now, I am seeing a whole lot of interconnecting lines going everywhere — to Todd, to Megan, to Mr. Boyd, to my dad — its all one big bundle of people, and they all have their own points of view. It could be easy to get lost, but somehow I seem to have my own opinions, as well. I am still here, but somehow I'm in it as *me*.

Because you were so there for me ... in a funny way, you were more help because you didn't try to help, you never gave an opinion about what I should do, but you did seem genuinely interested in me and my situation. Usually, with Mark, he either takes over or won't get involved, so he tries to talk me out of my feelings. What you did and what you didn't do were just right. They gave me the space to see the bigger picture, I guess.

The next week, Jenny arrived with a basket of vegetables from her garden and a decision to end therapy.

JENNY: I can do it myself, I think. You said you had confidence in me, and I thought when I got home, "Heck, if she sees me like that, why don't I just do it?" So I tried it, and it is working out. If I can't do it sometime, I'll come back. OK?"

She didn't. She did, however, keep in touch through Christmas cards and the occasional letter. Over the decade since I last saw her, she went to college and earned a fine arts degree, began to design for a major jewelry house, and rebuilt her relationship with her husband. Now, at age 51, she is making a good income and is close to her family in a way she had never been before. She has not needed any further psychotherapy, and although she occasionally experiences stage fright before making a major sales presentation, she otherwise is anxiety-free. More important, she still feels "like an adult." She says that she is "a deeper person somehow" and is beginning to think that she is going to make a "pretty awesome old lady one of these days."

Jenny had a transformative experience, apparently in just four sessions — a brief therapy success. But it wouldn't matter whether it had taken 10 session or even 30, it was the quality of the change that marks it as significant. It would miss her achievement altogether to evaluate what occurred in reductionist terms as "number of sessions," "symptom reduction," "problem solving," and certainly in terms of the managed-care industry's favorite standard, "returning her to premorbid functioning," and it would miss the importance of the presence of a significant Other, of me in my role as the provider of "psychological treatment."

In a very real sense, Jenny underwent an enlightenment experience. Who she was after the experience was qualitatively different from who she had been just the week before, and this change permeated her entire existence. Not only had she changed *what* she thought about the situation she was facing, but also changed *how* she was thinking.

Jenny had been operating from within mental processing frameworks inadequate for the complexity of her situation. It was as if she were attempting to navigate the complex psychological terrain of adult life with the very primitive maps she had drawn as a teenager. Epistemologically, she was in "over her head" (Kegan, 1994). She herself realized that she needed capacities she did not (yet) possess and worked furiously to find her own remedy. All those books, classes, talk shows, and her women's group had expanded her repertoire of conceptual options in important ways, but up until then had added more to the "quantity" of her knowledge base than to the quality of how she processed it.

When faced with contradictory life challenges, such as her unsatisfactory marriage and her simultaneous commitment to being a good mother, in which several of her well-established, but adolescent, cognitive-emotive patterns were in conflict, it seemed to Jenny that any solution from within one pattern would violate the requirements of another. The crisis over Todd's baseball playing had kicked the whole dilemma into high gear. She had been running around in mental circles looking for ways out of the impasse, and this had precipitated her anxiety attacks. Her level of physiological arousal had been raised significantly, and this had activated many, if not all, of the mental possibilities she had accumulated over a lifetime of experience. At home, without a supportive context in which to permit this process to take its own course, she was flooded with unbearable anxiety, but within the special conditions of the therapeutic setting, where she experienced herself as being met in the appreciative context of an unconditionally accepting "we," she was able to resist her impulse to retreat, and instead of failing yet again, was able to find her way out of the impasse. It is crucial to recognize that all this learning would have been lost had she been either "therapized or medicated out of her crisis.

As artists, scientists, and mystics have long known, states of high mental arousal, when not accompanied by too much fear or sense of threat, permit us to bring into focus, simultaneously, ordinarily disparate and disconnected fragments of knowing, state- and context-specific schematas, tidbits, unrelated ideas, narrative repertoires, odd-ball possibilities, unconscious connections, and strange and creative associations, and to make new connections. Neural pathways and cognitive subroutines, which develop separately at different stages and in response to specific experiential challenges, and which usually operate somewhat independently, become available to each other in such altered states. Emotional, cognitive, and even neurological reorganization can take place, and higher orders of mental functioning can be achieved. According to Pascual-Leone (1989), growth that creates advances in the level of mental functioning only occurs as "a *result of overcoming (i.e., reversing or accepting failure)*" because (deep cognitive-affective) structures do not change unless change is required (p. 275). By "accepting errors" in her characterization of the situation, "taking them as a challenge" (p. 276), broadening her perspective on a more comprehensive level, and becoming aware of her own existential involvement in the flow of her life, Jenny's breakthrough is archetypal of all higher orders of psychological growth.

Jenny is navigating a transformation from a way of being in which she is a passive recipient of life to one in which she is an active agent, from "subjective knower," where the only truth is her personal feelings, to something approaching "constructive knower," where reality is seen as a co-construction among multiple players (Belenky, Clinchy, Goldberger, & Tarule, 1986). In this one series of statements, we can hear her begin to see her connectedness to larger systems, her existential limits, and the dialectical relationships between the systems in which she is involved. She can see the tension between Todd's membership in the family, his relationships with his peers, and their relationship to the high school culture. Jenny begins to "dis-identify" with her own emotional responses ("getting perspective"), which she can now see are contaminated by out-of-awareness associations from her own (very different) childhood. She also begins to see that she has choices in the way she construes the world ("no right answers"), and begins to accept personal responsibility for the way in which she sees things, while accepting that others will make different choices. Whether such transformations are the result of psychotherapy, education, the ordinary challenges of life successfully faced, through participation in enlightenment traditions, rapidly during a crisis or over the long haul, is incidental. Jenny is on her way to becoming what Rogers calls one of the "the persons of tomorrow" (Rogers, 1977, p. 263).

Rogers believed that unless prevented by overwhelming and aversive circumstances, leaps of consciousness such as these could be *expected* to occur in therapy, in encounter groups, in community workshops, at home, at work, in church, temple, or mosque, because it is the *nature of*

Being to become. Like the South African prime minister Jan Christian Smuts, who, in 1926, on the heels of a political defeat, originated the concept of holism; physical chemist Ilya Prigiogine, who pioneered research on self-organizing systems; and physicist David Bohm, all of whom he felt kinship with, Rogers believed that complex systems, especially living systems, do not obey the laws of entropy, but rather move toward higher levels of organizational complexity. In this view, the "formative tendency" of the cosmos is eternally waiting for opportunities whereby the unseen, "implicate order" (Bohm) of the not yet Being can *become.*

RELATIONAL EMPATHY, READING THE GROUP'S MIND

By pushing the implications of such a metaphysics even further out, beyond rationalist–cognitivist explanations of breakthrough moments, which focus largely on what happens within the consciousness of individual persons, I want to consider some ways in which to understand the importance of relationships in this process.

I have discussed elsewhere that the source of a great deal of the suffering we hear about from our clients has to do with either their disconnection from mutual relationships with others or the violation and exploitation of such connections by others (O'Hara, 1984, 1989, 1997a, 1997b). Suffering happens because humans are fundamentally social beings so that to be disconnected is to be cut off from one's own humanity. We are composed of cells carrying DNA from both parents; for the first nine months, we are developed within the body of another person; we are nourished by the flesh of her body for months afterwards, every breath, thought, and movement; and every movement toward increasing wholeness takes place within the context of life with other human beings. Our place in social groups, our impact on others and their impact on us, and our making personal and collective sense out of it all are the nonstop life-and-death curriculum of conscious life.

Western culture's denial of this fundamental connectedness and relatedness to the eternal Whole, and our divorce from the Divinity, as some 15th-century opponents of the Copernican revolution saw it, perhaps lie at the heart of a great deal of modern psychological pain. A relationship with another who offers unconditional acceptance permits the small "I" of the individual self to experience itself as connected once more, to tune into and become a participant in orders of consciousness greater than itself. This "relational empathy" (O'Hara, 1997b) makes it possible to know the Other as an individual, as we do through "egocentric empathy," but also holistically through participation in larger "wholes."

To distinguish between "egocentric empathy" and "relational empathy," consider the following example.

I was working with a person-centered training group in Brazil, a particularly difficult group whose members were very competitive with one another, aggressive and uncooperative. Although everyone seemed willing to speak up and "deal with their stuff," nothing seemed to be happening. I had been a little detached for several minutes while group members tried unsuccessfully to work through a misunderstanding between Paulo and Carmen that was very painful for them, since they had been very close prior to this. I was having difficulty making an empathic connection with either Carmen or Paulo, so I tuned out from their conversation and into the group as a larger-order entity. I entered a sort of reverie in which the individuals in the group faded into the background and the patterns of interactions flowed on. I began to hallucinate images and to hear sounds that were apparently unconnected to what was happening in the room. Suddenly, and with crystal clarity, I saw Carmen as a small barefoot country girl. In my imagination (although not in fact), the robust-looking Carmen appeared undernourished and terrified. In the image, she was rocking back and forth, holding herself and weeping. Then there appeared a somewhat older boy about to bring a stick down on her head and a much younger boy who was trying to prevent it. The image faded and I came back into sharp focus.

I interrupted the free-for-all discussion to ask the couple, in a tone one would use to speak to small children, if either of them needed any help. Carmen moved quickly toward me, straight into my arms, and began sobbing as if her heart would break, while Paulo turned to the lap of my coleader and began to weep almost as deeply. As if on cue, other group members began to move closer to each other, holding hands or embracing. Tears flowed freely for several minutes. Later, when the members began to talk over what they had experienced, they shared fragments of images that were not very different from mine. One woman said she had felt the need to protect both Carmen and Paulo, but had no idea from what. Paulo said his frustration had been so intense because he felt a contradictory need to challenge Carmen and to protect her, and he couldn't do both. Finally, Carmen told a story of her early childhood that no one in the group knew about. She had been born to a poor sugar-plantation worker and had been adopted at the age of five by a wealthy family. She had been separated from her little brother, Paulo, and her stepbrother had been a bully. After this moment in the group, the conflict between Paulo and Carmen simply evaporated, and the dynamics of the group changed. In place of the heaviness that had characterized the group since the beginning, a lightness erupted. Laughter, playfulness, and creativity replaced the tense competition. The important "gender issues" that had required so much attention for the first days of the group suddenly, and without further work, were no longer important. The group was more cohesive, learning was accelerated, and like a team that had suddenly "clicked," the whole group was functioning on a far more creative level.

Over years of working with person-centered groups, as well as with individuals and families and in organizational settings, we have gradually come to trust relational empathy as a real, but underdeveloped, skill. We have begun to have confidence that these apparently unrelated hallucinations are ways of representing the implicit order that is always present, but rarely is discerned by individual-centered consciousness. Even when such relational patterns are recognized, we hesitate to give epistemic status to such knowledge. We call it "psychic," "paranormal," "miraculous," and by so doing, put it out of the reach of ordinary people. Worse still, at least in graduate training programs for therapists, we warn students of "psychic contagion," "loss of self," "boundary diffusion," and other such dangers that are said to await young therapists if they allow themselves to explore these realms. At the same time, we fail to offer them training in how to enter such states safely and creatively.

We have observed (O'Hara, 1983; Wood, 1984) that there are times in relationships, and in groups as large as several hundred members, when a resonance exists between the individual level of consciousness and the group level of consciousness, where individuals can "read the group's mind." This rarely happens early in a group, and it seems to require that the individuals present have allowed themselves to go beyond their previous ego boundaries and to make deep and authentic empathic connections with each other. But when it does happen everyone present recognizes that something very special is occurring. People report "knowing more than they could possibly know," "knowing what was to happen before it actually did," "feeling smarter and more aware than ever before," "feeling no separation between unconscious images and real events," "able to make connections they had never seen before," "speaking for the group," and so on. Descriptions of experiences in these groups have the sound and texture of the descriptions of "unity consciousness" about which poets, mystics, and philosophers have written over the ages. What differentiates these experiences from those of the mystics and spiritual practitioners who achieve such states only after long periods of mental preparation is that these moments happen in events that last as little as a day or two.

We believe that the very special context of person-centered therapy, which Rogers described almost 60 years ago, is one way in which people are able to tap into realms of knowledge that lie beyond the consciousness of any single individual, and that can be accessed through the open sacred space created within relationships. Professor Manton and Carl Rogers believed, and thanks to their mentor-ship, so do I, that such moments of eternity are reachable through relationships of unconditional love. Although not the only path — there are many more, some of them thousands of years old — but a good one, person-centered therapy provides both clients and therapists with a simple, but demanding, way to glimpse the divine at work in the world, and, more important, to participate.

References

Alexander, C. N., & Langer, E. J. (Eds.). (1990). *Higher stages of human development: Perspectives on adult growth.* New York: Oxford University Press.

Belenky, M. F., Clinchy, B. M., Goldberger, N. R., & Tarule, J. M. (1986). *Women's ways of knowing: Development of self, voice, and mind.* New York: Basic Books.

Bergin, A. E., & Garfield, S. L. (1994). Overview, trends, and future issues. In A. E. Bergin & S. L. Garfield (Eds.), *Handbook of psychotherapy and behavior change* (pp. 821–830). New York: Wiley.

Bohart, A., O'Hara, M., & Leitner, L. (1998). Empirically violated treatments: Disenfranchisement of humanistic and other psychotherapies. *Psychotherapy Research, 8*, 141–157.

Bohart, A., & Tallman, K. (1999). *How clients make therapy work: The process of self-healing.* Washington, DC: American Psychological Association:

Bowen, M., O'Hara, M. M., Rogers, C. R., & Wood, J. K. (1979). Learning in large groups: Implications for the future. *Education, 100*, 108–117.

Buber, M. (1970). *I and thou.* (W. Kaufman, trans.). New York: Scribner's Sons. (Originally published 1923.)

Cade, B., & O'Hanlon, W. H. (1993). *A brief guide to brief therapy*. New York: Norton.

Friedman, M. S. (1985). *The healing dialogue in psychotherapy*. New York: Jacob Aronson.

Geertz, C. (1979). From the native's point of view: On the nature of anthropological understanding. In P. Rabinow & W. M. Sullivan (Eds.), *Interpretive social psychology* (pp. 225–241). Berkeley: University of California Press.

Gergen, K. J. (1994). Exploring the postmodern: Perils or potentials? *The American Psychologist*, *49*(5), 412–414.

Gilligan, S. (1997). *The courage to love: Principles and practices of self-relations psychotherapy*. New York: Norton.

Harman, J. I. (1990). Unconditional confidence as a facilitative precondition. In G. Leitaer, J. Rombauts, & R. Van Balen (Eds.), *Client-centered and experiential psychotherapy in the nineties*. Louvain, Belgium: University of Louvain Press.

Kegan, R. (1994). *In over our heads: The mental demands of modern life*. Cambridge, MA: Harvard University Press.

Kirschenbaum, H. (1979). *On becoming Carl Rogers*. New York: Dell.

Kirschenbaum, H., & Henderson, V. L. (Eds.). (1989). *Carl Rogers: Dialogues*. Boston: Houghton Mifflin.

Kramer, R. (1995). Carl Rogers meets Otto Rank — and beyond. *Journal of Humanistic Psychology*, *35*(4), 54–110.

Kuhn, T. S. (1970). *The structure of scientific revolutions* (2nd ed.). Chicago: University of Chicago Press.

Luborsky, L., Singer, B., & Luborsky, L. (1975). Comparative studies of psychotherapies: Is it true that "everyone has won and all must have prizes"? *Archives of General Psychiatry*, *32*, 995–1008.

Mearns, D. (1994). *Developing person-centred counseling*. London: Sage.

Neimeyer, R. A., & Stewart, A. E. (2000). *Constructivist and narrative therapies*. In C. R. Snyder & R. E. Ingram (Eds.), *Handbook of psychotherapy* (pp. 337–357). New York: Wiley.

O'Hanlon, W. H. (1993). Possibility therapy: From iatrogenic injury to iatrogenic healing. In S. Gilligan & R. H. Prices (Eds.), *Therapeutic conversations*. New York: Norton.

O'Hara, M. (1983). Patterns of awareness: Consciousness and the group mind. *The Gestalt Journal*, *6*(2), 103–116.

O'Hara, M. M. (1984). Person-centered Gestalt: Towards a holistic synthesis. In R. F. Levant & J. M. Shlien (Eds.), *Client-centered therapy and the person-centered approach: New directions in theory, research and practice* (pp. 203–221). New York: Praeger.

O'Hara, M. (1989). Person-centered approach as conscientizacao: The works of Carl Rogers and Paulo Freire. *Journal of Humanistic Psychology, 29*(1), 11–35.

O'Hara, M. (1995). Carl Rogers: Scientist or mystic? *Journal of Humanistic Psychology, 35*(4), 40–53.

O'Hara, M. (1996). Rogers and Sylvia: A feminist analysis. In B. A. Farber, D. C. Brink, & P. M. Raskin (Eds.), *The psychotherapy of Carl Rogers: Cases and commentary* (pp. 284–300). New York: Guilford.

O'Hara, M. (1997a). Emancipatory therapeutic practice in a turbulent transmodern era: A work of retrieval. *Journal of Humanistic Psychology, 37*(3), 7–33.

O'Hara, M. (1997b). Relational empathy: From egocentric modernism to socio-centric postmodernism. In A. C. Bohart & L. S. Greenberg (Eds.), *Empathy reconsidered: New directions in psychotherapy* (pp. 295–320). Washington, DC: American Psychological Association.

Pascual-Leone, J. (1989). Reflections on life-span intelligence, consciousness, and ego-development. In C. N. Alexander & E. J. Langer (Eds.), *Higher stages of human development* (pp. 258–286). New York: Oxford University Press.

Rogers, C. R. (1942). *Counseling and psychotherapy: Newer concepts in practice.* New York: Houghton Mifflin.

Rogers, C. R. (1957). The necessary and sufficient conditions for therapeutic personality change. *Journal of Consulting Psychology, 21*, 95–103.

Rogers, C. R. (1977). *Carl Rogers on personal power.* New York: Delacorte.

Rogers, C. R. (1978). The formative tendency. *Journal of Humanistic Psychology, 18*(1), 23–26.

Rogers, C. R. (1980). *A way of being*. Boston: Houghton Mifflin.

Rogers, C. R., & Dymond, R. F. (Eds.). (1954). *Psychotherapy and personality change: Co-ordinated research studies in the client-centered approach.* Chicago: University of Chicago Press.

Rogers, C. R., & Sanford, R. C. (1989). Client-centered psychotherapy. In H. I. Kaplan & B. J. Sadock (Eds.), *Comprehensive textbook of psychiatry* (pp. 1482–1501). Baltimore: Williams & Wilkins.

Schmid, P. F. (1997). In N. Andrade (Ed.), *IV International Conference on Client-Centered Therapy and Experiential Psychotherapy* (p. 30). Lisbon, Portugal: University Católica Portuguesa.

Seeman, J. (1954). Counselor judgements of therapeutic progress and outcome. In C. R. Rogers & R. F. Dymond (Eds.), *Psychotherapy and personality change* (pp. 166–196). Chicago: University of Chicago Press:

Seligman, M. E. P. (1995). The effectiveness of psychotherapy: The *Consumer Reports* study. *The American Psychologist, 50*(12), 965–974.

Shlien, J. M. (1957). *An experimental investigation of time-limited, brief, client-centered therapy.* Doctoral dissertation, University of Chicago.

Shlien, J. (1997). Empathy in psychotherapy: A vital mechanism? Yes. Therapist's conceit? All too often. By itself enough? No. In A. Bohart & L. S. Greenberg (Eds.), *Empathy reconsidered: New directions in psychotherapy.* Washington, DC: American Psychological Association.

Standal, S. W., & van der Veen, F. (1957). Length of therapy in relation to counselor estimates of personal integration and other case variables. *Journal of Consulting Psychology, 21*(1), 1–9.

Taft, J. (1933/1973). *Dynamics of therapy in a controlled relationship.* Goucester, MA: Peter Smith.

Van Belle, H. A. (1990). Rogers' later move towards mysticism: Implications for client-centered therapy. In G. Lietare, J. Rombauts, & R. Van Balen (Eds.), *Client-centered and experiential psychotherapy in the nineties* (pp. 47–58). Louvain: University of Louvain Press.

Van Kalmthout, M. (1995). The religious dimensions of Rogers' work. *Journal of Humanistic Psychology, 35*(4), 23–39.

Wood, J. K. (1984). Communities for learning: A person-centered approach. In J. M. Shlien & R. F. Levant (Eds.), *Client-centered therapy and the person-centered approach: New directions in theory and practice* (pp. 297–316). New York: Praeger.

Wood, J. K. (1997). *Carl Rogers and transpersonal psychology.* Presented at the Sixth International Holistic and Transpersonal Congress, Aquas de Lindoia, Brazil.

22

Ericksonian Brief Psychotherapy in the New Millennium: Immediate-Early Genes in the Deep Psychobiology of Psychotherapy

Ernest Lawrence Rossi

The traditional psychotherapies, ranging from classical psychoanalysis to current cognitive-behavioral schools, usually conceptualize communication in terms of verbal interactions between the therapist and patient. The brain and body in the early behaviorist school, for example, were labeled a "black box" that need not be taken into account in describing human behavior. In contrast to this traditional approach, Milton H. Erickson (1948/1980) emphasized that it was the experiential "reassociation," "reorganization," and "resynthesis" of one's internal life that led to problem solving and healing as follows:

> The induction and maintenance of a trance serves to provide a special psychological state in which the patient can *reassociate* and *reorganize* his inner psychological complexities and utilize his own capacities in a manner in accord with his own experiential life ... Therapy results from an inner *resynthesis* of the patient's behavior

> achieved by the patient himself. It's true that direct suggestion can effect an alteration in the patient's behavior and result in a symptomatic cure, at least temporarily. However such a "cure" is simply a response to suggestion and does not entail that *reassociation* and *reorganization* of ideas, understandings, and memories so essential for actual cure. *It is the experience of reassociating and reorganizing his own experiential life that eventuates in a cure*, not the manifestation of responsive behavior which can, at best, satisfy only the observer. (p. 38, italics added)

How are we to understand Erickson's view of the reassocation and resynthesis of experiential life? Is it simply a process of change that takes place in a kind of subjective phenomenological space of cognitions, fantasies, and dreams, or does it involve transformations in the organic structure and functioning of the brain and body, as well? This chapter proposes that the current information revolution in psychology and medicine on the cellular–genomic level is creating a new foundation for the understanding of Erickson's view of "reassociation" and "resynthesis" as the essence of healing leading to lasting impressions in psychotherapy. Prominent researchers, for example, now regard immediate-early response genes (IEGs) as rapidly acting mediators between nature and nurture at the cellular–genomic level. The IEGs act as transducers, allowing brief signals from the external environment to regulate the expression of genes within the nucleus of life itself. It is now known that IEGs can transduce strong but brief signals of pain, trauma, stress, and novelty from the environment into enduring changes in the physical structure of the brain, as well as memory, learning, and behavior. This chapter explores how currently emerging understanding of the pathways of communication between mind and gene may become the psychobiological basis of Ericksonian brief therapy for creating lasting impressions.

IEGs AS THE FIRST RESPONSE TO EMOTIONAL AROUSAL

A generation ago, it was believed that genes were simply the units of physical heredity that were transmitted from one generation to another through sexual reproduction. Today, we know that different classes of genes have a number of other adaptive functions throughout the life cycle. A major class of genes, sometimes called immediate-early genes (or primary response genes or third messengers), that are actively turned on and off every second of our lives in response to physical and psychosocial stimuli, are important in the continual process of adaptation to our changing environment. Everything from physical trauma and toxins to temperature, psychosocial stress, food, and sexual stimuli in the environment can be signaled to neurons in the brain, where IEGs are turned on as the first step in the arousal of a creative response system at the molecular–genomic level, as illustrated in Figure 1.

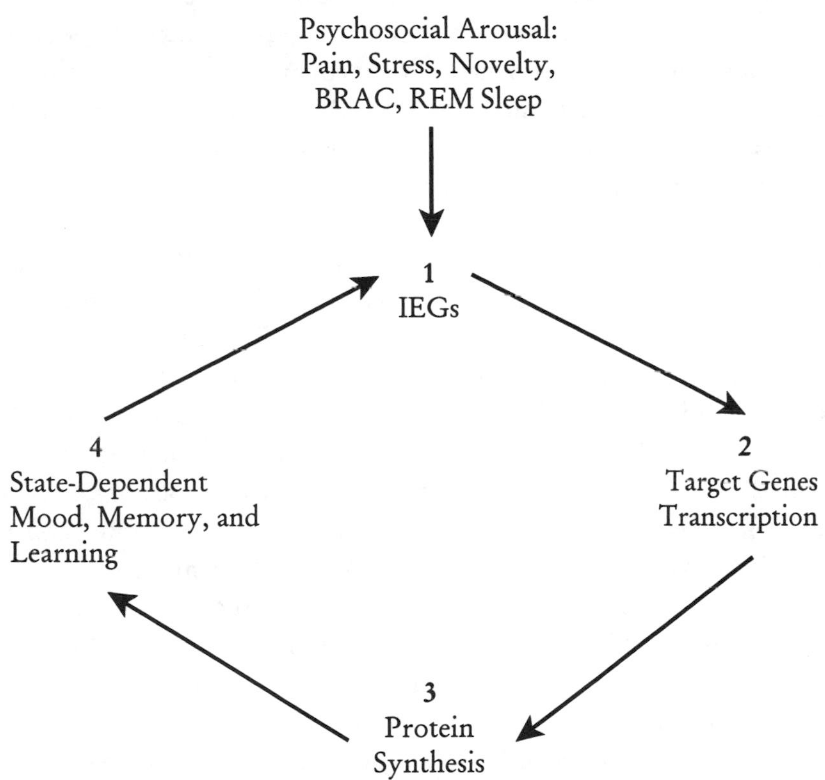

Figure 1. The mind–gene loop of mindbody communication in response to physical arousal and psychosocial stress is proposed as the essence of the creative response to emotional arousal and novel experiences in brief psychotherapy that can lead to lasting impressions and enduring changes in state dependent memory, learning, and behavior associated with healing.

In step 1, IEGs initiate a series of molecular–genomic transformations that can transduce relatively brief signals from the environment into lasting impressions in the physical structure of the developing nervous system throughout life. When neurons of the brain transmit electrochemical signals to each other, IEGs are activated immediately as the first step in an adaptive response at the cellular–genomic level (Dragunow, 1995; Tölle, Schadrack, & Zieglgansberger, 1995). *C-fos*, for example, is an IEG that is stimulated into activity by arousing or stressful environmental stimuli within neurons of the brain, where it leads to the production of a protein called "fos." Fos can then act as a transcription factor that turns on "target genes." That is, fos can bind on to the DNA molecule, where it can turn on target genes as illustrated in step 2 of Figure 1. These target genes are transcribed so that the information they contain can be sent to the cell in the form of messenger ribonucleic acid (mRNA). This mRNA then serves as a kind of blueprint for manufacturing the proteins in step 3 that are the bottom line for most processes of adaptation and healing on the material, energetic, and informational levels of life in response to psychosocial, as well as physical, stress and trauma (Rossi, 1986/1993, 1996, 1997a, 2002).

Many researchers now believe that memories, along with new experiences, are encoded in the central nervous system (CNS) by changes in the structure and formation of new proteins within neurons. IEGs function as transcription factors regulating downstream target genes that make the proteins within the neurons. Much current research is concerned with a number of families of IEGs involved with memory and learning, such as the egr family (also know as the zif 268 family, or krox -24 family). More than 100 IEGs have been reported so far. Although many of their functions still remain unknown, neuroscientists are exploring the complex range of interrelated biological and psychological functions that IEGs are already known to serve. It is precisely this simultaneous mediation of both the biological and psychological levels — the *psychobiological* — that recommends a central role for IEGs in understanding the foundations of mind-body medicine and psychotherapy, as illustrated in Figure 2.

In the neurons of the CNS, the IEGs are now recognized as general or universal transducers responding to many classes of noxious environmental stimuli by inducing adaptive changes in gene transcription to facilitate the healing of stress and trauma caused by mechanical or physical injury, severed neurons, epilepticus, spreading cortical depression, viral and bacterial infections, drug intoxication, and the like (Merchant, 1996). Studies

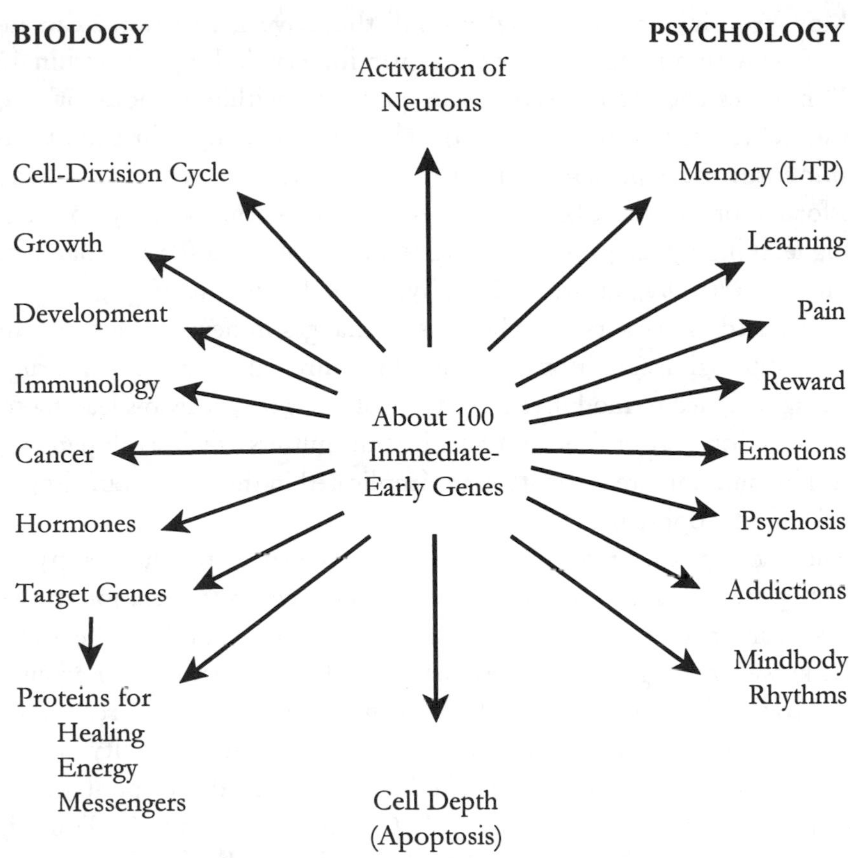

Figure 2. The interrelated psychological and biological functions mediated by IEGs in response to physical and psychosocial arousal and stress that suggest how IEGs may play a central role in mindbody communication and healing in short-term psychotherapy for lasting impressions. (From Rossi, 2002)

of the role of *c-fos* are currently changing the face of pain research, for example, in both acute and chronic pain, in phantom limb pain, and in hyperalgesia and allodynia. (Tölle, Schadrack, & Zieglgansberger, 1995). Drugs dealing with pain, as well as related addictive drugs, such as cocaine, amphetamine, and the opiates, are also mediated by IEGs. The implication is that IEGs are central in the expression of the emotions, moods, and behavioral addictions that are of prime interest in psychotherapy.

Most arousing environmental stimuli that have been studied can induce IEGs within minutes; their concentrations typically peak within 15 to 20 minutes and their effects are usually over within an hour or two (Rossi, 2002; Schlingensiepen, 1995). These rapid changes in gene transcription and new protein formation, however, can lead to enduring transformations in the CNS by converting short-term memory to long-lasting learning by the process of long term potentiation (Bailey, Bartsch, & Kandel, 1996; Dragunow, 1995; Tully, 1996). Immediate-early genes are now also used as markers or indicators of changes in neuronal activity in psychopathological conditions, such as schizophrenia. Antipsychotic drugs are being designed to modulate the effects of IEGs on pathways leading to the production and utilization of neurotransmitters, such as dopamine, serotonin, and noradrenaline, that are implicated in the "dopamine hypothesis" of schizophrenia.

There is as yet no research relating to hypnosis or psychotherapy to the IEG-protein cascade in healing. Recent research on the relation of the IEG c-fos and nerve growth factor-induced A (NGFI-A) in the wake–sleep cycle, however, suggests how they may be related to patterns of arousal and relaxation in hypnotherapy. It has been found "that the expression of c-fos during waking is strictly dependent on the level of activity of the noradrenergic system: "high levels of c-fos during forced and spontaneous waking and low levels during sleep" (Cirelli, Pompeiano, & Tononi, 1998, p. 46). It is tempting to speculate that such stimulation of the noradrenergic system and IEG expression may be the molecular–genetic basis of healing in hypnosis. This leads us to propose that a truly deep psychobiological model of how psychotherapy works at the cellular level to facilitate the lasting impressions of mindbody healing on a physical level as well as on the emotional and mental levels, must involve these molecular–genetic levels.

PATHWAYS OF MIND–GENE COMMUNICATION IN ANXIETY AND DEPRESSION

Much of conventional counseling and psychotherapy consists of talk at an ordinary level of attention and emotional arousal. Genuinely transforming psychological experiences of therapy, however, usually involves something more. Typically, the patient becomes emotionally aroused with highly focused attention when deeply significant psychological experiences are touched upon. Dramatic shifts in posture, mood, and emotional expressions, and tears, flushing, and breathing changes are all common accompaniments of the creative moments of psychological insight that can lead to lasting impressions and transformations of a patient's life (Rossi & Cheek, 1988, 1990). Such emotional arousal, illustrated as step 1 in Figure 1, has been described in great detail, with varying emphasis and interpretation, in the classical literature of hypnosis and depth psychotherapy as abreaction, catharsis, reliving and reframing of posttraumatic experiences, creative moments of transformation, and so on (Rossi, 1973a, 1973b, 1996, 2002).

The first step in mind–gene communication in such emotionally arousing processes of psychotherapy takes place in the limbic–hypothalamic–pituitary system, which is currently recognized as a major information transducer between the brain and the body. The pioneering physiologist Papez (1937) first traced the anatomical pathways by which emotional experiences of the brain were transduced into the physiological responses of the body in that system. The Scharrers (1940) and Harris (1948) then illustrated how the secretory cells within the hypothalamus could mediate molecular information transduction between brain and body. Cells within the hypothalamus transform the essentially electrochemical neural impulses of the neurons of the cerebral cortex that apparently encoded the phenomenological experience of "mind" and emotions into the hormonal messenger molecules of the endocrine system that are communicated to the body through the bloodstream in a cybernetic loop of information transduction, as described previously (Rossi, 1986/1993, 1996, 2002).

One of the first hormonal messenger molecules to be expressed in the hypothalamus in response to physical, as well as psychosocial, stress is corticotrophin-releasing factor (CRF). Within a minute, CRF signals the pituitary to release ACTH into the bloodstream as a primary messenger molecule, where it travels to the adrenals and signals them to release the next messenger, cortisol, into the bloodstream, where it can turn on cells throughout the entire body to activate their special functions to cope adaptively with stress. This major pathway from mind to molecules in response to stress has been called the hypothalamic–pituitary–adrenal (HPA) axis. During the emergence of stress, cortisol signals muscle cells to absorb fuel to facilitate the "fight or flight response," while CRF depresses appetite and sexuality and sharpens alertness to cope with the environmental stressor.

Several decades of neurobiological research have documented that when there is a chronic stressor, activating the HPA axis to the point where the organism no longer can cope, the conditions are being set for depression. It has been shown that the pituitary and the adrenal gland are actually enlarged because of the hyperactivation of the HPA axis in depressed patients. Microscopic examination of the brain tissues of these patients reveals that there has been a proliferation of CRF-producing neurons in the hypothalamus and an overexpression of the CRF gene, leading to an elevation of CRF in the cerebrospinal fluid and the typical behavior of depression in humans, such as insomnia, decreased appetite and libido, anxiety, and negative cognition.

Although this excessive production of CRF can be reduced by antidepressants and electroconvulsive treatments, there are unwanted side effects. This has led some psychobiologically oriented workers to call for brain-imaging studies with positron emission tomography (PET) to determine whether or not the activity of CRF-producing neurons and the expression of the CRF gene might not be modified by psychotherapy as well (Nemeroff, 1998). While such workers do not state it as explicitly as here, the direct implication of this research would be that appropriately focused mental activity in psychotherapy could modulate gene expression, as well as the anatomical structure of neurons in the hypothalamus of the human brain. This would clearly document how the mind can modulate molecules as well as how molecules can modulate the mind (Rossi, 1986/1993). This mutual modulation between mind and molecules is the essence of what has been called state-dependent memory, learning, and behavior (Rossi, 1990, 1996). This breakthrough in the Cartesian dichotomy between mind and body is well expressed by Andreasen (1997, p. 1592) as follows.

> A key point ... is that the anatomy of melancholy can be modified by both psychological and chemical/molecular experiences. The depressed state can often be reversed through treatment with drugs that affect the biogenic amine systems of the brain, but it can also be treated with cognitive therapies that attempt to reverse "negative sets," and combination therapies are perhaps the most effective of all. Depression may be a consequence of the plastic response of mind/brain to experience, and it may also remit because of either pharmacological or psychotherapeutic manipulations of brain plasticity.

The concept of gene-protein dynamics as the final common path to healing integrates traditional physical medicine with mind-body models and becomes an important criterion for evaluating all forms of therapeutic communication and healing — biofeedback, body work, meditation, imagery, active imagination, hypnosis, prayer, ritual, yoga, or whatever — with a common yardstick. Whatever the therapeutic method, we can test whether it has really facilitated healing with relatively simple assays that determine whether appropriate genes are expressed in the form of mRNAs (step 2 of Figure 1) that serve as "blueprints" for the synthesis of proteins. A dramatic example is provided by Schanberg (Pauk, Kuhn, Field, & Schanberg, 1986; Schanberg, personal communication, 1998), who found that "isolated very premature human babies ... showed marked gains in weight, development and sympatho-adrenal maturation" when they were massaged. He reports that in an animal model (preweaning rat pups), "The absence of nurturing touch suppresses ODC [ornithine decarboxylase] gene transcription by interfering with a cell's ability to transduce the hormone receptor-activated signal. This is accomplished by the down regulation of specific immediate early genes essential to the synthesis of this growth regulating enzyme." Such research literature implies that both touch and verbal suggestion can initiate gene-protein cascades to facilitate growth and healing at the cellular level. Further research may afford a new methodology for differentiating the relative merits of the many approaches to hypnosis and their therapeutic applications.

PSYCHOIMMUNOLOGY, STRESS, CANCER, AND IEGs

The most comprehensive demonstration of how psychosocial stress can modulate gene transcription was demonstrated by Ronald Glaser (Glaser, et al., 1990; Glaser, Lafuse, Bonneau, Atkinson, & Kiecolt-Glaser, 1993). His research helps us trace the effects of psychological stress (experienced by medical students during academic examinations) on the transcription of the interleukin-2 receptor gene and interleukin-2 production. These researchers, in essence documented the same path of information transduction illustrated in Figure 1 where (1) stress-activated IEGs in the limbic–hypothalamic–pituitary system lead to the release of hormones (primary messengers) that trigger (2) cell receptors to initiate a cascade of secondary messengers (cAMP) that mediate gene transcription of the interleukin-2 receptor target gene. This is then transcribed to form its mRNA "blueprint" for (3) the synthesis of the interleukin-2 protein that leads to the formation of (4) a new receptor that migrates to the cell surface and another messenger molecule of interleukin-2 that mediates communication among white blood cells of the immune system. Interleukin-2 can also reach the brain to modulate mind, memory, emotions, and behavior in a state-dependent manner (Rossi, 1986/1993, 1996, 2002).

A major challenge for fundamental research in psychobiologically oriented psychotherapy and holistic medicine is to document how a positive psychotherapeutic intervention designed to reduce psychosocial stress could lead to a facilitation of the transcription of the interleukin-2 receptor gene. This research would become a new paradigm of mind-body healing. It has profound significance for a general theory of mind-body communication and healing when we realize that other medical researchers (Rosenberg & Barry, 1992) have found that interleukin-2 is a messenger molecule of the immune system that signals white blood cells (cytotoxic T-cells) to attack pathogens and cancer cells. Thus, a purely medical model of research represented by Rosenberg and a holistic model, represented by Glaser, have found the same bottom line in mind-body communication at the level of gene expression in the field of psychoimmunology. It has been proposed that this will become the new criterion for evaluating all forms of mindbody healing in the future: biofeedback, body therapies, message, meditation, imagery, active imagination, hypnosis, prayer, ritual, or whatever. Whatever the holistic method of mindbody healing, we can test whether it really facilitated mindbody communication and healing simply by taking a blood sample to determine whether or not a healing gene transcription actually took place with the very easy and reliable test of whether mRNA is made so that new proteins and hormones could be synthesized for growth, healing, and new phenomenological experiences of consciousness (Rossi, 1973a, 1986/1993, 1996, 2002).

NEW PROTEIN SYNTHESIS IN STRESS, TRAUMA, AND HEALING

Todorov's (1990) research is the clearest current model of the structural, energy and informational dynamics of the cell in response to stress and trauma. His research outlines three major "blocks" or stages of gene transcription and translation in response to physical trauma and stress. The initial M (Metabolism) block proteins are those that are most quickly metabolized (*within a hour*) to process proteins required for energy dynamics. The next, R (Ribosomal) block proteins, are those involved in the mRNA translation processes *within a few hours*. The third stage produces the N (Nuclear) proteins, such as DNA polmerases and histones, in a slower process requiring *12 hours to a day or more*. I propose that a new research frontier for holistic medicine is to document how these three stages at the cellular–molecular level will also be found in response to psychosocial stress and its amelioration by psychotherapy.

These responses to trauma and stress are examples of the average time parameters for the general mind–gene communication loop framed on the right side of Figure 1. These time parameters illustrate the major chronobiological source of rhythms at the cellular–genomic level that mediates information transduction on all levels of mindbody communication. These psychobiological rhythms provide a new window on how the phenomenological experiences of mind and consciousness are related to processes at the molecular–genetic–cellular level in what has been called the unification hypothesis of chronobiology (Rossi & Lippincott, 1992; Lloyd & Rossi, 1992, 1993). That is, the domain of psychological time in minutes and hours as illustrated in Figure 1 relates the basic rest–activity cycle of human behavior to the processes of mindbody communication mediated by the slower neuroendocrine system of communication in sexual behavior. This contrasts with the more recent evolutionary form of rapid mindbody communication mediated by the CNS in small fractions of a second that are briefer than the usual phenomenological span of conscious human attention.

MESSENGER MOLECULES AND STATE-DEPENDENT MEMORY

Step 4 of Figure 1 indicates how messenger molecules that have their origin in the processing of the larger protein "mother molecules" in stage 3 may be stored within the cells of the brain and body as a kind of "molecular memory." These molecular messengers are released into the bloodstream, where they can complete the complex cybernetic loop of information transduction by passing through the blood–brain barrier (Davson & Segal, 1996) to modulate the brain's neural networks in a state-dependent manner. Recent research indicates that most forms of learning (Pavlovian,

Skinnerian, imprinting, sensitization, etc.) involve the four-step cascade of Figure 1. Insofar as these classical forms of learning are initiated with IEGs leading to the formation of messenger molecules, they *ipso facto* have a "state-dependent component" (Rossi, 1986/1993; Rossi & Cheek, 1988, 1990; Rossi, 1996, 2002).

This four step cascade of information transduction between arousal and stress, immediate-early genes, messenger molecules, and the state-dependent encoding of mindbody problems suggest a new research frontier for the psychobiological investigation of many classical psychoanalytic concepts, such as repression, dissociation, and emotional complexes. A new paradigm for such research has been provided by Cahill and associates (Cahill, Prins, Weber, & McGaugh, 1994), who compared the effects of the beta-adrenergic receptor antagonist propranolol hydrochloride on the long-term memory for an emotion-arousing and an emotionally neutral short story. Their results support the neuroscience paradigm of how enhanced memory associated with emotional experiences involves activation of the messenger molecules of the beta-adrenergic system. It would require only a simple extension of their method to document how the arousal phase of a psychobiologically oriented psychotherapy is mediated by the activation of similar messenger molecule–receptor systems.

A NEW PSYCHOBIOLOGICAL APPROACH TO PSYCHOTHERAPY

How long does it take to process one complete cycle of communication between mind and gene in Figure 1? Detailed research on the genetic, neuroendocrinal, and psychosocial levels suggests that the 90–120-minute ultradian rhythm (Lloyd & Rossi, 1992, 1993), originally described as the "basic rest–activity cycle" by Kleitman, is a more fundamental "work cycle of life" than the circadian cycle (the 24-hour rhythm). *Ultradian* in this context means any rhythm faster than the 24-hour circadian cycle; in this chapter, we focus on the major 90–120-minute ultradian rhythms on the genetic, endocrine, and cognitive-behavioral levels during sleeping and waking that have important implications for a new understanding of how all the systems of traditional psychophysiology are actually coordinated in time.

When the 90–120-minute ultradian cycle of mindbody communication of Figure 1 is unfolded over time we get graphs of the alternating ultradian rhythms of activity and rest on the genetic, endocrine and cognitive-behavioral, as illustrated on the lower part of Figure 3 (Rossi, 1996). This coordination of the diverse systems of traditional psychophysiology via their time parameters has been called the "Unification Hypothesis of Chronobiology" (Lloyd & Rossi, 1992; Rossi & Lippincott, 1992; Rossi, 1986/1993). This new understanding of the chronobiology of our natural psychophysiology from the molecular-genetic to the cognitive-behavioral levels may be taken as a new database for understanding the dynamics of mind-body communication and healing in psychotherapy.

The lower part of Figure 3 summarizes the alternating 90–120-minute ultradian rhythms of the awake and sleep states of an entire day in a simplified schematic manner. The ascending peaks of rapid eye movement (REM) sleep characteristic of nightly dreams every 90–120 minutes or so are illustrated along with the more variable ultradian rhythms of activity, adaptation, and rest in the daytime. Figure 3 also illustrates how many hormonal messenger molecules of the endocrine system such as *growth hormone*, the activating and stress hormone *cortisol*, and the sexual hormone *testosterone* have a typical circadian peak at different times of the 24-hour cycle. Because the nonlinear chronobiological release of many of these hormones (Rossi, 1988) is recognized as having profound state-dependent effects on memory, learning, emotions, and behavior throughout the day, it is important to consider their relevance for new models of psychotherapy.

Figure 3. (Top) The four stages of the creative process in psychobiologically oriented psychotherapy are a utilization of one of the natural 90–120-minute ultradian rhythms that take place throughout the 24-hour circadian rhythm of waking and sleeping shown below. It is proposed that the natural state of arousal in stage 2 of this creative process involves the activation of IEGs that initiate a cascade of mind–gene–protein synthesis that is the psychobiological essence of lasting impressions and enduring healing in brief psychotherapy. (Bottom) A simplified schematic of the alternating 90–120-minute ultradian rhythms of the awake and sleep states of an entire day. The ascending peaks of REM sleep characteristic of nightly dreams every 90–120 minutes or so are illustrated, along with the more variable ultradian

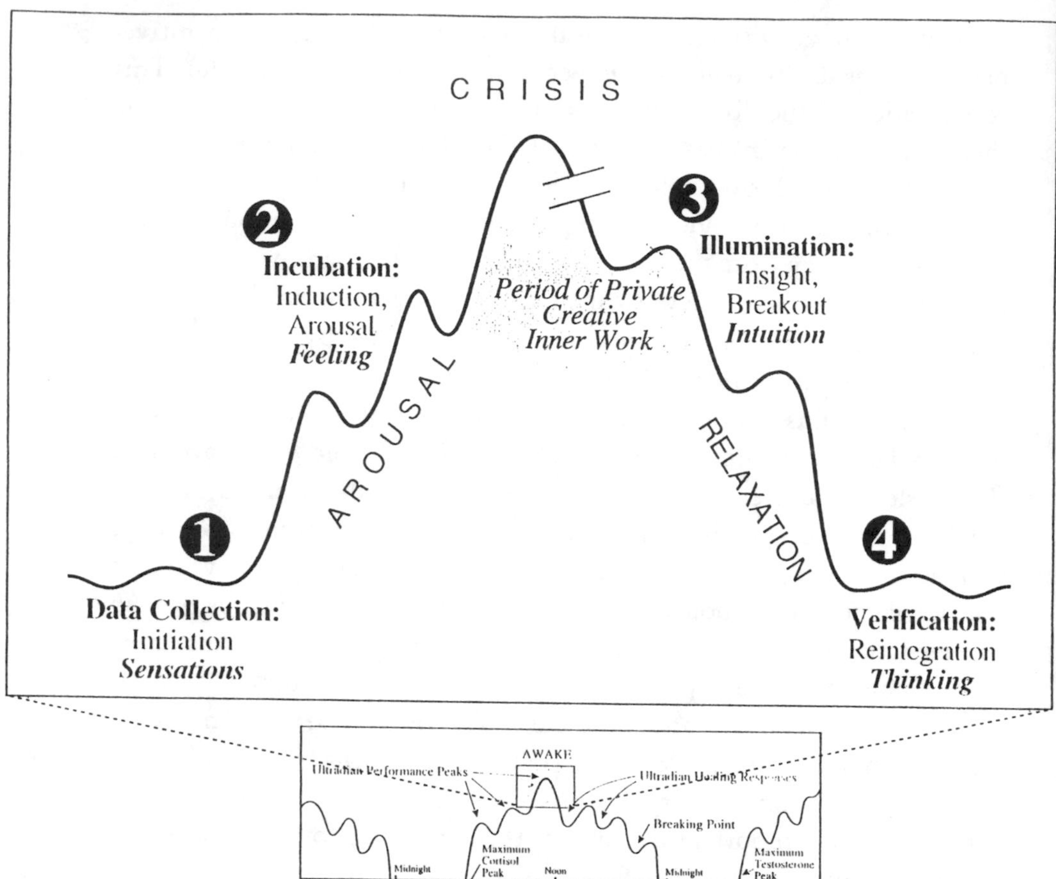

rhythms of activity, adaptation, and rest in the daytime. This figure also illustrates how many hormonal messenger molecules of the endocrine system, such as growth hormone, the activating and stress hormone cortisol, and the sexual hormone testosterone, have a typical circadian peak at different times of the 24-hour cycle. Because the nonlinear chronobiological release of many of these hormones is recognized as having a profound state-dependent effect on memory, learning, emotions, and behavior throughout the day, it is important to consider their relevance for new models of psychotherapy and the many approaches of holistic medicine and hypnotherapy (Rossi, 1996, 2002).

The upper part of Figure 3 illustrates my conjecture (Rossi, 1996) that the natural unit of psychobiologically oriented psychotherapy may be a utilization of one 90–120-minute ultradian cycle of activity and rest. In support of this idea, we may cite much research of the type illustrated by Iranmanesh, Lizarralde, Johnson, and Veldhuis (1989), for example, who documented how the ultradian peaks of cortisol secretion that lead to psychophysiological states of arousal every 90–120 minutes or so throughout the day (that I label as "Ultradian Performance Peaks" in Figure 3) are typically followed after about 20 minutes by ultradian peaks of beta-endorphin that lead to rest and relaxation that I label as "Ultradian Healing Responses" (Rossi, 1996; Rossi & Nimmons, 1991). It appears as if nature has built in a natural but flexible and highly adaptive ultradian rhythm of activity, rest, and healing, the "work cycle of life" mentioned above, every 90–120 minutes.

What, exactly, is the "work" that is done in each 90–120-minute ultradian cycle? I propose that the essence of such work is the formation of new proteins for a creative response to changing environmental conditions, stress and healing as described above particularly in the research of Todorov (1990). Twenty-five years ago (Rossi, 1972/1985/2002), I formulated "The Dream-Protein Hypothesis: Recent studies of learning and memory indicate that new experience is encoded by means of protein synthesis in brain tissue ... dreaming is a process of psychophysiological growth that involves the synthesis or modification of protein structures in the brain that serve as the organic basis for new developments in the personality" (Rossi, 1973a, p. 1094). While recent research has documented that new proteins are synthesized in some brain structures associated with REM dream sleep, such as the nucleus raphe dorsalis and the locus ceruleus (Sokolova, Taranova, & Kudriavtseva, 1992; Smith, Tenn, & Annett, 1991), the significance of such protein synthesis for humans during dreaming remains controversial (Flanagan, 1996). As a seminal hypothesis for Ericksonian approaches in the future, however, I would generalize the dream-protein hypothesis to include all states of creativity associated with the peak periods of arousal and insight generation in psychobiologically oriented psychotherapy as illustrated with clinical case histories elsewhere (Rossi, 1996, 2002). It will require extensive cooperation between psychotherapists and researchers to document this new psychobiological vision of the essence of Erickson's (1948/1980) synthetic approach as quoted above.

SUMMARY

To summarize, then, this chapter outlines an evolving view of how Milton Erickson's brief approaches to facilitating lasting impressions in the experience of reassociating, reorganizing, and resynthesizing emotional life "eventuates in a cure" on the molecular–genomic level. Current research on IEGs is providing a new database for understanding the fundamentals of the effects of novelty, pain, and stress on addictions, mood, depression, psychoimmunology, and a variety of issues of central concern to the psychotherapist. The pathways of mind–gene communication and healing that may lead to a new era of psychobiological healing whereby the mind could modulate the transcription and expression of certain classes of genes as the "bottom line" of healing are discussed. A psychobiological approach to hypnosis that is consistent with much of the classical theories of psychoanalysis and psychosomatic medicine, as well as the modern neuroscience of memory and learning at the cellular–genomic level, is proposed. This new integration of theory and research leads to a psychobiological model of how we may utilize the creative process in a manner that may seem visionary to some. Such a visionary ideal, however, may be what we need to develop truly new and inspired approaches to healing in the new millennium.

Note Added in Proof

Castes et al. (1999) reported that a 6-month program of relaxation, guided imagery, and self-esteem workshops with asthmatic children reduced the number of illness episodes and medication. The children had a significant increase in natural killers cells and other immune system factors associated with a reduction of psychosocial stress. *These children had an increase in gene expression of the T-cell receptor for interleukin-2 as hypothesized (on page 376 of this chapter to text the mind-gene parthway of healing in psychotherapy).* Eric Kandel (1998), who received the Noble Prize for Medicine in 2000, describes mind-gene concepts in this way.

> Insofar as psychotherapy or counseling is effective and produces long-term changes in behavior, it presumably does so through learning, by producing changes in *Gene Expression* that alter the strength of synaptic connections and structural changes that alter

the anatomical pattern of interconnections between nerve cells of the brain . . . *the regulation of gene expression by social factors makes all bodily functions, including functions of the brain, susceptible to social influences. These social influences will be biologically incorporated in the altered expressions of specific genes in specific nerve cells of specific regions of the brain.* (p. 460)

References

Andreasen, N. (1997). Linking mind and brain in the study of mental illness: A project for a scientific psychopathology. *Science, 275*, 1586–1593.

Bailey C. H., Bartsch, D., & Kandel, E. R. (1996). Toward a molecular definition of long-term memory storage. *Proceedings of the National Academy of Science. USA, 93*, 13445–13452.

Brey, D. (1995). Protein molecules as computational elements in living cells. *Nature, 376*, 307–312.

Cahill, L., Prins, B., Weber, M., & McGaugh, J. (1994). β-Adrenergic activation and memory for emotional events. *Nature, 371*(20), 702–704.

Castes, M., Hagel, I., Palenque, M., Canelones, P., Corano, A., & Lynch, N. (1999). Immunological changes associated with clinical improvements of asthmatic children subjected to psychosocial intervention. *Brain & Behavioral Immunology, 13*(1), 1–13.

Cirelli, C., Pompeiano, M., & Tononi, G. (1998). Immediate early genes as a tool to understand the regulation of the sleep–wake cycle: *In situ* hybridization, and antisense approaches. In R. Lydic (Ed.), *Molecular regulation of arousal states.* New York: CRC Press.

Davson, H., & Segal, M. (1996). *Physiology of the CFS and blood-brain barriers.* Boca Raton, FL: CRC Press.

Dragunow, M. (1995). Differential expression of immediate-early genes during synaptic plasticity, seizures and brain injury suggests specific functions for these molecules in brain neurons. In T. R. Tölle, J. Schadrack, and W. Zieglgansberger (Eds.), *Immediate early genes in the CNS.* New York: Springer-Verlag.

Erickson, M. (1948/1980). Hypnotic psychotherapy. In E. Rossi (Ed.), *The collected papers of Milton H. Erickson on hypnosis. Vol. 4. Innovative hypnotherapy* (pp. 35–48). New York: Irvington.

Flanagan, O. (1996). Deconstructing dreams: The spandrels of sleep. In S. Hameroff, A. Kaszniak, & A. Scott (Eds.), *Toward a science of consciousness: The first Tucson discussions and debates* (pp. 67–88). Cambridge, MA: MIT Press.

Glaser, R., Kennedy, S., Lafuse, W., Bonneau, R., Speicher, C., Hillhouse, J. & Kiecolt-Glaser, J. (1990). Psychological stress-induced modulation of interleukin 2 receptor gene expression and interleukin 2 production in peripheral blood leukocytes. *Archives of General Psychiatry, 47*, 707–712.

Glaser, R., Lafuse, W., Bonneau, R., Atkinson, C., & Kiecolt-Glaser, J. (1993). Stress-associated modulation of proto-oncogene expression in human peripheral blood leukocytes. *Behavioral Neuroscience, 107*, 525–529.

Hadamard, J. (1954). *The psychology of invention in the mathematical field.* New York: Dover.

Harris, G. (1948). Neural control of the pituitary gland. *Physiological Review, 28*, 139–179.

Iranmanesh, A., Lizarralde, G., Johnson, M., & Veldhuis, J. (1989). Circadian, ultradian, and episodic release of β-endorphin in men, and its temporal coupling with cortisol. *Journal of Clinical Endocrinology and Metabolism, 68*, 1019–1026.

Kandel, E. (1998). A new intellectual framework for psychiatry? *The American Journal of Psychiatry, 155*, 457–469.

Kraus, M., & Wolf, B. (1996). *Structured biological modeling: A new approach to biophysical cell biology.* Boca Raton, FL: CRC Press.

Lloyd, D., & Rossi, E. (1992). *Ultradian rhythms in life processes: A fundamental inquiry into chronobiology and psychobiology.* New York: Springer-Verlag.

Lloyd, D., & Rossi, E. (1993). Biological rhythms as organization and information. *Biological Reviews, 68*, 563–577.

Merchant, K. (Ed.). (1996). *Pharmacological regulation of gene expression in the CNS.* Boca Raton, FL: CRC Press.

Nemeroff, C. (1998). The neurobiology of depression. *Scientific American, 278*, 42–49.

Papez, J. (1937). A proposed mechanism of emotion. *Archives of Neurology and Psychiatry, 38*, 725–744.

Pauk, J., Kuhn, C., Field, T., & Schanberg, S. (1986). Positive effects of tactile versus kinesthetic or vistibular stimulation on neuroendocrine and ODC activity in maternally-deprived rat pups. *Life Sciences, 39*, 2081–2087.

Rosenberg, S., & Barry, J. (1992). *The transformed cell: Unlocking the mysteries of cancer.* New York: Putnam/Chapmans.

Rossi, E. (1972/1985/2000). *Dreams, consciousness, spirit* (3rd edition of *Dreams and the growth of personality*). Phoenix: Zeig, Tucker, & Theisen.

Rossi, E. (1973a). The dream-protein hypothesis. *American Journal of Psychiatry, 130*, 1094–1097.

Rossi, E. (1973b). Psychological shocks and creative moments in psychotherapy. *American Journal of Clinical Hypnosis, 16*, 9–22.

Rossi, E. (1986/1993). *The psychobiology of mind-body healing* (rev. ed.) New York: Norton.

Rossi, E. (1990). From mind to molecule: More than a metaphor. In J. Zeig & S. Gilligan (Eds.), *Brief therapy: Myths, methods and metaphors* (pp. 445–472). New York: Brunner/Mazel.

Rossi, E. (1996). *The symptom path to enlightenment: The new dynamics of self-organization in hypnotherapeutic work.* Pacific Palisades, CA: Palisades Gateway Publishing.

Rossi, E. (1997a). The symptom path to enlightenment: The psychobiology of Jung's constructive method. *Psychological Perspectives, 36*, 68–84.

Rossi, E. (1997b). The Feigenbaum scenario in a unified science of life and mind. *World Futures, 49*, 3–4; part II, *50*, 1–4.

Rossi, E. (1998). The Feigenbaum as a model of the limits of conscious information processing. *BioSystems, 40*, 1–10.

Rossi, E. (2002). *The psychobiology of gene expression: Neuroscience and neurogenesis in hypnosis and the healing arts.* New York: Norton.

Rossi, E., & Cheek, D. (1988). *Mind-body therapy: Ideodynamic healing in hypnosis.* New York: Norton.

Rossi, E., & Cheek, D. (1990). Ideomotor healing of burn injuries. In E. C. Hammond (Ed.), *Handbook of hypnotic suggestions and metaphors.* New York: Norton.

Rossi, E., & Lippincott, B. (1992). The wave nature of being: Ultradian rhythms and mind-body communication. In D. Lloyd & E. Rossi (Eds.), *Ultradian rhythms in life processes: A fundamental inquiry into chronobiology and psychobiology* (pp. 371–402). New York: Springer-Verlag.

Rossi, E., & Nimmons, D. (1991). *The twenty minute break: Using the new science of ultradian rhythms.* Phoenix: Zeig, Tucker, & Theisen.

Schacter, D. (1996). *Searching for memory: The brain, the mind and the past.* New York: Basic Books.

Schanberg, S. (1998). Early life experiences and the developing brain: consequences on mind and body. Presented at the Sedona Conference on the Science and Practice of Mindbody Interactions.

Scharrer, E., & Scharrer, B. (1940). Secretory cells within the hypothalamus. In research publications of the Association of Nervous and Mental Diseases. New York: Hafner.

Schlingensiepen, K., Kunst, M., Gerdes, W., & Brysch, W. (1995). Complementary expression patterns of c-jun and jun B in rat brain and analysis of their function with antisense oligonucleotides. In T. Tölle, J. Schadrack, W. Zieglgansberger (Eds.), *Immediate early genes in the CNS.* New York: Springer-Verlag.

Smith, C., Tenn, C., & Annett, R. (1991). Some biochemical and behavioral aspects of the paradoxical sleep window. *Canadian Journal of Psychology, 45*(2), 115–124.

Sokolova, N., Taranova, N., & Kudriavtseva, I. (1992). The normalizing pattern of some behavioral and neurochemical parameters after paradoxical sleep deprivation in rats. *Fiziologicheskii Zhurnal SSSR im I. M. Sechenova, 78*(5), 9–16.

Todorov, I. (1990). How cells maintain stability. *Scientific American, 263*, 66–75.

Tölle, T., Schadrack J., & Zieglgansberger, W. (Eds.) (1995). *Immediate early genes in the CNS.* New York: Springer-Verlag.

Tully, T. (1996). Discovery of genes involved with learning and memory: An experimental synthesis of Hirschian and Benzerian perspectives. *Proceedings of the National Academy of Science. USA*, *93*, 13460–13467.

23

Brief Therapy for Sexual Dysfunction

Joseph LoPiccolo

The mental health field first started writing about sexual issues in the Victorian Age just over 100 years ago. Richard Von Kraft Ebbing and Havelock Ellis published the first books on sexual issues. In those days, the accepted theory about the causes of sexual problems was what they called "moral degeneracy." Moral degeneracy basically meant excessive masturbation, any masturbation in childhood, or excessive masturbation or excessive sexual activity in adulthood. Treatment, therefore, was focused on prevention of all childhood masturbation. And, believe it or not, until about 1930, when the U.S. Patent Office stopped granting patents for them, there were about 40 different patented devices for preventing childhood masturbation. They consisted of a variety of restraining garments, strait-jackets, metal mittens, and types of handcuffs. My favorite one was a wonderfully complicated set of levers and pulleys. It was designed so that if the child's bed wiggled, a bell rang so that the parents could rush in and stop the child from doing this thing that was "destined" to give him or her terrible problems later in life.

For adults in those days it was thought that excessive sexual activity would cause problems. In fact, cornflakes and graham crackers were developed specifically to avoid stimulating sexual appetites. It was thought that if you had a bowl of cornflakes in the morning, you were less likely to feel very sexy later in the day. Cornflakes and graham crackers were specifically designed to be antiaphrodisiacs, to decrease sexual desires. Another antiaphrodisiac was long outdoor walks. The basic notion was that one was born with a finite capacity for arousal cycles, erections, and orgasms. If you used them up as a child or too rapidly as an adult, you would be out of luck for the rest of your life. There was even a mathematic formula for the health cost of sexual activity. One of the standard medical textbooks of the day touted the loss of one drop of semen was equivalent to the loss of seven drops of blood. That was remarkable precision.

Things changed a bit with Freud. In Freudian theory was the notion that there was a natural cycling through of oral, anal, and phallic stages to resolve one's Oedipal complex and to arrive at true, genital sexuality. If there was a fixation at one of the earlier stages, especially in an unresolved Oedipal stage, one would develop frigidity, erectile problems, premature ejaculation, homosexuality, or sexual deviance. The treatment, of course, was long-term psychoanalysis. One of the standard textbooks indicated, for example, that because "frigidity" involves unresolved penis envy, the problem could only be resolved with a psychoanalysis of a minimum of four times a week for a minimum of two years.

Ernest Hemingway made an apt comment about penis envy. He said the only validity he could see in the concept was that he had noticed as a child that it was easier for his father than it was for his mother to urinate when they went on a picnic in the woods.

Needless to say, analytic treatment never has proven to be noticeably successful in treating any form of sexual problem, regardless of the frequency or longevity of the treatment. Think of it this way: Will focusing on childhood events and Oedipal issues be sufficient to cure a man who has developed erectile dysfunctioning in his late 50s, after 25 years of perfectly adequate sexual functioning?

When I started doing sex therapy as an intern and asked one of my supervisors if I could try the Masters and Johnson approach, I was very surprised when he agreed, because he himself was an analyst. (He allows me to tell this story on the condition that I never divulge his name.) He was trained in Vienna. He eventually told me, "I'm an ego analyst. Freud's contribution is his work on the mechanism of defense. I already knew he was wrong about the sex stuff." I said, "If you don't mind me asking,

Professor, how?" He said, "Well, I've known that for years. Once, long ago, I had an experience that horrified me for just a few seconds."

He explained that one night he and his wife were making love and with some embarrassment, he told me that his little boy was right in the middle of the Oedipal phase, and he was showing all the Oedipal behaviors. The boy was in bed asleep and had been sleeping for a couple of hours. The professor and his wife were making love, and he told, with a bit of hesitancy, they were in a position they used occasionally. His wife was lying face down with a pillow under her hips. Her hips were raised, and he was sort of kneeling behind her but with her legs together, and his legs outside her so it was a nice tight fit, as he put it. He was thrusting away, when he heard a noise and looked up. There was his little boy standing in the doorway of their bedroom. He had been watching for quite some time. Here was his Oedipal boy viewing the primal scene! Clearly, he now was destined to be impotent, maybe a homosexual, maybe a pervert. All these horrors flashed through his mind. He knew that was what happened from a little boy seeing the primal scene while he is in the middle of the Oedipal phase. As their eyes locked, the little boy's face lit up. He burst into a big smile, and he yelled, "Atta boy, Daddy! Ride 'em, cowboy!" My professor said, "Right then, I knew Freud was wrong." So that is why he was willing for me to use the Masters and Johnson techniques.

To continue history: In the middle 1950s people like Wolpe, Salter, and Lazarus started some behavioral work. They saw that sexual dysfunctions were anxiety-related. They used systematic desensitization, and taught deep muscle relaxation. Patients would visualize sexual scenes and maintain relaxation. They would do the same at home, and there were some positive results. The method was moderately successful, but it did not have much impact on the field.

The real revolution, what I think of as "Modern Sex Therapy," came from Masters and Johnson, who published *Human Sexual Inadequacy* in 1970. Their work stressed two things. The first was the role of life experiences in terms of parental, religious, cultural, initial sexual experiences in terms of dating and so forth. The second was the self-maintaining vicious cycle mediated by anxiety, specifically performance anxiety, which was at the basis of many sexual dysfunctions. Performance anxiety would lead people to watch themselves rather than enjoy themselves. To get people out of the spectator role they developed some specific behavioral techniques. For premature ejaculation there was the pause and squeeze technique; for erectile failure, there was the stuffing the nonerect penis into the vagina to eliminate the performance anxiety cycle and so forth. The method was a combination of reducing anxiety plus particular sexual techniques.

Some of the behavior therapists got upset at Masters and Johnson, saying, "What they're doing is desensitization, just doing it in vivo at home rather than in the office with visualization and relaxation." That is not really a fair criticism because Masters and Johnson also taught skills rather than just reducing anxiety. There was a lot more to what they were doing than simple desensitization.

The next development was the cognitive-behavioral movement in psychotherapy, which stresses how people think about what is happening. Within sex therapy, that means looking at what are unrealistic expectations, self-image, distorted views of the opposite sex's needs and requirements, or tendencies to catastrophic thinking. Cognitive behavior therapy is now a mainstream part of sexual therapy. But initially these techniques were applied to treatment failures using Masters and Johnson methods. Reducing performance anxiety and teaching techniques of good sexual stimulation is not effective if the clients have unrealistic thoughts about themselves and their partner, and about what sex means. This is similar to telling a tense, depressed person, "Just relax and cheer up." For example, a woman might think she's not attractive because she doesn't look like models she sees in magazines. Therefore, she believes her husband can't really think of her as sexy. He might indeed have some thoughts that nice women aren't truly sexual. If you tell her it's okay to be sexy, and it's unrealistic to expect to look like a model, so she should use a vibrator on her clitoris and then her husband will do better with her, that isn't going to get you anywhere. Some cognitive work with the couple would be much more effective than simple sex therapy methods.

The next development is the LoPiccolo model, what I call, "Post-Modern Sex Therapy." Modern sex therapy really stressed anxiety reduction, cognitive therapy, and behavioral therapy. Now we must add a couple of other elements. There are essentially five categories of things needed for a functional analysis of both the original causes and the current maintaining causes of the dysfunction. To intervene as needed in a particular case, a therapist must customize treatment for each individual case. Automatic use of standardized protocols no longer is viable.

The first of the five elements is family of origin learning history. Sometimes this is relevant, sometimes it is not. What did they learn in the family of origin about sex, and what happened to them? This includes what they were told, and any incest-type experiences, ranging from "mild" forms of abuse to stories that, no matter how much armor I've developed over the years, make my skin crawl when I hear them. For example, I had a woman patient who was inorgasmic, and whose marriage was unconsummated due to her vaginismus. As a child, her father rubbed her back, stroked her, told her how much he loved her and how he wanted her to remain a virgin, so she could have a good husband, while he raped her anally so she would remain a virgin. He did this repeatedly, starting when she was about 12, and continuing until she finally ran away when she was 14 because she was tired of having to wear feminine pads all the time because she was bleeding from the anus. Now, is regular sex therapy going to be of much use to her? I think not. I cannot hear stories like that without getting very upset. Obviously, the family of origin therapy, and specific incest-survivor therapy, is going to be crucial in a case like this.

The second element of post modern therapy is systemic issues in the couple's relationship. Masters and Johnson, whose work is required reading for all who work with sexual dysfunction cases, screened all their couples and accepted for therapy only those with a happy marriage, who had circumscribed sexual problems. I see several hundred cases a year, and very few would pass that screening criteria. It is hard to find cases that only have an isolated sexual problem in the midst of an otherwise absolutely happy marriage. Sexual dysfunction is not just caused by the unhappy marriage. It is more complicated than that. The unhappy marriage is causing the sexual dysfunction, and the sexual dysfunction is causing the marriage to be unhappy. They both are cause and effect; they are intertwined with each other. It is a very rare case that I do not address both sexual and marital issues. I tell couples it is not even worthwhile trying to figure out which is cause and which is effect. There are cases, however, that I do turn down. There are some that it simply does not make any sense to try and do any sex work on. At one of the Erickson Foundation-sponsored conferences on sexuality and intimacy, John Gottman said there are cases he declines doing any marital work because it is clear that one of the partners, at least, wants to get their exit ticket punched. They want to be able to say, "I tried everything before the divorce, even went to marital therapy, and that didn't work." In these cases when the marriage is in such a shambles, it would be essentially a waste of time and money to try to do any sex work at all. But those cases are rare. Mostly, we're able to do sex and marital therapy at the same time.

The intrapsychic or cognitive issues are the third element that should be assessed. I don't mean intrapsychic in terms of psychoanalytic thinking. Recently I had one man, for example, who was told he was suffering from the classic Freudian "princess or prostitute syndrome." He was dividing women into one of those two categories, and he was told his current wife couldn't be both ways. He had selected her because he saw her as a princess, and he couldn't see her as sexual.

It was much more complicated than that. He had loved his first wife very dearly. He came home from a business trip, and his secretary walked into his office and burst into tears. She said she had been struggling during the last few days about whether or not to relate to him an incident she had seen, and finally decided she had no choice but to tell him.

She had come into the office Saturday to finish some work. He was due back to fly back home Sunday. The secretary came into his office and found my patient's then-wife and his business partner (and best friend) in the throes of intercourse on the couch in the office. The secretary couldn't deal with that and told him. A divorce resulted.

He was single for about two years and had met a very nice lady and married her. He loved her dearly, but didn't have any sexual desire for her. He could not see her as sexual because it was too scary to think that if he had sexual feelings toward her, that it would mean she was a sexual person and then maybe she would do something like his first wife did. Obviously, that situation was a real, cognitive issue we had to work with. And we did. The case was successfully treated. He did not divide women into princesses and prostitutes. It was much more complicated than that. It was a real cognitive issue of allowing himself to feel vulnerable to being sexual again with a woman, which meant she was a sexual person. We had to start from there.

The fourth element in the postmodern model might be called operant issues in the couple's day-to-day life environment. To put it in everyday language, it means dealing with reality. For example take a couple, both of whom are employed full time at jobs that are not just 9-to-5 jobs, but that are demanding jobs. They have three kids, each of whom is in various after-school clubs and activities and lessons. And they live and care for one of their aged, ill parents, who arguably should be living in some sort of supervised living environment rather than with them. When I inquired, as near as we could figure out, it had literally been weeks since they had so much as a moment for just the two of them alone when they were not exhausted nor saddled with responsibilities. Is there any real surprise that their sex life was basically a shambles?

We may wonder, of course, what things get prioritized in their lives, and why have things gotten to that point. And while that is a question worth asking, sometimes you simply need to help people try and find a way to get their sex life possible in the reality of things. Sometimes that can be very simple.

I had one couple, for example, where her inability to relax and get aroused was caused by her worry about the kids hearing or even coming into their bedroom and interrupting them. We used a very sophisticated intervention. We installed a lock for the bedroom door, and we bought a radio for their bedroom. We also got an intercom so that if there were a genuine emergency, the kids could buzz them. The intercom was set up in one direction, so the kids couldn't turn it on to be able to monitor their room without them knowing about it. We were able to deal with the reality and make an adjustment, such that we could do in therapy.

Finally, the fifth element is physiological or medical issues, since sex does involve both mind and body. We no longer ask, for some sexual difficulties, if the main problem is physiologic or psychologic because in some cases this is a nonquestion. There are almost *no* cases of male erectile problems that don't involve some degree of physiologic impairment. For some, it's a very small degree, but almost all cases have at least some degree of physiologic involvement. On the other hand, with premature ejaculation, there is *no* physiologic issue at all. No one has been able to show any physiologic abnormality of any sort in premature ejaculation, in even one single case.

I talked about this issue once with the late Helen Singer Kaplan, whose work I admired greatly. In her book (1974), in the section on premature ejaculation, there was a line about "evaluating medical causes." Because I had great respect for her, I asked, "What causes?" She answered, "Well, we don't know of any right now but I thought the week after the book was published somebody might finally find one, so I wanted to have that line there in case somebody did."

On the other hand, inhibited ejaculation — men with orgasm disorders

— may have a lot of organic involvement. Often, these men suffer from an undiagnosed neurologic disorder.

For women, it's the opposite. Virtually no women with orgasm problems have neurologic problems. Almost all female orgasm problems are psychological, not in terms of neurosis, but because of their response to life events, especially relationship issues. One of my female psychologist colleagues states it clearly: "If a woman can masturbate to orgasm easily and well but can't with her partner, it's really clear what the problem is, and it isn't her." The conflict isn't quite that simple, of course, because perhaps she is too inhibited to teach her partner, or it may be that he is not willing to listen and learn.

One of my patients brought me in a record I had never heard. The title was *I Wish I Was a Lesbian and Not a Hetero*. It is quite good. The woman talks about her heterosexuality, but complains that men are so horrible in terms of emotional relationships. She cannot imagine herself being in a sexual relationship with another woman, but she has had no luck at all emotionally with men. The patient brought in the record, but it was only partially related to her situation. Emotionally she did connect with her husband, but he was hopeless as a sexual partner for her. She could not teach him. He didn't seem to learn.

Sometimes it isn't funny. I had one case that presented the issue of whether or not a woman is normal if she cannot have orgasm during intercourse, which everybody in the sex therapy field says is not a requirement for sexual normality for women. If she can have an orgasm with her guy from him caressing her manually, or orally, or using a vibrator, and if she enjoys intercourse, there is no requirement that the two things happen at the same time. The research shows that about 50% of women have an orgasm during penile containment and 50% do not, and there are no personality or mental health correlates of having orgasm during intercourse or not. So we always just try and reassure people to go home and enjoy themselves. We tell them, "Don't wreck your sex life by trying to make the orgasm happen during intercourse. Enjoy it as it is."

I explained that to one couple, and the man said to me, "I've kept a logbook in my life. I had sex with more than 100 women before we got married, and my wife is the only one who didn't have orgasms during intercourse, so your numbers are wrong." He was a retired Navy officer and I said, "Let me guess. Since you were in the Navy, a good percentage of those ladies were port prostitutes?" He agreed. I said, "Well, just out of curiosity, how many weren't? Can you remember that?" He thought for a while and answered, "Well, other than my wife, three."

I didn't want to alienate him, but I said, "I can't myself say I've ever patronized a prostitute, but I've had several prostitutes as patients, and they have all told me exactly the same thing: They all tell me they never had an orgasm with a client in any way let alone during intercourse, but they always faked it because it meant return business or a good tip. I get the feeling you made it real clear to the gals you wanted them to have an orgasm during intercourse, and I suspect that your actual score is zero on this." He wasn't real happy with me telling him that, but this was an important reality for them to examine.

To summarize, then, there are five elements to address in postmodern sex therapy: Family of origin learning history, systemic issues in the couple's relationship, intra-psychic or cognitive issues, reality issues in daily life, and physiologic or medical issues.

In terms of medical issues, I might mention here the new oral medication for erectile failure: Viagra. In our practice, we have 50 or 60 men on Viagra. We had more than 100 men doing penile injections, and another 50 or 60 men using the vacuum pump to get erections. Virtually all these guys have shifted or are in the process of shifting to Viagra. The drug works on about 60 to 70% of men. I have done some work with Pfizer and do some teaching with physicians prescribing it, because of all the issues raised by the use of the drug. There were a little more than one million prescriptions written in July 1998 for Viagra. It has only been FDA-approved recently but the drug has received enormous popular press publicity, including national magazine cover story features. All sorts of marketing is being done, and our clinic has been swamped with calls.

Viagra is very useful, and it is clearly indicated in cases in which the man has any degree of physiologic/medical impairment of his erectile function. We also use it in sex therapy cases, to help alleviate performance anxiety in purely "psychogenic" cases of erectile failure. Some of these cases use the Viagra only a few times, at the start of the sex therapy. However, Viagra can also bring distressed couples to a crisis.

I saw a couple for initial evaluation of erectile failure, and she was looking very happy, and he was looking quite unhappy. She was a very nice looking young lady and very polite. I tried to draw him out and get him to say something, but I wasn't connecting with him at all. He finally asked me, "How many of those pills do I have to take?" I said, "As of today, they come in one strength: 50 mg. Some of our men take one, but most men take two. That seems to work quite a bit better." He cupped his two hands, making a bowl of them, and said, with her sitting there right next to him, "With her I could probably take this many pills without getting a hard-on!" She looked like she was either going to burst into tears, or jump out of the chair and run out of the room. My thought was, "Well, we obviously are not going to write a prescription for Viagra for them today." And now I knew exactly what sort of questions to start asking to explore what was really going on in the marriage. Sometimes the penis is saying something when it is not getting erections. And with him not getting the erection it was clearly saying, as his extremely hurtful remark vividly demonstrated, that the relationship basically was in a shambles. That was why he was not getting erections. When my urologist partner and I worked him up, there was nothing physiologically wrong with the man. He was really quite healthy. We send our patients home with a take home Rigiscan, which gives you a full night's recording of nocturnal penile tumescence. His penis was very diagnostic. Giving him Viagra would have been a real mistake, as this problem was purely relationship based.

What about men who are given the Viagra and it cures their erection problem, but they don't get their desire back? The causal relationship between lack of desire and lack of erection can be in either direction. That is, if a guy starts having erection problems, for most men, their desire disappears. After all, who wants to get into bed when you're likely to have another humiliating experience of being impotent? So, low desire develops as a result of erectile failure. But, on the other hand, there are men who have no desire. So when they get into bed, of course they don't get an erection because they don't want to be there in the first place. These men are attempting sex out of pressure from the wife, typically. We are now seeing cases in which the low drive/erectile failure man was able to avoid conflict with the wife by blaming his not wanting to make love on his "impotence." Now, with general practitioners writing prescriptions, when these men get the Viagra, it's "Oh, no. Now I've got that darn bottle of pills sitting there on the shelf, and my wife wants me to take those darn things." And that again will blow the relationship right out of the water.

Let me close by stating that Viagra represents one of what I see as the two major challenges facing the field of sex therapy — and perhaps the entire field of psychotherapy — at the current time. The first issue is the "medicalization" of what is an emotional/personal/ relationship as well as a medically based problem. Sexual functioning is the classic case of mind/body interaction, and simply having general practice physicians write prescriptions for medications to "cure" sexual problems, with no evaluation of the psychological functioning of the individual or the relationships involved, is producing problems that currently are making national headlines frequently.

The other problem facing our profession concerns the constraints placed upon our practices by "managed care." Most HMOs and other insurance plans have very short limits on the number of sessions for outpatient psychotherapy, and many plans will not pay for psychotherapy for sexual dysfunction diagnoses. It is very ironic that we are now in the position that when we at last have effective treatments for sexual dysfunction, our patients are to be denied access for financial reasons. Fortunately, with the aid of focused treatment, brief therapy can be very effective.

References

Ellis, H. (1910). *Studies in the psychology of sex*. Philadelphia: F. A. Davis.

Freud, S. (1905/1962). *Three essays on the theory of female sexuality*. New York: Avon.

Kaplan, H. S. (1974). *The new sex therapy*. New York: Brunner/Mazel.

Lazarus, A. A. (1965). The treatment of a sexually inadequate man. In L. P. Ullman & L. Krasner (Eds.), *Case studies in behavior modification* (pp. 223–240). New York: Holt.

LoPiccolo, J. (1992). Post-modern sex therapy for erectile failure. In R. C. Rosen & S. R. Leiblum (Eds.), *Erectile failure: Assessment and treatment* (pp. 171–197). New York: Guilford.

Masters, W. H., & Johnson, V. E. (1970). *Human sexual inadequacy*. Boston: Little-Brown.

Salter, A. (1949). *Conditioned reflex therapy*. New York: Creative Age.

Wolpe, J. (1958). *Psychotherapy by reciprocal inhibition*. Stanford, CA: Stanford University Press.

THE PERSON OF THE THERAPIST

24

The Experience of "Negative Otherness": How Shall We Treat Our Enemies?

Stephen Gilligan

Not too long ago, an American psychotherapist invited a Tibetan monk to his home for the weekend. During the visit, the therapist did what I guess one does when entertaining a Tibetan monk for the weekend — watch "The Exorcist," the movie in which the actress Linda Blair is possessed by a devil, who is then violently exorcised by a priest. Halfway through the movie, the therapist suddenly realized that Tibetans take their demons seriously — they have got a cartography of demonology more sophisticated than the psychiatrists' DSM-IV. He looked over at the monk, who was recoiling in horror at what he was seeing.

After the movie, the therapist expressed his apologies and hopes that the demon hadn't disturbed the monk too much. The monk replied that he wasn't disturbed by the demon, but rather liked him. The confused therapist pointed out that the monk had appeared to be upset, and that he was hiding his eyes. The monk again stated that he wasn't disturbed by the demon. "But why did you look upset?" asked the therapist.

"Oh, that," replied the monk. "I felt so bad for the priest because he so misunderstood the demon."

We all confront a lot of demons in the course of our lives. They may be the demons we call anger, depression, fear, or criticism. They may be the demons of addiction or compulsions, the demons of managed care or the patriarchal system, or the demons of social injustice. These demons may possess us, tell us we're worthless or no good, or induce us to sell our souls or prostitute ourselves.

Indeed, psychotherapy is, in large part, a conversation about our relationships to such enemies. These enemies embody what we might call "negative otherness." It is "otherness" in that it doesn't fit with our identity, ideals, values, hopes, or plans; it's negative in that it seems to want to negate our presence, our humanness, our integrity, our very lives. Without the presence of "negative others" — whether we think of them as internal states, behavioral patterns, external institutions, or other people or groups — we would have no basis for a psychotherapy conversation. So how we think about this negative otherness, how we understand our relationship to it, how we develop our responses to it, make a great deal of difference.

In long-ago times, the negative others were thought to be helpful. In *The Origin of Satan*, Elaine Pagels (1995) describes how the early Hebrew term for Satan meant "one who stands in the way of." It was thought that Satan was a great angel, a trusted servant of God who was sent down when God thought someone was on the wrong path. Satan was a bit of a trickster, a rascal who could engage you and get you out of your fixed ways so you could go back to where you belonged. This early Satan was not an enemy to be destroyed, but an honorable adversary who was there to help. It was only later that Satan was seen as outside the field of life, someone to be destroyed at any cost. I guess we should ask: Has this latter way of understanding Satan been helpful? Has it worked?

Also in earlier times, a struggle with a dragon appeared in many cultural myths. Again, the dragon was regarded as a presence that challenged you to grow up, to become a person, to learn how to negotiate crises skillfully. The dragon was not to be killed, but to be engaged in a way that would allow the transformation of both the person and the dragon. This was a dangerous undertaking, to be sure, for if one slipped, the results were catastrophic. But still, the relationship with the "negative other" of the dragon required not violence, but intelligence, courage, and self-transformation. It was only later, for example, in the Christian myth of St. George slaying the dragon, that the relationship shifted to violence and what Thomas Merton (1964) termed the "irreversibility of evil," — that is, the assumption that the enemy would never change, but would always stay in its state of "negative otherness" — an assumption that Merton described as the basis for the justification of violence.

Again I would ask, is the attitude of primarily opposing and destroying our enemies and their practices workable and helpful in the long run?

This is not a moot question, for the modern myth of the "negative other" — whether our enemies, or a symptom, or an out-of-control experience — as an inhuman "it" that requires violence to be changed lives deeply within us. It is a core assumption of the modernist era, one that has led to much suffering and injustice. But does it really change in postmodernism? It doesn't seem so. I would like to suggest that, in many ways, this "us versus them" or "self versus it" frame continues unabated in many postmodernist myths and practices. I further suggest that this metaphor is both unnecessary and unhelpful in many ways. What Deborah Tannen (1999) has called the "argument culture" can only lead to greater violence, less community, more suffering, and deeper hopelessness. But until we develop more effective ways of transforming conflict nonviolently, we will perpetuate and exacerbate suffering in the name of ending it once and for all.

It is easy to talk about honoring differences and multiple possibilities, but the real test comes in our relationship to our "enemies" — the people, institutions, experiences, and practices that seem to threaten our survival. For example, take a moment to think of some person, experience, system that you really can't stand. Maybe it's someone who hurt you. Maybe it's an unjust system, perhaps managed care. Maybe it's the ideology and practice of, say, racism. Maybe it's a part of you, some lazy presence within you that's stopping you from being an important person, some fearful presence that just doesn't understand your repeated pronouncements that there's nothing of which to be afraid.

It's not too hard to come up with examples, is it?

As you bring that "negative other" into your awareness, just notice what your internal response is. It could be many things: fear, anger, disgust, numbness. What fantasies do you entertain about engaging with negative others? Would you like to hurt them? Scream at them? Run from them? Teach them lessons they'll never forget? What do you do with those feelings, those fantasies, those thoughts, those reactions?

In traditional terms, we generally respond to an enemy or threat in one of two ways: We fight it or flee from it. To fight it, we try to dominate it, repress it, destroy it, demonize it, analyze it, numb it, dissociate it. In trying to flee from it, we check out, drug out, give up, feel anxious, become paralyzed, get depressed.

Neither of these response styles is very helpful in the long run. The negative other keeps attacking, the conflict keeps recurring, and our human presence keeps diminishing. Such is the legacy of the fight-or-flight response.

Postmodernism is, in a significant way, about more options, more possibilities, more truths, more perspectives. For the promise of postmodernism to be realized, we need to develop more practices and understandings about how to deal with conflicts and "negative otherness," within ourselves and between ourselves. Ghandi (in Merton, 1962) used to say that if the only alternative to passive submission to injustice were violence, he would recommend violence in virtually every case, for no one should have to endure oppression and injustice. But he suggested a third path of what he called *satyagraha* (or "the force of love"), which involved neither submission to nor violence against one's enemies, as a more helpful alternative.

In the martial art of aikido, this third way, this alternative to fight or flight, dominance or submission, is sometimes referred to as "flow." This is not a flow whereby whatever the other wants, the other gets. It's a flow that allows one to stay relationally connected during conflict, both with our adversaries and with ourselves, so that the conflict itself is a creative, nonviolent event that leads to new understandings, new conversations, and new realities.

I'm suggesting that this is one of the great challenges of psychotherapy, and one of the great contributions that therapy can make to our culture today: offering creative ways to transform conflictual relationships. We need to accept that conflict is natural, inevitable, and helpful to human progress, both individual and collective. This is not to say that you look for conflict or seek to provoke. On the contrary, our hope is that we can advance peace however and wherever possible, but that when conflict arises, we can accept it and work with it as an opportunity for real growth. Ther are various paths to accomplishing this.

One path is the practice of aikido, which can be roughly translated as "the path of resolving conflict by blending with energy." In aikido, you try to open your heart, mind, and soul to your attacker in ways that protect you and the attacker. The interest is in how to join the attacker's energy to transform it. It's a beautiful and challenging practice. For example, one of the major learnings is letting go of taking things so personally. My aikido teacher, Coryl Crane, is a fifth-degree black belt, and an inspiring person from whom to learn. One day in class, we had about eight big guys who were dealing with each other's attacks in the traditional aggressive American way, slamming each other around to teach lessons that would never be forgotten. Coryl knelt on the side of the mat, watching the spectacle unfold. At the end of class, as we bowed in front of the altar, she said, "I just want to mention one thing: A lot of you are taking this very personally. When people attack, you think they're attacking you. So you're either backing up or trying to oppose them."

"If you look at me," she said, "you can see that I wouldn't last two minutes with such an approach. So you just might consider that the attackers are not attacking you, they're just trying to get somewhere. And so, if you can get out of their way, then you can join them and help them to get to where they want to go, maybe lessening a little bit of the violence and agitation as you walk with them."

Is such an approach workable? Is it possible to work with violence and injustice without punishing people, without hurting them, without your getting hurt or being destroyed? Is it possible to open your heart, mind, and soul to negative otherness as a way to help both yourself and others? Of course, it is. We see examples of it everywhere — not only in famous lives, such as those of Martin Luther King, Nelson Mandela, Gandhi, or Jesus, but in the lives of countless lesser-known people. As the poet W. H. Auden wrote, love is the only rational response.

Our challenge, then, is to articulate what love looks like as a skill, as a vibrant practice not only of protecting life, but also of transforming it. It's an enormous challenge, to be sure, one made all the more difficult by our deeply held assumptions. The roots of modernist thinking run deep within our consciousness. Of the many possible ways of describing, defining, or deconstructing modernism, I would like to offer a single phrase to describe its core: *disembodied, isolated intellect.* The great accomplishment of modernism, for better and worse, was to separate the intellect from the present moment of the body, nature, and life itself. Once this separation was done, it was never undone. The mind was elevated to a supreme position of will and solitary intelligence: its task was to monitor, control, and dominate all that to which it related.

The hope was that if we could just think clearly and rationally enough, we could overcome the major problems of life. If we could just get the right idea, the proper text, the accurate theory, the clearest diagnosis, then we could control things. And if we could control and predict things, happiness would follow. Did it? Well, advances certainly were made in technology, in rational thinking, in materialistic comfort, in medicine, in the production of food. And extremely important differentiations were articulated between the fields of science, art, and religion, such that thinking and artistic expression were liberated from the dictates of the state.

But with these advances came certain pathologies. Modernism bred urbanism, a strange lifestyle in which concrete is poured over everything, people live within walls and cars all day, and we communicate primarily through machines. The disembodied intellect dictates a mind/nature split in which the body is objectified, the intellect is seen as the only valid intelligence, human life is primarily viewed in terms of utilitarian values (what's in it for me?), spirit and soul and heart–mind are denied, interconnectedness is rejected, nature is exploited, death is feared above all, materialism becomes a cult, relationships are seen in dominance–submission terms, ritual is ignored, and everything outside the self-identity is seen and feared as an "it." In short, the disembodied intellect leads to a disconnection and denial of the precious life of the present moment.

See how that feels after 30 years. Or 40 years. Or 450 years.

If we allow these disconnections and denials to continue unabated, postmodernism can easily deteriorate into what Charlene Spretnak (1997) has called "hypermodernism," or what Bruce Springsteen had in mind when he wrote the song, "57 Channels and There's Nothing On." It can become a practice of advanced consumerism and its main tool, television. More shallowness, more cynicism, more channels, more wasteland, more splintering into ever-growing factions without any common base. Less soulfulness, less mystery, less healing, less deep listening, less sitting still, less wisdom, less hope for peace and understanding. Granted, we're not sure what these words mean anymore, and we've almost forgotten how to use them poetically. But what I'm trying to point here is a postmodern practice of what psychologist Marion Woodman (1993) calls "embodied consciousness," a consciousness that is full of living energy, connected to the world and the present moment, filled with vitality, sensitive to shifting differences, discerning of subtle patterns, expressive of wondrous mystery. Embodied consciousness allows one to deal with differences creatively, without demonizing one's adversary or getting locked into fixed understandings or rigid positions. I am suggesting that without some conscious practices of embodied consciousness, the hopes and dreams of postmodernism will go down the tubes.

Embodied consciousness can be discussed in various different ways. I'd like to address two complementary aspects of it, the experience of a mind/body center and the experience of a relational field. It should be emphasized that these distinctions don't make that much sense in academic, literary, or intellectual contexts, which are the bases for most of the thinking and practice of psychotherapy and social change. They are distinctions that come from performance-art contexts, such as music, dance, oratory, and the martial arts.

The experience of a mind/body center is the experience of a nonintellectual intelligence and presence within one's self. It is a felt sense of dropping down under the words into a balanced, calm, aware connection with self and others. The experience of centering is described beautifully by the artist M. C. Richards (1962) in *Centering in Pottery, Poetry, and the Person*. The Chilean novelist Isabelle Allende (in Toms, 1994) has talked about how she writes primarily from her belly mind. When you hear great singers or speakers, you can sense immediately their connections to their centers, how they are expressing themselves from a deep connection.

The idea of a center is central to many cultures. Malidoma Some (1994), a member of the African Dagara tribe, describes in his autobiography how he was kidnapped by the French Jesuits in Africa when he was four years old. They tried to raise him to be a priest, but he escaped his captors in late adolescence and returned to his people. Some finally underwent his initiation rituals; he described the initial instructions given by the ritual elder as follows:

> Somehow what he said did not strange to me or — I found out later — to anyone. It was as if he were putting into words something we all knew, something we had never questioned and could never verbalize.
>
> What he said was this: the place where he was standing was the center. Each one of us possessed a center that he had grown away from after birth. To be born was to lose contact with our center and to grow from childhood to adulthood was to walk away from it. The center is both within and without. But we must real-

> ize it exists, find it, and be with it, for without the center we cannot tell who we are, where we come from, and where we are going.
>
> He explained that the purpose of Baor (the initiation process) was to find our center. This school specialized in repairing the wear and tear incurred in the course of 13 rainy seasons of life. I was 20. Had I been home all that time, I would have gone through this process seven years ago. I wondered if I was catching up too late but then thought, better late than never.
>
> No one's center is like someone else's. Find your own center, not the center of your neighbor; not the center of your father or mother or family or ancestor but that center which is yours and yours alone. (pp. 198-199)

The basic idea of a mind/body center is that there is a nonlinguistic presence within you that you can tune to, connect with, rest in, and receive from. It is not a linguistic distinction so much as a postlinguistic distinction, something that the poet Rilke (1981) perhaps had in mind when he said:

> It seems that things are more like me now,
> that I can see farther into paintings.
> I feel closer to what language cannot reach.

Dancers dance from their centers. Writers write from their centers. Political prisoners engage from their centers. I would hope that this skill would be available to the rest of us in our diverse situations.

In psychotherapy, this might be done in relation to the problem or complaint a client brings in. A complaint always involves a somatic component. That is, the problem always carries a disturbing feeling or lack of feeling somewhere in the body. Were this distress not there, I don't think most people would seek psychotherapy. They are not caught in a philosophical conundrum; they are experiencing suffering in their moment-to-moment life experience.

In our self-relations approach to therapy (Gilligan, 1997), we typically ask folks to notice, when they experience the problems, where they most feel the centers of disturbance in their bodies. Interestingly, most point to their hearts, solar plexus, or gut areas. Rather than regarding these as bad feelings that need to be removed, we become curious about listening to these felt centers of disturbances as ontological presences; that is, as the presence of another intelligence that is awakening in their lives. In other words, the onset of a symptom may be regarded as the awakening of a person's center. Therefore, we see problems and crises as positive events, as heralding the breakdown of the isolated intellect and the development of a more relational intelligence that is distributed throughout the mind/body.

For example, one of my clients was a man who said he was really depressed. He was 38 years old and had just gone through his second divorce. He was trying to start a new business, but wasn't into it. He was trying to date, but just wasn't into it. He was trying to connect with friends, but he just wasn't into it. He was very concerned because he couldn't get himself motivated to "get on with it." When I asked him what the problem was, he said "depression." When I asked where he felt the center of the depression feeling, he at first said that he felt nothing or had a big empty feeling. When I asked him to take some time to sense where he felt the center of the emptiness, he pointed to his solar plexus. When I asked him to listen to what that center of his experience was saying to him, he looked at me as though I were crazy. I asked him again, and he reported hearing a voice saying, "It's no use, nothing will ever work." I suggested that the voice that went with the felt sense in his belly perhaps spoke with a lot of integrity, and that it was worth listening to. The conversation continued to be organized around listening to the felt sense (Gendlin, 1978), and gradually its position of rejecting an old identity based on pleasing others emerged. In short, the depression in the belly transformed into a felt sense of acting with integrity, rather than following what his head identity had been conditioned to do.

In this view, the mind/body distress in a problem or complaint is indicative of the waking up of one's center. We welcome disturbances as signals of new life. But rather than trying to understand or interpret such disturbances from the head, we connect to and engage the language of the mind/body center. Through careful attentiveness, listening, and conversation, this center can be developed as a primary base for knowing and expressing identity.

Attending to a mind/body center has many other values as well. For example, it offers an important point for stabilizing attention, especially in stressful situations. In self-relations therapy, we ask the question: To whom or what or where do you give your first attention? First attention is like the cursor on the computer screen: you can move it around. For example, if a person is yelling at you, where do you focus: on the person yelling, on a memory from childhood that is activated by that yelling, on a theory or text that says that the person shouldn't yell? If it gets locked onto another person or an old memory, you become reactive rather than responsive; that other person or memory becomes the "higher power" that dictates your action. If it gets locked onto a text or theoretical model, you slip into ideology and fundamentalism, trying to force the world into your frame of reference. By letting your first attention gently drop and touch your center, whether it's in your heart or your belly, you can allow your attention to stabilize and still have the freedom to be flexible and responsive.

Mind/body centering is another way of talking about tuning into different types of intelligences. Centering in your heart yields a different type of thinking than does centering in your head. Centering in your belly tunes into a different brain, one that scientists are now calling the enteric nervous system, or brain in the stomach. The type of mental processing that comes from centering is quite different from just intellectual thinking. It tends to be more archetypal than personal, more intuitive than causal in its logic, more attuned to the present moment than to some grand theory about the ways things work.

Mind/body centering allows connection and responsiveness to other people, as well. It's what allows you to dance freely with a partner, not knowing what the next movement might be, but secure in knowing that you can find it in the moment. Centering allows you also to stay connected with yourself and a partner during conflict, so you can stay in tune with each moment. In aikido, we follow the relational principle of "heart to heart, mind to mind, center to center," which means that as you connect with your attacker in these ways, you can deal most effectively with protecting yourself and transforming the conflict. When you're just in your head, it's hard to stay connected to others, whoever they might be.

Mind/body centering also allows you to create a place or sanctuary for holding experiences. Without a place to go, experiences — like people — get a little agitated and crazy. The mind/body center can be used as a container in which any feeling, image, or presence can rest. It's sort of like when your six-year-old comes in with a skinned knee. She's crying as if there was no tomorrow. You allow her to climb into your lap, where your feeling is a container for hers. It allows her experience to play itself out.

In a similar way, we can ask, when you are visited by fear, anger, depression, or confusion, what you do with these visitors. One possibility is that you can give them place within your mind/body center. As you breathe, you can feel a sanctuary opening up in your belly, a safe place to which any experiential presence can come. Rather than having, say, a fear that permeates your body, you can let it rest in your sanctuary. You can then connect with it relationally, developing what Martin Buber (1923/1958) would call an "I–thou" relationship with it. This type of relationship is central to work in self-relations psychotherapy.

As you connect with your center, you also have a powerful place where you can move and extend your energies into the world. A center is a place in which to gather your strength, to focus your attention, to balance yourself. As you sink into it, your voice, your self, your presence are able to extend into the world. Again, this is obvious and inspiring in gifted performance artists: their energetic presence radiates into the world. We are all performance artists, of course. But when we lose connection with our centers, our expressions become less clear, less confident, less connected to life. By learning how to keep coming back and connecting with our centers, we can regain our power and keep it present in the land of the living.

This extension of the self into the world of the living leads us to the complement of the center, the relational field. The field is the larger space and context in which we live. When we feel connected to it and nurtured by it, we do all right. But when we lose connection to it, as when under stress, we tend to think and react in our isolated worlds with little effectiveness. The basic idea is that there is an intelligence greater than you. It's not about giving yourself, but about joining in an experience of communion with a wholeness deeper than your individual self. If you feel it and can listen to it, your capacity to act with effectiveness and integrity, especially in response to your enemies, is increased tremendously.

It's important to recognize that people know the experience of a relational field in different ways. You may know it through walking in the forest, and call it nature. You may know it by joining with others in social justice, and call it community. You may know it through athletic performance, and call it the zone. You may know it through prayer, and call it God. You may know it through an intimate relationship, and call it love.

There are many names for the field, but all involve an experience of being supported and guided by a deeper intelligence around you. If you want to find out how people know the field, ask them what they do to get back to themselves. For instance, you've worked all week and are really tired. What do you do to get back to yourself? Answers might include talking with friends, conscious breathing, going for a walk, meditating, playing or listening to music, knitting, reading, or gardening.

What happens when folks engage in such activities? For one thing, their intellectual self mellows out a bit. There's not so much chattering, controlling, agitating, conspiring, plotting. Second, people feel less of a need to control and more of a sense of relational connecting, curiosity, and quiet confidence. Third, if you ask people where their sense of self "ends" in such experiences — where their boundaries delineate self from non-self — most look puzzled by the questions, and then start moving their hands outward, saying, "It doesn't end. It is an expansive field that has no limit." The experience of this expansive, unitive feeling is what we call the field. Interestingly, as William James (1902/1982) and Aldous Huxley (1944) pointed out, this experience of unitive consciousness is a common element of so-called mystical experiences across many historical periods and many cultures.

It is one thing to know the field in positive circumstances, a place where you feel safe and accepted. Is it possible to stay connected and supported by the field under adversarial conditions? I think so. Although the general response to attack is to constrict your field, thus leaving you locked into a small space that is under the influence of negative otherness, you can train yourself to stay connected to both your center and the relational field even in difficult circumstances. When you stay connected to your center and the field, alienating, negative influences cannot take hold of you. What I'm saying is that connecting with a living field is about as good a technique for externalizing alien presences as you can find.

To me, a great example is Nelson Mandela. Reading his autobiography (Mandela, 1994) or watching him on television dancing at a political gathering, one cannot help but wonder what it is that he is connected to that allows him such grace and strength, such a lack of bitterness, throughout what he calls "the long walk to freedom." I would suggest that he is a beautiful example of somebody connected to the soulfulness of his center and to the depth and breadth of the larger field of life.

In aikido, we describe this connection with the maxim, "Drop into center, open into field." That is, when you're in a stressful situation, don't fixate on the stressor. Don't give first attention to the problem. Instead, drop down into your mind/body center as a base from which to listen, perceive, relax, and respond, and expand your awareness outward to connect with a field awareness that is bigger than the stressful event. Now your attention is not entrapped by the stressor; it's free to receive and give beyond the confines of the situation. This allows you to respond to conflict not in a dominant–submissive way, in which someone wins and someone loses, but in a relational way that protects both you and your attacker, and seeks to bring a resolution of whatever differences or agitation is present.

It's a simple but difficult challenge, something that T. S. Eliot called "a condition of complete simplicity costing not less than everything." Sometimes people say, "You're asking a lot." My response is: "What else are you doing? And what are the alternatives?"

What I've been suggesting so far is that throughout our lives, we will be confronted with "negative otherness," with what we perceive to be enemies. Negative otherness comes in all shapes and sizes, and has many names. It can be internal experiences, such as fear or anger, that grip us; addictive behaviors that overtake us; oppressive systems that try to dominate us; old memories that try to possess us; angry people who try to control us; or fixed ideas that try to seduce us. If you are alive, these experiences will continue to visit you. The question is: How will you respond to these negative others?

You can capitulate to them, you can try to oppose directly and eradicate them, or you can engage them relationally as opportunities for mutual growth. If we choose the third path, we need to overcome the modernist tradition of the disembodied intellect. We need to find ways to reconnect with a mind/body center and the relational field that surrounds us. By embodying consciousness and situating it in a larger relational field, we can become more attentive, more effective, more loving, and more skillful. We can find ways to work creatively and nonviolently with conflict, so that more connection to life and love may be made possible for all involved.

There are many examples of how this can be done. For example, Zen Roshi Bernie Glassman is one of the leading figures in what is called socially engaged Buddhism, an American movement that tries to intregrate Buddhist mindfulness training with social change. Glassman, a self-described Zen entrepreneur, owns a number of businesses, including a large bakery, that are run and managed by homeless and ex-homeless people in New York. He has established a multifaceted social service agency in Yonkers, N.Y., called the Greyston mandala.

Glassman (1999) has also developed a community called the Peacemaking Order, which has three basic tenets. The first is not knowing — being in the state of not knowing, letting go of fixed ideas. The second is bearing witness — totally immersing one's self in the situations in which one is involved. The third is "healing one's self and others" using the materials that result from bearing witness.

To apply these tenets, Glassman (1999) recommends entering into situations that you fear, situations in which you think it would be great if healing could happen. For example, Glassman and his students have sat for days at a time with homeless people on the streets of New York City, who then join the community, guided by the three tenets of opening up into not knowing, bearing witness, and healing one's self and others. On the basis of their experiences, they then initiate further action. For Glassman's businesses employing the homeless came out of the sittings with them.

Another project involved sitting in the Auschwitz concentration camp for a week or so, a gathering in which numerous people participated: Jews, Germans, Poles, Catholics. The experiences and subsequent action that came from sitting in a not-knowing mindfulness state in the middle of the concentration camp were quite extraordinary.

We as therapists need to continue to cultivate a similar openness as we sit with our clients, bearing witness in a not-knowing state to their homelessness, their Auschwitzes, their unnamed, unwitnessed experiences. This cannot be done via the disembodied intellect. By "dropping into center, opening into field," our capacity not only to tolerate but to help heal ourselves and others is greatly increased.

In connecting to center and to field, perhaps one of the best outcomes is that our awareness returns to the value of stillness and silence. Modernism is in no small part an emphasis on a linguistic universe, where talking and thinking and action, the yang of the universe, are given total priority. The ying principle of empty space, listening, receiving, and silence is ignored and marginalized.

I know that in some quarters it is heresy to suggest that something beyond linguistic construction exists, but isn't it obvious when you hold a baby or a dying person, anytime you connect in love or in wondrous amazement? Some deep presence, an extraordinary intelligence, lives in the gap between the words, the space between the notes, the silence in the conversation. We lost that connection in the language-dominated, yang-based world of modernism. In this regard, I hope that the postmodern world can become a postlinguistic one, where we use language to go beyond language, to what T. S. Eliot has called "a further union, a deeper communion" with ourselves and others. This is where the experiences of mind/body centering and relational field can help.

The Chilean poet Pablo Neruda said it this way in his poem entitled "Keeping Quiet":

> Now we will count to twelve
> and we will all keep still
> For once on the face of the
> earth, let's not speak in any language;
> let's stop for a second,
> and not move our arms so much.
>
> It would be an exotic moment
> without rush, without engines;
> we would all be together
> in a sudden strangeness.
>
> Fisherman in the cold sea
> would not harm whales
> and the man gathering salt
> would not look at his hurt hands.
>
> Those who prepare green wars,
> wars with gas, wars with fire,
> victories with no survivors,
> would put on clean clothes
> and walk about with their brothers
> in the shade, doing nothing.
>
> What I want should not be confused
> with total inactivity.
> Life is what it is about. . . .

If we were not so single-minded
about keeping our lives moving
and for once could do nothing,
perhaps a huge silence
might interrupt this sadness
of never understanding ourselves
and of threatening ourselves with
death.

Perhaps the earth can teach us
as when everything seems dead in winter
and later proves to be alive.

Now I'll count up to twelve
and you keep quiet and I will go.

References

Buber, M. (1923/1958). *I and thou* (R. G. Smith, trans.). New York: Scribner & Sons.

Gendlin, E. (1978). *Focusing*. New York: Bantam.

Gilligan, S. (1997). *The courage to love: Principles and practices of self-relations psychotherapy*. New York: Norton.

Glassman, B. (1999). *Bearing witness: A Zen master's lessons in making peace*. New York: Harmony Books.

Huxley, A. (1944). *The perennial philosophy*. New York: Harper & Row.

James, W. (1902/1982). *The varieties of religious experience*. London: Penguin Books.

Mandela, N. (1994). *The long walk to freedom*. London: Little, Brown.

Merton, T. (Ed.). (1962). *Gandhi on non-violence: A selection from the writings of Mahatma Gandhi*. New York: New Directions.

Neruda, P. (1969). Keeping quiet. In *Extravagaria* (A. Reid, trans.). London: Farrar, Straus & Giroux.

Pagels, E. (1995). *The origin of Satan*. New York: Vintage.

Richards, M. C. (1962). *Centering in pottery, poetry, and the person*. Middletown, CT: Wesleyan University Press.

Rilke, R. (1981). Moving forward. In R. Bly (Ed. & trans.), *Selected poems of Rainer Maria Rilke*. New York: Harper & Row.

Some, M. (1994). *Of water and spirit: Ritual, magic, and initiation in the life of an African shaman*. New York: Tarcher.

Spretnak, C. (1997). *The resurgence of the real: Body, nature, and place in a hypermodern world.* Reading, MA: Addison-Wesley.

Tannen, D. (1999). *The argument culture: Stopping America's war of words.* New York: Ballantine.

Toms, M. (1994). Writing from the belly: An interview with Isabel Allende. *Common Boundary, 12*(3), 16–23.

Woodman, M. (1993). *Conscious femininity: Interviews with Marion Woodman.* Toronto: Inner City Books.

25

The Last Session in Brief Therapy: Why and How to Say When

Michael F. Hoyt

"So teach us to number our days
that we may get us a heart of wisdom."
— *Moses (Psalm 90: 12)*

"Whoever loves, if he does not propose
The right true end of love, he's one that goes
To sea for nothing but to make him sick."
— *John Donne (1633) "Love's Progress"*

"It ain't over 'til it's over."
— *Yogi Berra* (Pepe, 1988)

Betwixt epigraphers times three lies the realm of termination.

Having previously written at length about the problems of a proper beginning (Budman, Hoyt, & Friedman, 1992), I want here to discuss some aspects of a proper ending of treatment. Finishing well both completes and perpetuates the good work that has preceded it. While we can recognize that termination in some ways may be a pseudo-event in that the work continues and formal treatment can be resumed intermittently (Bennett, 1983, 1984; Budman, 1990; Hoyt, 1990/1995; Cummings, 1990; Cummings & Sayama, 1995), it is important to end sessions and a course of therapy well. Done skillfully, we increase the likelihood that while the therapy may be brief, the benefit may be long term.[1]

Termination simply means "extracting the therapist from the equation of the successful relationship" (Gustafson, 1986, p. 279). In effect, we ask, and attempt to answer the question, session by session and therapy by therapy: "You have done well with me; how will you continue to do well without me?" My intention here is to provide a number of perspectives, drawing upon both my personal experience and the literature, that address the issues of *why* and *how* to say "*when.*"

WHY STOP?

Knowing that therapy will stop provides structure and direction. It focuses the mind. It shows respect for client autonomy and competence (and his or her checkbook), and conveys the existential implication to "get on with it" — that therapy, like life, does not involve an endless proliferation of time (Goldberg, 1975; Hoyt, 1990/1995).[2] As Nick Cummings has put it, our contract with patients should be to be available as long as they truly need us, and their contract should be to make us obsolete as soon as possible (Cummings & Sayama, 1995). Therapy can be brief by *design* or by *default* (Budman & Gurman, 1988, pp. 6–9); this is what Bloom (1992, p. 3) meant by *planned*: "treatment that is intended to accomplish a set of therapeutic objectives within a sharply limited time

---

[1] As Strupp and Binder (1984, p. 259) have noted, young therapists in particular may be insufficiently aware of the critical importance of termination for a number of reasons: it receives inadequate attention in many training programs; young therapists entering the profession may have been spared the personal experiences of separation and loss; and many therapies conducted by graduate students or residents are often ended not for clinical reasons, but because of service rotations or the end of a semester or academic year. It is not only beginning therapists, however, who may underestimate the importance of finishing well.

[2] Failure to accept endings can have far-reaching effects, as writers of various theoretical persuasions have noted (e.g., Mann, 1973; Tobin, 1976; Vorkoper, 1997). One can be left like the character eloquently described in Robert Hellenga's novel *The Sixteen Pleasures* (1995, p. 267): "He is in the same boat, drifting down the same river, but he has turned around. The boat is still travelling in the same direction, but instead of standing on the bow, looking straight ahead to see where he is going, he is standing in the stern, looking back at where he's been, and this is where he will remain for the rest of the journey."

frame." Unless is it forever, it will end — the pertinent questions then become *when?* and *how?* Talking ourselves out of a job should be our intention.

At times, patients sometimes can become "prisoners of psychotherapy" (Minsky, 1987), especially if the therapist is adept at theory-driven one-upsmanship (see Haley, 1969; Duncan, Hubble, & Miller, 1997) and insistently views the client's attempts to terminate a nonproductive treatment as "premature" (see Hoyt, 1993, 1994a). There are a number of "resistances" that therapists may have to "brief" therapy with its ever-present implication of ending, including the belief that "more is better," the confusion of therapists' interests with patients' interests, the temptation to hold on to that which is profitable and dependable, the need to be needed and difficulties with saying goodbye, resentment of externally imposed limits, and the avoidance of the paperwork involved in closing cases and opening new ones (Hoyt, 1985/1995, 1987). With apologies to Paul Simon (1975), we might sing (or hum, for the exhibitionistically challenged):

"Fifty Ways Not to Leave Your Client"

You just insist they come back, Jack,
Make a new treatment plan, Stan.
Avoid the topic of ending — be coy, Roy.
Tell them they're not ready, Freddie.
If they try to cancel, make a big fuss, Gus.
They still need to discuss much
Before they can leave, Steve.
("How could you do this to me?")
And don't forget your fee, Lee.

However, while we want to avoid fostering needless dependency, the goal is not just to be "brief" or "quick." Some clients need, and will benefit from, more extended or longer-term approaches, and many of the skills of brief therapy may be applicable (e.g., see Duncan, Hubble, & Miller, 1997; Kreider, 1998; O'Hanlon, 1990; Yapko, 1990). Indeed, it may be more accurate, following Budman and Gurman (1988) and Friedman (1997), to use the terms "time-sensitive" or "time-effective" rather than "brief." Therapy should not be "long" or "short." It should be sufficient, adequate, and appropriate: "measured not by its brevity or length, but whether it is efficient and effective in aiding people with their complaints or whether it wastes time" (Fisch, Weakland, & Segal, 1982, p. 156). Effectiveness "depends far less on the hours you put in than on what you put into those hours" (Lazarus, 1997, p. 6). The approach is characterized more by an attitude than by a particular length: "as few sessions as possible, not even one more than is necessary" is the way Steve de Shazer (1991, p. x) describes it. By its very nature, in brief therapy the issue of termination is always present. We need to "seize the moment" and "be here now." Time is of the essence. When we're thinking *brief*, "termination is our frame" (Goldfield, 1998, p. 243).[3]

I should note that while I use the term for continuity with the literature, I find the word "termination" somewhat troubling. Derived from the Latin *terminus*, meaning "an end, limit, or final goal," it seems so heavy and ominous, conjuring up images of Arnold Schwarznegger in *The Terminator* or, more darkly, of Final Solutions. We sometimes say that we are going to "terminate a case" or, even worse, "terminate a patient." What a different prospect, how more encouraging and respectful, if we speak of the ending phase as *completion* or *graduation* or *achievement*, or even simply as *stopping meeting*.[4]

The answer to the question of why we should stop also involves the issue of how best to use limited community resources, which one colleague, Carol Austad (1996), has highlighted in the provocative title of her book, *Is Long-Term Psychotherapy Unethical? Toward a Social Ethic in an Era of Managed Care*. While the terms *brief therapy* and *managed care* need

---

[3] Writing within the context of possible single-session therapies, Rosenbaum (in Hoyt, Rosenbaum, & Talmon, 1992, p. 80) emphasizes present-centeredness: "My desire is not to see everyone for one session; my desire is to see everyone for one full moment, as long as that takes." Gary Snyder (1980, p. 109) also reminds us not to hurry past the moment: "During the first year or two that I was at Daitoku-ji Sodo, out back working in the garden, helping put in a little firewood, or firing up the bath, I noticed a number of little improvements that could be made. Ultimately, I ventured to suggest to the head monks some labor- and time-saving techniques. They were tolerant of me for a while. Finally, one of them took me aside and said, 'We don't want to do things any better or any faster, because that's not the point — the point is that you live the whole life. If we speed up the work in the garden, you'll just have to spend that much more time sitting in the zendo, and your legs will hurt more.' It's all one meditation. The importance is in the right balance, and not how to save time in one place or another. I've turned that insight over and over ever since."

[4] Following Epston and White (1990, pp. 14–16), we can extend this deconstructive thrust to see the "termination as loss" metaphor as situated within a certain modern Western tradition that expects us to engage in "therapies of isolation" that encourage "relinquishing" and "letting go" as hallmarks of "individualism" and "mature separation." A different, "Hullo, again" approach, emphasizing a "reincorporation" metaphor and "therapies of inclusion" may be more useful and more natural in the resolution of grief (see Hoyt, 1983; White, 1988).

to be kept clearly distinct, I am in strong agreement with the need for greater efficacy and accountability (see Hoyt, 1995a; Hoyt & Friedman, 1998).[5] We need to be especially careful not to become overly enamored with the God of Efficiency, however — one only need read the section on devotion to efficiency in James Hillman's (1995, pp. 33–44) *Kinds of Power: A Guide to Its Intelligent Uses* to see where blind obedience to the calculated bottom line can take us.

LITERATURE ROUNDUP

Here are a few of the authors whose writings have contributed to my understanding of the process we call *termination.*

Sigmund Freud, known as the father of psychoanalysis, in some ways can also be thought of as a progenitor of brief therapy. His early cases (Breuer & Freud, 1893–1895/1955) ranged from a single session to several sessions to a few months, and his early techniques involved the frequent use of hypnosis, suggestion, directives, guidance, reassurance, and education — as well as interpretation (see Freud, 1910/1957, p. 111). Near the end of his career, he described analysis as "interminable" (Freud, 1937/1964). In his famous case of the "Wolf Man," Freud (1918/1953) introduced the idea of setting a termination date, a time past which doctor-patient contacts would not continue, as a way of both stimulating the patient's work and of extricating himself from what seemed to be an interminable therapeutic quagmire — a technique which Freud (1937/ 1964, p. 218) described as a "blackmailing device" that was likely, but without guarantee, "to be effective provided that one hits the right time for it."[6]

---

[5] "Managed care" is still largely a code word for "cost containment" (sometimes with attendant practices of "invisible rationing" requiring premature or inappropriate termination resulting in systematic undertreatment and possible patient abandonment — see Miller, 1996a, 1996b; Stern, 1993; Hoyt, 2000). De Shazer (quoted in Short, 1997, p. 18) has made his position clear: "We are *not* a response to managed care. We've been doing brief therapy for 30 years. We developed this a long time before managed care was even somebody's bad idea."

[6] For a report of a time that didn't seem "right," see Hoyt and Farrell (1983–1984). A number of brief-therapy advocates (e.g., O'Hanlon, 1991; Lipchik, 1994; Nylund & Corsiglia, 1994) have written against the use of rigid time limits as a method of "forcing" or curtailing treatment. Others, especially those attempting to adapt psychodynamic methods to briefer time frames (e.g., Appelbaum, 1975; Hoyt, 1979/1995, 1980; in press; Levenson, 1995; Malan, 1976; Mann, 1973), have found such methods useful — with carefully selected patients. In this regard, Strupp and Binder (1984, pp. 265–266) wisely caution "that the time limits be set *after* a therapeutic focus has at least begun to be outlined by the participants, because the introduction of a focus is more likely to provide the patient with a belief that there are circumscribed goals that can be achieved in the available time."

Franz Alexander and *Thomas French*, in their book *Psychoanalytic Therapy: Principles and Applications* (1946), described many groundbreaking innovations, including varying the therapist's demeanor with different types of patients to help generate what they termed "corrective emotional experiences," the application of a learning model and a call for new theoretical perspectives, alterations in the frequency of sessions and the use of interruptions in treatment to prepare for termination, and the limiting of therapy to deliberately brief contacts in selected cases. In Alexander's (1965) last significant paper, he reviewed these developments and commented:

> Very long treatments lasting over many years do not seem to be the most successful ones. On the other hand, many so-called "transference cures" after very brief contact have been observed to be lasting. . . . If one starts out treatment by saying to the patient that one can forget about time — that is the wrong emphasis. You encourage procrastination by this. Instead, one should say that we wish to complete treatment as fast as possible. Of course, we are not magicians, but our intention is to make therapy as brief as we can. It may last longer than we hope, but at least we make an attempt at shortening treatment. (pp. 90–91)

Lewis Wolberg (1965, p. 140), in *Short-Term Psychotherapy*, the first book published in North America on the subject (almost four decades ago), recommended:

> The best strategy, in my opinion, is to assume that every patient, irrespective of diagnosis, will respond to short-term treatment unless he proves himself refractory to it. If the therapist approaches each patient with the idea of doing as much as he can for him, within the space of, say, up to twenty treatment sessions, he will give the patient an opportunity to take advantage of short-term treatment to the limit of his potential. If this fails, he can always then resort to prolonged therapy.[7]

---

[7] Thirty years later, the well-known psychoanalyst Michael Franz Basch (1995) echoed this view in his last book, *Doing Brief Psychotherapy*:

> During the training of the dynamic psychotherapist, the idea becomes firmly imprinted that longer is better. Experience has taught me, however, that shorter is anything but second-best. In a majority of cases, short-term treatment, effectively applied, enables the

James Mann (1973), writing from an existential–analytic perspective in his book *Time-Limited Psychotherapy*, says:

> It is absolutely incumbent upon the therapist to deal directly with the reaction to termination in all its painful aspects and affects if he expects to help the patient come to some vividly effective understanding of the now inappropriate nature of his early unconscious conflict. ... Since anger, rage, guilt, and their accompaniments of frustration and fear are the potent factors that prevent positive internalization [of the therapist] and mature separation, it is these that must not be overlooked in this phase of the time-limited therapy. (p. 36)

Carl Whitaker (1987), whose family-therapy approach is sometimes called symbolic–experiential, emphasized the power of the moment. In his paper at the First Evolution of Psychotherapy Conference, he said:

> It is important to maintain the therapist's conviction that each appointment is both the first interview and the last interview. The first interview is, in essence, a blind date; and every subsequent interview opens the possibility of divorce or at least the separation between the family as foster child and the therapist as foster parent. (p. 81)

In *Midnight Musings of a Family Therapist*, Whitaker (1989) elaborated:

> The ending phase is a process in which the family's participation is subtle and critical. Their message may be, "Enough already," "Things are better," "Things are worse"; or the exposure of outside transferences with or without the stories: that is, "I almost forgot to come," "My job is going better," "My boss is a wonderful guy," "I'm falling in love with my wife." Essentially, they are saying that life is more important than psychotherapy.

---

patient to reach the same therapeutic goals as long-term psychotherapy, while offering the added advantage of relieving the patient's psychic stress that much sooner. Moreover, I believe that one cannot decide arbitrarily, on the basis of either symptoms or character structure, that a patient will not benefit from brief therapy. Indeed, it is my position that all patients who are not psychotic or suicidal should be thought of as candidates for brief psychotherapy until proven otherwise. (p. xi)

> The distortions that can occur during the ending phase include the family members' offer of new symptoms, their denial of change, the bribe of their fear of anxiety returning, a symbolic dropout. . . . , the presentation of a pseudo-symptom, a symptom in the therapist, the discovery or the presence of concealed hostility in the therapist or the family, the lack of humility in the therapist, or the pride of the therapist in being humble. When ending is successful, there evolves the arrangement for a future alliance (if needed), a discussion of the lining of the therapist's empty nest, his request for direct therapeutic help from the family members, his learning from their case and the sharing of his real-life fragments in terms of persons, his work, new cases, the money, and his inner video replay of their joint experience together. Finally, ending includes the therapist's dream of greatness and his dream of craziness, and his sharing with them of Plato's famous summary of the *Dialogues*, "Practice Dying." (p. 166)

Aaron Beck and his associates (Beck, Rush, Shaw, & Emery, 1979), in their book *Cognitive Therapy of Depression*, made their view clear:

> Because cognitive therapy is time-limited, the problems associated with termination are usually not as complex as those associated with longer forms of treatment. . . . The issue of termination should be touched on periodically throughout therapy. From the beginning the therapist stresses to the patient that he will *not* stay in treatment indefinitely, and that he will be shown how to handle his psychological problems on his own. . . . This sets the stage for the patient's becoming his own therapist. (p. 317)[8]

Bob and *Mary Goulding*, in their book *Changing Lives Through Redecision Therapy* (1979), highlight the importance of establishing a good change contract at the beginning of treatment (and sessions), often asking: "What are you willing to change today?" In discussing termination, the Gouldings expressed their views as follows:

---

[8] In *Nurturing Independent Learners*, Meichenbaum and Biemiller (1998) discuss many pedagogical strategies, with clear implications for therapists, for promoting acquisition, consolidation, and transfer of metacognitive development.

> Redecision is a beginning rather than an ending. After redecision, the person begins to think, feel and behave in new ways. At this point he may decide to terminate therapy. We applaud this choice. Our philosophy of treatment is that therapy should be as condensed and quick as possible and that termination is a triumph, like graduation. . . . Whatever the treatment format, we believe that the client should be encouraged to terminate when he has made the personal changes he wants to make, and should be welcomed back if he encounters difficulties he doesn't know how to solve on his own. This minimizes dependency and transference problems. (pp. 280–281)

Jay Haley, in his book *Problem-Solving Therapy* (1976), came right to the point:

> If therapy is to end properly, it must begin properly — by negotiating a solvable problem and discovering the social situation that makes the problem necessary. (p. 9)

Milton H. Erickson (1980) also emphasized the strategic importance of defining achievable goals:

> Long experience in psychotherapy has disclosed the wisdom of avoiding perfectionistic drives and wishes on the part of patients and of motivating them for the comfortable achievement of lesser goals. This then ensures not only the lesser goal but makes more possible the easy output of effort that can lead to a greater goal. Of even more importance is that the greater accomplishment then becomes more satisfyingly the patient's own rather than a matter of obedience to the therapist. (Volume 4, p. 190)

Richard Fisch, *John Weakland*, and *Lynn Segal* (1982), chief proponents (along with Paul Watzlawick) of the MRI strategic–interactional approach, put their termination criteria like this in their book *The Tactics of Change*:

> The therapist wishing to work briefly. . . . will be keeping the original complaint and the goal of treatment in mind, and will be looking for the attainment of that goal and for some expression by

> the client that his complaint has been resolved. The suggestion for terminating will most often be made by the therapist, usually with the expectation that the client will agree. Obviously, the client can also initiate termination for various reasons. Preferably, the client may propose that his problem has been resolved, and, in that case, the therapist is likely to agree to termination. But the converse can occur, the client expressing significant dissatisfaction with treatment and announcing that he is discontinuing the therapy. Or contingencies can arise that prevent the continuation of treatment: the client may have a job change that requires moving from the area, or financial problems may preclude further private therapy. Finally, time-limited treatment will automatically terminate when the agreed-upon number of sessions have run their course, although here the therapist will usually be the one to remind the client that such is the case. (pp. 176–177)

Steve de Shazer (1985, 1988), the prime developer of solution-focused therapy, has also emphasized the importance of establishing clear (relevant, measurable, difficult but achievable) goals at the outset of therapy. In his elegantly minimalistic way, he might ask the client, "How will we know when we can stop meeting like this?"

Insoo Kim Berg (1994), de Shazer's solution-focused collaborator, has elaborated some criteria and methods for termination, including goal achievement, designating a limited number of sessions, no movement in a case, and leaving things open-ended in response to outside restrictions. In her book *Family Based Services: A Solution-Focused Approach*, Berg wrote:

> Life is full of problems to be solved and your clients are no different from anyone else. If you wait until *all* the client's problems are solved, you will never end treatment. ... What is important to keep in mind is that "empowering" clients means equipping them with the tools to solve their own problems as far as possible. When they can't do it on their own, they need to know when to ask for help and where to go for help. Termination can occur when you are confident that the client will know when and where to go to seek help, and *not* when you are confident that he will never have problems. (p. 163)

Michael White, the co-author of *Narrative Means to Therapeutic Ends*, (White & Epston, 1990; also see Epston & White, 1990) responded as follows (White, 1995) when an interviewer asked him, "How do you define the point where therapy is finished?"

> The therapist becomes increasingly decentralised in the whole process, and eventually s/he is discharged from the therapy. The discharge of the therapist generally doesn't take long to happen, and it is rarely much of a surprise when it does happen. Although the therapist has played a very significant part. . . . s/he has also worked to ensure that those persons who seek help are the privileged co-authors in this collaboration. So, as persons go some way in the articulation and the experience of other ways of being and thinking that are available to them, as they experience some of the purposes, values, beliefs, commitments, and so on, that are associated with these alternative accounts of life, they approach a point at which the therapist's contribution is unnecessary. It makes perfect sense to discharge the therapist at this point, and this can be celebrated. (p. 20)

BUT NOT TOO FAST

While time is of the essence in brief therapy, we have to be mindful — especially with managed care providing a strong push for rapid turnover — that the quest for efficient goal attainment does not become a juggernaut toward termination. "Making the most of each session" may involve a pleasant urgency, but should not feel frantic or pell-mell. Too fast is too fast. Clients need adequate time to become involved, to get their bearings and set their direction. As James Broughton (1990, p. 212) wrote at the beginning of his poem, "Ways of Getting There":

> What makes you think
> you know your way around?
> You add the mileage
> but subtract the scenery.

There is a vital dialectic, a tension between opening and closing, between discovery and direction (see Hoyt, White, & Zimmerman, 2001).

While it's true, as they say in golf, that "If you don't know where the hole is, it's a long day on the course" (see Hoyt, 1996b), it's also true that too narrow a focus cuts us off from creativity and flexibility, from the unpredictable and fortuitous, from the serendipitous events that often occur within the therapeutic relationship. As narrative therapist Michael White has said (quoted in Hoyt & Combs, 1996):

> There is a certain pleasure or joy available to us in the knowledge that we can't know where we'll be at the end; in the sense that we can't know beforehand what we will be thinking at the end; in the idea that we can't know what new possibilities for action in the world might be available to us at that time. . . . If I knew where we would be at the end of the session, I don't think I would do this work. (p. 41)

Brief therapists want to "get right to it" and expect to "terminate" as soon as they do, but they should not be in such a rush as to miss the point of Broughton's closing poetic admonition:

> Why not for once
> wander off a path
> without caring how
> long it takes?
> You might bump into
> Time's older brother
> the one who never needs
> to go anywhere.

THE STRUCTURE OF (BRIEF) THERAPY

In other publications (e.g., Hoyt, 1990/1995; Hoyt & Miller, 2000), I have suggested that therapy (and sessions) can be conceptualized as having a structure of sequenced (epigenetic or pyramidal) phases, involving different tasks and skills, as shown in Figure 1. (The structure of therapy and session are the same when treatment comprises a single meeting.) Change may begin before the first meeting and, especially with skillful facilitation during the termination phases, may continue past the formal ending of treatment.

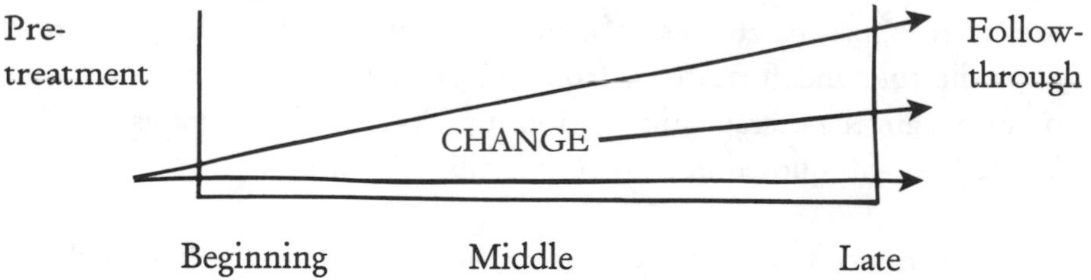

Figure 1: The structure of brief therapy (and each session).

Let's take a closer look (Figure 2) at some of the activities that may be involved in the ending phases of treatment (and sessions).

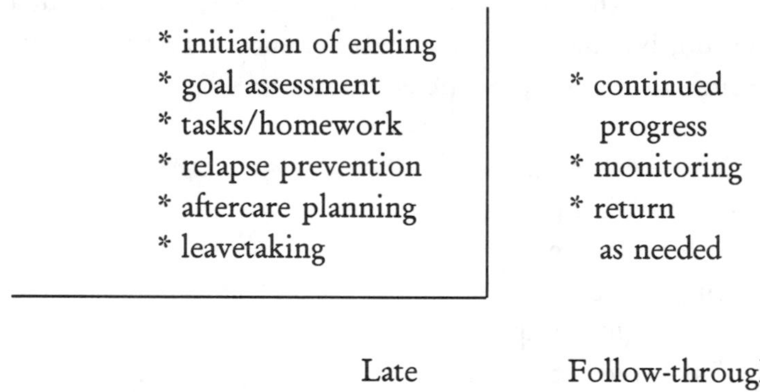

Figure 2: The ending (termination) phases of treatment (and sessions): Subtracting the therapist from the successful equation.

In the *late* phase of a course of therapy (and at the close of each session), there are a number of activities to which one must attend:

- *Initiation of ending*, shifting the discussion toward finishing, often with an explicit question such as, "Is there anything else that we should discuss today before talking about ending?"
- *Goal assessment*, the determination with the client of how well the purposes of therapy have been achieved, what may remain to be accom-

plished during therapist–patient meetings, and what does not appear to be achievable within the treatment context.[9] Attention should be directed to helping clients develop an understanding ("empowerment") that emphasizes their role in the attainment of treatment goals (see Eron & Lund, 1998, p. 394). Meta-discussion, reviewing and talking about it, may further enhance the egalitarian therapeutic relationship, "demystifying" treatment and depotentiating clinician–client transference dynamics (see Whitaker & Malone, 1953, pp. 212–214; Quintana, 1993; Coleman et al., 1998).

- *Tasks/homework*, the frequent direction, recommendation, or suggestion of activities for the client to carry out after the session (or therapy) — a hallmark of most forms of brief therapy (see Budman, Hoyt, & Friedman, 1992).
- *Good maintenance and relapse prevention*, the construction of mnemonics ("anchors") that will help clients recall and "encore" (see Goulding, in Hoyt, 1995b) therapeutic gains; as well as contingency planning to avoid the possible return of the presenting problem, sometimes including discussions about the temptations of "self-sabatoge" and inoculating predictions of difficult challenges, with the framing of possible "slips" as opportunities to apply therapeutic lessons.
- *Aftercare planning*, including discussions of life post-therapy and indications for possible return to treatment.
- *Leave-taking*, well-wishing, and saying "goodbye," including acknowledgment and validation of feelings (client's and clinician's) about ending. As Karl Lewin (1970, pp. 224–226) has written, "Before the interviews can be discontinued, the relationship which the patient has made with the doctor must be resolved. . . . If the patient wants to keep anything of the doctor, he must learn to introject him, to take him inside, to convert him from an external object into a part of himself." This is also what Milton Erickson (quoted in Zeig, 1980, frontispiece) seems to have had in mind when he said, "And my voice goes everywhere with you, and changes into the voice of your parents, your teachers, your playmates and the voices of the wind and of the rain."

[9] When (and how) best to assess the results of a therapy is a multifaceted question that goes beyond the scope of the present discussion. It should be noted, however, that while the most common time for such assessment is at the end of the last session, brief therapists recognize that change often continues and extends beyond the last meeting and thus we will need to see what happens after the session before assessing its impact (outcome: change and durability) (Hoyt, 1995a, p. 331).

In the *follow-through* phase of a course of therapy (and after the close of each session), there also are a number of activities of which to attend:

- *Continued progress*, the realization of the encouraging message (and possible "seeding" — see Haley, 1973, p. 34; Zeig, 1990) that growth will continue past the formal ending date — indeed, that the application of some of the lessons of therapy can occur only after the end of therapist–patient meetings.
- *Monitoring*, continued evaluation by the client regarding the status of success, coping, and possible setbacks. The therapist (or agency or case manager) may also elicit feedback via patient-satisfaction and outcome-assessment questionnaires or telephone calls — contacts that ethically should be prearranged with the client's consent.
- *Return as needed*, the door being left open if the client wishes to return for the same or another problem — sometimes knowing that help will be available if truly needed helps clients weather some challenges without additional therapy and thus further appreciate their own strengths and coping abilities.

As Poynter (1998) nicely summarized:

> Both the clinical and the procedural tasks involved in the termination phase are critical. Procedurally, this is the major milestone for measurement of effectiveness (though measurements are taken at different points), initiation of aftercare plans, composition of data for statistical analysis, and coordination of care arrangements if the client will be continuing in medication management. Clinically, the closure process involves elucidating integration of the changes, framing unfinished issues, and clarifying relapse prevention. The part of the clinical closure process that involves integrating intrapsychic changes that have occurred in treatment is the overriding task of the termination phase, and therefore it should be pursued as a simultaneous consideration during the process of accomplishing all of the other tasks. (pp. 132–133)

Termination can sometimes also produce other benefits. Again, as Poytner (1998) observed:

> [Although focused] on remediation to previous levels of functioning, the process of accomplishing this invariably generates many other — usually desirable — changes as well. During the change process new understandings are often developed, new and enhanced coping mechanisms are usually generated, interpersonal roles and boundaries may be reorganized, dysfunctional patterns are frequently broken, and better defenses and coping mechanisms emerge. Especially when therapy is brief, this leaves many loose ends. My experience is that clients usually continue to undergo intrapsychic reorganization after formal counseling has concluded, and that reorganization can produce substantial additional growth.[10] (pp. 132–133)

It is important to distinguish life goals from therapy goals (see Ticho, 1972), and to recognize that we often simply need to meet with clients until they are "unstuck" and back "on track" (O'Hanlon & Wilk, 1987, pp. 178–179; Walter & Peller, 1994) rather than waiting for everything to be settled. Sometimes a process will be set in motion or amplified but not completely resolved during a session or course of treatment — both the therapist and the patient may need to live with a certain amount of suspense.[11] The Milan Family Therapy Group (Selvini-Palazzoli, 1980; Selvini-Palazzoli, Boscolo, Cecchin, & Prata, 1978) make a similar point. As Boscolo and Bertrando (1993) wrote in their book, *The Times of Time*:

> We often terminate therapy or consultation when the therapist or team sees highly significant change in clients: more fluent communication and information flow, greater ability to "see" different solutions to the same problem, an improvement in emotional at-

---

[10] The importance of highlighting for the patient the possibilities for continued growth and integration after the formal end of brief treatment was well delineated by Wolberg (1965, pp. 189–191): "The termination of short-term therapy is predicated on the principle that while immediate accomplishments may be modest (symptom relief, for example) the constant application by the patient of the lessons he has learned will probably bring further substantial changes. Deep personality alterations may require years of reconditioning which may go on outside of a formal treatment situation. . . . Where treatment is to be terminated, I find it helpful to warn the patient that, while he may feel better, there will be required of him a consistent application of what he has learned in therapy to insure a more permanent resolution of his deeper problems."

[11] As Wittgenstein said (1980, p. 77e; quoted by de Shazer in Hoyt, 1996b, p. 81): "Anything your reader can do for himself, leave to him."

> mosphere, and above all, a new ability to resolve conflicts. The problems and symptoms that were brought in for therapy may still partly be present, but the assumptions that would ensure their continuation are beginning to crumble. In short, when we see what we, in our jargon, call an "about-turn in the system," we tell our clients that our work is done. (p. 195)

It is especially important to leave the door open for possible return. As my Kaiser colleague, Bob Rosenbaum, wrote (in Rosenbaum, Hoyt, & Talmon, 1990/1995):

> In terminating the session, the. . . . therapist may help a client remember to remember, forget to remember, remember to forget, or forget to remember. . . . The degree of closure appropriate to a termination covers a wide range and is influenced by the extent to which the therapy was seeking resolution of some issue or attempting to open up new possibilities. . . . Some clients will need to put the therapist behind them and get on with their lives; others will need to recall the therapist or some words of the therapist with a high degree of vividness. Because some . . . clients will in the future seek further therapy, it is important to structure the termination in such a way that a decision for more treatment will be seen by the patient as an opportunity for further growth, rather than an indicator of failure. Whether the termination turns out to be for just a few weeks or forever, though, it still involves saying goodbye to the client, and all goodbyes have some degree of both grief and healing, sorrow and hope. (pp. 184–185)

TERMINATION: TIPS, TALES, AND TWISTS

"Parting is such sweet sorrow."

— William Shakespeare, *Romeo and Juliet*
(Act II, Scene 2, line 185)

"All is well ended, if this suit be won,
That you express content; which we will pay,
With strife to please you, day exceeding day:
Ours be your patience then, and yours our part;

> Your gentle hands lend us, and take our hearts.
>
> — William Shakespeare, *All Well's That Ends Well* (Epilogue)

Termination is not always a big issue — at least not for clients! Often the ending goes well and smoothly. We and the client co-create achievable goals; techniques are specific, integrated, and as eclectic as needed; treatment is focused, the therapist appropriately active, and the client responsible for making changes; each session is valuable; therapy ends as soon as possible; and the client carries on, and can return to treatment as needed.

I often find it helpful at the end of sessions:

- To stop a bit earlier than the allotted 50 minutes if we have reached a good point — a "solution" or "victory" — rather than trying to fill the time and risking getting back into "problem talk" without sufficient opportunity to achieve success and finish on a positive note (see Goulding & Goulding, 1979; Friedman, 1997, p. 228).
- To signal that the session is coming to a close by a change in my posture, by ritualistically fiddling with my computer or appointment book, and by future-paced phrases, such as "Before we stop in a couple of minutes, when I'll walk you back to the waiting room, let's discuss what's next ..."
- To ask, "Would you like to make another appointment now, or wait and see how things go and call me as needed?"
- To make only one appointment at a time, the implication being that each session is valuable in itself and that we may not need more than one (see Ecker & Hulley, 1996, p. 136).[12]
- To ask patients when they would like to have their next appointment, framing the question within a range that seems appropriate (e.g., "Would you like to make our next appointment for about three weeks, or six weeks, or wait a bit longer?").[13]

---

[12] As a variant (learned from observing Carl Whitaker), one can also cultivate the patient's initiative and involvement by asking, at the end of a session, "Do you want to keep the appointment next week? We could cancel it if you don't want to work."

[13] See Hoyt (1990/1995) for an extended discussion of the timing of sessions and related issues. Additional leads may be found in Kramer (1990), Kupers (1988), Pinkerton & Rockwell (1990), Quintana (1993), Shectman (1986), and Wright & Leahey (1994).

- Alternatively, to suggest to patients that they practice whatever activities or tasks we have discussed, and that they wait until they have completed their "homework" before calling me for the next appointment (leaving the door open, of course, that they can also call if some problem or emergency arises).
- To taper the frequency of sessions, emphasize the idea of intermittent treatment and an "open door," and consider continuous but not intensive meetings as some possible "termination" strategies for efficiently working with clients who may require ongoing or extended contact. Getting the job done, appropriate care, is paramount. Remember: *brief* does not always mean quick.
- To keep in mind, as we walk to the door and down the hallway, that every word counts — one patient (see Hoyt & Farrell, 1983–1984) reported that my casual farewell, "Hey, man, take care of yourself," had enormous positive meaning to him.

We can expect the termination phase to carry more significance and to be potentially more complicated when there has been an extended therapeutic relationship ("The bigger the Hello, the bigger the Goodbye"), when an impasse has been reached in which significant problems continue without resolution, and when the ending stirs up other issues of loss — for client, clinician, or both. Numerous voices — from the Buddha's "Discourse on the Four Noble Truths" to Freud's (1916) essay, "On Transience," to Cat Stevens' (1973) sweet song, "Oh Very Young" — have given eloquent expression to the human desire for attachment and our reluctance to let go and say goodbye.

Even if we know it will someday end, the work together may make the goodbye harder still. There may be an arousal of dependency and underlying separation–individuation issues, with possible recrudescence of presenting symptomatology.[14] There may be countertransference pulls to avoid ending, to "rescue" the patient, to cram extra work into the last session or two; alternatively, the last session may be particularly flat as participants prematurely detach to avoid a genuine ending. Do client and

---

[14] According to Mann (1973), termination will often stimulate four underlying themes, which he conceptualizes as unresolved mourning, activity versus passivity, independence versus dependence, and adequate versus diminished self-esteem.

therapist seek "timelessness" (open-ended or long-term treatment) to avoid change and maintain dependency? Do client and therapist seek an "instant cure" to avoid contact and vulnerability? Is time "squeezed" or "squandered"? Does change occur? How does the patient respond to the impending termination of treatment? How does the therapist respond?

Please allow me to relate a few brief clinical vignettes to enliven some of the preceding, to provide some nuance and implication, and to prepare for us to terminate. Some are instances when things went fairly straightforward; others are termination tales with a twist. My structure here is thematically architectonic; my purpose illustrative and pragmatic.

Case 1. A couple sought assistance because of some waning of affection as well as "communication problems" and some specific conflicts regarding housework. In three sessions, we identified their preferences, largely through use of the Miracle Question (de Shazer, 1985, 1988) and detailed inquiry into times ("exceptions") when their "presenting problems" had not been present, practiced some more agreeable methods of communicating and resolving conflicts, and secured a commitment from both partners to engage in several preferred activities over the next month. We then scheduled a brief telephone follow-up contact, at which time the partners reported that they were doing better, that their affection had been "rekindled," and that they did not feel they needed to make another appointment. They agreed to call back on an as-needed basis.

Case 2. I met Mr. DeSoto with his adult daughter, and then met with him every six–eight weeks for almost two years. He mourned the death of his wife, relocated his residence, and maintained and eventually extended various social connections, including some recreational and service associations as well as a new romance. Things were going quite well and I was looking forward to our next appointment. That day, I found a receptionist's message in my box that simply read: "Mr. DeSoto canceled. No need for future appointment." My first thought was, "*How can he do this to me?*" I was quite hurt — he hadn't seemed at all like an "ingrate" — and he wasn't. I phoned him and we had a pleasant chat. As he thanked me for my help, I realized that our meetings had become more important to me than to him. My theory-driven idea that he had ducked termination to avoid reminders of losing his wife gave way to my realization that I had been "in denial" about my impending "obsolescence."

Case 3. Sam was a 67-year-old man when I first met him as he was sitting in a wheelchair next to his wife in the waiting room of the HMO Psychiatry Department. As I described in my 1995 book, *Brief Therapy and Managed Care* (Hoyt, 1995a, pp. 320–323), we had an intensive single-session encounter that resulted in his using his abilities to overcome his fear of falling and to get on with living in a manner he found more satisfying.

This was not the end of the story, of course. Consistent with the HMO therapy principle of intermittent treatment throughout the life cycle (Bennett, 1983, 1984; Cummings, 1990; Cummings & Sayama, 1995; Hoyt, 1990/1995), I met with Sam on several subsequent occasions — when he felt discouraged, when health problems put him in the hospital, when his physical condition required him to make the adjustment to life in a nursing home. I also had various encounters with his wife, who would leave me long, rambling phone messages to keep me in the loop. She let me know when Sam's illnesses reached the end stage and he was getting ready to die, and she put Sam's son on the phone so that we might talk. I was able to answer some questions, make sure that Sam's wife and son were O.K., convey something of my appreciation for Sam, and let the son know how warmly his father had spoken of him. I also requested that they remember me to Sam, and told them to call if I could be of assistance. A few days later, I received a message from Sam's wife that Sam was dead. I called her and wrote a condolence letter, and subsequently met with her and her sons.

Case 4. Mary was a bright, attractive young woman who had been deeply wounded by her parents' divorce. A person of strong religious convictions and herself a committed partner and parent, her father's affair, some conflicts with her own husband, and a series of panic attacks had torn the fabric of her worldview.

Our meetings were sometimes like intense *dharma* discussions, a mutually respectful struggle to construct a meaningful and workable world view. I liked her a lot — her intelligence and spunk, her incisive verbal manner, and her Scriptural knowledge and spiritual passion were all challenges that required me to stretch and learn a great deal. In leavetaking, she told me that she had been dubious about coming to therapy, expecting to be judged rather than accepted, and that she felt that she had been both "blessed" and "lucky" that Fortune and the Lord had brought us together. I told her that I had felt "lucky" and "blessed," too.

A few months later, her husband called and requested an appointment to see me. He was late for the session, which he claimed he had wanted in order to get help for his "Type A" compulsiveness. He scheduled a second appointment, but left the waiting room before being seen. When I called him, he said that he had had the flu and was feeling ill, and that he would contact me again when his schedule permitted. I haven't heard from him yet.

Many more months went by, almost a year, and then Mary called. We met, mostly as a "follow-up." She reported that things were all right, told me about her kids and her job at the church, and said that she and her husband were working out their problems with some counsel from an older couple they knew. She made a second appointment for two weeks later, and kept it, but said that she didn't really know why she had made it, that "I guess I just wanted to see you and touch bases." We chatted, and wished each other well — and I left the door open.[15]

Case 5. When you've done all you can do, it is time to stop. It can be a bit awkward, especially if you're heavily invested in being helpful and the client does not seem to be satisfied, but in such instances, most clients won't want to stick around anyway. In one situation, however, despite a lack of continuing therapeutic movement, the woman wouldn't take "No" for an answer. She continued to request appointments, during which she "Yes, butted" and "No, butted" and I tried harder and harder (using "Go slow" injunctions, looking for new goals, reframing, externalizing, seeking her theory of change, confronting and interpreting, making a one-down declaration of my impotence, and so forth), all to no avail. Finally, I decided to heed Grove and Haley's (1993) strategic advice:

> HALEY: ... He could tell her something that isn't appropriate, or that won't help her. ...
>
> GROVE: So that he doesn't have to feel like he's rejecting her. She'll reject him, instead of him rejecting her.
>
> HALEY: Right. Tell him it's important that she disengage from him, rather than having him disengage from her. (pp. 64–65)

[15] I'm reminded of Rosenbaum's observation (in Hoyt, Rosenbaum, & Talmon, 1992, pp. 75–76): "Perhaps we meet once, and the client thinks about it for the rest of her life. Perhaps we meet once, the client forgets me, and I think about her for the rest of my life."

I was also fortified by rereading the recommendation made by Whitaker and Malone (1953):

> Where termination of the relationship has resisted all other technical approaches, the therapy may be administratively ended by the therapist with the flat statement to the patient that he will not see the patient after a specific number of further interviews have ensued. Since the administrative ending occurs thus only after the process of therapy has been completed. ... [such an] ending is a declaration of faith in the patient and a statement of the limitations of the therapist's capacity. (pp. 215–216)

I stopped trying so damn hard. After a couple more sessions, I was about to announce that I would only meet with her another time or two, when she beat me to it. Therapy had been of some help in relieving her sense of torpor and unhappiness, she said, and she was ready to move on, and so she didn't wish to make another appointment.

Case 6. It usually is best when therapy meetings end by mutual agreement. Sometimes, however, a patient leaves abruptly or doesn't keep an appointment. While we shouldn't immediately assume that there has been a "treatment failure," such an unplanned termination at least suggests that we have missed a clue or that something has changed in the patient's status since we met last and scheduled the (not kept) appointment.[16] In such instances, we may call and/or send a letter, for reasons of clinical treatment, to fill our schedule, and for medical–legal coverage if the patient may be at serious adverse risk.

An interesting method of writing a letter to repair a badly ended therapy has been described by Omer (1991):[17]

---

[16] In studying the possibilities of single-session therapy, my colleagues and I (Hoyt, 1994b; Hoyt, Rosenbaum, & Talmon, 1992; Rosenbaum, Hoyt, & Talmon, 1990; Talmon, 1990) found by doing follow-up interviews that many times when patients canceled, didn't show up, or seemed to "disappear" after an initial session, they did so because they had obtained what they had come for at the first meeting. Their not returning for a second session was not a "premature termination" nor an indication of a "treatment failure," but rather because the therapy had been useful and sufficient. It should be noted that termination after one session is the most common length of treatment, occurring in 20–50% of cases.

[17] This is different from the end-of-session letters used by the Milan Family Therapy group (e.g., Selvini-Palazzoli, 1980) or by narrative therapists (e.g., White & Epston, 1990; Epston, 1994; Nylund & Thomas, 1994).

> The therapist's significance for clients does not stop when sessions cease. The therapist stays in their memory, fueling anger, disappointment, and feelings of rejection. Changing their perception of the therapist's attitude and behavior, even after therapy has been formally discontinued, is therefore bound to have repercussions. The post-therapy letter. . . . aims at changing the client's perception of the therapist so as to counter the ill effects of the negative ending, to provide an opening for renewed contact (by client or therapist), and, hopefully, to serve as a therapeutic intervention in itself. . . . The letter gives the therapist a good reason for calling the client or family some weeks or months later and asking them how they feel about it and how they are doing in general. (pp. 484–486)

In one instance, attending to the many specific guidelines and cautions that Omer provides, I wrote the following to a client whom I had offended by suggesting that his workplace difficulties were caused by his being overly rigid in his responses to his supervisor and co-workers:

> Dear Fred,
>
> I have been giving a lot of thought to what we discussed at our last meeting and I have reached the conclusion that I misunderstood what you said and your motivations. I now see things differently, appreciating how important honesty is to you. Being true to yourself is vital, and my mistake was to suggest that you should do anything that would compromise your integrity. It will be interesting to learn how you maintain this vital interest while dealing with such an imperfect world. I would be glad to have an honest discussion about these challenges with you.
>
> — Dr. H.

I waited a month, then telephoned the patient. He was surprised that I had reached out, and agreed to another appointment. We met several more times, and he later thanked me for seeing things from his side and for being helpful, and remarked that he had decided to reconsider his ideas when I had been willing to reconsider mine.

Case 7. A woman, now 92 years of age, became my patient because of what her internist described as "mild depression." A long-retired school teacher, she maintained various cultural and family interests and an extraordinary ability to experience the joys of life despite some flagging of her energy and a nagging forgetfulness. An avid reader and music lover, her memory lapses increasingly frustrated her. During one meeting, she lamented how much she had lost, how "dumb" she felt not to have names and ideas easily at her fingertips. As she gently berated herself as "mixed up" and "getting an empty head," I fished around on my desk, found a sheet of paper, and read to her:

> This is thy hour O Soul,
> Thy free flight into the wordless,
> Away from books, away from art,
> The day erased, the lesson done,
> Thee fully forth emerging, silent, gazing,
> Pondering the themes thou lovest best:
> Night, sleep, death and the stars.
>
> — Walt Whitman, "A Clear Midnight"
> (1891–1892/1992, p. 596)

She looked at me, paused, and then recited from memory:

> Grow old along with me!
> The best is yet to be,
> The last of life, for which the first was made:
> Our times are in His hand
> Who saith 'A whole I planned,
> Youth shows but half; trust God: see all nor be afraid!'
>
> — Robert Browning, "Rabbi Ben Ezra"
> (1864/1997, p. 304)[18]

---

[18] Thus wrote C. P. Cavafy (1911/1975, p. 32):

> When suddenly, at midnight, you hear
> an invisible procession going by
> with exquisite music, voices
> [. . .]
> go firmly to the window
> and listen with deep emotion,
> but not with the whining, the pleas of a coward;
> listen — your final pleasure — to the voices,
> to the exquisite music of that strange procession,
> and say goodbye to her, to the Alexandria you are losing.

We continue to meet periodically.

Case 8. A 42-year-old woman, a physician's assistant with a personal and family history of depression, came to the Psychiatry Department. A one-session intake interview determined that on two previous occasions she had responded well to treatment with antidepressants — three years earlier she had taken the medication for about a year, and a year prior she had resumed it for about a month. In both instances, she had unilaterally discontinued it, however, despite marked benefits and an absence of side effects, because she felt that as a strong woman, she "should" be able to handle problems without pills. She again was depressed, irritable, and sleeping poorly.

Discussion revealed that she was highly competent and had achieved a great deal of success (career, family, friends, travel, and so forth), even though she had come from a very rough beginning. When I asked how she had done so well, she identified a grandmother who had cared for her and taught her to set goals and assume responsibility, plus her own intelligence, an academic flair, and good fortune. As we talked, she quickly figured out that her otherwise useful drive toward self-sufficiency kept her, inappropriately, from allowing herself to benefit from medication. "Meds," I pointed out, did not obviate her responsibility or take away from her success; indeed, they could support her achievements. This "reframing" helped her to accept and continue to benefit from referral to a prescribing psychiatrist. It was all the psychotherapy she needed.[19]

Case 9. Were it not for the twinkle in his eye, one might mistake Mr. Burton for an unreconstructed cantankerous curmudgeon. Himself now elderly, irritable, and in pain, he was the no-nonsense son of a Texas sheriff. Failing health (emphysema, congestive heart failure, some small strokes) had landed him in a nursing facility, where he suffered not lightly the stupidities and incompetencies of the semiattentive staff. We joined through some salty "man-to-man" banter and certain shared intolerances, plus my appreciation of his stylish hats and many fascinating life experi-

[19] From the perspective of a narrative constructivist, I think of the appropriate use of psychopharmacology to support clients' self-empowerment as restoring restorying (Hoyt, 1998, p. 18). Medication may allow thinking to focus and mood to abate enough for clients to get on with the "reauthoring" and living of their lives. Respectful collaboration and informed consent ("invitation, not imposition") are paramount, of course.

ences and his appreciation of my practical suggestions regarding how to better manage the nursing staff. His long-time companion, Judy (whom he had met and courted 25 years earlier in San Francisco) was his partner in life. She was considerably younger than Mr. Burton. Every night after work, she went to the nursing home, where they had dinner together and visited. She brought him to our sessions and joined us.

Mr. Burton's condition progressively weakened over time. His pain got worse, his boredom increased, his breathing became more difficult, and he and Judy were enjoying their nightly visits less and less. He was hesitant to attend another therapy session. We did some work on pain reduction, including both hypnotherapy and a call to his physician to adjust medications. Utilizing his interest in the Old West, I suggested they get a VCR so that they could watch movies together in his room. We discussed his favorite actors and films. Mr. Burton made an allusion to the great film *Shane* — when I caught the reference and answered in kind, he decided to come back and see me again.

Finally, however, he declared that he didn't think he would come back, saying, "There's nothing more you can do for me, Doc." Judy did not look pleased — she knew they were in the ebb tide and that the end was not too far. "Well, you're right, Mr. Burton, I'm not sure what else I may be able to do. And, of course, you're the Boss; you have the right to fire me whenever you want. But instead of getting rid of me, why not just put me on 'pause' and keep me handy?" Judy brought up that they had been enjoying watching videos together. We talked Westerns for a bit, and then she mentioned that they had gone to the theater to see *Titantic*. Mr. Burton had been sleeping more lately, but he had managed to stay awake pretty much throughout the long film. We talked about it. When Judy asked what part I liked best, I went on about the scene near the beginning, when the young man so cleverly talks the depressed woman off the ship rail. "How about you?" I finally asked. She liked that scene, and others, but she said that what had really moved her was the ending, when the woman (now much older) climbed back on to the rail and threw the long-treasured jewel overboard. But, Judy added, she didn't like seeing it sink.

M.H.: Yeah, but the movie didn't end there. Remember what the woman did then?

JUDY: She went back to bed.

M.H.: Right. And do you remember her room?

JUDY: (*She thought a minute.*) He had all those photos around her bed, the pictures of all the things she had done, things that she and Jack [the movie's protagonist] had planned to do together.

M.H.: Right. There were pictures of her good memories, of her in different countries, in front of a ferris wheel, in front of a small plane — (*Judy interrupted.*)

JUDY: — and there was a picture of her riding a horse. (*She paused, her eyes brimming with tears, and looked at Mr. Burton ... and he looked at me and nodded approvingly*).

ENOUGH (FOR NOW): UNTIL WE MEET AGAIN

"The temple bell stops.
But the sound keeps coming out of the flowers."
— Matsuo Basho, 1644–1694
(quoted in Dodge, 1983)

When it is done well, the therapy may be brief, but the benefit may be long-term. Getting the job done, finishing successfully, is what counts. In golf they say, "You drive for show, but you putt for dough" (Hoyt, 1996b, p. 315). In therapy, we call it "termination," knowing *how* and *why* to say "*when*." To make treatment no longer than necessary, we have to *pay attention to ending*.

I recall that Milton Erickson (Rosen, 1982) sometimes would say, "My voice will go with you." I also recall that Ishi (Kroeber, 1961, p. 238), the last aboriginal survivor of California's First Nation Yana people, would say, instead of goodbye, "You stay, I'll go." In leavetaking, dear reader, allow me to thank you for your continuing attention. I leave you with this poem from Charles Bukowski (1996, p. 131) called "Defining the Magic."

a good poem is like a cold beer
when you need it,
a good poem is a hot turkey

sandwich when you're
hungry,
a good poem is a gun when
the mob corners you,
a good poem is something that
allows you to walk through the streets of
death,
a good poem can make death melt like
hot butter,
a good poem can frame agony and
hang it on a wall,
a good poem can let your feet touch
China,
a good poem can make a broken mind
fly,
a good poem can let you shake hands
with Mozart,
a good poem can let you shoot craps
with the devil
and win,
a good poem can do almost anything,
and most important
a good poem knows when to
stop.

Acknowledgments

A version of this chapter previously appeared in M. F. Hoyt, *Some Stories Are Better than Others: Doing What Works in Brief Therapy and Managed Care*. Philadelphia: Brunner/Mazel, 2000. Used here by agreement.

Excerpts from the James Broughton poem, "Ways of Getting There," which appeared in *Special Deliveries: New and Selected Poems* (Seattle, WA: Broken Moon Press, 1990), are used by permission of Joel Singer.

The poem "defining the magic" by Charles Bukowski (copyright 1996 by Linda Lee Bukowski), which appeared in *Betting on the Moon: Poems and Stories* (Santa Rosa, CA: Black Sparrow Press, 1996), is used by permission of Black Sparrow Press.

References

Alexander, F. (1965). Psychoanalytic contributions to short-term psychotherapy. In L. R. Wolberg (Ed.), *Short-term psychotherapy* (pp. 84–126). New York: Grune & Stratton.

Alexander, F., & French, T. M. (1946). *Psychoanalytic therapy: Principles and applications*. New York: Ronald Press.

Appelbaum, S. A. (1975). Parkinson's law in psychotherapy. *International Journal of Psychoanalytic Psychotherapy*, *4*, 426–436.

Austad, C. S. (1996). *Is long-term psychotherapy unethical? Toward a social ethic in an era of managed care*. San Francisco: Jossey-Bass.

Basch, M. F. (1995). *Doing brief psychotherapy*. New York: Basic Books.

Beck, A. T., Rush, A. J., Shaw, B. F., & Emery, G. (1979). *Cognitive therapy of depression*. New York: Guilford.

Bennett, M. J. (1983). Focal psychotherapy — terminable and interminable. *American Journal of Psychotherapy*, *37*, 365–375.

Bennett, M. J. (1984). Brief psychotherapy and adult development. *Psychotherapy*, *21*, 171–177.

Berg, I. K. (1994). *Family-based services: A solution-focused approach*. New York: Norton.

Bloom, B. L. (1992). *Planned short-term psychotherapy: A clinical handbook*. Boston: Allyn & Bacon.

Boscolo, L., & Bertrando, P. (1993). *The times of time*. New York: Norton.

Breuer, J., & Freud, S. (1893–1895). Studies in hysteria. In *The standard edition of the complete psychological works of Sigmund Freud* (Vol. 2, pp. 3–305). London: Hogarth, 1955.

Broughton, J. (1990). Ways of getting there. In *Special deliveries: New and selected poems* (p. 212). Seattle: Broken Moon Press.

Browning, R. (1864/1997). Rabbi Ben Ezra. In R. Roberts (Ed.), *Robert Browning* (pp. 304–310). Oxford: Oxford University Press.

Budman, S. H. (1990). The myth of termination in brief therapy: Or, it ain't over until it's over. In J. K. Zeig & S. G. Gilligan (Eds.), *Brief therapy: Myths, methods, and metaphors* (pp. 206–218). New York: Brunner/Mazel.

Budman, S. H., & Gurman, A. S. (1988). *Theory and practice of brief therapy*. New York: Guilford.

Budman, S. H., Hoyt, M. F., & Friedman, S. (Eds.) (1992). *The first session in brief therapy*. New York: Guilford.

Bukowski, C. (1996). Defining the magic. In *Betting on the muse: Poems and stories* (p. 131). Santa Barbara, CA: Black Sparrow Press.

Cavafy, C. P. (1911/1975). The god abandons Antony. In *C. P. Cavafy: Selected poems* (p. 32) (E. Keeley & P. Sherrard, trans.). Princeton, NJ: Princeton University Press.

Coleman, S. M., Combs, G., DeLaurenti, B., DeLaurenti, P., Freedman, J., Larimer, D., & Shulman, D. (1998). Minimizing hierarchy in therapeutic relationships: A reflecting team approach. In M. F. Hoyt (Ed.), *The handbook of constructive therapies* (pp. 276–292). San Francisco: Jossey-Bass.

Cummings, N. A. (1990). Brief intermittent psychotherapy throughout the life cycle. In J. K. Zeig & S. G. Gilligan (Eds.), *Brief therapy: Myths, methods, and metaphors* (pp. 169–184). New York: Brunner/Mazel.

Cummings, N. A., & Sayama, M. (1995). *Focused psychotherapy: A casebook of brief, intermittent psychotherapy throughout the life cycle.* New York: Brunner/Mazel.

de Shazer, S. (1985). *Keys to solution in brief therapy.* New York: Norton.

de Shazer, S. (1988). *Clues: Investigating solutions in brief therapy.* New York: Norton.

de Shazer, S. (1991). Foreword. In Y. M. Dolan, *Resolving sexual abuse: Solution-focused therapy and Ericksonian hypnosis for adult survivors* (pp. ix–x). New York: Norton.

Dodge, J. (1983). *Fup.* Berkeley, CA: City Miner Books.

Donne, J. (1633/1971). Love's progress. (Elegy 18) In A. J. Smith (Ed.), *The complete English poems.* London: Penguin.

Duncan, B. L., Hubble, M. A., & Miller, S. D. (1997). *Psychotherapy with "impossible" cases: The efficient treatment of therapy veterans.* New York: Norton.

Ecker, B., & Hulley, L. (1996). *Depth-oriented brief therapy.* San Francisco: Jossey-Bass.

Epston, D. (1994). Extending the conversation. *Family Therapy Networker, 18*(6), 30–37, 62–63.

Epston, D., & White, M. (1990). Consulting your consultants: The documentation of alternative knowledges. *Dulwich Centre Newsletter*, no. 4. Reprinted in *Experience, contradiction, narrative and imagination: Selected papers of David Epston and Michael White, 1989–1991* (pp. 11–26). Adelaide, Australia: Dulwich Centre Publications.

Erickson, M. H. (1980). In E. L. Rossi (Ed.), *The collected papers of Milton H. Erickson, Vol. 4.* New York: Irvington.

Eron, J. B., & Lund, T. W. (1998). Narrative solutions in couple therapy. In F. M. Dattilio (Ed.), *Case studies in couple and family therapy* (pp. 371–400). New York: Guilford.

Fisch, R., Weakland, J. H., & Segal, L. (1982). *The tactics of change: Doing therapy briefly.* San Francisco: Jossey-Bass.

Freud, S. (1910/1957). The future prospects of psycho-analytic therapy. In *The standard edition of the complete psychological works of Sigmund Freud* (Vol. 11, pp. 139–151). London: Hogarth.

Freud, S. (1916/1957). On transience. In *The standard edition of the complete psychological works of Sigmund Freud* (Vol. 14, pp. 303–307). London: Hogarth.

Freud, S. (1918/1953). From the history of an infantile neurosis. In *The standard edition of the complete psychological works of Sigmund Freud* (Vol. 17, pp. 3–122). London: Hogarth. 1953.

Freud, S. (1937/1964). Analysis terminable and interminable. In *The standard edition of the complete psychological works of Sigmund Freud* (Vol. 23, pp. 211–253). London: Hogarth.

Friedman, S. (1997). *Time-effective psychotherapy: Maximizing outcomes in an era of minimized resources.* Boston: Allyn & Bacon.

Goldberg, C. (1975). Termination — a meaningful pseudodilemma in psychotherapy. *Psychotherapy: Theory, Research & Practice, 12*, 341–343.

Goldfield, J. (1998). "Master of faster" and "The problem talks back." In M. F. Hoyt (Ed.), *The handbook of constructive therapies* (pp. 241–248). San Francisco: Jossey-Bass.

Goulding, M. M., & Goulding, R. L. (1979). *Changing lives through redecision therapy.* New York: Grove Press.

Grove, D. R., & Haley, J. (1993). *Conversations on therapy: Popular problems and uncommon solutions.* New York: Norton.

Gustafson, J. P. (1986). *The complex secret of brief psychotherapy.* New York: Norton.

Haley, J. (1969). The art of psychoanalysis. In *The power tactics of Jesus Christ and other essays* (pp. 9–26). New York: Avon.

Haley, J. (1973). *Uncommon therapy: The psychiatric techniques of Milton H. Erickson, M.D.* New York: Norton.

Haley, J. (1976). *Problem-solving therapy: New strategies for effective family therapy.* San Francisco: Jossey-Bass.

Hellenga, R. (1995). *The sixteen pleasures.* New York: Delta.

Hillman, J. (1995). *Kinds of power: A guide to its intelligent uses.* New York: Doubleday.

Hoyt, M. F. (1979). Aspects of termination in a brief time-limited psychotherapy. *Psychiatry, 42*, 208–219. Reprinted in M. F. Hoyt, *Brief therapy and managed care* (pp. 183–204). San Francisco: Jossey-Bass, 1995.

Hoyt, M. F. (1980). Therapist and patient actions in "good" psychotherapy sessions. *Archives of General Psychiatry, 37*, 159–161.

Hoyt, M. F. (1983). Concerning remorse: With special attention to its defensive function. *Journal of the American Academy of Psychoanalysis, 11*, 435–444.

Hoyt, M. F. (1985). Therapist resistances to short-term dynamic psychotherapy. *Journal of the American Academy of Psychoanalysis, 13*, 93–112. Reprinted in M. F. Hoyt, *Brief therapy and managed care* (pp. 219–235). San Francisco: Jossey-Bass, 1995.

Hoyt, M. F. (1987). Resistances to brief therapy. *American Psychologist, 42*, 408–409.

Hoyt, M. F. (1990). On time in brief therapy. In R. A. Wells & V. J. Giannetti (Eds.), *Handbook of the brief psychotherapies* (pp. 115–143). New York: Plenum. Reprinted in M. F. Hoyt, *Brief therapy and managed care: Readings for contemporary practice* (pp. 69–104). San Francisco: Jossey-Bass, 1995.

Hoyt, M. F. (1993). Termination in the case of Gary: Overdue, not premature. *Psychotherapy, 30*, 536–537.

Hoyt, M. F. (1994a). Therapeutic flexibility in the case of Gary: Too little, too late. *Psychotherapy, 31*, 545–546.

Hoyt, M. F. (1994b). Single-session solutions. In M. F. Hoyt (Ed.), *Constructive therapies* (pp. 140–159). New York: Guilford. Reprinted in M. F. Hoyt (1995), *Brief therapy and managed care* (pp. 141–162). San Francisco: Jossey-Bass.

Hoyt, M. F. (1995a). *Brief therapy and managed care: Readings for contemporary practice*. San Francisco: Jossey-Bass.

Hoyt, M. F. (1995b). Contact, contract, change, encore: A conversation with Bob Goulding. *Transactional Analysis Journal, 25*(4), 300–311. Reprinted in M. F. Hoyt, *Interviews with brief therapy experts* (pp. 121–143). New York: Brunner/Routledge, 2001.

Hoyt, M. F. (1996a). Solution building and language games: A conversation with Steve de Shazer. In M. F. Hoyt (Ed.), *Constructive therapies, Vol. 2* (pp. 60–86). New York: Guilford. Reprinted in M. F. Hoyt, *Interviews with brief therapy experts* (pp. 158–183). New York: Brunner/Routledge, 2001.

Hoyt, M. F. (1996b). A golfer's guide to brief therapy (with footnotes for baseball fans). In M. F. Hoyt (Ed.), *Constructive therapies, Vol. 2* (pp. 306–318). New York: Guilford. Reprinted in M. F. Hoyt, *Some stories are better than others* (pp. 5–15). Philadelphia: Brunner/Mazel, 2000.

Hoyt, M. F. (1998). Introduction. In M. F. Hoyt (Ed.), *The handbook of constructive therapies* (pp. 1–27). San Francisco: Jossey-Bass.

Hoyt, M. F. (2000). *Some stories are better than others: Doing what works in brief therapy and managed care*. Philadelphia: Brunner/Mazel.

Hoyt, M. F. (in press). Brief psychotherapies. In A. S. Gurman & S. B. Messer (Eds.), *Essential psychotherapies: Theory and practice* (2nd ed.). New York: Guilford.

Hoyt, M. F., & Combs, G. (1996). On ethics and the spiritualities of the surface: A conversation with Michael White. In M. F. Hoyt (Ed.), *Constructive therapies,*

Vol. 2 (pp. 33–59). New York: Guilford. Reprinted in M. F. Hoyt, *Interviews with brief therapy experts* (pp. 71–96). New York: Brunner/Routledge, 2001.

Hoyt, M. F., & Farrell, D. (1983–1984). Countertransference difficulties in a time-limited psychotherapy. *International Journal of Psychoanalytic Psychotherapy, 10,* 191–203.

Hoyt, M. F., & Friedman, S. (1998). Dilemmas of postmodern practice under managed care and some pragmatics for increasing the likelihood of treatment authorization. *Journal of Systemic Therapies, 17*(3), 1–11. Reprinted in M. F. Hoyt, *Some stories are better than others* (pp. 109–117). Philadelphia: Brunner/Mazel, 2000.

Hoyt, M. F., & Miller, S. D. (2000). Stage-appropriate change-oriented brief therapy strategies. In J. Carlson & L. Sperry (Eds.), *Brief therapy strategies with individuals and couples.* Phoenix, AZ: Zeig/Tucker. Reprinted in M. F. Hoyt, *Some stories are better than others* (pp. 207–235). Philadelphia: Brunner/Mazel, 2000.

Hoyt, M. F., Rosenbaum, R. L., & Talmon, M. (1992). Planned single-session psychotherapy. In S. H. Budman, M. F. Hoyt, & S. Friedman, (Eds.), *The first session in brief therapy* (pp. 59–86). New York: Guilford.

Hoyt, M. F., White, M., & Zimmerman, J. (2001). Direction and dismay: A conversation about power and politics in narrative therapy with Michael White and Jeff Zimmerman. In M. F. Hoyt, *Interviews with brief therapy experts* (pp. 265–293). New York: Brunner/Routledge, 2001.

Kramer, S. A. (1990). *Positive endings in psychotherapy: Bringing meaningful closure to therapeutic relationships.* San Francisco: Jossey–Bass.

Kreider, J. W. (1998). Solution-focused ideas for briefer therapy with longer-term clients. In M. F. Hoyt (Ed.), *The handbook of constructive therapies* (pp. 341–357). San Francisco: Jossey-Bass.

Kroeber, T. (1961). *Ishi in two worlds: A biography of the last wild Indian in North America.* Berkeley: University of California Press.

Kupers, T. A. (1988). *Ending therapy: The meaning of termination.* New York: New York University Press.

Lazarus, A. A. (1997). *Brief but comprehensive psychotherapy: The multimodal way.* New York: Springer.

Levenson, H. (1995). *Time-limited dynamic psychotherapy: A guide to clinical practice.* New York: Basic Books.

Lewin, K. K. (1970). *Brief psychotherapy: Brief encounters.* St. Louis, MO: Warren H. Green.

Lipchik, E. (1994). The rush to be brief. *Family Therapy Networker, 18*(2), 34–39.

Malan, D. H. (1976). *The frontier of brief psychotherapy.* New York: Plenum.

Mann, J. (1973). *Time-limited psychotherapy.* Cambridge, MA: Harvard University Press.

Meichenbaum, D., & Biemiller, A. (1998). *Nurturing independent learners: Helping students take charge of their learning.* Cambridge, MA: Brookline Books.

Miller, I. J. (1996a). Managed care is harmful to outpatient mental health services: A call for accountability. *Professional Psychology: Research & Practice, 27,* 349–363.

Miller, I. J. (1996b). Some "short-term therapy values" are a formula for invisible rationing. *Professional Psychology: Research & Practice, 27,* 577–582.

Minsky, T. (1987). Prisoners of psychotherapy. *New York, 20,* 34–40.

Nylund, D., & Corsiglia, V. (1994). Becoming solution-focused forced in brief therapy: Remembering something important we already knew. *Journal of Systemic Therapies, 13*(1), 5–12.

Nylund, D., & Thomas, J. (1994). The economics of narrative. *Family Therapy Networker, 18*(6), 38–39.

O'Hanlon, W. H. (1990). Debriefing myself: When a brief therapist does long-term work. *Family Therapy Networker, 14*(2), 48–50.

O'Hanlon, W. H. (1991). Not strategic, not systemic: Still clueless after all these years. *Journal of Strategic and Systemic Therapies, 10,* 105–109.

O'Hanlon, W. H., & Wilk, J. (1987). *Shifting contexts: The generation of effective psychotherapy.* New York: Guilford.

Omer, H. (1991). Writing a post-scriptum to a badly ended therapy. *Psychotherapy, 28,* 484–492.

Pepe, P. (1988). *The wit and wisdom of Yogi Berra.* Westport, CT: Meekler Books.

Pinkerton, R. S., & Rockwell, W. J. K. (1990). Termination in brief psychotherapy: The case for an eclectic approach. *Psychotherapy, 27*(3), 362–365.

Poynter, W. L. (1998). *The textbook of behavioral managed care: From concept through management to treatment.* Washington, DC: Brunner/Mazel (Taylor & Francis).

Quintana, S. M. (1993). Toward an expanded and updated conceptualization of termination: Implications for short-term, individual psychotherapy. *Professional Psychology: Research and Practice, 24*(4), 426–432.

Rosen, S. (1982). *My voice will go with you: The teaching tales of Milton H. Erickson.* New York: Norton.

Rosenbaum, R., Hoyt, M. F., & Talmon, M. (1990). The challenge of single-session therapies: Creating pivotal moments. In R. A. Wells & V. J. Giannetti (Eds.), *Handbook of the brief psychotherapies* (pp. 165–189). New York: Plenum. Reprinted in M. F. Hoyt, *Brief therapy and managed care* (pp. 105–139). San Francisco: Jossey-Bass, 1995.

Selvini-Palazzoli, M. (1980). Why a long interval between sessions? In M. Andolfi & I. Zwerling (Eds.), *Dimensions of family therapy.* New York: Guilford.

Selvini-Palazzoli, M., Boscolo, L., Cecchin, G., & Prata, G. (1978). *Paradox and counterparadox.* New York: Jason Aronson.

Shectman, F. (1986). Time and the practice of psychotherapy. *Psychotherapy, 23*(4), 521–525.

Short, D. (1997). Interview: Steve de Shazer and Insoo Kim Berg. *The Milton H. Erickson Foundation Newsletter, 17*(2), 1, 18–20.

Simon, P. (1975). 50 ways to leave your lover. Song on album, *Still crazy after all these years*. New York: Columbia Records (BMI).

Snyder, G. (1980). *The real work: Interviews and talks, 1964–1979*. New York: New Directions.

Stern, S. (1993). Managed care, brief therapy, and therapeutic integrity. *Psychotherapy, 30*, 162–175.

Stevens, C. (1973). Oh very young. Song on album, *Greatest hits*. Beverly Hills, CA: A & M Records (ASCAP).

Strupp, H. H., & Binder, J. L. (1984). *Psychotherapy in a new key: A guide to time-limited dynamic psychotherapy*. New York: Basic Books.

Talmon, M. (1990). *Single session therapy*. San Francisco: Jossey-Bass.

Ticho, E. A. (1972). Termination of psychoanalysis: Treatment goals, life goals. *Psychoanalytic Quarterly, 41*, 315–333.

Tobin, S. A. (1976). Saying goodbye in Gestalt therapy. In C. Hatcher & P. Himelstein (Eds.), *The handbook of gestalt therapy* (pp. 371–383). New York: Jason Aronson.

Vorkoper, C. F. (1997). The importance of saying goodbye. In C. E. Lennox (Ed.), *Redecision therapy: A brief, action-oriented approach* (pp. 95–108). Northvale, NJ: Jason Aronson.

Walter, J. L., & Peller, J. E. (1994). "On track" in solution-focused brief therapy. In M. F. Hoyt (Ed.), *Constructive therapies* (pp. 111–125). New York: Guilford.

Whitaker, C. A. (1987). The dynamics of the American family as deduced from 20 years of family therapy: The family unconscious. In J. K. Zeig (Ed.), *The evolution of psychotherapy* (pp. 75–83). New York: Brunner/Mazel.

Whitaker, C. A. (1989). *Midnight musings of a family therapist*. New York: Norton.

Whitaker, C. A., & Malone, T. P. (1953). Some techniques in brief psychotherapy. In *The roots of psychotherapy* (pp. 194–230). New York: Blakiston.

White, M. (1988/1989). Saying hullo again: The incorporation of the lost relationship in the resolution of grief. *Dulwich Centre Newsletter*, Spring. Reprinted in M. White, *Selected papers* (pp. 29–36). Adelaide, Australia: Dulwich Centre Publications.

White, M. (1995). *Re-authoring lives: Interviews and essays*. Adelaide, Australia: Dulwich Centre Publications.

White, M., & Epston, D. (1990). *Narrative means to therapeutic ends*. New York: Norton.

Whitman, W. (1891–1892/1992). A clear midnight. In *Leaves of grass* (p. 596). (J. Hollander, intro.) New York: Vintage.

Wittgenstein, L. (1980). *Culture and value* (P. Winch, trans.). Chicago: University of Chicago Press.

Wolberg, L. R. (1965). The technic of short-term psychotherapy. In L. R. Wolberg (Ed.), *Short-term psychotherapy* (pp. 127–200). New York: Grune & Stratton.

Wright L. M., & Leahey, M. (1994, Spring). *Finishing well: Tips for terminating treatment.* Presented at Family Therapy Networker Conference, Washington, DC.

Yapko, M. (1990). Brief therapy tactics in longer-term psychotherapies. In J. K. Zeig & S. G. Gilligan (Eds.), *Brief therapy: Myths, methods, and metaphors* (pp. 185–195). New York: Brunner/Mazel.

Zeig, J. K. (Ed.) (1980). *A teaching seminar with Milton H. Erickson.* New York: Brunner/Mazel.

Zeig, J. K. (1990). Seeding. In J. K. Zeig & S. G. Gilligan (Eds.), *Brief therapy: Myths, methods, and metaphors* (pp. 221–246). New York: Brunner/Mazel.

26

The Personal Life of the Psychotherapist: An Evolving Research Project[1]

Michael J. Mahoney

For many years now, I have been interested in the relationship between the personal experiences and the development of therapists as they relate to the range of experiences and developments in their psychotherapy clients. When, with great fortuity, I became a client of Milton Erickson in 1967, my concern was with this very theme, at a personal level (Mahoney, 1997b). I was concerned about my "appropriateness" — but, more fundamentally, my own "worthiness" — to serve and work as a psychologist. My nuclear question, asked with great and anxious reluctance in the last few minutes of our session, was whether I had the "right" to presume to guide other people in their personal lives when the formidable limitations in my own navigational skills were so apparent to me. Dr. Erickson responded by reminding me that "some of the best football coaches in this country have never played the game." Note that he did not say to me that perfect mental health was not a prerequisite for being a good therapist. Nor did he say, for that matter, that my experience with the existential pains of self-consciousness might actually serve

[1] Some of this material is elaborated in M. J. Mahoney, *Constructive psychotherapy: Exploring principles and practices* (in press). New York: Guilford.

me well in my services to others. In a way, he said something like, "The inexperienced and still-learning may also be great teachers." Years later, I was reminded of his message in a Zen koan: "We often teach best that which we most need to learn."

I am still fascinated with elaborations of my first questions about the relationships between therapists' and clients' lives. They *are* connected, I believe. Psychotherapists can, and often do, make a significant lifelong difference in the lives of their clients. Clients also make significant lifelong differences in the lives of their therapists. One cannot be involved in so many lives, in so many human tragedies, in so much suffering, struggle, and development without being affected personally. And, even though I feel that my graduate mentoring and internship were outstanding, I was not prepared for the challenges and complexities of daily clinical supervision and practice. I felt overwhelmed by the complexity of my clients. They did not meet the simplistic expectations of the textbook examples that I had read. They were alive and unique and very unpredictable. They exhibited diverse patterns of distress and dysfunction, and their expressions of their concerns and the particulars of their momentary attention not only changed between sessions, but also within sessions, many times. The same client seemed to want and need different things at different moments. I felt unbearably stretched. Sensing a need to develop more quickly in my own capacities to serve, I began confining my private practice to "difficult" clients, persons who had been in psychotherapy at least twice before they contacted me. To be sure, they accelerated my development — and deepened my patience. They taught me more than I can possibly describe, and I am deeply grateful.

Later, I began to devote most of my private practice to clients who were themselves mental health professionals. My motivations for this move (in the mid-1980s) were probably multiple. To begin with, I wanted to serve people who were serving. I knew that my time was limited, and I wanted to serve some servers (who sorely needed it). Second, I wanted to learn what they were learning and to share what I was learning. And I had a sense that our work together would be fundamental and challenging. I think I was right about that. I am deeply grateful to my clients, both "fellow" therapists and others, for their invaluable lessons about life and its living. Many times I have felt overwhelmed, and I have wondered what I might possibly offer. Many times I was surprised by my clients' felt value of my presence, even in silence. I spent many sleepless nights —

as I still do — trying to distill some wisdom from their collective teachings. Although slowly, I hope I may be doing so.

THE IMPORTANCE OF THE TOPIC

Given the fact that there are so many other topics that are in need of research, what is the importance of investigating the personal lives of psychotherapists? Is it not self-serving and self-centered for psychotherapy researchers to study practitioners' personal lives? There are several relevant responses to these questions. It is, of course, understandable that therapists would be interested in the quality of their own lives. But there are, I believe, other important reasons for this research. The first is that considerable research now suggests that the person and personal qualities of the psychotherapist are important factors in the success of psychotherapy (Lambert, 1989; Mahoney, 1991). Therapist variables, separated statistically from variability associated with theoretical orientations and actual techniques of psychotherapy practice, are second only to client variables in predicting the outcome of psychotherapy across the full spectrum of psychological disorders. Hence it is important that we understand more about the personal qualities and personal lives of individuals who are more, and less, helpful as practitioners.

Another reason for this line of research is the unique opportunities it creates for studying human psychological development. Recent investigations suggest that the work demands of being a psychotherapist appear to be associated with an amplification and acceleration of normal psychological development. If this is the case, then studying the personal development of therapists across their careers may help us to better understand basic patterns and processes in human development. Therapists often live very challenging lives, lives involving an unusual frequency and diversity of clients, life circumstances, and treatment challenges. If their life challenges accelerate and amplify the more general processes of human development, then therapists become an unusually rich and promising source of information about change processes.

Interestingly, research on the personal life of the psychotherapist and the effects of therapy on the practitioner has been remarkably sparse. The classic research review by James Guy (1987) stands out as a valuable compendium. Other books and articles have accumulated in the ensuing years, and many of them contain valuable information (Boice & Myers, 1987;

Deutsch, 1985; Elliott & Guy, 1993; Farber, 1983, 1985; Farber & Heifetz, 1982; Freud, 1937/1964; Freudenberger, 1983; Garfield & Kurtz, 1974, 1975a, 1975b, 1976; Hellman & Morrison, 1987; Henry, Sims, & Spray, 1971, 1973; Kottler, 1986; Mahoney, 1991, 1995, 1997a; Mahoney & Fernandez-Alvarez, 1998; Miller, 1998; Prochaska & Norcross, 1983; Radeke & Mahoney, 2000; Sarason, 1981; Thoreson, Miller, & Krauskopf, 1989).

After many attempts by my colleagues and myself to assess differences in the epistemological assumptions and positions of behaviorists and cognitivists in the 1970s, my interests evolved toward more basic assumptions, common experiences, and felt conceptual commitments. I still asked about theoretical orientation(s), but these were clearly less predictive of patterns of responding than were other parameters of self-identification. What are some of those patterns? This chapter reflects my current reflections and continuing interest in the human beings who serve as psychotherapists and the impact of their work on their own development. My discussion is around some of the basic questions about psychotherapists and their personal lives.

WHAT KIND OF PERSON IS THE PSYCHOTHERAPIST?

The simplest answer to that question is that the person of the psychotherapist is always unique and fundamentally human — a kind of person who shares with all other humans the capacities to be happy, to suffer, to struggle, to lose and regain a sense of personal balance and life meaning, and to continue developing throughout life. Once you have met one psychotherapist, you have met one psychotherapist. Individual differences across shared patterns demand to be acknowledged (Allport, 1961; Kelly, 1955; Lamiell, 1987; Mahoney, 1991). One can cite descriptive statistics, but these are always gross (and sometimes misleading) generalizations about the particulars (Hermans, 1988). Measures of central tendency cannot capture the individualities involved. People are people — even therapists! I cannot adequately express my gratitude to the therapists I have worked with for what they have taught me, especially, and particularly, about their uniqueness. We each inevitably meet other members of our profession whom we do not like (and might even wonder how they possibly got licensed). They may be challenges to our identities. We also meet many, many kindred souls who — like us — are struggling on an everyday basis to serve, to understand, and to make peace with the demons inside us that question why we try and whether or not we help.

One of the popular lay stereotypes of psychotherapists is that they are generally neurotic and unhappy individuals who have come from troubled childhoods and who have entered the profession either to understand themselves or to avoid their own problems by focusing on the problems of other people (Guy, 1987). Is this an accurate caricature? Do therapists usually come from unhappy homes and tragic childhoods? Statistically speaking, no, and the sparsity of existing data makes it difficult to say much more. Preliminary data suggest that psychotherapists do report a higher frequency of childhood sexual abuse than do those colleagues whose primary work is research (Radeke & Mahoney, 2000). Likewise, a large survey of women professionals in the United States has suggested that — relative to women in other professions — women psychotherapists report higher frequencies of having experienced abuse, loss, or family dysfunction during their childhoods (Elliott & Guy, 1993). It is important to note, however, that as adults, women therapists were no less happy or adjusted than their nontherapist peers. In a variety of surveys whose results are still being integrated, reports of abuse and loss during childhood have been significantly more common among female (versus male) therapists. Male therapists have been somewhat more likely than their female peers to report that their fathers had exhibited alcohol, drug, or mental problems while the therapists were children.

Despite this apparent theme of some (although not most) therapists as having come from dysfunctional family origins, the vast majority report having had happy childhoods.[2] Likewise, in terms of current life satisfaction, most therapists report being basically happy and healthy, even in the face of the considerable challenges associated with their work. Some data suggest that therapists may experience greater overall life satisfaction and friendships than do their research peers (Radeke & Mahoney, 2000). Most therapists report liking themselves and their work, as well as where they live. Interestingly, the dimension with which they are least satisfied is

[2] We should be open, of course, to biases in these self-reports, as well as to professionally hewed perspective, i.e., every childhood has included disappointments, frustrations, and psychological tensions, and the experienced therapist may learn to reevaluate his or her own childhood more positively in light of witnessing the stark tragedies and abuses reported by many psychotherapy clients.

their bodies. However, there are no comparable data from other professions or careers with which to compare this finding.

HOW STRESSFUL IS BEING A PSYCHOTHERAPIST?

A consistent finding across virtually all existing surveys of psychotherapists is that they experience their work as practitioners as being very stressful at times, and sometimes much of the time. These stresses may be more strongly associated with some specializations (e.g., trauma and personality disorders; cf. Miller, 1998), but they are rarely absent from any form of therapeutic work. When asked about sources of stress in their lives, therapists' most common responses to this question include a range of clinical situations. Rank orderings from several recent surveys suggest that the most difficult and stressful situations for many therapists are the following:

1. Resistance to treatment
2. Suicide attempts by clients
3. Client death by suicide
4. Clients' exhibiting paranoia or delusions
5. Client anger toward the therapist
6. Premature termination of treatment
7. Clients' violent behavior toward others
8. Clients' violent behavior toward the therapist
9. The death of a client (nonsuicidal)
10. Hospitalizing a client against his or her will

Other common sources of stress were such things as financial insecurity, the changing demands of "managed-health-care" policies, excessive paperwork, being overextended in felt responsibility, inadequate staffing, and interpersonal conflicts with co-workers or management. These are, of course, understandable stressors for any therapist.

What Are the Most Common Problems of Psychotherapists?

Several surveys have elicited data on the frequency with which psychotherapists report various personal problems. In two surveys of psychiatrists, for example, over 90% reported having suffered "special emotional problems" resulting from their roles as therapists, with 73% having experienced moderate to incapacitating anxiety in their first years of practice and 58% experiencing serious depression (Guy, 1987; Guy & Liaboe, 1986). Likewise, Deutsch (1985) found that 82% of his sample of 264 therapists had suffered relationship difficulties. Depression was also commonly reported (57%), and reports of substance abuse and suicide attempts were not insignificant (11% and 2% respectively). Therapists attending the 1996 Brief Therapy Conference in San Francisco (Mahoney, 1999) reported generally lower rates of these problems (relationship difficulties, 39%; anxiety, 34%; depression, 30%; concerns about alcohol use, 12.5%; concerns about drug use, 1.3%). In a South American survey (Mahoney & Fernandez-Alvarez, 1998), the most common personal concerns of therapists during the previous year were financial security (48%), anxiety (30%), physical exhaustion (31%), weight problems (22%), family problems (17%), loneliness (14%), low confidence or self-esteem (13%), depression (12%), perfectionism (10%), and emotional exhaustion (10%). These findings were paralleled to some degree in a regional survey (Radeke & Mahoney, 2000) that found that the most common personal concerns of practitioners were financial security (36.3%), relationship problems (34.2%), sleep problems (28.1%), depression (27.4%), and shyness (27.4%). Differences in these estimates may reflect a number of factors related to sampling and methodology.

Again, less important than averages and percentages are individual factors and response patterns. Many therapists report a sense of loneliness in that their work requires them to act as confidantes to whom their clients reveal their secret suffering. It is not unusual for therapists to feel helpless or frustrated about their inability to be of much help to some clients, given the clients' current life circumstances (at home, in relationships, and at work), their enduring patterns of dysfunctional coping, and what they perceive as options for change. The numerical rankings of sources of stresses and the personal problems of therapists are less important, I believe, than are their clusters and therapists' preparedness to cope with them. Anxiety, depression, and exhaustion are often associated with low self-esteem and relationship difficulties. The frequency of these personal concerns among psychotherapy practitioners does not appear to exceed estimates of their prevalence in the general population. Moreover, the causes and effects of these personal concerns are decidedly conjectural. We should be careful not to presume that any degree or form of distress or dysfunction on the part of the therapist necessarily diminishes his or her ability to provide satisfactory professional services. Many therapists report that their personal problems actually have made them more empathic with clients and more patient about change processes. Nevertheless, we should not deny the likelihood that serious and ongoing personal difficulties can lead to the impairment of services, and that this is an issue that deserves our personal and collective professional attention. The effect of the therapists' own plights on their delivery of professional services, however, have yet to be adequately measured, and estimates vary widely. My concern — based on my work with therapists both as clients and as supervisees — is that many highly competent therapists hinder themselves unnecessarily by setting unreasonable standards for their own personal adjustment, whereas less competent practitioners are inclined to blame their clients for a lack of progress that probably stems from a poor therapeutic relationship and the therapist's personal limitations. The latter, in my experience, are less likely to seek personal therapy or peer feedback.

What Are the Effects of Therapy on the Therapist's Life?

This has been one of the least frequently asked questions in research on the personal life of the psychotherapist. Ironically, much of that research has focused almost exclusively on stress, burnout, and impairment. The underlying assumption seems to have been that therapy necessarily and unilaterally depletes or otherwise damages the practitioner. In more recent, and perhaps more balanced, inquiries, it appears that the undeniable challenges of practicing psychotherapy are often accompanied by positive benefits. In response to the question, "How has being a psychotherapist influenced your personal life?," for example, the majority of respondents in several surveys emphasized enrichment much more than impairment (Mahoney, 1999; Mahoney & Fernandez-Alvarez, 1998; Radeke & Mahoney, 2000). These findings are corroborated by interviews and self-reports from independent sources (Skovholt & Rønnestad, 1992). The most common responses to the question, in approximate order (across surveys) of strength of response, were that being a psychotherapist:

1. "has made me more respectful of individual differences."
2. "has increased my appreciation for human relationships."
3. "has increased my self-awareness."
4. "has made me more tolerant of ambiguity."

5. "has accelerated my psychological development."
6. "has left me with vivid memories of clients' triumphs."
7. "has made me wiser."
8. "has made me a better person."
9. "has depleted me emotionally."
10. "has increased my capacity to enjoy life."
11. "has resulted in changes in my value system."
12. "has felt like a form of spiritual service."

Negative responses were significantly less common (e.g., feelings of cynicism, helplessness, premature aging). Moreover, the ratio of positive to negative effects generally increased with years of experience as a psychotherapist and were not related to therapists' theoretical orientations.

The finding that even nonreligious therapists sometimes experience psychotherapy as a form of spiritual service is an intriguing one that deserves further clarification. There are increasing signs of a consensus that psychotherapy is a value-laden endeavor (Cushman, 1995). Virtually all world religions have traditionally included prescriptions and proscriptions relating to morals, values, and virtues. Over the past several decades, spirituality has been distinguished from traditional religiosity, and spiritual issues in psychotherapy have been more directly addressed (e.g., Vaughan, 1991).

A recent survey attempted to clarify the meaning of the term "spiritual" for experts in death studies (services to the dying and grieving) and experts in spiritual studies (Mahoney & Graci, 1999). Preliminary findings suggest that the meaning is changing. In its contemporary use, the term appears to include charity (a sense of giving, service), community (a sense of connection, relationship), compassion, forgiveness (and peace), hope, learning opportunities, love, meaning or purpose in life, and morality (a sensitivity to right and wrong). Under this broad and evolving definition of "spirituality," it is no longer surprising that many therapists might experience and conduct their work as a form of spiritual practice (Epstein, 1995; Rosenbaum, 1999). For millennia and across continents and cultures, healers and helpers have offered counsel and comfort to people who are suffering and seeking meaning in their lives (Walsh, 1990). As culturally sanctioned life counselors, it is only natural that psychotherapy practitioners should feel both challenged and changed by their work.

CAREGIVING AND CAREGIVER

In some of the reported surveys, therapists were asked about their self-care patterns and priorities. It seems clear that our work as professional caregivers entails considerable stress. This raises the issue of self-care – an issue that survey respondents in general highlighted. Although personal therapy is not the only form that such self-care might assume, it is a frequent one. Most therapists who have been in therapy report positive experiences. However, the available evidence suggests that psychotherapy may be underutilized by psychotherapists, and for various reasons. Many therapists seem to feel that they cannot afford the emotional and financial investment of being in personal therapy. Others do not know therapists who are not friends or colleagues (which raises dual-role complexities). Still others are reluctant to ask for the same kind of help that they themselves offer as practitioners. Whatever the reasons, there are indications that psychotherapists may be receiving less care than may be wise for persons involved in such a challenging profession.

I personally believe that life-span developmental issues and self-care priorities should be addressed in graduate school and in continuing professional education (Mahoney, 1991, 1998). Indeed, I believe that many of the lessons we hope to teach our clients can be augmented by our practicing them on ourselves (e.g., time management, exercise, recreation, compassion). In so doing, we may also reduce the aura of mystique so often associated with therapy and encourage more realistic and humane images of ourselves.

DISCUSSION

When I reflect on possibly general patterns in the life and development of practioners, I find myself focusing on only a few themes. In general therapists feel that their development has been accelerated by their work, and that they have attained a degree of wisdom as a result. Although many do struggle long and hard with such issues as anxiety, burnout, depression, insecurities (including finances and self-confidence), and life meaning, the vast majority report being happy, healthy, and enriched by their effort.

This brief overview is selective, of course, and it raises many more questions than it answers. It is my hope, however, that it serves to illustrate the promise and potential contributions of studying how we as psychotherapists see ourselves and our professional roles. Particularly important, I believe, are intensive longitudinal studies of individual therapists and the impact of their work on their personal lives (and vice versa). As a culturally sanctioned authority on human problems and human experience, the psychotherapist participates in the lives of thousands of individuals over the course of his or her career. That participation includes vicarious experiences, numerous challenges that were unanticipated, and countless situations of ambiguity and stress. By studying the emotionally amplified and accelerated lives of psychotherapists, we may improve our understanding of the very principles and processes that lie at the heart of our work.

References

Allport, G. W. (1961). *Pattern and growth in personality*. New York: Holt, Rinehart & Winston.

Bergin, A. E., & Garfield, S. L. (1994). *Handbook of psychotherapy and behavior change (4th ed.).* New York: Wiley.

Boice, R., & Myers, P. E. (1987). Which setting is happier, academe or private practice? *Professional Psychology: Research and Practice, 18*, 526–529.

Casement, P. (1985). *On learning from the patient.* London: Tavistock.

Cushman, P. (1995). *Constructing the self, constructing America: A cultural history of psychotherapy*. Reading, MA: Addison-Wesley.

Deutsch, C. J. (1985). A survey of therapists' personal problems and treatment. *Professional Psychology: Research and Practice, 16*(2), 305–315.

Elliott, D. M., & Guy, J. D. (1993). Mental health professionals versus non-mental-health professionals: Childhood trauma and adult functioning. *Professional Psychology: Research and Practice, 24*, 83–90.

Epstein, M. (1995). *Thoughts without a thinker: Psychotherapy from a Buddhist perspective.* New York: Basic Books.

Farber, B. A. (1983). The effects of psychotherapeutic practice upon the psychotherapists. *Psychotherapy: Theory, Research and Practice, 20,* 174–182.

Farber, B. A. (1985). Clinical psychologists' perceptions of psychotherapeutic work. *Clinical Psychologist, 38,* 10–13.

Farber, B. A., & Heifetz, L. (1982). The process and dimensions of burnout in psychotherapists. *Professional Psychology, 13*, 293–302.

Freud, S. (1937/1964). Analysis terminable and interminable. In J. Strachey (Ed. and trans.), *The standard edition of the complete works of Sigmund Freud (Vol. 23).* London: Hogarth.

Freudenberger, H. J. (1983). Hazards of psychotherapeutic practice. *Psychotherapy in Private Practice, 1,* 83–89.

Garfield S. L., & Bergin, A. E. (1986). *Handbook of psychotherapy and behavior change: An empirical analysis.* New York: John Wiley.

Garfield, S. L., & Kurtz, R. M. (1974). A survey of clinical psychologists: Characteristics, activities and orientations. *The Clinical Psychologist, 28,* 7–10.

Garfield, S. L., & Kurtz, R. M. (1975a). Training and career satisfaction among clinical psychologists. *The Clinical Psychologist, 28,* 6–9.

Garfield, S. L., & Kurtz, R. M. (1975b). The clinical psychologists: A survey of selected attitudes and views. *The Clinical Psychologist, 28,* 4–7.

Garfield, S. L., & Kurtz, R. M. (1976). Personal therapy for the psychotherapist: Some findings and issues. *Psychotherapy: Theory, Research and Practice, 13,* 188–192.

Geller, J. D., & Spector, P. D. (Eds.) (1987). *Psychotherapy: Portraits in fiction.* Northvale, NJ: Jason Aronson.

Goldberg, C. (1992). *The seasoned psychotherapist: Triumph over diversity.* New York: Norton.

Guy, J. D. (1987). *The personal life of the psychotherapist.* New York: Wiley.

Guy, J. D., Poelstra, P. L., & Stark, M. J. (1989). Personal distress and therapeutic effectiveness: National survey of psychologists practicing psychotherapy. *Professional Psychology: Research and Practice, 20,* 48–50.

Guy, J. D., & Liaboe, G. P. (1986). Personal therapy for the experienced psychotherapist: A discussion of its usefulness and utilisation. *Clinical Psychologist, 39,* 30–23.

Harner, M. (1982). *The way of the shaman.* New York: Bantam.

Hellman, I. D., & Morrison, T. L. (1987). Practice setting and type of caseload as factors in psychotherapist stress. *Psychotherapy, 24,* 427–433.

Hellman, I. D., Morrison, T. L., & Abramowitz, S. I. (1987). Therapist experience and the stresses of psychotherapeutic work. *Psychotherapy, 24,* 171–177.

Henry, W., Sims, J., & Spray, S. L. (1971). *The fifth profession.* San Francisco: Jossey-Bass.

Henry, W., Sims, J., & Spray, S. L. (1973). *Public and private lives of psychotherapists.* San Francisco: Jossey-Bass.

Hermans, H. J. M. (1988). On the integration of nomothetic and idiographic research methods in the study of personal meaning. *Journal of Personality, 56,* 785–812.

Holt, R. R., & Luborsky, L. (1958). *Personality patterns of psychiatrists.* New York: Basic Books.

Kelly, E. L. (1961). Clinical psychology - 1960. Report of survey of findings. *Division of Clinical Psychology of the American Psychological Association, 14*, 1–11.

Kelly, G. A. (1955). *The psychology of personal constructs.* New York: Norton.

Kopp, S. B. (1976). *Guru: Metaphors from a psychotherapist.* New York: Bantam.

Kottler, J. A. (1986). *On being a therapist.* San Francisco: Jossey-Bass.

Kottler, J. A. (1991). *The compleat therapist.* San Francisco: Jossey-Bass.

Lambert, M. J. (1989). The individual therapist's contribution to psychotherapy process and outcome. *Clinical Psychology Review, 9*, 469–485.

Lamiell, J. T. (1987). *The psychology of personality: An epistemological inquiry.* New York: Columbia University Press.

MacDevitt, J. W. (1987). Therapists' personal therapy and professional self-awareness. *Psychotherapy, 24*, 693–703.

Maeder, T. (1989). *Children of psychiatrists and other psychotherapists.* New York: Harper & Row.

Mahoney, M. J. (1991). *Human change processes.* New York: Basic Books.

Mahoncy, M. J. (1995). Thc psychological burdens of being a constructive psychotherapist. In R. A. Neimeyer & M. J. Mahoney (Eds.), *Constructivism in psychotherapy* (pp. 385–399). Washington, DC: American Psychological Association.

Mahoney, M. J. (1997a). Brief moments and enduring effects: Personal reflections on time and timing in psychotherapy. In W. J. Matthews & J. Edgette (Eds.), *Current thinking and research in brief therapy: Solutions, strategies, narratives* (pp. 25–38). New York: Brunner/Mazel.

Mahoney, M. J. (1997b). Psychotherapists' personal problems and self-care patterns. *Professional Psychology: Research and Practice, 28*(1), 14–16.

Mahoney, M. J. (1998). Essential themes in the training of psychotherapists. *Constructivism in the Human Sciences, 3*, 36–54.

Mahoney, M. J. (1999). *The personal lives and lessons of psychotherapists.* Manuscript in progress.

Mahoney, M. J. (in press). *Constructive psychotherapy: Exploring principles and practices.* New York: Guilford.

Mahoney, M. J., & Fernandez-Alvarez, H. (1998). La vida personal del psicoterapeuta (The personal life of the psychotherapist). *Avances en Psicología Clínica Latinoamericana, 16*, 9–22.

Mahoney, M. J., & Graci, G. M. (1999). The meanings and correlates of spirituality: An exploratory survey of experts. *Death Studies, 23*, 521–528.

Miller, L. (1998). Our own medicine: Traumatized psychotherapists and the stresses of doing therapy. *Psychotherapy, 35*, 137–146.

Nevels, L. A., & Coché, J. M. (1993). *Powerful wisdom: Voices of distinguished women psychotherapists*. San Francisco: Jossey-Bass.

Norcross, J. C., & Guy, J. D. (in press). *Leaving it at the office*. New York: Guilford.

Norcross, J. C., Strausser-Kirtland, D., & Missar, C. D. (1988). The processes and outcomes of psychotherapists' personal treatment experiences. *Psychotherapy, 25*, 36–43.

Prochaska, J. O., & Norcross, J. C. (1983). Contemporary psychotherapists: A national survey of characteristics, practices, orientations, and attitudes. *Psychotherapy: Theory, Research and Practice, 20*(2), 161–173.

Radeke, J. T., & Mahoney, M. J. (2000). Comparing the personal lives of psychotherapists and research psychologists. *Professional Psychology: Research and Practice, 31,* 82–84.

Ram Dass & Gorman, P. (1986). *How can I help? Stories and reflections on service.* New York: Random House.

Rosenbaum, R. (1999). *Zen and the heart of psychotherapy*. London: Taylor & Francis.

Sarason, S. B. (1981). *Psychology misdirected.* New York: Free Press.

Scott, C. D., & Hawk, J. (Eds.) (1986). *Heal thyself: The health care of health care professionals*. New York: Brunner/Mazel.

Skovholt, T. M., & Rønnestad, M. H. (1992). *The evolving professional self: Stages and themes in therapist and counselor development*. New York: Wiley.

Thoreson, R. W., Miller, M., & Krauskopf, D. J. (1989). The distressed psychologist: Prevalence and treatment considerations. *Professional Psychology: Research and Practice, 20*, 153–158.

Vaughan, F. (1991). Spiritual issues in psychotherapy. *Journal of Transpersonal Psychology, 23*, 105–119.

Walsh, R. N. (1990). *The spirit of shamanism*. Los Angeles: Tarcher.